AMERICAN INSTITUTIONS.

MOUNT VERNON.

AMERICAN INSTITUTIONS

AND THEIR

INFLUENCE.

BY

ALEXIS DE TOCQUEVILLE.

WITH NOTES,

BY HON. JOHN C. SPENCER.

NEW YORK:
PUBLISHED BY A. S. BARNES & CO.,
NO. 51 JOHN-STREET.
CINCINNATI:—H. W. DERBY & COMPANY.
1851.

ADVERTISEMENT.

THE American publishers of M. De Tocqueville's "Democracy in America," have been frequently solicited to furnish the work in a form adapted to seminaries of learning, and at a price which would secure its more general circulation, and enable trustees of School District Libraries, and other libraries, to place it among their collections. Desirous to attain these objects, they have consulted several gentlemen, in whose judgment they confided, and particularly the editor of the American editions, to ascertain whether the work was capable of abridgment or condensation, so as to bring the expense of its publication within the necessary limits. They are advised that the nature of the work renders it impossible to condense it by omitting any remarks or illustrations of the author upon any subject discussed by him, even if common justice to him did not forbid any such attempt; and that the only mode of reducing its bulk, is to exclude wholly such subjects as are deemed not to be essential.

It will be recollected that the first volume was originally published separately, and was complete in itself. It treated of the influence of democracy upon the political institutions of the United States, and exhibited views of the nature of our government, and of their complicated machinery, so new, so striking, and so just, as to excite the admiration and even the wonder of our countrymen. It was universally admitted to be the best, if not the first systematic and philosophic view of the great principles of our constitutions which has been presented to the world. As a treatise upon the spirit of our governments, it was full and finished, and was deemed worthy of being introduced as a text-book in some of our Seminaries of Learning. The publication of the first volume alone would therefore seem to be sufficient to accomplish in the main the objects of the publishers above stated.

And upon a careful re-examination of the second volume, this impression is confirmed. It is entirely independent of the first volume, and is in no way essential to a full understanding of the principles and views contained in that volume. It discusses the effects of the democratic principle upon the tastes, feelings, habits, and manners of the Americans; and although deeply interesting and valuable, yet the observations of the author on these subjects are better calculated for foreign countries than for our own citizens. As he wrote for Europe they were necessary to his plan. They follow naturally and properly the profound views which had already been presented, and which they carry out and illustrate. But they furnish no new developments of those views, nor any facts that would be new to us.

The publishers were therefore advised that the printing of the first volume complete and entire, was the only mode of attaining the object they had in view. They have accordingly determined to adopt that course, intending, if the public sentiment should require it, hereafter to print the second volume in the same style, so that both may be had at the same moderate price.

A few notes, in addition to those contained in the former editions, have been made by the American editor, which upon a reperusal of the volume seemed useful if not necessary: and some statistical results of the census of 1840 have been added, in connection with similar results given by the author from returns previous to that year.

PREFACE TO THE AMERICAN EDITION.

THE following work of M. DE TOCQUEVILLE has attracted great attention throughout Europe, where it is universally regarded as a sound, philosophical, impartial, and remarkably clear and distinct view of our political institutions, and of our manners, opinions, and habits, as influencing or influenced by those institutions. Writers, reviewers, and statesmen of all parties, have united in the highest commendations of its ability and integrity. The people, described by a work of such a character, should not be the only one in Christendom unacquainted with its contents. At least, so thought many of our most distinguished men, who have urged the publishers of this edition to reprint the work, and present it to the American public. They have done so in the hope of promoting among their countrymen a more thorough knowledge of their frames of government, and a more just appreciation of the great principles on which they are founded.

But it seemed to them that a reprint in America of the views of an author so well entitled to regard and confidence, without any correction of the few errors or mistakes that might be found, would be in effect to give authenticity to the whole work, and that foreign readers, especially, would consider silence, under such circumstances, as strong evidence of the accuracy of its statements. The preface to the English edition, too, was not adapted to this country, having been written, as it would seem, in reference to the political questions which agitate Great Britain. The publishers, therefore, applied to the writer of this, to furnish them with a short preface, and such notes upon the text as might appear necessary to correct any erroneous impressions. Having had the honor of a personal acquaintance with M. DE TOCQUEVILLE while he was in this country; having discussed with him many of the topics treated of in this book; having entered deeply into the feelings and sentiments which guided and impelled him in his task, and having formed a high admiration of his character and of this production, the writer felt under some obligation to aid in procuring for one whom he ventures to call his friend, a hearing from those who were the subjects of his observations. These circumstances furnish to his own mind an apology for undertaking what no one seemed willing to attempt, notwithstanding his want of practice in literary composition, and notwithstanding the impediments of professional avocations, constantly recurring, and interrupting that strict and continued examination of the work, which became necessary, as well to detect any errors of the author, as any misunderstanding or misrepresentation of his meaning by his translator. If the same circumstances will atone in the least for the imperfections of what the editor has contributed to this edition, and will serve to mitigate the severity of judgment upon those contributions, it is all he can hope or ask.

The NOTES are confined, with very few exceptions, to the correction of what appeared to be misapprehensions of the author in regard to some matters of fact, or some principles of law, and to explaining his meaning where the translator had misconceived it. For the latter purpose the original was consulted; and it affords great pleasure to bear witness to the general fidelity with which Mr. Reeve has transferred the author's ideas from French into English. He has not been a literal translator, and this has been the cause of the very few errors which have been discovered: but he has been more and better: he has caught the spirit of M. De Tocqueville, has understood the sentiment he meant to express, and has clothed it in the language which M. De Tocqueville would have himself used, had he possessed equal facility in writing the English language.

Being confined to the objects before mentioned, the reader will not find any comments on the theoretical views of our author. He has discussed many subjects on which very different opinions are entertained in the United States; but with an ability, a candor, and an evident devotion to the cause of truth, which will commend his views to those who most radically dissent from them. Indeed, readers of the most discordant opinions will find that he frequently agrees with both sides, and as frequently differs from them. As an instance, his remarks on slavery will not be found to coincide throughout with the opinions either of abolitionists or of slaveholders: but they will be found to present a masterly view of a most perplexing and interesting subject, which seems to cover the whole ground, and to lead to the melancholy conclusion of the utter impotency of human effort to eradicate this acknowledged evil. But on this, and on the various topics of the deepest interest which are discussed in this work, it was thought that the American readers would be fully competent to form their own opinions, and to detect any errors of the author. if such there are, without any attempt of the present editor to enlighten them. At all events, it is to be hoped that the citizens of the United States will patiently read, and candidly consider, the views of this accomplished foreigner, however hostile they may be to their own preconceived opinions or prejudices. He says: "There are certain truths which Americans can only learn from strangers, or from experience." Let us, then, at least listen to one who admires us and our institutions, and whose complaints, when he makes any, are, that we have not perfected our own glorious plans, and that there are some things yet to be amended. We shall thus furnish a practical proof, that public opinion in this country is not so intolerant as the author may be understood to represent it. However mistaken he may be, his manly appeal to our understandings and to our consciences, should at least be heard. "If ever," he says, "these lines are read in America, I am well assured of two things: in the first place, that all who peruse them will raise their voice to condemn me; and, in the second place, that very many of them will acquit me at the bottom of their consciences." He is writing on that very sore subject, the tyranny of public opinion in the United States.

Fully to comprehend the scope of the present work, the author's motive and object in preparing it should be distinctly kept in view. He has written, not for America, but for France. "It was not, then, merely to satisfy a legitimate curiosity," he says, "that I have examined America: my wish has been to find instruction, by which we might ourselves profit."—"I sought the image of democracy itself, with its inclinations, its character, its prejudices, and its passions, in order to learn what *we* have to hope or fear from its progress." He thinks that the principle of democracy has sprung into new life throughout Europe, and particularly in France, and that it is advancing with a firm and steady march to the control of all civilized governments. In his own country, he had seen a recent attempt to repress its energies within due bounds, and to prevent the consequences of its excesses. And it seems to be a main object with him, to ascertain whether these bounds can be relied upon; whether the dikes and embankments of human contrivance can keep within any appointed channel this mighty and majestic stream. Giving the fullest confidence to his declaration, that his book "is written to favor no particular views and with no design of serving or attacking any party," it is yet evident that his mind has been very open to receive impressions unfavorable to the admission into France of the unbounded and unlimited democracy which reigns in these United States. A knowledge of this inclination of his mind will necessarily induce some caution in his readers, while perusing those parts of the work which treat of the effects of our democracy upon the stability of our government and its administration. While the views of the author, respecting the application of the democratic principle, in the extent that it exists with us, to the institutions of France, or to any of the European nations, are of the utmost importance to the people and statesmen of those countries, they are scarcely less entitled to the attention of Americans. He has exhibited, with admirable skill, the causes and circumstances which prepared our forefathers, gradually, for the enjoyment of free institutions, and which enable them to sustain, without abusing, the utmost liberty that was ever enjoyed by any people. In tracing these causes, in examining how far they continue to influence our conduct, manners, and opinions, and in searching for the means of preventing their decay or destruction, the intelligent American reader will find no better guide than M. De Tocqueville.

Fresh from the scenes of the "three days" revolution in France, the author came among us to observe, carefully and critically, the operation of the new principle on which the happiness of his country, and, as he seems to believe, the destinies of the civilized world, depend. Filled with the love of liberty, but remembering the atrocities which, in its name, had been committed under former dynasties at home, he sought to discover the means by which it was regulated in America, and reconciled with social order. By his laborious investigations, and minute observations of the history of the settlement of the country, and of its progress through the colonial state to independence, he found the object of his inquiry in the manners, habits, and opinions, of a people who had been gradually prepared, by a long course of peculiar circumstances, and by their local position, for self-government; and he has explained, with a pencil of light, the mystery that has baffled Europeans and perplexed Americans. He exhibits us, in our present condition, a new, and to Europeans, a strange people. His views of our political institutions are more general, comprehensive, and philosophic than have been presented by any writer, domestic or foreign. He has traced them from their source, democracy—the power of the people—and has steadily pursued this foundation-principle in all its forms and modifications: in the frame of our governments, in their administration by the different executives, in our legislation, in the arrangement of our judiciary, in our manners, in religion, in the freedom and licentiousness of the press, in the influence of public opinion, and in various subtle recesses, where its existence was scarcely suspected. In all these, he analyzes and dissects the tendencies of democracy; heartily applauds where he can, and faithfully and independently gives warning of dangers that he foresees. No one can read the result of his observations without better and clearer perceptions of the structure of our governments, of the great pillars on which they rest, and of the dangers to which they are exposed: nor without a more profound and more intelligent admiration of the harmony and beauty of their formation, and of the safeguards provided for preserving and transmitting them to a distant posterity. The more that genera. and indefinite notions of our own liberty, greatness, happiness, &c., are made to give place to precise and accurate knowledge of the true merits of our institutions, the peculiar objects they are calculated to attain or promote, and the means provided for that purpose, the better will every citizen be enabled to discharge his great political duty of guarding those means against the approach of corruption, and of sustaining them against the violence of party commotions. No foreigner has ever exhibited such a deep, clear, and correct insight of the machinery of our complicated systems of federal and state governments. The most intelligent Europeans are confounded with our *imperium in imperio;* and their constant wonder is, that these systems are not continually jostling each other. M. De Tocqueville has clearly perceived, and traced correctly and distinctly, the orbits in which they move, and has described, or rather defined, our federal government, with an accurate precision, unsurpassed even by an American pen. There is no citizen of this country who will not derive instruction from our author's account of our national government, or, at least, who will not find his own ideas systematised, and rendered more fixed and precise, by the perusal of that account.

Among other subjects discussed by the author, that of the *political influence* of the institution of trial by jury, is one of the most curious and interesting. He has certainly presented it in a light entirely new, and as important as it is new. It may be that he has exaggerated its influence as "a gratuitous public school;" but if he has, the error will be readily forgiven.

His views of religion, as connected with patriotism, in other words, with the democratic principle, which he steadily keeps in view, are conceived in the noblest spirit of philanthropy, and cannot fail to confirm the principles already so thoroughly and universally entertained by the American people. And no one can read his observations on the union of "church and state," without a feeling of deep gratitude to the founders of our government, for saving us from such a prolific source of evil.

These allusions to topics that have interested the writer, are not intended as an enumeration of the various subjects which will arrest the attention of the American reader. They have been mentioned rather with a view of exciting an appetite for the whole feast, than as exhibiting the choice dainties which cover the board.

It remains only to observe, that in this edition the constitutions of the United States and of the state of New York, which had been published at large in the original and in the English edition, have been omitted, as they are documents to which every American reader has access. The map which the author annexed to his work, and which has been hitherto omitted, is now for the first time inserted in the American edition, to which has been added the census of 1840.

TABLE OF CONTENTS.

INTRODUCTION.

AMONG the novel objects that attracted my attention during my stay in the United States, nothing struck me more forcibly than the general equality of conditions. I readily discovered the prodigious influence which this primary fact exercises on the whole course of society, by giving a certain direction to public opinion, and a certain tenor to the laws; by imparting new maxims to the governing powers, and peculiar habits to the governed.

I speedily perceived that the influence of this fact extends far beyond the political character and the laws of the country, and that it has no less empire over civil society than over the government; it creates opinions, engenders sentiments, suggests the ordinary practices of life, and modifies whatever it does not produce.

The more I advanced in the study of American society, the more I perceived that the equality of conditions is the fundamental fact from which all others seem to be derived, and the central point at which all my observations constantly terminated.

I then turned my thoughts to our own hemisphere, where I imagined that I discerned something analogous to the spectacle which the New World presented to me. I observed that the equality of conditions is daily advancing towards those extreme limits which it seems to have reached in the United States; and that the democracy which governs the American communities, appears to be rapidly rising into power in Europe.

I hence conceived the idea of the book which is now before the reader.

It is evident to all alike that a great democratic revolution is going on among us; but there are two opinions as to its nature and consequences. To some it appears to be a novel accident, which as such may still be checked; to others it seems irresistible, because it is the most uniform, the most ancient, and the most permanent tendency which is to be found in history.

Let us recollect the situation of France seven hundred years ago, when the territory was divided among a small number of families, who were the owners of the soil and the rulers of the inhabitants; the right of governing descended with the family inheritance from generation to generation; force was the only means by which man could act on man; and landed property was the sole source of power.

Soon, however, the political power of the clergy was founded, and began to exert itself; the clergy opened its ranks to all classes, to the poor and the rich, the villain and the lord; equality penetrated into the government through the church, and the being who, as a serf, must have vegetated in perpetual bondage, took his place as a priest in the midst of nobles, and not unfrequently above the heads of kings.

The different relations of men became more complicated and more numerous, as society gradually became more stable and more civilized. Thence the want of civil laws was felt; and the order of legal functionaries soon rose from the obscurity of the tribunals and their dusty chambers, to appear at the court of the monarch, by the side of the feudal barons in their ermine and their mail.

While the kings were ruining themselves by their great enterprises, and the nobles exhausting their resources by private wars, the lower orders were enriching themselves by commerce. The influence of money began to be perceptible in state affairs. The transactions of business opened a new road to power, and the financier rose to a station of political influence in which he was at once flattered and despised.

Gradually the spread of mental acquirements, and the increasing taste for literature and art, opened chances of success to talent; science became the means of government, intelligence led to social power, and the man of letters took a part in the affairs of the state.

The value attached to the privileges of birth, decreased in the exact proportion in which new paths were struck out to advancement. In the eleventh century nobility was beyond all price; in the thirteenth it might be purchased; it was conferred for the first time in 1270; and equality was thus introduced into the government by the aristocracy itself.

In the course of these seven hundred years, it sometimes happened that, in order to resist the authority of the crown, or to diminish the power of their rivals, the nobles granted a certain share of political rights to the people. Or, more frequently, the king permitted the lower orders to enjoy a degree of power, with the intention of repressing the aristocracy.

In France the kings have always been the most active and the most constant of levellers. When they were strong and ambitious, they spared no pains to raise the people to the level of the nobles; when they were temperate or weak, they allowed the people to rise above themselves. Some assisted the democracy by their talents, others by their vices. Louis XI. and Louis XIV. reduced every rank beneath the throne to the same subjection; Louis XV. descended, himself and all his court, into the dust.

As soon as land was held on any other than a feudal tenure, and personal property began in its turn to confer influence and power, every improvement which was introduced in commerce or manufacture, was a fresh element of the equality of conditions. Henceforward every new discovery, every new want which it engendered, and every new desire which craved satisfaction, was a step toward the universal level. The taste for luxury, the love of war, the sway of fashion, the most superficial, as well as the deepest passions of the human heart, co-operated to enrich the poor and to empoverish the rich.

From the time when the exercise of the intellect became the source of strength and of wealth, it is impossible not to consider every addition to science, every fresh truth, and every new idea, as a germe of power placed within the reach of the people. Poetry, eloquence, and memory, the grace of wit, the glow of imagination, the depth of thought, and all the gifts which are bestowed by Providence with an equal hand, turned to the advantage of the democracy; and even when they were in the possession of its adversaries, they still served its cause by throwing into relief the natural greatness of man; its conquests spread, therefore, with those of civilisation and knowledge; and literature became an arsenal, where the poorest and weakest could always find weapons to their hand.

In perusing the pages of our history, we shall scarcely meet with a single great event, in the lapse of seven hundred years, which has not turned to the advantage of equality.

The crusades and the wars of the English decimated the nobles, and divided their possessions; the erection of communes introduced an element of democratic liberty into the bosom of feudal monarchy; the invention of firearms equalized the villain and the noble on the field of battle; printing opened the same resources to the minds of all classes; the post was organized so as to bring the same information to the door of the poor man's cottage and to the gate of the palace; and protestantism proclaimed that all men are alike able to find the road to heaven. The discovery of America offered a thousand new paths to fortune, and placed riches and power within the reach of the adventurous and the obscure.

If we examine what has happened in France at intervals of fifty years, beginning with the eleventh century, we shall invariably perceive that a twofold revolution has taken place in the state of society. The noble has gone down on the social ladder, and the *roturier* has gone up; the one descends as the other rises. Every half-century brings them nearer to each other, and they will very shortly meet.

Nor is this phenomenon at all peculiar to France. Whithersoever we turn our eyes, we shall discover the same continual revolution throughout the whole of Christendom.

The various occurrences of national existence have everywhere turned to the advantage of democracy; all men have aided it by their exertions; those who have intentionally labored in its cause, and those who have served it unwittingly—those who have fought for it, and those who have declared themselves its opponents—have all been driven along in the same track, have all labored to one end, some ignorantly, and some unwillingly; all have been blind instruments in the hands of God.

The gradual development of the equality of conditions is, therefore, a providential fact, and it possesses all the characteristics of a divine decree: it is universal, it is durable, it constantly eludes all human interference, and all events as well as all men contribute to its progress.

Would it, then, be wise to imagine that a social impulse which dates from so far back, can be checked by the efforts of a generation? Is it credible that the democracy which has annihilated the feudal system, and vanquished kings, will respect the citizen and the capitalist? Will it stop now that it has grown so strong and its adversaries so weak?

None can say which way we are going, for all terms of comparison are wanting: the equality of conditions is more complete in the Christian countries of the present day, than it has been at any time, or in any part of the world; so that the extent of what already exists prevents us from foreseeing what may be yet to come.

The whole book which is here offered to the public, has been written under the impression of a kind of religious dread, produced in the author's mind by the contemplation of so irresistible a revolution, which has advanced for centuries in spite of such amazing obstacles, and which is still proceeding in the midst of the ruins it has made.

It is not necessary that God himself should speak in order to disclose to us the unquestionable signs of his will; we can discern them in the habitual course of nature, and in the invariable tendency of events; I know, without a special revelation, that the planets move in the orbits traced by the Creator's fingers.

If the men of our time were led by attentive observation and by sincere reflection, to acknowledge that the gradual and progressive development of social equality is at once the past and future of their history, this solitary truth would confer the sacred character of a divine decree upon the change. To attempt to check democracy would be in that case to resist the will of God; and the nations would then be constrained to make the best of the social lot awarded to them by Providence.

The Christian nations of our age seem to me to present a most alarming spectacle; the impulse which is bearing them along is so strong that it cannot be stopped, but it is not yet so rapid that it cannot be guided: their fate is in their hands; yet a little while and it may be so no longer.

The first duty which is at this time imposed upon those who direct our affairs is to educate the democracy; to warm its faith, if that be possible; to purify its morals; to direct its energies; to substitute a knowledge of business for its inexperience, and an acquaintance with its true interests for its blind propensities; to adapt its government to time and place, and to modify it in compliance with the occurrences and the actors of the age.

A new science of politics is indispensable to a new world.

This, however, is what we think of least; launched in the middle of a rapid stream, we obstinately fix our eyes on the ruins which may still be descried upon the shore we have left, while the current sweeps us along, and drives us backward toward the gulf.

In no country in Europe has the great social revolution which I have been describing, made such rapid progress as in France; but it has always been borne on by chance. The heads of the state have never had any forethought for its exigences, and its victories have been obtained without their consent or without their knowledge. The most powerful, the most intelligent, and the most moral classes of the nation have never attempted to connect themselves with it in order to guide it. The people have consequently been abandoned to its wild propensities, and it has grown up like those outcasts who receive their education in the public streets, and who are unacquainted with aught but the vices and wretchedness of society. The existence of a democracy was seemingly unknown, when, on a sudden, it took possession of the supreme power. Everything was then submitted to its caprices; it was worshipped as the idol of strength; until, when it was enfeebled by its own excesses, the legislator conceived the rash project of annihilating its power, instead of instructing it and correcting its vices; no attempt was made to fit it to govern, but all were bent on excluding it from the government.

The consequence of this has been that the democratic revolution has been effected only in the material parts of society, without that concomitant change in laws, ideas, customs, and manners, which was necessary to render such a revolution beneficial. We have gotten a democracy, but without the conditions which lessen its vices, and render its natural advantages more prominent; and although we already perceive the evils it brings, we are ignorant of the benefits it may confer.

While the power of the crown, supported by the aristocracy, peaceably governed the nations of Europe, society possessed, in the midst of its wretchedness, several different advantages which can now scarcely be appreciated or conceived.

The power of a part of his subjects was an insurmountable barrier to the tyranny of the prince; and the monarch who felt the almost divine character which he enjoyed in the eyes of the multitude, derived a motive for the just use of his power from the respect which he inspired.

High as they were placed above the people, the nobles could not but take that calm and benevolent interest in its fate which the shepherd feels toward his flock; and without acknowledging the poor as their equals, they watched over the destiny of those whose welfare Providence had intrusted to their care.

The people, never having conceived the idea of a social condition different from its own, and entertaining no expectation of ever ranking with its chiefs, received benefits from them without discussing their rights. It grew attached to them when they were clement and just, but it submitted without resistance or servility to their exactions, as to the inevitable visitations of the arm of God. Custom, and the manners of the time, had moreover created a species of law in the midst of violence, and established certain limits to oppression.

As the noble never suspected that any one would attempt to deprive him of the privileges which he believed to be legitimate, and as the serf looked upon his own inferiority as a consequence of the immutable order of nature, it is easy to imagine that a mutual exchange of good-will took place between two classes so differently gifted by fate. Inequality and wretchedness were then to be found in society; but the souls of neither rank of men were degraded.

Men are not corrupted by the exercise of power or debased by the habit of obedience; but by the exercise of power which they believe to be illegal, and by obedience to a rule which they consider to be usurped and oppressive.

On one side were wealth, strength, and leisure, accompanied by the refinement of luxury, the elegance of taste, the pleasures of wit, and the religion of art. On the other were labor, and a rude ignorance; but in the midst of this coarse and ignorant multitude, it was not uncommon to meet with energetic passions, generous sentiments, profound religious convictions, and independent virtues.

The body of a state thus organized, might boast of its stability, its power, and above all, of its glory.

But the scene is now changed, and gradually the two ranks mingle; the divisions which once severed mankind, are lowered; property is divided, power is held in common, the light of intelligence spreads, and the capacities of all classes are equally cultivated; the state becomes democratic, and the empire of democracy is slowly and peaceably introduced into the institutions and manners of the nation.

I can conceive a society in which all men would profess an equal attachment and respect for the laws of which they are the common authors; in which the authority of the state would be respected as necessary, though not as divine; and the loyalty of the subject to the chief magistrate would not be a passion, but a quiet and rational persuasion. Every individual being in the possession of rights which he is sure to retain, a kind of manly reliance and reciprocal courtesy would arise between all classes, alike removed from pride and meanness.

The people, well acquainted with its true interests, would allow, that in order to profit by the advantages of society, it is necessary to satisfy its demands. In this state of things, the voluntary association of the citizens might supply the individual exertions of the nobles, and the community would be alike protected from anarchy and from oppression.

I admit that in a democratic state thus constituted, society will not be stationary; but the impulses of the social body may be regulated and directed forward; if there be less splendor than in the halls of an aristocracy, the contrast of misery will be less frequent also; the pleasures of enjoyment may be less excessive, but those of comfort will be more general; the sciences may be less perfectly cultivated, but ignorance will be less common; the impetuosity of the feelings will be repressed, and the habits of the nation softened; there will be more vices and fewer crimes.

In the absence of enthusiasm and of an ardent faith, great sacrifices may be obtained from the members of a commonwealth by an appeal to their understandings and their experience: each individual will feel the same necessity for uniting with his fellow-citizens to protect his own weakness; and as he knows that if they are to assist he must co-operate, he will readily perceive that his personal interest is identified with the interest of the community.

The nation, taken as a whole, will be less brilliant, less glorious, and perhaps less strong; but the majority of the citizens will enjoy a greater degree of prosperity, and the people will remain quiet, not because it despairs of melioration, but because it is conscious of the advantages of its condition.

If all the consequences of this state of things were not good or useful, society would at least have appropriated all such as were useful and good; and having once and for ever renounced the social advantages of aristocracy, mankind would enter into possession of all the benefits which democracy can afford.

But here it may be asked what we have adopted in the place of those institutions, those ideas, and those customs of our forefathers which we have abandoned.

The spell of royalty is broken, but it has not been succeeded by the majesty of the laws; the people have learned to despise all authority. But fear now extorts a larger tribute of obedience than that which was formerly paid by reverence and by love.

I perceive that we have destroyed those independent beings which were able to cope with tyranny single-handed; but it is the government that has inherited the privileges of which families, corporations, and individuals, have been deprived; the weakness of the whole community has, therefore, succeeded to that influence of a small body of citizens, which, if it was sometimes oppressive, was often conservative.

The division of property has lessened the distance which separated the rich from the poor; but it would seem that the nearer they draw to each other, the greater is their mutual hatred, and the more vehement the envy and the dread with which they resist each other's claims to power; the notion of right is alike insensible to both classes, and force affords to both the only argument for the present, and the only guarantee for the future.

The poor man retains the prejudices of his forefathers without their faith, and their ignorance without their virtues; he has adopted the doctrine of self-interest as the rule of his actions, without understanding the science which controls it, and his egotism is no less blind than his devotedness was formerly.

If society is tranquil, it is not because it relies upon its strength and its well-being, but because it knows its weakness and its infirmities; a single effort may cost it its life; everybody feels the evil, but no one has courage or energy enough to seek the cure; the desires, the regret, the sorrows, and the joys of the time, produce nothing that is visible or permanent, like the passions of old men which terminate in impotence.

We have, then, abandoned whatever advantages the old state of things afforded, without receiving any compensation from our present condition; having destroyed an aristocracy, we seem inclined to survey its ruins with complacency, and to fix our abode in the midst of them.

The phenomena which the intellectual world presents, are not less deplorable. The democracy of France, checked in its course or abandoned to its lawless passions, has overthrown whatever crossed its path, and has shaken all that it has not destroyed. Its control over society has not been gradually introduced, or peaceably established, but it has constantly advanced in the midst of disorder, and the agitation of a conflict. In the heat of the struggle each partisan is hurried beyond the limits of his opinions by the opinions and the excesses of his opponents, until he loses sight of the end of his exertions, and holds a language which disguises his real sentiments or secret instincts. Hence arises the strange confusion which we are beholding.

I cannot recall to my mind a passage in history more worthy of sorrow and of pity than the scenes which are happening under our eyes; it is as if the natural bond which unites the opinions of man to his tastes, and his actions to his principles, was now broken; the sympathy which has always been acknowledged between the feelings and the ideas of mankind, appears to be dissolved, and all the laws of moral analogy to be abolished.

Zealous Christians may be found among us, whose minds are nurtured in the love and knowledge of a future life, and who readily espouse the cause of human liberty, as the source of all moral greatness. Christianity, which has de-declared that all men are equal in the sight of God, will not refuse to acknowledge that all citizens are equal in the eye of the law. But, by a singular concourse of events, religion is entangled in those institutions which democracy assails, and it is not unfrequently brought to reject the equality it loves, and to curse that cause of liberty as a foe, which it might hallow by its alliance.

By the side of these religious men I discern others whose looks are turned to the earth more than to heaven; they are the partisans of liberty, not only as the source of the noblest virtues, but more especially as the root of all solid advantages; and they sincerely desire to extend its sway, and to impart its blessings to mankind. It is natural that they should hasten to invoke the assistance of religion, for they must know that liberty cannot be established without morality, nor morality without faith; but they have seen religion in the ranks of their adversaries, and they inquire no farther; some of them attack it openly, and the remainder are afraid to defend it.

In former ages slavery has been advocated by the venal and slavish-minded, while the independent and the warm-hearted were struggling without hope to save the liberties of mankind. But men of high and generous characters are now to be met with, whose opinions are at variance with their inclinations, and who praise that servility which they have themselves never known. Others, on the contrary, speak in the name of liberty as if they were able to feel its sanctity and its majesty, and loudly claim for humanity those rights which they have always disowned.

There are virtuous and peaceful individuals whose pure morality, quiet habits, affluence, and talents, fit them to be the leaders of the surrounding population; their love of their country is sincere, and they are prepared to make the greatest sacrifices to its welfare, but they confound the abuses of civilisation with its benefits, and the idea of evil is inseparable in their minds from that of novelty.

Not far from this class is another party, whose object is to materialise mankind, to hit upon what is expedient without heeding what is just; to acquire knowledge without faith, and prosperity apart from virtue; assuming the title of the champions of modern civilisation, and placing themselves in a station which they usurp with insolence, and from which they are driven by their own unworthiness.

Where are we then ?

The religionists are the enemies of liberty, and the friends of liberty attack religion; the high-minded and the noble advocate subjection, and the meanest and most servile minds preach independence; honest and enlightened citizens are opposed to all progress, while men without patriotism and without principles, are the apostles of civilisation and of intelligence.

Has such been the fate of the centuries which have preceded our own? and has man always inhabited a world, like the present, where nothing is linked together, where virtue is without genius, and genius without honor; where the love of order is confounded with a taste for oppression, and the holy rites of freedom with a contempt of law; where the light thrown by conscience on human actions is dim, and where nothing seems to be any longer forbidden or allowed, honorable or shameful, false or true?

I cannot, however, believe that the Creator made man to leave him in an endless struggle with the intellectual miseries which surround us: God destines a calmer and a more certain future to the communities of Europe; I am unacquainted with his designs, but I shall not cease to believe in them because I cannot fathom them, and I had rather mistrust my own capacity than his justice.

There is a country in the world where the great revolution which I am speaking of seems nearly to have reached its natural limits; it has been effected with ease and simplicity, say rather that this country has attained the consequences of the democratic revolution which we are undergoing, without having experienced the revolution itself.

The emigrants who fixed themselves on the shores of America in the beginning of the seventeenth century, severed the democratic principle from all the principles which repressed it in the old communities of Europe, and transplanted it unalloyed to the New World. It has there been allowed to spread in perfect freedom, and to put forth its consequences in the laws by influencing the manners of the country.

It appears to me beyond a doubt, that sooner or later we shall arrive, like the Americans, at an almost complete equality of conditions. But I do not conclude from this, that we shall ever be necessarily led to draw the same political consequences which the Americans have derived from a similar social organization. I am far from supposing that they have chosen the only form of government which a democracy may adopt; but the identity of the efficient cause of laws and manners in the two countries is sufficient to account for the immense interest we have in becoming acquainted with its effects in each of them.

It is not, then, merely to satisfy a legitimate curiosity that I have examined America; my wish has been to find instruction by which we may ourselves profit. Whoever should imagine that I have intended to write a panegyric would be strangely mistaken, and on reading this book, he will perceive that such was not my design: nor has it been my object to advocate any form of government in particular, for I am of opinion that absolute excellence is rarely to be found in any legislation; I have not even affected to discuss whether the social revolution, which I believe to be irresistible, is advantageous or prejudicial to mankind; I have acknowledged this revolution as a fact already accomplished or on the eve of its accomplishment; and I have selected the nation, from among those which have undergone it, in which its development has been the most peaceful and the most complete, in order to discern its natural consequences, and, if it be possible, to distinguish the means by which it may be rendered profitable. I confess that in America I saw more than America; I sought the image of democracy itself, with its inclinations, its character, its prejudices, and its passions, in order to learn what we have to fear or to hope from its progress.

In the first part of this work I have attempted to show the tendency given to the laws by the democracy of America, which is abandoned almost without restraint to its instinctive propensities; and to exhibit the course it prescribes to the government, and the influence it exercises on affairs. I have sought to discover the evils and the advantages which it produces. I have examined the precautions used by the Americans to direct it, as well as those which they have not adopted, and I have undertaken to point out the causes which enable it to govern society.

It was my intention to depict, in a second part, the influence which the equality of conditions and the rule of democracy exercise on the civil society, the habits, the ideas, and the manners of the Americans; I begin, however, to feel less ardor for the accomplishment of this project, since the excellent work of my friend and travelling companion M. de Beaumont has been given to the world.* I do not know whether I have succeeded in making known what I saw in America, but I am certain that such has been my sincere desire, and that I have never, knowingly, moulded facts to ideas, instead of ideas to facts.

Whenever a point could be established by the aid of written documents, I have had recourse to the original text, and to the most authentic and approved works.† I have cited my authorities in the notes, and any one may refer to them. Whenever an opinion, a political custom, or a remark on the manners of the country was concerned, I endeavored to consult the most enlightened men I met with. If the point in question was important or doubtful, I was not satisfied with one testimony, but I formed my opinion on the evidence of several witnesses. Here the reader must necessarily believe me upon my word. I could frequently have quoted names which are either known to him, or which deserve to be so, in proof of what I advance; but I have carefully abstained from this practice. A stranger frequently hears important truths at the fireside of his host, which the latter would perhaps conceal even from the ear of friendship; he consoles himself with his guest, for the silence to which he is restricted, and the shortness of the traveller's stay takes away all fear of his indiscretion. I carefully noted every conversation of this nature as soon as it occurred, but these notes will never leave my writing-case; I had rather injure the success of my statements than add my name to the list of those strangers who repay the generous hospitality they have received by subsequent chagrin and annoyance.

I am aware that, notwithstanding my care, nothing

* This work is entitled, Marie, ou l'Esclavage aux Etats-Unis.

† Legislative and administrative documents have been furnished me with a degree of politeness which I shall always remember with gratitude. Among the American functionaries who thus favored my inquiries I am proud to name Mr. Edward Livingston, then Secretary of State and late American minister at Paris. During my stay at the session of Congress, Mr. Livingston was kind enough to furnish me with the greater part of the documents I possess relative to the federal government. Mr. Livingston is one of those rare individuals whom one loves, respects, and admires, from their writings, and to whom one is happy to incur the debt of gratitude on further acquaintance.

will be easier than to criticise this book, if any one ever chooses to criticise it.

Those readers who may examine it closely will discover the fundamental idea which connects the several parts together. But the diversity of the subjects I have had to treat is exceedingly great, and it will not be difficult to oppose an isolated fact to the body of facts which I quote, or an isolated idea to the body of ideas I put forth. I hope to be read in the spirit which has guided my labors, and that my book may be judged by the general impression it leaves, as I have formed my own judgment not on any single reason, but upon the mass of evidence.

It must not be forgotten that the author who wishes to be understood is obliged to push all his ideas to their utmost theoretical consequences, and often to the verge of what is false or impracticable; for if it be necessary sometimes to quit the rules of logic in active life, such is not the case in discourse, and a man finds that almost as many difficulties spring from inconsistency of language, as usually arise from consistency of conduct.

I conclude by pointing out myself what many readers will consider the principal defect of the work. This book is written to favor no particular views, and in composing it I have entertained no design of serving or attacking any party: I have undertaken not to see differently, but to look farther than parties, and while they are busied for the morrow, I have turned my thoughts to the future.

AMERICAN INSTITUTIONS.

CHAPTER I.

EXTERIOR FORM OF NORTH AMERICA.

North America divided into two vast regions, one inclining toward the Pole, the other toward the Equator.—Valley of the Mississippi.—Traces of the Revolutions of the Globe.—Shore of the Atlantic Ocean, where the English Colonies were founded.—Difference in the Appearance of North and of South America at the Time of their Discovery.—Forests of North America.—Prairies.—Wandering Tribes of Natives.—Their outward Appearance, Manners, and Language.—Traces of an Unknown People.

North America presents in its external form certain general features, which it is easy to discriminate at the first glance.

A sort of methodical order seems to have regulated the separation of land and water, mountains and valleys. A simple but grand arrangement is discoverable amid the confusion of objects and the prodigious variety of scenes.

This continent is divided, almost equally, into two vast regions, one of which is bounded, on the north by the arctic pole, and by the two great oceans on the east and west. It stretches toward the south, forming a triangle, whose irregular sides meet at length below the great lakes of Canada.

The second region begins where the other terminates, and includes all the remainder of the continent.

The one slopes gently toward the pole, the other toward the equator.

The territory comprehended in the first regions descends toward the north with so imperceptible a slope that it may almost be said to form a level plain. Within the bounds of this immense tract of country there are neither high mountains nor deep valleys. Streams meander through it irregularly; great rivers mix their currents, separate and meet again, disperse and form vast marshes, losing all trace of their channels in the labyrinth of waters they have themselves created; and thus, at length, after innumerable windings, fall into the polar seas. The great lakes which bound this first region are not walled in, like most of those in the Old World, between hills and rocks. Their banks are flat, and rise but a few feet above the level of their waters; each of them thus forming a vast bowl filled to the brim. The slightest change in the structure of the globe would cause their waters to rush either toward the pole or to the tropical sea.

The second region is more varied on its surface, and better suited for the habitation of man. Two long chains of mountains divide it from one extreme to the other; the Allegany ridge takes the form of the shores of the Atlantic ocean; the other is parallel with the Pacific.

The space which lies between these two chains of mountains contains 1,341,649 square miles.* Its surface is therefore about six times as great as that of France.

This vast territory, however, forms a single valley, one side of which descends gradually from the rounded summits of the Alleganies, while the other rises in an uninterrupted course toward the tops of the Rocky mountains.

At the bottom of the valley flows an immense river, into which the various streams issuing from the mountains fall from all parts. In memory of their native land, the French formerly called this the river St. Louis. The Indians, in their pompous language, have named it the Father of Waters, or the Mississippi.

The Mississippi takes its source above the limit of the two great regions of which I have spoken, not far from the highest point of the table-land where they unite. Near the same spot rises another river,† which empties itself into the polar seas. The course of the Mississippi is at first devious: it winds several times toward the north, whence it rose; and, at length, after having been delayed in lakes and marshes, it flows slowly onward to the south.

Sometimes quietly gliding along the argillaceous bed which nature has assigned to it; sometimes swollen by storms, the Mississippi waters 2,500 miles in its course.‡ At the dis-

* Darby's "View of the United States." † Mackenzie's river.
‡ Warden's "Description of the United States."

tance of 1,364 miles from its mouth this river attains an average depth of fifteen feet; and it is navigated by vessels of 300 tons burden for a course of nearly 500 miles. Fifty-seven large navigable rivers contribute to swell the waters of the Mississippi; among others the Missouri, which traverses a space of 2,500 miles; the Arkansas of 1,300 miles; the Red river 1,000 miles; four whose course is from 800 to 1000 miles in length, viz., the Illinois, the St. Peter's, the St. Francis, and the Moingona; besides a countless number of rivulets which unite from all parts their tributary streams.

The valley which is watered by the Mississippi seems formed to be the bed of this mighty river, which like a god of antiquity dispenses both good and evil in its course. On the shores of the stream nature displays an inexhaustible fertility; in proportion as you recede from its banks, the powers of vegetation languish, the soil becomes poor, and the plants that survive have a sickly growth. Nowhere have the great convulsions of the globe left more evident traces than in the valley of the Mississippi: the whole aspect of the country shows the powerful effects of water, both by its fertility and by its barrenness. The waters of the primeval ocean accumulated enormous beds of vegetable mould in the valley, which they levelled as they retired. Upon the right shore of the river are seen immense plains, as smooth as if the husbandman had passed over them with his roller. As you approach the mountains, the soil becomes more and more unequal and sterile; the ground is, as it were, pierced in a thousand places by primitive rocks, which appear like the bones of a skeleton whose flesh is partly consumed. The surface of the earth is covered with a granitic sand, and huge irregular masses of stone, among which a few plants force their growth, and give the appearance of a green field covered with the ruins of a vast edifice. These stones and this sand discover, on examination, a perfect analogy with those which compose the arid and broken summits of the Rocky mountains. The flood of waters which washed the soil to the bottom of the valley, afterward carried away portions of the rocks themselves; and these, dashed and bruised against the neighboring cliffs, were left scattered like wrecks at their feet.*

The valley of the Mississippi is, upon the whole, the most magnificent dwelling-place prepared by God for man's abode; and yet it may be said that at present it is but a mighty desert.

* See Appendix A.

On the eastern side of the Alleganies, between the base of these mountains and the Atlantic ocean, lies a long ridge of rocks and sand, which the sea appears to have left behind as it retired. The mean breadth of this territory does not exceed one hundred miles; but it is about nine hundred miles in length. This part of the American continent has a soil which offers every obstacle to the husbandman, and its vegetation is scanty and unvaried.

Upon this inhospitable coast the first united efforts of human industry were made. This tongue of arid land was the cradle of those English colonies which were destined one day to become the United States of America. The centre of power still remains there; while in the backward States the true elements of the great people, to whom the future control of the continent belongs, are secretly springing up.

When the Europeans first landed on the shores of the Antilles, and afterwards on the coast of South America, they thought themselves transported into those fabulous regions of which poets had sung. The sea sparkled with phosphoric light, and the extraordinary transparency of its waters discovered to the view of the navigator all that had hitherto been hidden in the deep abyss.* Here and there appeared little islands perfumed with odoriferous plants, and resembling baskets of flowers, floating on the tranquil surface of the ocean. Every object which met the sight, in this enchanting region, seemed prepared to satisfy the wants, or contribute to the pleasures of man. Almost all the trees were loaded with nourishing fruits, and those which were useless as food, delighted the eye by the brilliancy and variety of their colors. In groves of fragrant lemon-trees, wild figs, flowering myrtles, acacias, and oleanders, which were hung with festoons of various climbing-plants, covered with flowers, a multitude of birds unknown in Europe displayed their bright plumage, glittering with purple and azure, and mingled their warbling in the harmony of a world teeming with life and motion.†

Underneath this brilliant exterior death was concealed. The air of these climates had so enervating an influence

* Malte Brun tells us (vol. v., p. 726) that the water of the Caribbean sea is so transparent, that corals and fish are discernible at a depth of sixty fathoms. The ship seemed to float in the air, the navigator became giddy as his eye penetrated through the crystal flood, and beheld submarine gardens, or beds of shells, or gilded fishes gliding among tufts and thickets of seaweed.

† See Appendix B.

that man, completely absorbed by the present enjoyment, was rendered regardless of the future.

North America appeared under a very different aspect; there, everything was grave, serious, and solemn; it seemed created to be the domain of intelligence, as the south was that of sensual delight. A turbulent and foggy ocean washed its shores. It was girded round by a belt of granitic rocks, or by wide plains of sand. The foliage of its woods was dark and gloomy; for they were composed of firs, larches, evergreen oaks, wild olive-trees, and laurels.

Beyond this outer belt lay the thick shades of the central forests, where the largest trees which are produced in the two hemispheres grow side by side. The plane, the catalpa, the sugar-maple, and the Virginian poplar, mingled their branches with those of the oak, the beech, and the lime.

In these, as in the forests of the Old World, destruction was perpetually going on. The ruins of vegetation were heaped upon each other; but there was no laboring hand to remove them, and their decay was not rapid enough to make room for the continual work of reproduction. Climbing-plants, grasses and other herbs, forced their way through the moss of dying trees; they crept along their bending trunks, found nourishment in their dusty cavities, and a passage beneath the lifeless bark. Thus decay gave its assistance to life, and their respective productions were mingled together. The depths of these forests were gloomy and obscure, and a thousand rivulets, undirected in their course by human industry, preserved in them a constant moisture. It was rare to meet with flowers, wild fruits, or birds, beneath their shades. The fall of a tree overthrown by age, the rushing torrent of a cataract, the lowing of the buffalo, and the howling of the wind, were the only sounds which broke the silence of nature.

To the east of the great river the woods almost disappeared; in their stead were seen prairies of immense extent. Whether nature in her infinite variety had denied the germes of trees to these fertile plains, or whether they had once been covered with forests, subsequently destroyed by the hand of man, is a question which neither tradition nor scientific research has been able to resolve.

These immense deserts were not, however, devoid of human inhabitants. Some wandering tribes had been for ages scattered among the forest shades or the green pastures of the prairie. From the mouth of the St. Lawrence to the Delta of the Mississippi, and from the Atlantic to the Pacific ocean, these savages possessed certain points of resemblance which bore witness of their common origin: but at the same time they differed from all other known races of men:* they were neither white like the Europeans, nor yellow like most of the Asiatics, nor black like the negroes. Their skin was reddish brown, their hair long and shining, their lips thin, and their cheek-bones very prominent. The languages spoken by the North American tribes were various as far as regarded their words, but they were subject to the same grammatical rules. Those rules differed in several points from such as had been observed to govern the origin of language.

The idiom of the Americans seemed to be the product of new combinations, and bespoke an effort of the understanding, of which the Indians of our days would be incapable.†

The social state of these tribes differed also in many respects from all that was seen in the Old World. They seemed to have multiplied freely in the midst of their deserts, without coming in contact with other races more civilized than their own.

Accordingly, they exhibited none of those indistinct, incoherent notions of right and wrong, none of that deep corruption of manners that is usually joined with ignorance and rudeness among nations which, after advancing to civilisation, have relapsed into a state of barbarism. The Indian was indebted to no one but himself; his virtues, his vices, and his prejudices, were his own work; he had grown up in the wild independence of his nature.

If, in polished countries, the lowest of the people are rude and uncivil, it is not merely because they are poor and ignorant, but that, being so, they are in daily contact with rich and enlightened men. The sight of their own hard lot and of their weakness, which are daily contrasted with the happiness and power of some of their fellow creatures, excites

* With the progress of discovery, some resemblance has been found to exist between the physical conformation, the language, and the habits of the Indians of North America, and those of the Tongous, Mantchous, Moguls, Tartars, and other wandering tribes of Asia. The land occupied by these tribes is not very distant from Behring's strait; which allows of the supposition, that at a remote period they gave inhabitants to the desert continent of America. But this is a point which has not yet been clearly elucidated by science. See Malte Brun, vol. v.; the works of Humboldt; Fischer, "Conjecture sur l'Origine des Américains;" Adair, "History of the American Indians."

† See Appendix C.

in their hearts at the same time the sentiments of anger and of fear: the consciousness of their inferiority and of their dependence irritates while it humiliates them. This state of mind displays itself in their manners and language; they are at once insolent and servile. The truth of this is easily proved by observation; the people are more rude in aristocratic countries than elsewhere; in opulent cities than in rural districts. In those places where the rich and powerful are assembled together, the weak and the indigent feel themselves oppressed by their inferior condition. Unable to perceive a single chance of regaining their equality, they give up to despair, and allow themselves to fall below the dignity of human nature.

This unfortunate effect of the disparity of conditions is not observable in savage life; the Indians, although they are ignorant and poor, are equal and free.

At the period when Europeans first came among them, the natives of North America were ignorant of the value of riches, and indifferent to the enjoyments which civilized man procures to himself by their means. Nevertheless there was nothing coarse in their demeanor; they practised an habitual reserve, and a kind of aristocratic politeness.

Mild and hospitable when at peace, though merciless in war beyond any known degree of human ferocity, the Indian would expose himself to die of hunger in order to succor the stranger who asked admittance by night at the door of his hut—yet he could tear in pieces with his hands the still quivering limbs of his prisoner. The famous republics of antiquity never gave examples of more unshaken courage, more haughty spirits, or more intractable love of independence, than were hidden in former times among the wild forests of the New World.* The Europeans produced no great impression when they landed upon the shores of North America: their presence engendered neither envy nor fear. What influence could they possess over such men as we have described? The Indian could live without wants, suffer without complaint, and pour out his death-song at the

* We learn from President Jefferson's "Notes upon Virginia," p. 148, that among the Iroquois, when attacked by a superior force, aged men refused to fly, or to survive the destruction of their country; and they braved death like the ancient Romans when their capital was sacked by the Gauls. Further on, p. 150, he tells us, that there is no example of an Indian, who, having fallen into the hands of his enemies, begged for his life; on the contrary, the captive sought to obtain death at the hands of his conquerors by the use of insult and provocation.

stake.* Like all the other members of the great human family, these savages believed in the existence of a better world, and adored, under different names, God, the Creator of the universe. Their notions on the great intellectual truths were, in general, simple and philosophical.†

Although we have here traced the character of a primitive people, yet it cannot be doubted that another people, more civilized and more advanced in all respects, had preceded it in the same regions.

An obscure tradition, which prevailed among the Indians to the north of the Atlantic, informs us that these very tribes formerly dwelt on the west side of the Mississippi. Along the banks of the Ohio, and throughout the central valley, there are frequently found, at this day, *tumuli* raised by the hands of men. On exploring these heaps of earth to their centre, it is usual to meet with human bones, strange instruments, arms and utensils of all kinds, made of a metal, or destined for purposes, unknown to the present race.

The Indians of our time are unable to give any information relative to the history of this unknown people. Neither did those who lived three hundred years ago, when America was first discovered, leave any accounts from which even an hypothesis could be formed. Tradition—that perishable, yet ever-renewed monument of the pristine world—throws no light upon the subject. It is an undoubted fact, however, that in this part of the globe thousands of our fellow-beings had lived. When they came hither, what was their origin, their destiny, their history, and how they perished, no one can tell.

How strange does it appear that nations have existed, and afterward so completely disappeared from the earth, that the remembrance of their very name is effaced: their languages are lost; their glory is vanished like a sound without an echo; but perhaps there is not one which has not left behind it a tomb in memory of its passage. The most durable monument of human labor is that which recalls the wretchedness and nothingness of man.

Although the vast country which we have been describing

* See "Histoire de la Louisiane," by Lepage Dupratz; Charlevoix, "Histoire de la Nouvelle France;" "Lettres du Rev. G. Hecwelder;" "Transactions of the American Philosophical Society," v. i.; Jefferson's "Notes on Virginia," pp. 135–190. What is said by Jefferson is of especial weight, on account of the personal merit of the writer, and of the matter-of-fact age in which he lived.

† See Appendix D.

was inhabited by many indigenous tribes, it may justly be said, at the time of its discovery by Europeans, to have formed one great desert. The Indians occupied, without possessing it. It is by agricultural labor that man appropriates the soil, and the early inhabitants of North America lived by the produce of the chase. Their implacable prejudices, their uncontrolled passions, their vices, and still more, perhaps, their savage virtues, consigned them to inevitable destruction. The ruin of these nations began from the day when Europeans landed on their shores: it has proceeded ever since, and we are now seeing the completion of it. They seemed to have been placed by Providence amid the riches of the New World to enjoy them for a season, and then surrender them. Those coasts, so admirably adapted for commerce and industry; those wide and deep rivers; that inexhaustible valley of the Mississippi; the whole continent, in short, seemed prepared to be the abode of a great nation, yet unborn.

In that land the great experiment was to be made by civilized man, of the attempt to construct society upon a new basis; and it was there, for the first time, that theories hitherto unknown, or deemed impracticable, were to exhibit a spectacle for which the world had not been prepared by the history of the past.

CHAPTER II.

ORIGIN OF THE ANGLO-AMERICANS AND ITS IMPORTANCE, IN RELATION TO THEIR FUTURE CONDITION.

Utility of knowing the Origin of Nations in order to understand their social Condition and their Laws.—America the only Country in which the Starting-Point of a great People has been clearly observable.—In what respects all who emigrated to British America were similar.—In what they differed.—Remark applicable to all the Europeans who established themselves on the shores of the New World.—Colonization of Virginia.—Colonization of New England.—Original Character of the first inhabitants of New England.—Their Arrival.—Their first Laws.—Their social Contract.—Penal Code borrowed from the Hebrew Legislation.—Religious Fervor.—Republican Spirit.—Intimate Union of the Spirit of Religion with the Spirit of Liberty.

After the birth of a human being, his early years are obscurely spent in the toils or pleasures of childhood. As he grows up, the world receives him, when his manhood begins, and he enters into contact with his fellows. He is then studied for the first time, and it is imagined that the germe of the vices and the virtues of his maturer years is then formed.

This, if I am not mistaken, is a great error. We must begin higher up; we must watch the infant in his mother's arms; we must see the first images which the external world casts upon the dark mirror of his mind; the first occurrences which he beholds; we must hear the first words which awaken the sleeping powers of thought, and stand by his earliest efforts, if we would understand the prejudices, the habits, and the passions, which will rule his life. The entire man is, so to speak, to be seen in the cradle of the child.

The growth of nations presents something analogous to this; they all bear some marks of their origin; and the circumstances which accompanied their birth and contributed to their rise, affect the whole term of their being.

If we were able to go back to the elements of states, and to examine the oldest monuments of their history, I doubt not that we should discover the primary cause of the prejudices, the habits, the ruling passions, and in short of all that constitutes what is called the national character: we should then find the explanation of certain customs which now seem at variance with prevailing manners, of such laws as conflict with established principles, and of such incoherent opinions as are here and there to be met with in society, like those fragments of broken chains which we sometimes see hanging from the vault of an edifice, and supporting nothing. This might explain the destinies of certain nations which seem borne along by an unknown force to ends of which they themselves are ignorant. But hitherto facts have been wanting to researches of this kind: the spirit of inquiry has only come upon communities in their latter days; and when they at length turned their attention to contemplate their origin, time had already obscured it, or ignorance and pride adorned it with truth-concealing fables.

America is the only country in which it has been possible to study the natural and tranquil growth of society, and where the influence exercised on the future condition of states by their origin is clearly distinguishable.

At the period when the people of Europe landed in the New World, their national characteristics were already completely formed; each of them had a physiognomy of its own; and as they had already attained that stage of civilisation at which men are led to study themselves, they have transmitted to us a faithful picture of their opinions, their manners, and their laws. The men of the sixteenth century are almost as well known to us as our contemporaries. America consequently exhibits in the broad light of day the phenomena which the ignorance or rudeness of earlier ages conceals from our researches. Near enough to the time when the states of America were founded to be accurately acquainted with their elements, and sufficiently removed from that period to judge of some of their results. The men of our own day seem destined to see farther than their predecessors into the series of human events. Providence has given us a torch which our forefathers did not possess, and has allowed us to discern fundamental causes in the history of the world which the obscurity of the past concealed from them.

If we carefully examine the social and political state of America, after having studied its history, we shall remain perfectly convinced that not an opinion, not a custom, not a law, I may even say not an event, is upon record which the origin of that people will not explain. The readers of this book will find the germe of all that is to follow in the present chapter, and the key to almost the whole work.

The emigrants who came at different periods to occupy the territory now covered by the American Union, differed from each other in many respects; their aim was not the same, and they governed themselves on different principles.

These men had, however, certain features in common, and they were all placed in an analogous situation. The tie of language is perhaps the strongest and most durable that can unite mankind. All the emigrants spoke the same tongue; they were all offsets from the same people. Born in a country which had been agitated for centuries by the struggles of faction, and in which all parties had been obliged in their turn to place themselves under the protection of the laws, their political education had been perfected in this rude school, and they were more conversant with the notions of right, and the principles of true freedom, than the greater part of their European contemporaries. At the period of the first emigrations, the parish system, that fruitful germe of free institutions, was deeply rooted in the habits of the English; and with it the doctrine of the sovereignty of the people had been introduced even into the bosom of the monarchy of the house of Tudor.

The religious quarrels which have agitated the Christian world were then rife. England had plunged into the new order of things with headlong vehemence. The character of its inhabitants, which had always been sedate and reflecting, became argumentative and austere. General information had been increased by intellectual debate, and the mind had received a deeper cultivation. While religion was the topic of discussion, the morals of the people were reformed. All these national features are more or less discoverable in the phisiognomy of those adventurers who came to seek a new home on the opposite shores of the Atlantic.

Another remark, to which we shall hereafter have occasion to recur, is applicable not only to the English, but to the French, the Spaniards, and all the Europeans who successively established themselves in the New World. All these European colonies contained the elements, if not the development of a complete democracy. Two causes led to this result. It may safely be advanced, that on leaving the mother-country the emigrants had in general no notion of superiority over one another. The happy and the powerful do not go into exile, and there are no surer guarantees of equality among men than poverty and misfortune. It happened, however, on several occasions that persons of rank were driven to America by political and religious quarrels. Laws were made to establish a gradation of ranks; but it was soon found that the soil of America was entirely opposed to a territorial aristocracy. To bring that refractory land into cultivation, the constant and interested exertions of the owner himself were necessary; and when the ground was prepared, its produce was found to be insufficient to enrich a master and a farmer at the same time. The land was then naturally broken up into small portions, which the proprietor cultivated for himself. Land is the basis of an aristocracy, which clings to the soil that supports it; for it is not by privileges alone, nor by birth, but by landed property handed down from generation to generation, that an aristocracy is constituted. A nation may present immense fortunes and extreme wretchedness; but unless those fortunes are territorial, there is no aristocracy, but simply the class of the rich and that of the poor.

All the British colonies had then a great degree of similarity at the epoch of their settlement. All of them, from their first beginning, seemed destined to behold the growth, not of the aristocratic liberty of their mother-country, but of that freedom of the middle and lower orders of which the history of the world has as yet furnished no complete example.

In this general uniformity several striking differences were however discernible, which it is necessary to point out. Two branches may be distinguished in the Anglo-American family, which have hitherto grown up without entirely commingling; the one in the south, the other in the north.

Virginia received the first English colony; the emigrants took possession of it in 1607. The idea that mines of gold and silver are the sources of national wealth, was at that time singularly prevalent in Europe; a fatal delusion, which has done more to impoverish the nations which adopted it, and has cost more lives in America, than the united influence of war and bad laws. The men sent to Virginia* were seekers of gold, adventurers without resources and without character, whose turbulent and restless spirits endangered the infant colony,† and rendered its progress uncertain. The artisans and agriculturists arrived afterward; and although they were a more moral and orderly race of men, they were in nowise above the level of the inferior classes in England.‡ No lofty conceptions, no intellectual system directed the foundation of these new settlements. The colony was scarcely established when slavery was introduced,§ and this was the main circumstance which has exercised so prodigious an influence on the character, the laws, and all the future prospects of the south.

Slavery, as we shall afterward show, dishonors labor; it introduces idleness into society, and, with idleness, ignorance and pride, luxury and distress. It enervates the powers of the mind, and benumbs the activity of man. The influence

* The charter granted by the crown of England, in 1609, stipulated, among other conditions, that the adventurers should pay to the crown a fifth of the produce of all gold and silver mines. See Marshall's "Life of Washington," vol i., pp. 18-66.

† A large portion of the adventurers, says Stith (History of Virginia), were unprincipled young men of family, whom their parents were glad to ship off, discharged servants, fraudulent bankrupts, or debauchees: and others of the same class, people more apt to pillage and destroy than to assist the settlement, were the seditious chiefs who easily led this band into every kind of extravagance and excess. See for the history of Virginia the following works:—

"History of Virginia, from the first Settlements in the year 1624," by Smith.

"History of Virginia," by William Stith.

"History of Virginia, from the earliest Period," by Beverley.

‡ It was not till some time later that a certain number of rich English capitalists came to fix themselves in the colony.

§ Slavery was introduced about the year 1620, by a Dutch vessel, which landed twenty negroes on the banks of the river James. See Chalmer.

of slavery, united to the English character, explains the manners and the social condition of the southern states.

In the north, the same English foundation was modified by the most opposite shades of character; and here I may be allowed to enter into some details. The two or three main ideas which constitute the basis of the social theory of the United States, were first combined in the northern British colonies, more generally denominated the states of New England.* The principles of New England spread at first to the neighboring states; they then passed successively to the more distant ones; and at length they embued the whole confederation. They now extend their influence beyond its limits over the whole American world. The civilisation of New England has been like a beacon lit upon a hill, which, after it has diffused its warmth around, tinges the distant horizon with its glow.

The foundation of New England was a novel spectacle, and all the circumstances attending it were singular and original. The large majority of colonies have been first inhabited either by men without education and without resources, driven by their poverty and their misconduct from the land which gave them birth, or by speculators and adventurers greedy of gain. Some settlements cannot even boast so honorable an origin: St. Domingo was founded by buccaneers; and, at the present day, the criminal courts of England supply the population of Australia.

The settlers who established themselves on the shores of New England all belonged to the more independent classes of their native country. Their union on the soil of America at once presented the singular phenomenon of a society containing neither lords nor common people, neither rich nor poor. These men possessed, in proportion to their number, a greater mass of intelligence than is to be found in any European nation of our own time. All, without a single exception, had received a good education, and many of them were known in Europe for their talents and their acquirements. The other colonies had been founded by adventurers without family; the emigrants of New England brought with them the best elements of order and morality, they landed in the desert accompanied by their wives and children. But what most especially distinguished them was the aim of their under-

* The states of New England are those situated to the east of the Hudson; they are now six in number: 1. Connecticut; 2. Rhode Island; 3. Massachusetts; 4. Vermont; 5. New Hampshire; 6. Maine.

taking. They had not been obliged by necessity to leave their country, the social position they abandoned was one to be regretted, and their means of subsistence were certain. Nor did they cross the Atlantic to improve their situation, or to increase their wealth ; the call which summoned them from the comforts of their homes was purely intellectual; and in facing the inevitable sufferings of exile, their object was the triumph of an idea.

The emigrants, or, as they deservedly styled themselves, the pilgrims, belonged to that English sect, the austerity of whose principles had acquired for them the name of puritans. Puritanism was not merely a religious doctrine, but it corresponded in many points with the most absolute democratic and republican theories. It was this tendency which had aroused its most dangerous adversaries. Persecuted by the government of the mother-country, and disgusted by the habits of a society opposed to the rigor of their own principles, the puritans went forth to seek some rude and unfrequented part of the world, where they could live according to their own opinions, and worship God in freedom.

A few quotations will throw more light upon the spirit of these pious adventurers than all we can say of them. Nathaniel Morton,* the historian of the first years of the settlement, thus opens his subject:—

"Gentle Reader : I have for some length of time looked upon it as a duty incumbent, especially on the immediate successors of those that have had so large experience of those many memorable and signal demonstrations of God's goodness, viz., the first beginning of this plantation in New England, to commit to writing his gracious dispensations on that behalf; having so many inducements thereunto, not only otherwise, but so plentifully in the Sacred Scriptures : that so, what we have seen, and what our fathers have told us (Psalm lxxviii., 3, 4), we may not hide from our children, showing to the generations to come the praises of the Lord; that especially the seed of Abraham his servant, and the children of Jacob his chosen (Psalm cv., 5, 6), may remember his marvellous works in the beginning and progress of the planting of New England, his wonders and the judgments of his mouth; how that God brought a vine into this wilderness; that he cast out the heathen and planted it; that he made

* "New England's Memorial," p. 13. Boston, 1826. See also "Hutchinson's History," vol. ii., p. 440.

room for it, and caused it to take deep root; and it filled the land (Psalm lxxx., 8, 9). And not onely so, but also that he hath guided his people by his strength to his holy habitation, and planted them in the mountain of his inheritance in respect of precious gospel enjoyments: and that as especially God may have the glory of all unto whom it is most due; so also some rays of glory may reach the names of those blessed saints, that were the main instruments and the beginning of this happy enterprise."

It is impossible to read this opening paragraph without an involuntary feeling of religious awe; it breathes the very savor of gospel antiquity. The sincerity of the author heightens his power of language. The band, which to his eyes was a mere party of adventurers, gone forth to seek their fortune beyond the seas, appears to the reader as the germe of a great nation wafted by Providence to a predestined shore.

The author thus continues his narrative of the departure of the first pilgrims:—

"So they left that goodly and pleasant city of Leyden, which had been their resting-place for above eleven years; but they knew that they were pilgrims and strangers here below, and looked not much on these things, but lifted up their eyes to Heaven, their dearest country, where God hath prepared for them a city (Heb. xi., 16), and therein quieted their spirits. When they came to Delfs-Haven they found the ship and all things ready; and such of their friends as could come with them, followed after them, and sundry came from Amsterdam to see them shipt, and to take their leaves of them. One night was spent with little sleep with the most, but with friendly entertainment and Christian discourse, and other real expressions of true Christian love. The next day they went on board, and their friends with them, where truly doleful was the sight of that sad and mournful parting, to hear what sighs and sobs and prayers did sound among them; what tears did gush from every eye, and pithy speeches pierced each other's heart, that sundry of the Dutch strangers that stood on the key as spectators could not refrain from tears. But the tide (which stays for no man) calling them away that were thus loath to depart, their reverend pastor falling down on his knees, and they all with him, with watery cheeks commended them with most fervent prayers unto the Lord and his blessing; and then, with mutual embraces and many tears, they took their leaves one of another, which proved to be the last leave to many of them."

The emigrants were about 150 in number, including the women and the children. Their object was to plant a colony on the shores of the Hudson; but after having been driven about for some time in the Atlantic ocean, they were forced to land on that arid coast of New England which is now the site of the town of Plymouth. The rock is still shown on which the pilgrims disembarked.*

"But before we pass on," continues our historian, "let the reader with me make a pause, and seriously consider this poor people's present condition, the more to be raised up to admiration of God's goodness toward them in their preservation: for being now passed the vast ocean, and a sea of troubles before them in expectation, they had now no friends to welcome them, no inns to entertain or refresh them, no houses, or much less towns to repair unto to seek for succor; and for the season it was winter, and they that know the winters of the country know them to be sharp and violent, subject to cruel and fierce storms, dangerous to travel to known places, much more to search unknown coasts. Besides, what could they see but a hideous and desolate wilderness, full of wilde beasts, and wilde men? and what multitudes of them there were, they then knew not: for which way soever they turned their eyes (save upward to Heaven) they could have but little solace or content in respect of any outward object; for summer being ended, all things stand in appearance with a weather-beaten face, and the whole country full of woods and thickets represented a wild and savage hue; if they looked behind them, there was the mighty ocean which they had passed, and was now as a main bar or gulph to separate them from all the civil parts of the world."

It must not be imagined that the piety of the puritans was of a merely speculative kind, or that it took no cognizance of the course of worldly affairs. Puritanism, as I have

* This rock is become an object of veneration in the United States. I have seen bits of it carefully preserved in several towns of the Union. Does not this sufficiently show that all human power and greatness is in the soul of man? Here is a stone which the feet of a few outcasts pressed for an instant, and this stone becomes famous; it is treasured by a great nation, its very dust is shared as a relic; and what is become of the gateways of a thousand palaces?

already remarked, was scarcely less a political than a religious doctrine. No sooner had the emigrants landed on the barren coast, described by Nathaniel Morton, than their first care was to constitute a society, by passing the following act :*—

"In the name of God, Amen! We, whose names are underwritten, the loyal subjects of our dread sovereign lord King James, &c., &c., having undertaken for the glory of God and advancement of the Christian faith, and the honor of our king and country, a voyage to plant the first colony in the northern parts of Virginia: do by these presents solemnly and mutually, in the presence of God and one another, covenant and combine ourselves together into a civil body politic, for our better ordering and preservation, and furtherance of the ends aforesaid: and by virtue hereof do enact, constitute, and frame, such just and equal laws, ordinances, acts, constitutions, and officers, from time to time, as shall be thought most meet and convenient for the general good of the colony: unto which we promise all due submission and obedience," &c.†

This happened in 1620, and from that time forward the emigration went on. The religious and political passions which ravished the British empire during the whole reign of Charles I., drove fresh crowds of sectarians every year to the shores of America. In England the stronghold of puritanism was in the middle classes, and it was from the middle classes that the majority of the emigrants came. The population of New England increased rapidly; and while the hierarchy of rank despotically classed the inhabitants of the mother-country, the colony continued to present the novel spectacle of a community homogeneous in all its parts. A democracy, more perfect than any which antiquity had dreamed of, started in full size and panoply from the midst of an ancient feudal society.

The English government was not dissatisfied with an emigration which removed the elements of fresh discord and of future revolutions. On the contrary, everything was done to encourage it, and little attention was paid to the destiny of

* "New England Memorial," p. 37.

† The emigrants who founded the state of Rhode Island in 1638, those who landed at New Haven in 1637, the first settlers in Connecticut in 1639, and the founders of Providence in 1640, began in like manner by drawing up a social contract, which was submitted to the approval of all the interested parties. See "Pitkin's History," pp. 42, 47.

those who sought a shelter from the rigor of their country's laws on the soil of America. It seemed as if New England was a region given up to the dreams of fancy, and the unrestrained experiments of innovators.

The English colonies (and this is one of the main causes of their prosperity) have always enjoyed more internal freedom and more political independence than the colonies of other nations; but this principle of liberty was nowhere more extensively applied than in the states of New England.

It was generally allowed at that period that the territories of the New World belonged to that European nation which had been the first to discover them. Nearly the whole coast of North America thus became a British possession toward the end of the sixteenth century. The means used by the English government to people these new domains were of several kinds: the king sometimes appointed a governor of his own choice, who ruled a portion of the New World in the name and under the immediate orders of the crown;* this is the colonial system adopted by the other countries of Europe. Sometimes grants of certain tracts were made by the crown to an individual or to a company,† in which case all the civil and political power fell into the hands of one or more persons, who, under the inspection and control of the crown, sold the lands and governed the inhabitants. Lastly, a third system consisted in allowing a certain number of emigrants to constitute a political society under the protection of the mother-country, and to govern themselves in whatever was not contrary to her laws. This mode of colonization, so remarkably favorable to liberty, was adopted only in New England.‡

* This was the case in the state of New York.

† Maryland, the Carolinas, Pennsylvania, and New Jersey, were in this situation. See Pitkin's History, vol. i., pp. 11–31.

‡ See the work entitled, "*Historical Collection of State Papers and other Authentic Documents intended as Materials for a History of the United States of America*," by Ebenezer Hazard, Philadelphia, 1792, for a great number of documents relating to the commencement of the colonies, which are valuable from their contents and their authenticity; among them are the various charters granted by the king of England, and the first acts of the local governments.

See also the analysis of all these charters given by Mr. Story, judge of the supreme court of the United States, in the introduction to his Commentary on the Constitution of the United States. It results from these documents that the principles of representative government and the external forms of political liberty were introduced into all the colonies at their origin These principles were more fully acted upon in the North than in the South, but they existed everywhere.

In 1628,* a charter of this kind was granted by Charles I. to the emigrants who went to form the colony of Massachusetts. But, in general, charters were not given to the colonies of New England till they had acquired a certain existence. Plymouth, Providence, New Haven, the state of Connecticut, and that of Rhode Island,† were founded without the co-operation, and almost without the knowledge of the mother-country. The new settlers did not derive their incorporation from the head of the empire, although they did not deny its supremacy; they constituted a society of their own accord, and it was not till thirty or forty years afterward, under Charles II., that their existence was legally recognised by a royal charter.

This frequently renders it difficult to detect the link which connected the emigrants with the land of their forefathers, in studying the earliest historical and legislative records of New England. They perpetually exercised the rights of sovereignty; they named their magistrates, concluded peace or declared war, made police regulations, and enacted laws, as if their allegiance was due only to God.‡ Nothing can be more curious, and at the same time more instructive than the legislation of that period; it is there that the solution of the great social problem which the United States now present to the world is to be found.

Among these documents we shall notice as especially characteristic, the code of laws promulgated by the little state of Connecticut in 1650.§

The legislators of Connecticut‖ begin with the penal laws, and, strange to say, they borrow their provisions from the text of holy writ.

"Whoever shall worship any other God than the Lord," says the preamble of the code, "shall surely be put to death." This is followed by ten or twelve enactments of the same kind, copied verbatim from the books of Exodus,

* See Pitkin's History, p. 35. See the History of the Colony of Massachusetts Bay, by Hutchinson, vol. i., p. 9.

† See Pitkin's History, pp. 42, 47.

‡ The inhabitants of Massachusetts had deviated from the forms which are preserved in the criminal and civil procedure of England: in 1650 the decrees of justice were not yet headed by the royal style. See Hutchinson, vol. i., p. 452.

§ Code of 1650, p. 28 Hartford, 1830.

‖ See also in Hutchinson's History, vol. i., pp. 435, 456, the analysis of the penal code adopted in 1648, by the colony of Massachusetts: this code is drawn up on the same principles as that of Connecticut.

Leviticus, and Deuteronomy. Blasphemy, sorcery, adultery,* and rape were punished with death; an outrage offered by a son to his parents, was to be expiated by the same penalty. The legislation of a rude and half-civilized people was thus transferred to an enlightened and moral community. The consequence was, that the punishment of death was never more frequently prescribed by the statute, and never more rarely enforced toward the guilty.

The chief care of the legislators, in this body of penal laws, was the maintenance of orderly conduct and good morals in the community: they constantly invaded the domain of conscience, and there was scarcely a sin which they did not subject to magisterial censure. The reader is aware of the rigor with which these laws punished rape and adultery; intercourse between unmarried persons was likewise severely repressed. The judge was empowered to inflict a pecuniary penalty, a whipping, or marriage,† on the misdemeanants; and if the records of the old courts of New Haven may be believed, prosecutions of this kind were not infrequent. We find a sentence bearing date the first of May, 1660, inflicting a fine and a reprimand on a young woman who was accused of using improper language, and of allowing herself to be kissed.‡ The code of 1650 abounds in preventive measures. It punishes idleness and drunken- with severity.§ Innkeepers are forbidden to furnish more than a certain quantity of liquor to each customer; and simple lying, whenever it may be injurious,|| is checked by a fine or a flogging. In other places, the legislator, entirely forgetting the great principles of religious toleration which

Adultery was also punished with death by the law of Massachusetts; and Hutchinson, vol. i., p. 441, says that several persons actually suffered for this crime. He quotes a curious anecdote on this subject, which occurred in the year 1663. A married woman had had criminal intercourse with a young man; her husband died, and she married the lover. Several years had elapsed, when the public began to suspect the previous intercourse of this couple; they were thrown into prison, put upon trial, and very narrowly escaped capital punishment.

† Code of 1650, p. 48. It seems sometimes to have happened that the judge superadded these punishments to each other, as is seen in a sentence pronounced in 1643 (New Haven Antiquities, p. 114), by which Margaret Bedford, convicted of loose cond ıct, was condemned to be whipped, and afterward to marry Nicolas Jemmings her accomplice.

‡ New Haven Antiquities, p. 104. See also **Hutchinson's History** for several causes equally extraordinary.

§ Code of 1650, pp. 50, 57.

|| Ibid, p. 64.

he had himself upheld in Europe, renders attendance on divine service compulsory,* and goes so far as to visit with severe punishment,† and even with death, the Christians who chose to worship God according to a ritual differing from his own.‡ Sometimes indeed, the zeal of his enactments induces him to descend to the most frivolous particulars: thus a law is to be found in the same code which prohibits the use of tobacco.§ It must not be forgotten that these fantastical and vexatious laws were not imposed by authority, but that they were freely voted by all the persons interested, and that the manners of the community were even more austere and more puritanical than the laws. In 1649 a solemn association was formed in Boston to check the worldly luxury of long hair.‖

These errors are no doubt discreditable to the human reason; they attest the inferiority of our nature, which is incapable of laying firm hold upon what is true and just, and is often reduced to the alternative of two excesses. In strict connection with this penal legislation, which bears such striking marks of a narrow sectarian spirit, and of those religious passions which had been warmed by persecution, and were still fermenting among the people, a body of political laws is to be found, which, though written two hundred years ago, is still ahead of the liberties of our age.

The general principles which are the groundwork of modern constitutions—principles which were imperfectly known in Europe, and not completely triumphant even in Great Britain, in the seventeenth century—were all recognised and determined by the laws of New England: the in-

* Ibid, p. 44.

† This was not peculiar to Connecticut. See for instance the law which, on the 13th of September, 1644, banished the ana-baptists from the state of Massachusetts. (Historical Collection of State Papers, vol. i., p. 538.) See also the law against the quakers, passed on the 14th of October, 1656. "Whereas," says the preamble, "an accursed race of heretics called quakers has sprung up," &c. The clauses of the statute inflict a heavy fine on all captains of ships who should import quakers into the country. The quakers who may be found there shall be whipped and imprisoned with hard labor. Those members of the sect who should defend their opinions shall be first fined, then imprisoned, and finally driven out of the province. (Historical Collection of State Papers, vol. i., p. 630.)

‡ By the penal law of Massachusetts, any catholic priest who should set foot in the colony after having been once driven out of it, was liable to capital punishment.

§ Code of 1650, p. 96.

‖ New England's Memorial, p. 316. See Appendix E.

tervention of the people in public affairs, the free voting of taxes, the responsibility of authorities, personal liberty, and trial by jury, were all positively established without discussion.

From these fruitful principles, consequences have been derived and applications have been made such as no nation in Europe has yet ventured to attempt.

In Connecticut the electoral body consisted, from its origin, of the whole number of citizens; and this is readily to be understood,* when we recollect that this people enjoyed an almost perfect equality of fortune, and a still greater uniformity of capacity.† In Connecticut, at this period, all the executive functionaries were elected, including the governor of the state.‡ The citizens above the age of sixteen were obliged to bear arms; they formed a national militia, which appointed its own officers, and was to hold itself at all times in readiness to march for the defence of the country.§

In the laws of Connecticut, as well as in those of New England, we find the germe and gradual development of that township independence, which is the life and mainspring of American liberty at the present day. The political existence of the majority of the nations of Europe commenced in the superior ranks of society, and was gradually and always imperfectly communicated to the different members of the social body. In America, on the other hand, it may be said that the township was organized before the county, the county before the state, the state before the Union.

In New England, townships were completely and definitively constituted as early as 1650. The independence of the township was the nucleus around which the local interests, passions, rights, and duties, collected and clung. It gave scope to the activity of a real political life, most thoroughly democratic and republican. The colonies still recognised the supremacy of the mother-country; monarchy was still the law of the state; but the republic was already established in every township.

The towns named their own magistrates of every kind, rated themselves, and levied their own taxes.|| In the town-

* Constitution of 1638, p. 17.

† In 1641 the general assembly of Rhode Island unanimously declared that the government of the state was a democracy, and that the power was vested in the body of free citizens, who alone had the right to make the laws and to watch their execution. Code of 1650, p. 70

‡ Pitkin's History, p. 47.

§ Constitution of 1638, p. 12.

|| Code of 1650, p. 80.

ships of New England the law of representation was not adopted, but the affairs of the community were discussed, as at Athens, in the market-place, by a general assembly of the citizens.

In studying the laws which were promulgated at this first era of the American republics, it is impossible not to be struck by the remarkable acquaintance with the science of government, and the advanced theory of legislation, which they display. The ideas there formed of the duties of society toward its members, are evidently much loftier and more comprehensive than those of the European legislators at that time: obligations were there imposed which were elsewhere slighted. In the states of New England, from the first, the condition of the poor was provided for;* strict measures were taken for the maintenance of roads, and surveyors were appointed to attend to them;† registers were established in every parish, in which the results of public deliberations, and the births, deaths, and marriages of the citizens were entered;‡ clerks were directed to keep these registers;§ officers were charged with the administration of vacant inheritances, and with the arbitration of litigated landmarks; and many others were created whose chief functions were the maintenance of public order in the community.‖ The law enters into a thousand useful provisions for a number of social wants which are at present very inadequately felt in France.

But it is by the attention it pays to public education that the original character of American civilisation is at once placed in the clearest light. "It being," says the law, "one chief project of Satan to keep men from the knowledge of the Scripture by persuading from the use of tongues, to the end that learning may not be buried in the graves of our forefathers, in church and commonwealth, the Lord assisting our endeavors, . . ."¶ Here follow clauses establishing schools in every township, and obliging the inhabitants, under pain of heavy fines, to support them. Schools of a superior kind were founded in the same manner in the more populous districts. The municipal authorities were bound to enforce the sending of children to school by their parents; they were empowered to inflict fines upon all who refused compliance; and in cases of continued resistance, society assumed the

* Code of 1650, p. 78.
† Code of 1750, p. 94.
‡ See Hutchinson's History, vol. i. p. 455.
§ Ibid, p. 86.
‖ Ibid, p. 40.
¶ Code of 1650, p. 90.

place of the parent, took possession of the child, and deprived the father of those natural rights which he used to so bad a purpose. The reader will undoubtedly have remarked the preamble of these enactments: in America, religion is the road to knowledge, and the observance of the divine laws leads men to civil freedom.

If, after having cast a rapid glance over the state of American society in 1650, we turn to the condition of Europe, and more especially to that of the continent, at the same period, we cannot fail to be struck with astonishment. On the continent of Europe, at the beginning of the seventeenth century, absolute monarchy had everywhere triumphed over the ruins of the oligarchical and feudal liberties of the middle ages. Never were the notions of right more completely confounded than in the midst of the splendor and literature of Europe ; never was there less political activity among the people ; never were the principles of true freedom less widely circulated, and at that very time, those principles, which were scorned or unknown by the nations of Europe, were proclaimed in the deserts of the New World, and were accepted as the future creed of a great people. The boldest theories of the human reason were put into practice by a community so humble, that not a statesman condescended to attend to it ; and a legislation without precedent was produced off-hand by the imagination of the citizens. In the bosom of this obscure democracy, which had as yet brought forth neither generals, nor philosophers, nor authors, a man might stand up in the face of a free people, and pronounce amid general acclamations the following fine definition of liberty :*—

"Nor would I have you to mistake in the point of your own liberty. There is a liberty of corrupt nature, which is affected both by men and beasts to do what they list ; and this liberty is inconsistent with authority, impatient of all restraint ; by this liberty '*sumus omnes deteriores* ;' 't is the grand enemy of truth and peace, and all the ordinances of God are bent against it. But there is a civil, a moral, a federal liberty, which is the proper end and object of authority ; is a liberty for that only which is just and good : for this liberty you are to stand with the hazard of your very lives,

* Mather's Magnalia Christi Americana, vol. ii., p. 13. This speech was made by Winthrop ; he was accused of having committed arbitrary actions during his magistracy, but after having made the speech of which the above is a fragment, he was acquitted by acclamation, and from that time forward he was always re-elected governor of the state. See Marshall, vol. i., p. 166.

and whatsoever crosses it, is not authority, but a distemper thereof. This liberty is maintained in a way of subjection to authority; and the authority set over you will, in all administrations for your good, be quietly submitted unto by all but such as have a disposition to shake off the yoke and lose their true liberty, by their murmuring at the honor and power of authority."

The remarks I have made will suffice to display the character of Anglo-American civilisation in its true light. It is the result (and this should be constantly present to the mind) of two distinct elements, which in other places have been in frequent hostility, but which in America have admirably incorporated and combined with one another. I allude to the spirit of religion and the spirit of liberty.

The settlers of New England were at the same time ardent sectarians and daring innovators. Narrow as the limits of some of their religious opinions were, they were entirely free from political prejudices.

Hence arose two tendencies, distinct but not opposite, which are constantly discernible in the manners as well as in the laws of the country.

It might be imagined that men who sacrificed their friends, their family, and their native land, to a religious conviction, were absorbed in the pursuit of the intellectual advantages which they purchased at so dear a rate. The energy, however, with which they strove for the acquirements of wealth, moral enjoyment, and the comforts as well as the liberties of the world, was scarcely inferior to that with which they devoted themselves to Heaven.

Political principles, and all human laws and institutions were moulded and altered at their pleasure; the barriers of the society in which they were born were broken down before them; the old principles which had governed the world for ages were no more; a path without a turn, and a field without a horizon, were opened to the exploring and ardent curiosity of man; but at the limits of the political world he checks his researches, he discreetly lays aside the use of his most formidable faculties, he no longer consents to doubt or to innovate, but carefully abstaining from raising the curtain of the sanctuary, he yields with submissive respect to truths which he will not discuss.

Thus in the moral world, everything is classed, adapted, decided, and foreseen; in the political world everything is agitated, uncertain, and disputed: in the one is a passive, though a voluntary obedience; in the other an independence, scornful of experience and jealous of authority.

These two tendencies, apparently so discrepant, are far from conflicting; they advance together, and mutually support each other.

Religion perceives that civil liberty affords a noble exercise to the faculties of man, and that the political world is a field prepared by the Creator for the efforts of the intelligence. Contented with the freedom and the power which it enjoys in its own sphere, and with the place which it occupies, the empire of religion is never more surely established than when it reigns in the hearts of men unsupported by aught besides its native strength.

Religion is no less the companion of liberty in all its battles and its triumphs; the cradle of its infancy, and the divine source of its claims. The safeguard of morality is religion, and morality is the best security of law as well as the surest pledge of freedom.*

REASONS OF CERTAIN ANOMALIES WHICH THE LAWS AND CUSTOMS OF THE ANGLO-AMERICANS PRESENT.

Remains of aristocratic Institutions in the midst of a complete Democracy.—Why?—Distinction carefully to be drawn between what is of Puritanical and what is of English Origin.

THE reader is cautioned not to draw too general or too absolute an inference from what has been said. The social condition, the religion, and the manners of the first emigrants undoubtedly exercised an immense influence on the destiny of their new country. Nevertheless it was not in their power to found a state of things originating solely in themselves; no man can entirely shake off the influence of the past, and the settlers, unintentionally or involuntarily, mingled habits derived from their education and from the traditions of their country, with those habits and notions which were exclusively their own. To form a judgment on the Anglo-Americans of the present day, it is therefore necessary carefully to distinguish what is of puritanical from what is of English origin.

Laws and customs are frequently to be met with in the United States which contrast strongly with all that surrounds them. These laws seem to be drawn up in a spirit contrary to the

* See Appendix F.

prevailing tenor of the American legislation; and these customs are no less opposed to the general tone of society. If the English colonies had been founded in an age of darkness, or if their origin was already lost in the lapse of years, the problem would be insoluble.

I shall quote a single example to illustrate what I advance.

The civil and criminal procedure of the Americans has only two means of action—committal or bail. The first measure taken by the magistrate is to exact security from the defendant, or, in case of refusal, to incarcerate him: the ground of the accusation, and the importance of the charges against him are then discussed.

It is evident that a legislation of this kind is hostile to the poor man, and favorable only to the rich. The poor man has not always a security to produce, even in a civil cause: and if he is obliged to wait for justice in prison, he is speedily reduced to distress. The wealthy individual, on the contrary, always escapes imprisonment in civil causes; nay, more, he may readily elude the punishment which awaits him for a delinquency, by breaking his bail. So that all the penalties of the law are, for him, reducible to fines.* Nothing can be more aristocratic than this system of legislation. Yet in America it is the poor who make the law, and they usually reserve the greatest social advantages to themselves. The explanation of the phenomenon is to be found in England; the laws of which I speak are English,† and the Americans have retained them, however repugnant they may be to the tenor of their legislation, and the mass of their ideas.

Next to its habits, the thing which a nation is least apt to change is its civil legislation. Civil laws are only familiarly known to legal men, whose direct interest it is to maintain them as they are, whether good or bad, simply because they themselves are conversant with them. The body of the nation is scarcely acquainted with them: it merely perceives their action in particular cases; but it has some difficulty in seizing their tendency, and obeys them without reflection.

I have quoted one instance where it would have been easy to adduce a great number of others.

The surface of American society is, if I may use the expression, covered with a layer of democracy, from beneath which the old aristocratic colors sometimes peep. (*a*)

* Crimes no doubt exist for which bail is inadmissible, but they are few in number.

† See Blackstone; and Delolme, book i., chap. x.

(*a*) The author is not quite accurate in this statement. A person

CHAPTER III.

SOCIAL CONDITION OF THE ANGLO-AMERICANS.

A social condition is commonly the result of circumstances, sometimes of laws, oftener still of these two causes united; but wherever it exists, it may justly be considered as the source of almost all the laws, the usages, and the ideas,

accused of crime is, in the first instance, arrested by virtue of a warrant issued by the magistrate, upon a complaint granted upon proof of a crime having been committed by the person charged. He is then brought before the magistrate, the complainant examined in his presence, other evidence adduced, and he is heard in explanation or defence. If the magistrate is satisfied that a crime has been committed, and that the accused is guilty, the latter is then, and then only, required to give security for his appearance at the proper court to take his trial, if an indictment shall be found against him by a Grand Jury of twenty-three of his fellow-citizens. In the event of his inability or refusal to give the security he is incarcerated, so as to secure his appearance at a trial.

In France, after the preliminary examination, the accused, unless absolutely discharged, is in all cases incarcerated, to secure his presence at the trial. It is the relaxation of this practice in England and the United States, in order to attain the ends of justice at the least possible inconvenience to the accused, by accepting what is deemed an adequate pledge for his appearance, which our author considers hostile to the poor man and favorable to the rich. And yet it is very obvious, that such is not its design or tendency. Good character, and probable innocence, ordinarily obtain for the accused man the required security. And if they do not, how can complaint be justly made that others are not treated with unnecessary severity, and punished in anticipation, because some are prevented by circumstances from availing themselves of a benign provision so favorable to humanity, and to that innocence which our law presumes, until guilt is proved? To secure the persons of suspected criminals, that they may abide the sentence of the law, is indispensable to all jurisprudence. And instead of reproof for aristocratic tendency, our system deserves credit for having ameliorated, as far as possible, the condition of persons accused. That this amelioration cannot be made in all instances, flows from the necessity of the case.

It would be a mistake to suppose, as the author seems to have done, that the forfeiture of the security given, exonerates the accused from punishment. He may be again arrested and detained in prison, as security would not ordinarily be received from a person who had given such evidence of his guilt as would be derived from his attempt to escape. And the difficulty of escape is rendered so great by our constitutional provisions for the delivery, by the different states, of fugitives from justice, and by our treaties with England and France for the same purpose, that the instances of successful evasion are few and rare.

which regulate the conduct of nations: whatever it does not produce, it modifies.

It is, therefore, necessary, if we would become acquainted with the legislation and the manners of a nation, to begin by the study of its social condition.

THE STRIKING CHARACTERISTIC OF THE SOCIAL CONDITION OF THE ANGLO-AMERICANS IS ITS ESSENTIAL DEMOCRACY.

The first Emigrants of New England.—Their Equality.—Aristocratic Laws introduced in the South.—Period of the Revolution.—Change in the Law of Descent.—Effects produced by this Change.—Democracy carried to its utmost Limits in the new States of the West.—Equality of Education.

MANY important observations suggest themselves upon the social condition of the Anglo-Americans; but there is one which takes precedence of all the rest. The social condition of the Americans is eminently democratic; this was its character at the foundation of the colonies, and is still more strongly marked at the present day.

I have stated in the preceding chapter that great equality existed among the emigrants who settled on the shores of New England. The germe of aristocracy was never planted in that part of the Union. The only influence which obtained there was that of intellect; the people were used to reverence certain names as the emblems of knowledge and virtue. Some of their fellow-citizens acquired a power over the rest which might truly have been called aristocratic, if it had been capable of invariable transmission from father to son.

This was the state of things to the east of the Hudson: to the southwest of that river, and in the direction of the Floridas, the case was different. In most of the states situated to the southwest of the Hudson some great English proprietors had settled, who had imported with them aristocratic principles and the English law of descent. I have explained the reasons why it was impossible ever to establish a powerful aristocracy in America; these reasons existed with less force to the southwest of the Hudson. In the south, one man, aided by slaves, could cultivate a great extent of country: it was therefore common to see rich landed proprietors. But their influence was not altogether aristocratic as that term is understood in Europe, since they possessed no privileges; and the cultivation of their estates being carried on by slaves, they had no tenants depending on them, and consequently no patronage. Still, the great proprietors south of the Hudson constituted a superior class, having ideas and tastes of its own, and forming the centre of political action. This kind of aristocracy sympathized with the body of the people, whose passions and interests it easily embraced; but it was too weak and too short-lived to excite either love or hatred for itself. This was the class which headed the insurrection in the south, and furnished the best leaders of the American revolution.

At the period of which we are now speaking, society was shaken to its centre: the people, in whose name the struggle had taken place, conceived the desire of exercising the authority which it had acquired; its democratic tendencies were awakened; and having thrown off the yoke of the mother-country, it aspired to independence of every kind. The influence of individuals gradually ceased to be felt, and custom and law united together to produce the same result.

But the law of descent was the last step to equality. I am surprised that ancient and modern jurists have not attributed to this law a greater influence on human affairs.* It is true that these laws belong to civil affairs: but they ought nevertheless to be placed at the head of all political institutions; for, while political laws are only the symbol of a nation's condition, they exercise an incredible influence upon its social state. They have, moreover, a sure and uniform manner of operating upon society, affecting, as it were, generations yet unknown.

Through their means man acquires a kind of preternatural power over the future lot of his fellow-creatures. When the legislator has once regulated the law of inheritance, he may rest from his labor. The machine once put in motion will go on for ages, and advance, as if self-guided, toward a given point. When framed in a particular manner, this law unites, draws together, and vests property and power in a few hands: its tendency is clearly aristocratic. On opposite principles

* I understand by the law of descent all those laws whose principal object it is to regulate the distribution of property after the death of its owner. The law of entail is of this number: it certainly prevents the owner from disposing of his possessions before his death; but this is solely with a view of preserving them entire for the heir. The principal object, therefore, of the law of entail is to regulate the descent of property after the death of its owner: its other provisions are merely means to this end.

its action is still more rapid; it divides, distributes, and disperses both property and power. Alarmed by the rapidity of its progress, those who despair of arresting its motion endeavor to obstruct by difficulties and impediments; they vainly seek to counteract its effect by contrary efforts: but it gradually reduces or destroys every obstacle, until by its incessant activity the bulwarks of the influence of wealth are ground down to the fine and shifting sand which is the basis of democracy. When the law of inheritance permits, still more when it decrees, the equal division of a father's property among all his children, its effects are of two kinds: it is important to distinguish them from each other, although they tend to the same end.

In virtue of the law of partible inheritance, the death of every proprietor brings about a kind of revolution in property: not only do his possessions change hands, but their very nature is altered; since they are parcelled into shares, which become smaller and smaller at each division. This is the direct, and, as it were, the physical effect of the law. It follows, then, that in countries where equality of inheritance is established by law, property, and especially landed property, must have a tendency to perpetual diminution. The effects, however, of such legislation would only be perceptible after a lapse of time, if the law was abandoned to its own working; for supposing a family to consist of two children (and in a country peopled as France is, the average number is not above three), these children, sharing among them the fortune of both parents, would not be poorer than their father or mother.

But the law of equal division exercises its influence not merely upon the property itself, but it affects the minds of the heirs, and brings their passions into play. These indirect consequences tend powerfully to the destruction of large fortunes, and especially of large domains.

Among the nations whose law of descent is founded upon the right of primogeniture, landed estates often pass from generation to generation without undergoing division. The consequence of which is, that family feeling is to a certain degree incorporated with the estate. The family represents the estate, the estate the family; whose name, together with its origin, its glory, its power, and its virtues, is thus perpetuated in an imperishable memorial of the past, and a sure pledge of the future.

When the equal partition of property is established by law, the intimate connection is destroyed between family feeling and the preservation of the paternal estate; the property ceases to represent the family; for, as it must inevitably be divided after one or two generations, it has evidently a constant tendency to diminish, and must in the end be completely dispersed. The sons of the great landed proprietor, if they are few in number, or if fortune befriend them, may indeed entertain the hope of being as wealthy as their father, but not that of possessing the same property as he did; their riches must necessarily be composed of elements different from his.

Now, from the moment when you divest the land-owner of that interest in the preservation of his estate which he derives from association, from tradition, and from family pride, you may be certain that sooner or later he will dispose of it; for there is a strong pecuniary interest in favor of selling, as floating capital produces higher interest than real property, and is more readily available to gratify the passions of the moment.

Great landed estates which have once been divided, never come together again; for the small proprietor draws from his land a better revenue in proportion, than the large owner does from his; and of course he sells it at a higher rate.* The calculations of gain, therefore, which decided the rich man to sell his domain, will still more powerfully influence him against buying small estates to unite them into a large one.

What is called family pride is often founded upon an illusion of self-love. A man wishes to perpetuate and immortalize himself, as it were, in his great-grandchildren. Where the *esprit de famille* ceases to act, individual selfishness comes into play. When the idea of family becomes vague, indeterminate, and uncertain, a man thinks of his present convenience; he provides for the establishment of the succeeding generation, and no more.

Either a man gives up the idea of perpetuating his family, or at any rate he seeks to accomplish it by other means than that of a landed estate.

Thus not only does the law of partible inheritance render it difficult for families to preserve their ancestral domains entire, but it deprives them of the inclination to attempt it, and compels them in some measure to co-operate with the law in their own extinction.

* I do not mean to say that the small proprietor cultivates his land better, but he cultivates it with more ardor and care; so that he makes up by his labor for his want of skill.

The law of equal distribution proceeds by two methods: by acting upon things, it acts upon persons; by influencing persons, it affects things. By these means the law succeeds in striking at the root of landed property, and dispersing rapidly both families and fortunes.*

Most certainly is it not for us, Frenchmen of the nineteenth century, who daily behold the political and social changes which the law of partition is bringing to pass, to question its influence. It is perpetually conspicuous in our country, overthrowing the walls of our dwellings and removing the landmarks of our fields. But although it has produced great effects in France, much still remains for it to do. Our recollections, opinions, and habits, present powerful obstacles to its progress.

In the United States it has nearly completed its work of destruction, and there we can best study its results. The English laws concerning the transmission of property were abolished in almost all the states at the time of the revolution. The law of entail was so modified as not to interrupt the free circulation of property.† The first having passed away, estates began to be parcelled out; and the change became more and more rapid with the progress of time. At this moment, after a lapse of little more than sixty years, the aspect of society is totally altered; the families of the great landed proprietors are almost all commingled with the general mass. In the state of New York, which formerly contained many of these, there are but two who still keep their heads above the stream; and they must shortly disappear. The sons of these opulent citizens have become merchants, lawyers, or physicians. Most of them have lapsed into obscurity. The

* Land being the most stable kind of property, we find, from time to time, rich individuals who are disposed to make great sacrifices in order to obtain it, and who willingly forfeit a considerable part of their income to make sure of the rest. But these are accidental cases. The preference for landed property is no longer found habitually in any class but among the poor. The small land-owner, who has less information, less imagination, and fewer passions, than the great one, is generally occupied with the desire of increasing his estate; and it often happens that by inheritance, by marriage, or by the chances of trade, he is gradually furnished with the means. Thus, to balance the tendency which leads men to divide their estates, there exists another, which incites them to add to them. This tendency, which is sufficient to prevent estates from being divided *ad infinitum*, is not strong enough to create great territorrial possessions, certainly not to keep them up in the same family.

† See Appendix G.

last trace of hereditary ranks and distinctions is destroyed—the law of partition has reduced all to one level.

I do not mean that there is any deficiency of wealthy individuals in the United States; I know of no country, indeed, where the love of money has taken stronger hold on the affections of men, and where a profounder contempt is expressed for the theory of the permanent equality of property. But wealth circulates with inconceivable rapidity, and experience shows that it is rare to find two succeeding generations in the full enjoyment of it.

This picture, which may perhaps be thought overcharged, still gives a very imperfect idea of what is taking place in the new states of the west and southwest. At the end of the last century a few bold adventurers began to penetrate into the valleys of the Mississippi, and the mass of the population very soon began to move in that direction: communities unheard of till then were seen to emerge from their wilds: states, whose names were not in existence a few years before, claimed their place in the American Union; and in the western settlements we may behold democracy arrived at its utmost extreme. In these states, founded off hand, and as it were by chance, the inhabitants are but of yesterday. Scarcely known to one another, the nearest neighbors are ignorant of each other's history. In this part of the American continent, therefore, the population has not experienced the influence of great names and great wealth, nor even that of the natural aristocracy of knowledge and virtue. None are there to wield that respectable power which men willingly grant to the remembrance of a life spent in doing good before their eyes. The new states of the west are already inhabited; but society has no existence among them.

It is not only the fortunes of men which are equal in America; even their acquirements partake in some degree of the same uniformity. I do not believe there is a country in the world where, in proportion to the population, there are so few uninstructed, and at the same time so few learned individuals. Primary instruction is within the reach of everybody; superior instruction is scarcely to be obtained by any. This is not surprising; it is in fact the necessary consequence of what we have advanced above. Almost all the Americans are in easy circumstances, and can therefore obtain the elements of human knowledge.

In America there are comparatively few who are rich enough to live without a profession. Every profession requires an apprenticeship, which limits the time of instruction to the early years of life. At fifteen they enter upon their calling, and thus their education ends at the age when ours begins. Whatever is done afterward, is with a view to some special and lucrative object; a science is taken up as a matter of business, and the only branch of it which is attended to is such as admits of an immediate practical application.

[This paragraph does not fairly render the meaning of the author. The original French is as follows:—

"En Amérique il y a peu de riches; presque tous les Américains ont donc besoin d'exercer une profession. Or, toute profession exige an apprentissage. Les Américains ne peuvent donc donner a la culture générale de l'intelligence que les premières années de la vie: à quinze ans, ils entrent dans une carrière: ainsi leur education finit le plus souvent à l'époque où la nôtre commence."

What is meant by the remark, that "at fifteen they enter upon a career, and thus their education is very often finished at the epoch when ours commences," is not clearly perceived. Our professional men enter upon their course of preparation for their respective professions, wholly between eighteen and twenty-one years of age. Apprentices to trades are bound out, ordinarily, at fourteen, but what general education they receive is after that period. Previously, they have acquired the mere elements of reading, writing, and arithmetic. But it is supposed there is nothing peculiar to America, in the age at which apprenticeship commences. In England, they commence at the same age, and it is believed that the same thing occurs throughout Europe. It is feared that the author has not here expressed himself with his usual clearness and precision.—*American Editor.*]

In America most of the rich men were formerly poor: most of those who now enjoy leisure were absorbed in business during their youth; the consequence of which is, that when they might have had a taste for study they had no time for it, and when the time is at their disposal they have no longer the inclination.

There is no class, then, in America in which the taste for intellectual pleasures is transmitted with hereditary fortune and leisure, and by which the labors of the intellect are held in honor. Accordingly there is an equal want of the desire and the power of application to these objects.

A middling standard is fixed in America for human knowledge. All approach as near to it as they can; some as they rise, others as they descend. Of course, an immense multitude of persons are to be found who entertain the same number of ideas on religion, history, science, political economy, legislation, and government. The gifts of intellect proceed directly from God, and man cannot prevent their unequal distribution. But in consequence of the state of things which we have here represented, it happens, that although the capacities of men are widely different, as the Creator has doubtless intended they should be, they are submitted to the same method of treatment.

In America the aristocratic element has always been feeble from its birth; and if at the present day it is not actually destroyed, it is at any rate so completely disabled that we can scarcely assign to it any degree of influence in the course of affairs.

The democratic principle, on the contrary, has gained so much strength by time, by events, and by legislation, as to have become not only predominant but all-powerful. There is no family or corporate authority, and it is rare to find even the influence of individual character enjoy any durability.

America, then, exhibits in her social state a most extraordinary phenomenon. Men are there seen on a greater equality in point of fortune and intellect, or in other words, more equal in their strength, than in any other country of the world, or, in any age of which history has preserved the remembrance.

POLITICAL CONSEQUENCES OF THE SOCIAL CONDITION OF THE ANGLO-AMERICANS.

THE political consequences of such a social condition as this are easily deducible.

It is impossible to believe that equality will not eventually find its way into the political world as it does everywhere else. To conceive of men remaining for ever unequal upon one single point, yet equal on all others, is impossible; they must come in the end to be equal upon all.

Now I know of only two methods of establishing equality in the political world: every citizen must be put in possession of his rights, or rights must be granted to no one. For nations which have arrived at the same stage of social existence as the Anglo-Americans, it is therefore very difficult to discover a medium between the sovereignty of all and the absolute power of one man: and it would be vain to deny that the social condition which I have been describing is equally liable to each of these consequences.

There is, in fact, a manly and lawful passion for equality, which excites men to wish all to be powerful and honored. This passion tends to elevate the humble to the rank of the great; but there exists also in the human heart a depraved taste for equality, which impels the weak to attempt to lower the powerful to their own level, and reduces men to prefer equality in slavery to inequality with freedom. Not that those nations whose social condition is democratic naturally despise liberty ; on the contrary, they have an instinctive love of it. But liberty is not the chief and constant object of their desires ; equality is their idol : they make rapid and sudden efforts to obtain liberty, and if they miss their aim, resign themselves to their disappointment ; but nothing can satisfy them except equality, and rather than lose it they resolve to perish.

On the other hand, in a state where the citizens are nearly on an equality, it becomes difficult for them to preserve their independence against the aggression of power. No one among them being strong enough to engage singly in the struggle with advantage, nothing but a general combination can protect their liberty : and such a union is not always to be found.

From the same social position, then, nations may derive one or the other of two great political results ; these results are extremely different from each other, but they may both proceed from the same cause.

The Anglo-Americans are the first who, having been exposed to this formidable alternative, have been happy enough to escape the dominion of absolute power. They have been allowed by their circumstances, their origin, their intelligence, and especially by their moral feeling, to establish and maintain the sovereignty of the people.

CHAPTER IV.

THE PRINCIPLE OF THE SOVEREIGNTY OF THE PEOPLE IN AMERICA.

It predominates over the whole of Society in America.—Application made of this Principle by the Americans even before their Revolution.—Development given to it by that Revolution.—Gradual and irresistible Extension of the elective Qualification.

WHENEVER the political laws of the United States are to be discussed, it is with the doctrine of the sovereignty of the people that we must begin.

The principle of the sovereignty of the people, which is to be found, more or less, at the bottom of almost all human institutions, generally remains concealed from view. It is obeyed without being recognised, or if for a moment it be brought to light, it is hastily cast back into the gloom of the sanctuary.

" The will of the nation" is one of those expressions which have been most profusely abused by the wily and the despotic of every age. To the eyes of some it has been represented by the venal suffrages of a few of the satellites of power; to others, by the votes of a timid or an inter ·ed minority; and some have even discovered it in the silence of a people, on the supposition that the fact of submission established the right of command.

In America, the principle of the sovereignty of the people is not either barren or concealed, as it is with some other nations; it is recognised by the customs and proclaimed by the laws; it spreads freely, and arrives without impediment at its most remote consequences. If there be a country in the world where the doctrine of the sovereignty of the people can be fairly appreciated, where it can be studied in its application to the affairs of society, and where its dangers and its advantages may be foreseen, that country is assuredly America.

I have already observed that, from their origin, the sovereignty of the people was the fundamental principle of the greater number of the British colonies in America. It was far, however, from then exercising as much influence on the government of society as it now does. Two obstacles, the one external, the other internal, checked its invasive progress.

It could not ostensibly disclose itself in the laws of the colonies, which were still constrained to obey the mother-country; it was therefore obliged to spread secretly, and to gain ground in the provincial assemblies, and especially in the townships.

American society was not yet prepared to adopt it with all its consequences. The intelligence of New England, and the wealth of the country to the south of the Hudson (as I have shown in the preceding chapter), long exercised a sort of aristocratic influence, which tended to limit the exercise of social authority within the hands of a few. The public functionaries were not universally elected, and the citizens were not all of them electors. The electoral franchise was everywhere placed within certain limits, and made dependant on a certain qualification, which was exceedingly low in the north, and more considerable in the south.

The American revolution broke out, and the doctrine of the sovereignty of the people, which had been nurtured in the townships, took possession of the state; every class was enlisted in its cause; battles were fought, and victories obtained for it; until it became the law of laws.

A scarcely less rapid change was effected in the interior of society, where the law of descent completed the abolition of local influences.

At the very time when this consequence of the laws and of the revolution became apparent to every eye, victory was irrevocably pronounced in favor of the democratic cause. All power was, in fact, in its hands, and resistance was no longer possible. The higher orders submitted without a murmur and without a struggle to an evil which was thenceforth inevitable. The ordinary fate of falling powers awaited them; each of their several members followed his own interest; and as it was impossible to wring the power from the hands of a people which they did not detest sufficiently to brave, their only aim was to secure its good-will at any price. The most democratic laws were consequently voted by the very men whose interests they impaired; and thus, although the higher classes did not excite the passions of the people against their order, they accelerated the triumph of the new state of things; so that, by a singular change, the democratic impulse was found to be most irresistible in the very states where the aristocracy had the firmest hold.

The state of Maryland, which had been founded by men of rank, was the first to proclaim universal suffrage,* and to introduce the most democratic forms into the conduct of its government.

When a nation modifies the elective qualification, it may easily be foreseen that sooner or later that qualification will be entirely abolished. There is no more invariable rule in the history of society: the farther electoral rights are extended, the more is felt the need of extending them; for after each concession the strength of the democracy increases, and its demands increase with its strength. The ambition of those who are below the appointed rate is irritated in exact proportion to the great number of those who are above it. The exception at last becomes the rule, con-

* See the amendments made to the constitution of Maryland in 1801 and 1809.

cession follows concession, and no stop can be made short of universal suffrage.

At the present day the principle of the sovereignty of the people has acquired, in the United States, all the practical development which the imagination can conceive. It is unencumbered by those fictions which have been thrown over it in other countries, and it appears in every possible form according to the exigency of the occasion. Sometimes the laws are made by the people in a body, as at Athens; and sometimes its representatives, chosen by universal suffrage, transact business in its name, and almost under its immediate control.

In some countries a power exists which, though it is in a degree foreign to the social body, directs it, and forces it to pursue a certain track. In others the ruling force is divided, being partly within and partly without the ranks of the people. But nothing of the kind is to be seen in the United States; there society governs itself for itself. All power centres in its bosom; and scarcely an individual is to be met with who would venture to conceive, or, still more, to express, the idea of seeking it elsewhere. The nation participates in the making of its laws by the choice of its legislators, and in the execution of them by the choice of the agents of the executive government; it may almost be said to govern itself, so feeble and so restricted is the share left to the administration, so little do the authorities forget their popular origin and the power from which they emanate.*

CHAPTER V.

NECESSITY OF EXAMINING THE CONDITION OF THE STATES BEFORE THAT OF THE UNION AT LARGE.

It is proposed to examine in the following chapter, what is the form of government established in America on the principle of the sovereignty of the people; what are its resources, its hindrances, its advantages, and its dangers. The first difficulty which presents itself arises from the complex nature of the constitution of the United States, which consists of two distinct social structures, connected, and, as it were,

* See Appendix H.

encased, one within the other; two governments, completely separate, and almost independent, the one fulfilling the ordinary duties, and responding to the daily and indefinite calls of a community, the other circumscribed within certain limits, and only exercising an exceptional authority over the general interests of the country. In short, there are twenty-four small sovereign nations, whose agglomeration constitutes the body of the Union. To examine the Union before we have studied the states, would be to adopt a method filled with obstacles. The Federal government of the United States was the last which was adopted; and it is in fact nothing more than a modification or a summary of these republican principles which were current in the whole community before it existed, and independently of its existence. Moreover, the federal government is, as I have just observed, the exception; the government of the states is the rule. The author who should attempt to exhibit the picture as a whole, before he had explained its details, would necessarily fall into obscurity and repetition.

The great political principles which govern American society at this day, undoubtedly took their origin and their growth in the state. It is therefore necessary to become acquainted with the state in order to possess a clew to the remainder. The states which at present compose the American Union, all present the same features as far as regards the external aspect of their institutions. Their political or administrative existence is centred in three foci of action, which may not inaptly be compared to the different nervous centres which convey motion to the human body. The township is in the lowest order, then the county, and lastly the state; and I propose to devote the following chapter to the examination of these three divisions.

THE AMERICAN SYSTEM OF TOWNSHIPS AND MUNICIPAL BODIES.*

Why the Author begins the Examination of the Political Institutions with the Township.—Its Existence in all Nations.—Difficulty of Establishing and Preserving Independence.—Its Importance.—Why the Author has selected the Township System of New England as the main Object of his Inquiry.

* [It is by this periphrasis that I attempt to render the French expressions "*Commune*" and "*Système Communal.*" I am not aware that any English word precisely corresponds to the general term of the original. In France every association of human dwellings forms

It is not undesignedly that I begin this subject with the township. The village or township is the only association which is so perfectly natural, that wherever a number of men are collected, it seems to constitute itself.

The town, or tithing, as the smallest division of a community, must necessarily exist in all nations, whatever their laws and customs may be: if man makes monarchies, and establishes republics, the first association of mankind seems constituted by the hand of God. But although the existence of the township is coeval with that of man, its liberties are not the less rarely respected and easily destroyed. A nation is always able to establish great political assemblies, because it habitually contains a certain number of individuals fitted by their talents, if not by their habits, for the direction of affairs. The township is, on the contrary, composed of coarser materials, which are less easily fashioned by the legislator. The difficulties which attend the consolidation of its independence rather augment than diminish with the increasing enlightenment of the people. A highly-civilized community spurns the attempts of a local independence, is disgusted at its numerous blunders, and is apt to despair of success before the experiment is completed. Again, no immunities are so ill-protected from the encroachments of the supreme power as those of municipal bodies in general: they are unable to struggle, single-handed, against a strong or an enterprising government, and they cannot defend their cause with success unless it be identified with the customs of the nation and supported by public opinion. Thus, until the independence of townships is amalgamated with the manners of a people, it is easily destroyed; and it is only after a long existence in the laws that it can be thus amalgamated. Municipal freedom eludes the exertions of man; it is rarely created; but it is, as it were, secretly and spontaneously

a *commune*, and every commune is governed by a *maire* and a *conseil municipal*. In other words, the *mancipium* or municipal privilege, which belongs in England to chartered corporations alone, is alike extended to every commune into which the cantons and departments of France were divided at the revolution. Thence the different application of the expression, which is general in one country and restricted in the other. In America, the counties of the northern states are divided into townships, those of the southern into parishes; besides which, municipal bodies, bearing the name of corporations, exist in the cities. I shall apply these several expressions to render the term *commune*. The word "parish," now commonly used in England, belongs exclusively to the ecclesiastical division; it denotes the limits over which a *parson's* (*personæ ecclesiæ* or perhaps *parochianus*) rights extend.—*Translator's Note.*]

engendered in the midst of a semi-barbarous state of society. The constant action of the laws and the national habits, peculiar circumstances, and above all, time, may consolidate it; but there is certainly no nation on the continent of Europe which has experienced its advantages. Nevertheless, local assemblies of citizens constitute the strength of free nations. Municipal institutions are to liberty what primary schools are to science; they bring it within the people's reach, they teach men how to use and how to enjoy it. A nation may establish a system of free government, but without the spirit of municipal institutions it cannot have the spirit of liberty. The transient passions, and the interests of an hour, or the chance of circumstances, may have created the external forms of independence; but the despotic tendency which has been repelled will, sooner or later, inevitably reappear on the surface.

In order to explain to the reader the general principles on which the political organisations of the counties and townships of the United States rest, I have thought it expedient to choose one of the states of New England as an example, to examine the mechanism of its constitution, and then to cast a general glance over the country.

The township and the county are not organized in the same manner in every part of the Union; it is, however, easy to perceive that the same principles have guided the formation of both of them throughout the Union. I am inclined to believe that these principles have been carried farther in New England than elsewhere, and consequently that they offer greater facilities to the observations of a stranger.

The institutions of New England form a complete and regular whole; they have received the sanction of time, they have the support of the laws, and the still stronger support of the manners of the community, over which they exercise the most prodigious influence; they consequently deserve our attention on every account.

LIMITS OF THE TOWNSHIP.

THE township of New England is a divison which stands between the *commune* and the *canton* of France, and which corresponds in general to the English tithing, or town. Its average population is from two to three thousand;* so that,

* In 1830, there were 305 townships in the state of Massachusetts,

on the one hand, the interests of the inhabitants are not likely to conflict, and, on the other, men capable of conducting its affairs are always to be found among its citizens.

AUTHORITIES OF THE TOWNSHIP IN NEW ENGLAND.

The People the Source of all Power here as Elsewhere.—Manages its own Affairs. No Corporation.—The greater part of the Authority vested in the Hands of the Selectmen.—How the Selectmen act. Town-meeting.—Enumeration of the public Officers of the Township. Obligatory and remunerated Functions.

In the township, as well as everywhere else, the people is the only source of power; but in no stage of government does the body of citizens exercise a more immediate influence. In America, the people is a master whose exigences demand obedience to the utmost limits of possibility.

In New England the majority acts by representatives in the conduct of the public business of the state; but if such an arrangement be necessary in general affairs, in the township, where the legislative and administrative action of the government is in more immediate contact with the subject, the system of representation is not adopted. There is no corporation; but the body of electors, after having designated its magistrates, directs them in anything that exceeds the simple and ordinary executive business of the state.*

This state of things is so contrary to our ideas, and so different from our customs, that it is necessary for me to adduce some examples to explain it thoroughly.

The public duties in the township are extremely numerous and minutely divided, as we shall see farther on; but the large proportion of administrative power is vested in the hands of a small number of individuals called "the selectmen."†

The general laws of the state impose a certain number of obligations on the selectmen, which may they fulfil without

and 610,014 inhabitants; which gives an average of about 2,000 inhabitants to each township.

* The same rules are not applicable to the great towns, which generally have a mayor, and a corporation divided into two bodies; this, however, is an exception which requires a sanction of a law. See the act of 22d February, 1822, for appointing the authorities of the city of Boston. It frequently happens that small towns as well as cities are subject to a peculiar administration. In 1832, 104 townships in the state of New York were governed in this manner.—*Williams's Register.*

† Three selectmen are appointed in the small townships, and nine in

the authorization of the body they govern, but which they can only neglect on their own responsibility. The law of the state obliges them, for instance, to draw up the list of electors in the townships; and if they omit this part of their functions, they are guilty of a misdemeanor. In all the affairs, however, which are determined by the town-meeting, the selectmen are the organs of the popular mandate, as in France the maire executes the decree of the municipal council. They usually act upon their own responsibility, and merely put in practice principles which have been previously recognised by the majority. But if any change is to be introduced in the existing state of things, or if they wish to undertake any new enterprise, they are obliged to refer to the source of their power. If, for instance, a school is to be established, the selectmen convoke the whole body of electors on a certain day at an appointed place; they explain the urgency of the case; they give their opinion on the means of satisfying it, on the probable expense, and the site which seems to be most favorable. The meeting is consulted on these several points; it adopts the principle, marks out the site, votes the rate, and confides the execution of its resolution to the selectmen.

The selectmen alone have the right of calling a town-meeting; but they may be requested to do so: if the citizens are desirous of submitting a new project to the assent of the township, they may demand a general convocation of the inhabitants; the selectmen are obliged to comply, but they have only the right of presiding at the meeting.*

The selectmen are elected every year in the month of April or of May. The town-meeting chooses at the same time a number of municipal magistrates, who are intrusted with important administrative functions. The assessors rate the township; the collectors receive the rate. A constable is appointed to keep the peace, to watch the streets, and to forward the execution of the laws; the town-clerk records all the town votes, orders, grants, births, deaths, and marriages; the treasurer keeps the funds; the overseer of the poor performs the difficult task of superintending the action of the poor laws; committee-men are appointed to attend to the

the large ones. See "The Town Officer," p. 186. See also the principal laws of the state of Massachusetts relative to the selectmen:—

Act of the 20th February, 1786, vol. i., p. 219; 24th February, 1796, vol. i., p. 488, 7th March, 1801, vol. ii., p. 45; 16th June, 1795, vol. i., p. 475; 12th March, 1808, vol. ii., p. 186; 28th February, 1787, vol. i., p. 302; 22d June, 1797, vol. i., p. 539.

* See laws of Massachusetts, vol. i., p. 150. Act of the 25th March, 1786.

schools and to public instruction; and the road-surveyors, who take care of the greater and lesser thoroughfares of the township, complete the list of the principal functionaries. They are, however, still farther subdivided; and among the municipal officers are to be found parish commissioners, who audit the expenses of public worship; different classes of inspectors, some of whom are to direct the citizens in case of fire; tithing-men, listers, haywards, chimney-viewers, fence-viewers to maintain the bounds of property, timber-measurers, and sealers of weights and measures.*

There are nineteen principal offices in a township. Every inhabitant is constrained, on pain of being fined, to undertake these different functions; which, however, are almost all paid, in order that the poor citizens may be able to give up their time without loss. In general the American system is not to grant a fixed salary to its functionaries. Every service has its price, and they are remunerated in proportion to what they have done.

EXISTENCE OF THE TOWNSHIP.

Every one the best Judge of his own Interest.—Corollary of the Principle of the Sovereignty of the People.—Application of these Doctrines in the Townships of America.—The Township of New England is Sovereign in that which concerns itself alone; subject to the State in all other matters.—Bond of Township and the State.—In France the Government lends its Agents to the *Commune*.—In America the Reverse occurs.

I HAVE already observed, that the principle of the sovereignty of the people governs the whole political system of the Anglo-Americans. Every page of this book will afford new instances of the same doctrine. In the nations by which the sovereignty of the people is recognised, every individual possesses an equal share of power, and participates alike in the government of the state. Every individual is therefore supposed to be as well informed, as virtuous, and as strong, as any of his fellow-citizens. He obeys the government, not because he is inferior to the authorities which conduct it, or that he is less capable than his neighbor of governing himself,

* All these magistrates actually exist; their different functions are all detailed in a book called, "The Town Officer," by Isaac Goodwin, Worcester, 1827; and in the Collection of the General Laws of Massachusetts, 3 vols., Boston, 1823.

but because he acknowledges the utility of an association with his fellow-men, and because he knows that no such association can exist without a regulating force. If he be a subject in all that concerns the mutual relations of citizens, he is free and responsible to God alone for all that concerns himself. Hence arises the maxim that every one is the best and the sole judge of his own private interest, and that society has no right to control a man's actions, unless they are prejudicial to the common weal, or unless the common weal demands his co-operation. This doctrine is universally admitted in the United States. I shall hereafter examine the general influence which it exercises on the ordinary actions of life: I am now speaking of the nature of municipal bodies.

The township, taken as a whole, and in relation to the government of the country, may be looked upon as an individual to whom the theory I have just alluded to is applied. Municipal independence is therefore a natural consequence of the principle of the sovereignty of the people in the United States, all the American republics recognise it more or less; but circumstances have peculiarly favored its growth in New England.

In this part of the Union the impulsion of political activity was given in the townships; and it may almost be said that each of them originally formed an independent nation. When the kings of England asserted their supremacy, they were contented to assume the central power of the state. The townships of New England remained as they were before; and although they are now subject to the state, they were at first scarcely dependent upon it. It is important to remember that they have not been invested with privileges, but that they seem, on the contrary, to have surrendered a portion of their independence to the state. The townships are only subordinate to the state in those interests which I shall term *social*, as they are common to all the citizens. They are independent in all that concerns themselves; and among the inhabitants of New England I believe that not a man is to be found who would acknowledge that the state has any right to interfere in their local interests. The towns of New England buy and sell, prosecute or are indicted, augment or diminish their rates, without the slightest opposition on the part of the administrative authority of the state.

They are bound, however, to comply with the demands of the community. If the state is in need of money, a town can neither give nor withhold the supplies. If the state projects a road, the township cannot refuse to let it cross its territory;

if a police regulation is made by the state, it must be enforced by the town. A uniform system of instruction is organised all over the country, and every town is bound to establish the schools which the law ordains. In speaking of the administration of the United States, I shall have occasion to point out the means by which the townships are compelled to obey in these different cases: I here merely show the existence of the obligation. Strict as this obligation is, the government of the state imposes it in principle only, and in its performance the township resumes all its independent rights. Thus, taxes are voted by the state, but they are assessed and collected by the township; the existence of a school is obligatory, but the township builds, pays, and superintends it. In France the state collector receives the local imposts; in America the town collector receives the taxes of the state. Thus the French government lends its agents to the commune; in America, the township is the agent of the government. This fact alone shows the extent of the differences which exist between the two nations.

PUBLIC SPIRIT OF THE TOWNSHIPS OF NEW ENGLAND.

How the Township of New England wins the Affections of its Inhabitants.—Difficulty of creating local public Spirit in Europe.—The Rights and Duties of the American Township favorable to it.—Characteristics of Home in the United States.—Manifestations of public Spirit in New England.—Its happy Effects.

In America, not only do municipal bodies exist, but they are kept alive and supported by public spirit. The township of New England possesses two advantages which infallibly secure the attentive interest of mankind, namely, independence and authority. Its sphere is indeed small and limited, but within that sphere its action is unrestrained; and its independence would give to it a real importance, even if its extent and population did not ensure it.

It is to be remembered that the affections of men are generally turned only where there is strength. Patriotism is not durable in a conquered nation. The New Englander is attached to his township, not only because he was born in it, but because it constitutes a strong and free social body of which he is a member, and whose government claims and deserves the exercise of his sagacity. In Europe, the absence of local public spirit is a frequent subject of regret to those who are in power; every one agrees that there is no surer guarantee of order and tranquillity, and yet nothing is more difficult to create. If the municipal bodies were made powerful and independent, the authorities of the nation might be disunited, and the peace of the country endangered. Yet, without power and independence, a town may contain good subjects, but it can have no active citizens. Another important fact is, that the township of New England is so constituted as to excite the warmest of human affections, without arousing the ambitious passions of the heart of man. The officers of the county are not elected, and their authority is very limited. Even the state is only a second-rate community, whose tranquil and obscure administration offers no inducement sufficient to draw men away from the circle of their interests into the turmoil of public affairs. The federal government confers power and honor on the men who conduct it; but these individuals can never be very numerous. The high station of the presidency can only be reached at an advanced period of life; and the other federal functionaries are generally men who have been favored by fortune, or distinguished in some other career. Such cannot be the permanent aim of the ambitious. But the township serves as a centre for the desire of public esteem, the want of exciting interests, and the taste for authority and popularity, in the midst of the ordinary relations of life: and the passions which commonly embroil society, change their character when they find a vent so near the domestic hearth and the family circle.

In the American states power has been disseminated with admirable skill, for the purpose of interesting the greatest possible number of persons in the common weal. Independently of the electors who are from time to time called into action, the body politic is divided into innumerable functionaries and officers, who all, in their several spheres, represent the same powerful corporation in whose name they act. The local admintstration thus affords an unfailing source of profit and interest to a vast number of individuals.

The American system, which divides the local authority among so many citizens, does not scruple to multiply the functions of the town officers. For in the United States, it is believed, and with truth, that patriotism is a kind of devotion, which is strengthened by ritual observance. In this manner the activity of the township is continually perceptible; it is daily manifested in the fulfilment of a duty, or the exercise of a right; and a constant though gentle motion is thus kept up in society which animates without disturbing it.

The American attaches himself to his home, as the mountaineer clings to his hills, because the characteristic features of his country are there more distinctly marked than elsewhere. The existence of the townships of New England is in general a happy one. Their government is suited to their tastes, and chosen by themselves. In the midst of the profound peace and general comfort which reign in America, the commotions of municipal discord are infrequent. The conduct of local business is easy. The political education of the people has long been complete; say rather that it was complete when the people first set foot upon the soil. In New England no tradition exists of a distinction of ranks; no portion of the community is tempted to oppress the remainder; and the abuses which may injure isolated individuals are forgotten in the general contentment which prevails. If the government is defective (and it would no doubt be easy to point out its deficiencies), the fact that it really emanates from those it governs, and that it acts, either ill or well, casts the protecting spell of a parental pride over its faults. No term of comparison disturbs the satisfaction of the citizen: England formerly governed the mass of the colonies, but the people was always sovereign in the township, where its rule is not only an ancient, but a primitive state.

The native of New England is attached to his township because it is independent and free; his co-operation in its affairs ensures his attachment to its interest; the well-being it affords him secures his affection; and its welfare is the aim of his ambition and of his future exertions; he takes a part in every occurrence in the place; he practises the art of government in the small sphere within his reach; he accustoms himself to those forms which can alone ensure the steady progress of liberty; he imbibes their spirit; he acquires a taste for order, comprehends the union of the balance of powers, and collects clear practical notions on the nature of his duties and the extent of his rights.

THE COUNTIES OF NEW ENGLAND.

The division of the counties in America has considerable analogy with that of the arrondissements of France. The limits of the counties are arbitrarily laid down, and the various districts which they contain have no necessary connexion, no common traditional or natural sympathy; their object is simply to facilitate the administration of public affairs.

The extent of the township was too small to contain a system of judicial institutions; each county has, however, a court of justice,* a sheriff to execute its decrees, and a prison for criminals. There are certain wants which are felt alike by all the townships of a county; it is therefore natural that they should be satisfied by a central authority. In the state of Massachusetts this authority is vested in the hands of several magistrates who are appointed by the governor of the state, with the advice† of his council.‡ The officers of the county have only a limited and occasional authority, which is applicable to certain predetermined cases. The state and the townships possess all the power requisite to conduct public business. The budget of the county is only drawn up by its officers, and is voted by the legislature.§ There is no assembly which directly or indirectly represents the county; it has, therefore, properly speaking, no political existence.

A twofold tendency may be discerned in the American constitutions, which impels the legislator to centralize the legislative, and to disperse the executive power. The township of New England has in itself an indestructible element of independence; but this distinct existence could only be fictitiously introduced into the county, where its utility had not been felt. All the townships united have but one representation, which is the state, the centre of the national authority: beyond the action of the township and that of the nation, nothing can be said to exist but the influence of individual exertion.

* See the act of 14th February, 1821. Laws of Massachusetts, vol. i., p. 551.

† See the act of 20th February, 1819. Laws of Massachusetts, vol ii., p. 494.

‡ The council of the governor is an elective body.

§ See the act of 2d November, 1791. Laws of Massachusetts, vol i., p. 61.

ADMINISTRATION IN NEW ENGLAND.

Administration not perceived in America.—Why?—The Europeans believe that Liberty is promoted by depriving the social Authority of some of its Rights; the Americans, by dividing its Exercise.—Almost all the Administration confined to the Township, and divided among the town Officers.—No trace of an administrative Hierarchy to be perceived either in the Township, or above it.—The Reason of this.—How it happens that the Administration of the State is uniform.—Who is empowered to enforce the Obedience of the Township and the County to the Law.—The introduction of judicial Power into the Administration.—Consequence of the Extension of the elective Principle to all Functionaries.—The Justice of the Peace in New England.—By whom Appointed.—County Officer.—Ensures the Administration of the Townships.—Court of Sessions.—Its Action.—Right of Inspection and Indictment disseminated like the other administrative Functions.—Informers encouraged by the division of Fines.

Nothing is more striking to a European traveller in the United States than the absence of what we term government, or the administration. Written laws exist in America, and one sees that they are daily executed; but although everything is in motion, the hand which gives the impulse to the social machine can nowhere be discovered. Nevertheless, as all people are obliged to have recourse to certain grammatical forms, which are the foundation of human language, in order to express their thoughts; so all communities are obliged to secure their existence by submitting to a certain portion of authority, without which they fall a prey to anarchy. This authority may be distributed in several ways, but it must always exist somewhere.

There are two methods of diminishing the force of authority in a nation.

The first is to weaken the supreme power in its very principle, by forbidding or preventing society from acting in its own defence under certain circumstances. To weaken authority in this manner is what is generally termed in Europe to lay the foundations of freedom.

The second manner of diminishing the influence of authority does not consist in stripping society of any of its rights, nor in paralysing its efforts, but in distributing the exercise of its privileges among various hands, and in multiplying functionaries, to each of whom the degree of power necessary for him to perform his duty is intrusted. There may be nations whom this distribution of social powers might lead to anarchy; but in itself it is not anarchical. The action of authority is indeed thus rendered less irresistible, and less perilous, but it is not totally suppressed.

The revolution of the United States was the result of a mature and deliberate taste for freedom, not of a vague or ill-defined craving for independence. It contracted no alliance with the turbulent passions of anarchy; but its course was marked, on the contrary, by an attachment to whatever was lawful and orderly.

It was never assumed in the United States that the citizen of a free country has a right to do whatever he pleases: on the contrary, social obligations were there imposed upon him more various than anywhere else; no idea was ever entertained of attacking the principles, or of contesting the rights of society; but the exercise of its authority was divided, to the end that the office might be powerful and the officer insignificant, and that the community should be at once regulated and free. In no country in the world does the law hold so absolute a language as in America; and in no country is the right of applying it vested in so many hands. The administrative power in the United States presents nothing either central or hierarchical in its constitution, which accounts for its passing unperceived. The power exists, but its representative is not to be discerned.

We have already seen that the independent townships of New England protect their own private interests; and the municipal magistrates are the persons to whom the execution of the laws of the state is most frequently intrusted.* Beside the general laws, the state sometimes passes general police regulations; but more commonly the townships and town officers, conjointly with the justices of the peace, regulate the minor details of social life, according to the necessities of the different localities, and promulgate such enactments as concern the health of the community, and the peace as well as morality of the citizens.† Lastly, these municipal magistrates provide of their own accord and without any

* See "The Town Officer," especially at the words SELECTMEN, ASSESSORS, COLLECTORS, SCHOOLS, SURVEYORS OF HIGHWAYS. I take one example in a thousand: the state prohibits travelling on a Sunday; the *tything-men,* who are town-officers, are especially charged to keep watch and to execute the law. See the laws of Massachusetts, vol. i., p. 410.

The selectmen draw up the lists of electors for the election of the governor, and transmit the result of the ballot to the secretary of the state. See act of 24th February, 1796; *Ib.*, vol. i., p. 488.

† Thus, for instance, the selectmen authorise the construction of drains, point out the proper sites for slaughter-houses and other trades which are a nuisance to the neighborhood. See the act of 7th June, 1785; Laws of Massachusetts, vol. i., p. 193.

delegated powers, for those unforeseen emergencies which frequently occur in society.*

It results, from what we have said, that in the state of Massachusetts the administrative authority is almost entirely restricted to the township,† but that it is distributed among a great number of individuals. In the French commune there is properly but one official functionary, namely, the maire; and in New England we have seen that there are nineteen. These nineteen functionaries do not in general depend upon one another. The law carefully prescribes a circle of action to each of these magistrates; and within that circle they have an entire right to perform their functions independently of any other authority. Above the township scarcely any trace of a series of official dignities is to be found. It sometimes happens that the county officers alter a decision of the townships, or town magistrates,‡ but in general the authorities of the county have no right to interfere with the authorities of the township,§ except in such matters as concern the county.

The magistrates of the township, as well as those of the county, are bound to communicate their acts to the central government in a very small number of predetermined cases.|| But the central government is not represented by an individual whose business it is to publish police regulations and ordinances enforcing the execution of the laws; to keep up

* The selectmen take measures for the security of the public in case of contagious disease, conjointly with the justices of the peace. See the act of 22d June, 1797; vol. i., p. 539.

† I say *almost*, for there are various circumstances in the annals of a township which are regulated by the justice of the peace in his individual capacity, or by the justices of the peace, assembled in the chief town of the county; thus licenses are granted by the justices. See the act of 28th Feb., 1787; vol. i., p. 297.

‡ Thus licenses are only granted to such persons as can produce a certificate of good conduct from the selectmen. If the selectmen refuse to give the certificate, the party may appeal to the justices assembled in the court of sessions; and they may grant the license. See the act of 12th March, 1808; vol. ii., p. 186.

The townships have the right to make by-laws, and to enforce them by fines which are fixed by law; but these by-laws must be approved by the court of sessions. See the act of 23d March, 1786; vol. i., p. 254.

§ In Massachusetts the county-magistrates are frequently called upon to investigate the acts of the town-magistrates; but it will be shown farther on that this investigation is a consequence, not of their administrative, but of their judicial power.

|| The town committees of schools are obliged to make an annual report to the secretary of the state on the condition of the School. See the act of 10th March, 1827; vol. iii., p. 183.

a regular communication with the officers of the township and the county; to inspect their conduct, to direct their actions, or reprimand their faults. There is no point which serves as a centre to the radii of the administration.

What, then, is the uniform plan on which the government is conducted, and how is the compliance of the counties and their magistrates, or the townships and their officers, enforced? In the states of New England the legislative authority embraces more subjects than it does in France; the legislator penetrates to the very core of the administration; the law descends to the most minute details; the same enactment prescribes the principle and the method of its application, and thus imposes a multitude of strict and rigorously defined obligations on the secondary functionaries of the state. The consequence of this is, that if all the secondary functionaries of the administration conform to the law, society in all its branches proceeds with the greatest uniformity; the difficulty remains of compelling the secondary functionaries of the administration to conform to the law. It may be affirmed that, in general, society has only two methods of enforcing the execution of the laws at its disposal; a discretionary power may be intrusted to a superior functionary of directing all the others, and of cashiering them in case of disobedience; or the courts of justice may be authorized to inflict judicial penalties on the offender: but these two methods are not always available.

The right of directing a civil officer pre-supposes that of cashiering him if he does not obey orders, and of rewarding him by promotion if he fulfils his duties with propriety. But an elected magistrate can neither be cashiered nor promoted. All elective functions are inalienable until their term is expired. In fact, the elected magistrate has nothing either to expect or to fear from his constituents; and when all public offices are filled by ballot, there can be no series of official dignities, because the double right of commanding and of enforcing obedience can never be vested in the same individual, and because the power of issuing an order can never be joined to that of inflicting a punishment or bestowing a reward.

The communities therefore in which the secondary functionaries of the government are elected, are perforce obliged to make great use of judicial penalties as a means of administration. This is not evident at first sight; for those in power are apt to look upon the institution of elective functionaries as one concession, and the subjection of the elective magistrate to the judges of the land as another. They are equally averse to both these innovations; and as they are more pressingly solicited to grant the former than the latter, they accede to the election of the magistrate, and leave him independent of the judicial power. Nevertheless, the second of these measures is the only thing that can possibly counterbalance the first; and it will be found that an elective authority which is not subject to judicial power will, sooner or later, either elude all control or be destroyed. The courts of justice are the only possible medium between the central power and the administrative bodies; they alone can compel the elected functionary to obey, without violating the rights of the elector. The extension of judicial power in the political world ought therefore to be in the exact ratio of the extension of elective offices; if these two institutions do not go hand in hand, the state must fall into anarchy or into subjection.

It has always been remarked that habits of legal business do not render men apt to the exercise of administrative authority. The Americans have borrowed from the English, their fathers, the idea of an institution which is unknown upon the continent of Europe: I allude to that of justices of the peace.

The justice of the peace is a sort of *mezzo termine* between the magistrate and the man of the world, between the civil officer and the judge. A justice of the peace is a well-informed citizen, though he is not necessarily versed in the knowledge of the laws. His office simply obliges him to execute the police regulations of society; a task in which good sense and integrity are of more avail than legal science. The justice introduces into the administration a certain taste for established forms and publicity, which renders him a most unserviceable instrument of despotism; and, on the other hand, he is not blinded by those superstitions which render legal officers unfit members of a government. The Americans have adopted the system of English justices of the peace, but they have deprived it of that aristocratic character which is discernible in the mother-country. The governor of Massachusetts* appoints a certain number of justices of the peace in every county, whose functions last seven years.† He farther designates three individuals from among the whole

* We shall hereafter learn what a governor is; I shall content myself with remarking in this place, that he represents the executive power of the whole state.

† See the constitution of Massachusetts, chap. ii., § 1; chap. iii., § 3.

body of justices, who form in each county what is called the court of sessions. The justices take a personal share in public business; they are sometimes ihtrusted with administrative functions in conjunction with elected officers;* they sometimes constitute a tribunal, before which the magistrates summarily prosecute a refractory citizen or the citizens inform against the abuses of the magistrate. But it is in the court of sessions that they exercise their most important functions. This court meets twice a year in the county town; in Massachusetts it is empowered to enforce the obedience of the greater number† of public officers.‡ It must be observed that in the state of Massachusetts the court of sessions is at the same time an administrative body, properly so called, and a political tribunal. It has been asserted that the county is a purely administrative division. The court of sessions presides over that small number of affairs which, as they concern several townships, or all the townships of the county in common, cannot be intrusted to any of them in particular.§ In all that concerns county business, the duties of the court of sessions are therefore purely administrative; and if in its investigations it occasionally borrows the forms of judicial procedure, it is only with a view to its own information,|| or

* Thus, for example, a stranger arrives in a township from a country where a contagious disease prevails, and he falls ill. Two justices of the peace can, with the assent of the selectmen, order the sheriff of the county to remove and take care of him. Act of 22d June, 1797; vol. i., p. 540.

In general the justices interfere in all the important acts of the administration, and give them a semi-judicial character.

† I say *the greater number* because certain administrative misdemeanors are brought before the ordinary tribunals. If, for instance, a township refuses to make the necessary expenditure for its schools, or to name a school-committee, it is liable to a heavy fine. But this penalty is pronounced by the supreme judicial court or the court of common pleas. See the act of 10th March, 1827; laws of Massachusetts, vol. iii., p. 190. Or when a township neglects to provide the necessary war-stores. Act of 21st February, 1822; *Id.* vol. ii., p. 570.

‡ In their individual capacity, the justices of the peace take a part in the business of the counties and townships. The more important acts of the municipal government are rarely decided upon without the co-operation of one of their body.

§ These affairs may be brought under the following heads: 1. The erection of prisons and courts of justice. 2. The county budget, which is afterward voted by the state. 3. The assessment of the taxes so voted. 4. Grants of certain patents. 5. The laying down and repairs of the county roads.

|| Thus, when a road is under consideration, almost all difficulties are disposed of by the aid of the jury.

as a guarantee to the community over which it presides. But when the administration of the township is brought before it, it almost always acts as a judicial body, and in some few cases as an administrative assembly.

The first difficulty is to procure the obedience of an authority so entirely independent of the general laws of the state as the township is. We have stated that assessors are annually named by the town meetings, to levy the taxes. If a township attempts to evade the payment of the taxes by neglecting to name its assessors, the court of sessions condemns it to a heavy penalty.* The fine is levied on each of the inhabitants; and the sheriff of the county, who is an officer of justice, executes the mandate. Thus it is that in the United States the authority of the government is mysteriously concealed under the forms of a judicial sentence; and the influence is at the same time fortified by that irresistible power with which men have invested the formalities of law.

These proceedings are easy to follow, and to understand. The demands made upon a township are in general plain and accurately defined; they consist in a simple fact without any complication, or in a principle without its application in detail.† But the difficulty increases when it is not the obedience of the township, but that of the town officers, which is to be enforced. All the reprehensible actions of which a public functionary may be guilty are reducible to the following heads:—

He may execute the law without energy or zeal;

He may neglect to execute the law;

He may do what the law enjoins him not to do.

The last two violations of duty can alone come under the cognizance of a tribunal; a positive and appreciable fact is the indispensable foundation of an action at law. Thus, if the selectmen omit to fulfil the legal formalities usual to town elections, they may be condemned to pay a fine;‡ but

* See the act of the 20th February, 1786; laws of Massachusetts, vol. i., p. 217.

† There is an indirect method of enforcing the obedience of a township. Suppose that the funds which the law demands for the maintenance of the roads have not been voted; the town-surveyor is then authorized, *ex-officio*, to levy the supplies. As he is personally responsible to private individuals for the state of the roads, and indictable before the court of sessions, he is sure to employ the extraordinary right which the law gives him against the township. Thus by threatening the officer, the court of sessions exacts compliance from the town. See the act of 5th March, 1787; laws of Massachasetts, vol. i., p. 305

‡ Laws of Massachusetts, vol. 2., p. 45.

when the public officer performs his duty without ability, and when he obeys the letter of the law without zeal or energy, he is at least beyond the reach of judicial interference. The court of sessions, even when it is invested with its administrative powers, is in this case unable to compel him to a more satisfactory obedience. The fear of removal is the only check to these quasi offences; and as the court of sessions does not originate the town authorities, it cannot remove functionaries whom it does not appoint. Moreover, a perpetual investigation would be necessary to convict the subordinate officer of negligence or lukewarmness; and the court of sessions sits but twice a year, and then only judges such offences as are brought before its notice. The only security for that active and enlightened obedience, which a court of justice cannot impose upon public officers, lies in the possibility of their arbitrary removal. In France this security is sought for in powers exercised by the heads of the administration; in America it is sought for in the principle of election.

Thus, to recapitulate in a few words what I have been showing:—

If a public officer in New England commits a crime in the exercise of his functions, the ordinary courts of justice are always called upon to pass sentence upon him.

If he commits a fault in his official capacity, a purely administrative tribunal is empowered to punish him; and, if the affair is important or urgent, the judge supplies the omission of the functionary.*

Lastly, if the same individual is guilty of one of those intangible offences, of which human justice has no cognizance, he annually appears before a tribunal from which there is no appeal, which can at once reduce him to insignificance, and deprive him of his charge. This system undoubtedly possesses great advantages, but its execution is attended with a practical difficulty which it is important to point out.

I have already observed, that the administrative tribunal, which is called the court of sessions, has no right of inspection over the town officers. It can only interfere when the conduct of a magistrate is specially brought under its notice; and this is the delicate part of the system. The Americans of New England are unacquainted with the office of public

* If, for instance, a township persists in refusing to name its assessors, the court of sessions nominates them; and the magistrates thus appointed are invested with the same authority as elected officers See the act quoted above, 20th February, 1787.

prosecutor in the court of sessions,* and it may readily be perceived that it could not have been established without difficulty. If an accusing magistrate had merely been appointed in the chief town of each county, and if he had been unassisted by agents in the townships, he would not have been better acquainted with what was going on in the county than the members of the court of sessions. But to appoint agents in each township, would have been to centre in his person the most formidable of powers, that of a judicial administration. Moreover, laws are the children of habit, and nothing of the kind exists in the legislation of England. The Americans have therefore divided the officers of inspection and of prosecution as well as all the other functions of the administration. Grand-jurors are bound by the law to apprize the court to which they belong of all the misdemeanors which may have been committed in their county.† There are certain great offences which are officially prosecuted by the state;‡ but more frequently the task of punishing delinquents devolves upon the fiscal officer, whose province it is to receive the fine; thus the treasurer of the township is charged with the prosecution of such administrative offences as fall under his notice. But a more especial appeal is made by American legislation to the private interest of the citizen,§ and this great principle is constantly to be met with in studying the laws of the United States. American legislators are more apt to give men credit for intelligence than for honesty; and they rely not a little on personal cupidity for the execution of the laws. When an individual is really and sensibly injured by an administrative abuse, it is natural that his personal interest should induce him to prosecute. But if a legal formality be required which, however advantageous to the community, is of small importance to individnals, plaintiffs may be less easily found; and thus, by a tacit agreement, the laws might fall into disuse. Reduced by their system to this extremity, the Americans are obliged to encourage informers by bestowing on them a portion of the penalty in certain cases;‖ and

* I say the court of sessions, because in common courts there is a magistrate who exercises some of the functions of a public prosecutor.

† The grand-jurors are, for instance, bound to inform the court of the bad state of the roads. Laws of Massachusetts, vol. i., p. 308.

‡ If, for instance, the treasurer of the county holds back his account Laws of Massachusetts, vol. i., p. 406.

§ Thus, if a private individual breaks down or is wounded in consequence of the badness of a road, he can sue the township or the county for damages at the sessions. Laws of Massachusetts, vol. i., p. 309.

‖ In cases of invasion or insurrection, if the town officers neglect to

to ensure the execution of the laws by the dangerous expedient of degrading the morals of the people.

The only administrative authority above the county magistrates is, properly speaking, that of the government.

GENERAL REMARKS ON THE ADMINISTRATION OF THE UNITED STATES.

Difference of the States of the Union in their Systems of Administration.—Activity and Perfection of the local Authorities decreases towards the South.—Power of the Magistrates increases; that of the Elector diminishes.—Administration passes from the Township to the County.—States of New York, Ohio, Pennsylvania.—Principles of Administration applicable to the whole Union.—Election of public Officers, and Inalienability of their Functions.—Absence of Gradation of Ranks.—Introduction of judicial Resources into the Administration.

I HAVE already premised that after having examined the constitution of the township and the county of New England in detail, I should take a general view of the remainder of the Union. Townships and a local activity exist in every state; but in no part of the confederation is a township to be met with precisely similar to those in New England. The more we descend toward the south, the less active does the business of the township or parish become; the number of magistrates, of functions, and of rights, decreases; the population exercises a less immediate influence on affairs; town-meetings are less frequent, and the subjects of debates less numerous. The power of the elected magistrate is augmented, and that of the elector diminished, while the public spirit of the local communities is less awakened and less influential.*

furnish the necessary stores and ammunition for the militia, the township may be condemned to a fine of from two to five hundred dollars. It may readily be imagined that in such a case it might happen that no one cared to prosecute: hence the law adds that all the citizens may indict offences of this kind, and that half the fine shall belong to the plaintiff. See the act of 6th March, 1810; vol. ii., p. 236. The same clause is frequently to be met with in the laws of Massachusetts. Not only are private individuals thus incited to prosecute public officers, but the public officers are encouraged in the same manner to bring the disobedience of private individuals to justice. If a citizen refuses to perform the work which has been assigned to him upon a road, the road-surveyor may prosecute him, and he receives half the penalty for himself. See the laws above quoted, vol. i., p. 308.

* For details, see Revised Statutes of the state of New York, part I,

These differences may be perceived to a certain extent in the state of New York; they are very sensible in Pennsylvania; but they become less striking as we advance to the northwest. The majority of the emigrants who settle in the northwestern states are natives of New England, and they carry the habits of their mother-country with them into that which they adopt. A township in Ohio is by no means dissimilar from a township in Massachusetts.

We have seen that in Massachusetts the principal part of the public administration lies in the township. It forms the common centre of the interests and affections of the citizens. But this ceases to be the case as we descend to states in which knowledge is less generally diffused, and where the township consequently offers fewer guarantees of a wise and active administration. As we leave New England, therefore, we find that the importance of the town is gradually transferred to the county, which becomes the centre of administration, and the intermediate power between the government and the citizen. In Massachusetts the business of the town is conducted by the court of sessions, which is composed of a *quorum* named by the governor and his council; but the county has no representative assembly, and its expenditure is voted by the national (*a*) legislature. In the great state of New York, on the contrary, and in those of Ohio and Pennsylvania, the inhabitants of each county choose a certain number of representatives, who constitute the assembly of the county.* The county assembly has the right of taxing the inhabitants to a certain extent; and in this respect it enjoys the privileges of a real legislative body: at the same

chap. xi., vol. i., pp. 336–364, entitled, "Of the Powers, Duties, and Privileges of Towns."

See in the digest of the laws of Pennsylvania, the words, ASSESSORS, COLLECTOR, CONSTABLES, OVERSEER OF THE POOR, SUPERVISORS OF HIGHWAYS: and in the acts of a general nature of the state of Ohio, the act of 25th February, 1834, relating to townships, p. 412; beside the peculiar dispositions relating to divers town officers, such as township's clerks, trustees, overseers of the poor, fence-viewers, appraisers of property, township's treasurer, constables, supervisors of highways.

(*a*) The author means the state legislature. The congress has no control over the expenditure of the counties or of the states.

* See the Revised Statutes of the state of New York, part i., chap. xi., vol. i., p. 410. *Idem*, chap. xii., p. 366: also in the acts of the state of Ohio, an act relating to county commissioners, 25th February, 1824, p. 263. See the Digest of the Laws of Pennsylvania, at the words, COUNTY-RATES AND LEVIES, p. 170.

In the state of New York, each township elects a representative, who has a share in the administration of the county as well as in that of the township.

time it exercises an executive power in the county, frequently directs the administration of the townships, and restricts their authority within much narrower bounds than in Massachusetts.

Such are the principal differences which the systems of county and town administration present in the federal states. Were it my intention to examine the provisions of American law minutely, I should have to point out still farther differences in the executive details of the several communities. But what I have already said may suffice to show the general principles on which the administration of the United States rests. These principles are differently applied; their consequences are more or less numerous in various localities; but they are always substantially the same. The laws differ, and their outward features change, but their character does not vary. If the township and the county are not everywhere constituted in the same manner, it is at least true that in the United States the county and the township are always based upon the same principle, namely, that every one is the best judge of what concerns himself alone, and the person most able to supply his private wants. The township and the county are therefore bound to take care of their special interests: the state governs, but it does not interfere with their administration. Exceptions to this rule may be met with, but not a contrary principle.

The first consequence of this doctrine has been to cause all the magistrates to be chosen either by, or at least from among the citizens. As the officers are everywhere elected or appointed for a certain period, it has been impossible to establish the rules of a dependent series of authorities; there are almost as many independent functionaries as there are functions, and the executive power is disseminated in a multitude of hands. Hence arose the indispensable necessity of introducing the control of the courts of justice over the administration, and the system of pecuniary penalties, by which the secondary bodies and their representatives are constrained to obey the laws. The system obtains from one end of the Union to the other. The power of punishing the misconduct of public officers, or of performing the part of the executive, in urgent cases, has not, however, been bestowed on the same judges in all the states. The Anglo-Americans derived the institution of justices of the peace from a common source; but although it exists in all the states, it is not always turned to the same use. The justices of the peace everywhere participate in the administration of the townships and the counties,* either as public officers or as the judges of public misdemeanors, but in most of the states the more important classes of public offences come under the cognisance of the ordinary tribunals.

The election of public officers, or the inalienability of their functions, the absence of a gradation of powers, and the introduction of a judicial control over the secondary branches of the administration, are the universal characteristics of the American system from Maine to the Floridas. In some states (and that of New York has advanced most in this direction) traces of a centralised administration begin to be discernible. In the state of New York the officers of the central government exercise, in certain cases, a sort of inspection of control over the secondary bodies.† At other times they constitute a court of appeal for the decision of affairs.‡ In the state of New York judicial penalties are less

* In some of the southern states the county-courts are charged with all the details of the administration. See the Statutes of the State of Tennessee, *arts.* JUDICIARY, TAXES, &c.

† For instance, the direction of public instruction centres in the hands of the government. The legislature names the members of the university, who are denominated regents; the governor and lieutenant-governor of the state are necessarily of the number. Revised Statutes, vol. i., p. 455. The regents of the university annually visit the colleges and academies, and make their report to the legislature. Their superintendence is not inefficient, for several reasons: the colleges in order to become corporations stand in need of a charter, which is only granted on the recommendation of the regents: every year funds are distributed by the state for the encouragement of learning, and the regents are the distributors of this money. See chap. xv., "Public Instruction," Revised Statutes, vol i., p. 455.

The school commissioners are obliged to send an annual report to the superintendent of the state. *Idem*, p. 448.

A similar report is annually made to the same person on the number and condition of the poor. *Idem*, p. 631.

‡ If any one conceives himself to be wronged by the school commissioners (who are town-officers), he can appeal to the superintendent of the primary schools, whose decision is final. Revised Statutes, vol. i., p. 487.

Provisions similar to those above cited are to be met with from time to time in the laws of the state of New York: but in general these attempts at centralisation are weak and unproductive. The great authorities of the state have the right of watching and controlling the subordinate agents, without that of rewarding or punishing them. The same individual is never empowered to give an order and to punish disobedience; he has therefore the right of commanding, without the means of exacting compliance. In 1830 the superintendent of schools complained in his annual report addressed to the legislature, that several school commissioners had neglected, notwithstanding his application, to furnish him with the accounts which were due. He added, that if this omission continued, he should be obliged to prosecute them, as the law directs, before the proper tribunals.

used than in other parts as a means of administration; and the right of prosecuting the offences of public officers is vested in fewer hands.* The same tendency is faintly observable in some other states;† but in general the prominent feature of the administration in the United States is its excessive local independence.

OF THE STATE.

I HAVE described the townships and the administration: it now remains for me to speak of the state and government. This is ground I may pass over rapidly, without fear of being misunderstood; for all I have to say is to be found in written forms of the various constitutions, which are easily to be procured.‡ These constitutions rest upon a simple and rational theory; their forms have been adopted by all constitutional nations, and are become familiar to us.

In this place, therefore, it is only necessary for me to give a short analysis; I shall endeavor afterward to pass judgment upon what I now describe.

LEGISLATIVE POWER OF THE STATE.

Division of the Legislative Body into two Houses.—Senate.—House of Representatives.—Different functions of these two Bodies.

THE legislative power of the state is vested in two assemblies, the first of which generally bears the name of the senate.

The senate is commonly a legislative body; but it sometimes becomes an executive and judicial one. It takes a part in the government in several ways, according to the constitution of the different states;§ but it is in the nomination of

* Thus the district-attorney is directed to recover all fines below the sum of fifty dollars, (a) unless such a right has been specially awarded to another magistrate. Revised Statutes, vol. i., p. 383.

† Several traces of centralisation may be discovered in Massachusetts, for instance, the committees of the town-schools are directed to make an annual report to the secretary of state. See Laws of Massachusetts, vol. i., p. 367.

‡ See the constitution of New York.

§ In Massachusetts the Senate is not invested with any administrative functions.

(a) The words below the sum of fifty dollars should be omitted in the above note.

public functionaries that it most commonly assumes an executive power. It partakes of judicial power in the trial of certain political offences, and sometimes also in the decision of certain civil cases.* The number of its members is always small. The other branch of the legislature, which is usually called the house of representatives, has no share whatever in the administration, and only takes a part in the judicial power inasmuch as it impeaches public functionaries before the senate.

The members of the two houses are nearly everywhere subject to the same conditions of election. They are chosen in the same manner, and by the same citizens.

The only difference which exists between them is, that the term for which the senate is chosen, is in general longer than that of the house of representatives. The latter seldom remain in office longer than a year; the former usually sit two or three years.

By granting to the senators the privilege of being chosen for several years, and being renewed seriatim, the law takes care to preserve in the legislative body a nucleus of men already accustomed to public business, and capable of exercising a salutary influence upon the junior members.

The Americans, plainly, did not desire, by this separation of the legislative body into two branches, to make one house hereditary and the other elective; one aristocratic and the other democratic. It was not their object to create in the one a bulwark to power, while the other represented the interests and passions of the people. The only advantages which result from the present constitution of the United States, are, the division of the legislative power, and the consequent check upon political assemblies; with the creation of a tribunal of appeal for the revision of the laws.

Time and experience, however, have convinced the Americans that if these are its only advantages, the division of the legislative power is still a principle of the greatest necessity. Pennsylvania was the only one of the United States which at first attempted to establish a single house of assembly; and Franklin himself was so far carried away by the necessary consequences of the principle of the sovereignty of the people, as to have concurred in the measure; but the Pennsylvanians were soon obliged to change the law, and to create two houses. Thus the principle of the division of the legislative power was finally established, and its necessity may henceforward be regarded as a demonstrated truth.

* As in the state of New York.

This theory, which was nearly unknown to the republics of antiquity—which was introduced into the world almost by accident, like so many other great truths—and misunderstood by several modern nations, is at length become an axiom in the political science of the present age.

THE EXECUTIVE POWER OF THE STATE.

Office of Governor in an American State.—The Place he occupies in relation to the Legislature.—His Rights and his Duties.—His Dependence on the People.

The executive power of the state may with truth be said to be *represented* by the governor, although he enjoys but a portion of its rights. The supreme magistrate, under the title of governor, is the official moderator and counsellor of the legislature. He is armed with a suspensive veto, which allows him to stop, or at least to retard, its movements at pleasure. He lays the wants of the country before the legislative body, and points out the means which he thinks may be usefully employed in providing for them; he is the natural executor of its decrees in all the undertakings which interest the nation at large.* In the absence of the legislature, the governor is bound to take all necessary steps to guard the state against violent shocks and unforeseen dangers.

The whole military power of the state is at the disposal of the governor. He is commander of the militia and head of the armed force. When the authority, which is by general consent awarded to the laws, is disregarded, the governor puts himself at the head of the armed force of the state, to quell resistance and to restore order.

Lastly, the governor takes no share in the administration of townships and counties, except it be indirectly in the nomination of justices of the peace, which nomination he has not the power to revoke.†

The governor is an elected magistrate, and is generally chosen for one or two years only; so that he always continues to be strictly dependent on the majority who returned him.

* Practically speaking, it is not always the governor who executes the plans of the legislature; it often happens that the latter, in voting a measure, names special agents to superintend the execution of it.

† In some of the states the justices of the peace are not nominated by the governor.

POLITICAL EFFECTS OF THE SYSTEM OF LOCAL ADMINISTRATION IN THE UNITED STATES.

Necessary Distinction between the general Centralisation of Government, and the Centralisation of the local Administration.—Local Administration not centralized in the United States; great general Centralisation of the Government.—Some bad Consequences resulting to the United States from the local Administration.—Administrative Advantages attending the Order of things.—The Power which conducts the Government is less regular, less enlightened, less learned, but much greater than in Europe.—Political Advantages of this Order of things.—In the United States the Interests of the Country are everywhere kept in View.—Support given to the Government by the Community.—Provincial Institutions more necessary in Proportion as the social Condition becomes more democratic.—Reason of this.

Centralisation is become a word of general and daily use, without any precise meaning being attached to it. Nevertheless, there exist two distinct kinds of centralisation, which it is necessary to discriminate with accuracy.

Certain interests are common to all parts of a nation, such as the enactment of its general laws, and the maintenance of its foreign relations. Other interests are peculiar to certain parts of the nation; such, for instance, as the business of different townships. When the power which directs the general interests is centred in one place, or in the same persons, it constitutes a central government. The power of directing partial or local interests, when brought together, in like manner constitutes what may be termed a central administration.

Upon some points these two kinds of centralisation coalesce; but by classifying the objects which fall more particularly within the province of each of them, they may easily be distinguished.

It is evident that a central government acquires immense power when united to administrative centralisation. Thus combined, it accustoms men to set their own will habitually and completely aside; to submit, not only for once or upon one point, but in every respect, and at all times. Not only, therefore, does the union of power subdue them by force, but it affects them in the ordinary habits of life, and influences each individual, first separately, and then collectively.

These two kinds of centralisation mutually assist and attract each other: but they must not be supposed to be inseparable. It is impossible to imagine a more completely central government than that which existed in France under

Louis XIV.; when the same individual was the author and the interpreter of the laws, and being the representative of France at home and abroad, he was justified in asserting that the state was identified with his person. Nevertheless, the administration was much less centralized under Louis XIV., than it is at the present day.

In England the centralisation of the government is carried to great perfection; the state has the compact vigor of a man, and by the sole act of its will it puts immense engines in motion, and wields or collects the efforts of its authority. Indeed, I cannot conceive that a nation can enjoy a secure or prosperous existence without a powerful centralisation of government. But I am of opinion that a central administration enervates the nations in which it exists by incessantly diminishing their public spirit. If such an administration succeeds in condensing at a given moment on a given point all the disposable resources of a people, it impairs at least the renewal of those resources. It may ensure a victory in the hour of strife, but it gradually relaxes the sinews of strength. It may contribute admirably to the transient greatness of a man, but it cannot ensure the durable prosperity of a people.

If we pay proper attention, we shall find that whenever it is said that a state cannot act because it has no central point, it is the centralisation of the government in which it is deficient. It is frequently asserted, and we are prepared to assent to the proposition, that the German empire was never able to bring all its powers into action. But the reason was, that the state has never been able to enforce obedience to its general laws, because the several members of that great body always claimed the right, or found the means, of refusing their co-operation to the representatives of the common authority, even in the affairs which concerned the mass of the people; in other words, because there was no centralisation of government. The same remark is applicable to the middle ages; the cause of all the confusion of feudal society was that the control, not only of local but of general interests, was divided among a thousand hands, and broken up in a thousand different ways; the absence of a central government prevented the nations of Europe from advancing with energy in any straightforward course.

We have shown that in the United States no central administration, and no dependent series of public functionaries, exist. Local authority has been carried to lengths which no European nation could endure without great inconvenience, and which have even produced some disadvantageous consequences in America. But in the United States the centralisation of the government is complete; and it would be easy to prove that the national power is more compact than it has ever been in the old monarchies of Europe. Not only is there but one legislative body in each state; not only does there exist but one source of political authority; but numerous district assemblies and county courts have in general been avoided, lest they should be tempted to exceed their administrative duties and interfere with the government. In America the legislature of each state is supreme; nothing can impede its authority; neither privileges, nor local immunities, nor personal influence, nor even the empire of reason, since it represents that majority which claims to be the sole organ of reason. Its own determination is, therefore, the only limit to its action. In juxtaposition to it, and under its immediate control, is the representative of the executive power, whose duty it is to constrain the refractory to submit by superior force. The only symptom of weakness lies in certain details of the action of the government. The American republics have no standing armies to intimidate a discontented minority; but as no minority has as yet been reduced to declare open war, the necessity of an army has not been felt. The state usually employs the officers of the township or the county, to deal with the citizens. Thus, for instance, in New England the assessor fixes the rate of taxes; the collector receives them; the town treasurer transmits the amount to the public treasury; and the disputes which may arise are brought before the ordinary courts of justice. This method of collecting taxes is slow as well as inconvenient, and it would prove a perpetual hindrance to a government whose pecuniary demands were large. In general it is desirable that in whatever materially affects its existence, the government should be served by officers of its own, appointed by itself, removable at pleasure, and accustomed to rapid methods of proceeding. But it will always be easy for the central government, organized as it is in America, to introduce new and more efficacious modes of action proportioned to its wants.

The absence of a central government will not, then, as has often been asserted, prove the destruction of the republics of the New World; far from supposing that the American governments are not sufficiently centralized, I shall prove hereafter that they are too much so. The legislative bodies daily encroach upon the authority of the government, and their tendency, like that of the French convention, is to appropriate it entirely to themselves. Under these circumstances the social power is constantly changing hands, because it is subordinate to the power of the people, which is too apt to forget the maxims of wisdom and of foresight in the consciousness of its strength: hence arises its danger; and thus its vigor, and not its impotence, will probably be the cause of its ultimate destruction.

The system of local administration produces several different effects in America. The Americans seem to me to have outstepped the limits of sound policy, in isolating the administration of the government; for order, even in second-rate affairs, is a matter of national importance.* As the state has no administrative functionaries of its own, stationed on different parts of its territory, to whom it can give a common impulse, the consequence is that it rarely attempts to issue any general police regulations. The want of these regulations is severely felt, and is frequently observed by Europeans. The appearance of disorder which prevails on the surface, leads them at first to imagine that society is in a state of anarchy; nor do they perceive their mistake till they have gone deeper into the subject. Certain undertakings are of importance to the whole state; but they cannot be put in execution, because there is no national administration to direct them. Abandoned to the exertions of the towns or counties, under the care of elected or temporary

* The authority which represents the state ought not, I think, to waive the right of inspecting the local administration, even when it does not interfere more actively. Suppose, for instance, that an agent of the government was stationed at some appointed spot, in the county, to prosecute the misdemeanors of the town and county officers, would not a more uniform order be the result, without in any way compromising the independence of the township? Nothing of the kind, however, exists in America; there is nothing above the county courts, which have, as it were, only an accidental cognizance of the offences they are meant to repress.

[This note seems to have been written without reference to the provision existing, it is believed in every state of the Union, by which a local officer is appointed in each county, to conduct all public prosecutions at the expense of the state. And in each county, a grand-jury is assembled three or four times at least in every year, to which all who are aggrieved have free access, and where every complaint, particularly those against public officers, which has the least color of truth, is sure to be heard and investigated.

Such an agent as the author suggests would soon come to be considered a public informer, the most odious of all characters in the United States; and he would lose all efficiency and strength. With the provision above mentioned, there is little danger that a citizen, oppressed by a public officer, would find any difficulty in becoming his own informer, and inducing a rigid inquiry into the alleged misconduct.—*American Editor.*]

agents, they lead to no result, or at least to no durable benefit.

The partisans of centralisation in Europe maintain that the government directs the affairs of each locality better than the citizens could do it for themselves: this may be true when the central power is enlightened, and when the local districts are ignorant; when it is as alert as they are slow; when it is accustomed to act, and they to obey. Indeed, it is evident that this double tendency must augment with the increase of centralisation, and that the readiness of the one, and the incapacity of the others, must become more and more prominent. But I deny that such is the case when the people is as enlightened, as awake to its interests, and as accustomed to reflect on them, as the Americans are. I am persuaded, on the contrary, that in this case the collective strength of the citizens will always conduce more efficaciously to the public welfare than the authority of the government. It is difficult to point out with certainty the means of arousing a sleeping population, and of giving it passions and knowledge which it does not possess; it is, I am well aware, an arduous task to persuade men to busy themselves about their own affairs; and it would frequently be easier to interest them in the punctilios of court etiquette than in the repairs of their common dwelling. But whenever a central administration affects to supersede the persons most interested, I am inclined to suppose that it is either misled, or desirous to mislead. However enlightened and however skilful a central power may be, it cannot of itself embrace all the details of the existence of a great nation. Such vigilance exceeds the powers of man. And when it attempts to create and set in motion so many complicated springs, it must submit to a very imperfect result, or consume itself in bootless efforts.

Centralisation succeeds more easily, indeed, in subjecting the external actions of men to a certain uniformity, which at last commands our regard, independently of the objects to which it is applied, like those devotees who worship the statue and forget the deity it represents. Centralisation imparts without difficulty an admirable regularity to the routine of business; rules the details of the social police with sagacity; represses the smallest disorder and the most petty misdemeanors; maintains society in a *statu quo*, alike secure from improvement and decline; and perpetuates a drowsy precision in the conduct of affairs, which is hailed by the heads of the administration as a sign of perfect order and public tranquillity;* in short, it excels more in prevention than in action. Its force deserts it when society is to be disturbed or accelerated in its course; and if once the co-operation of private citizens is necessary to the furtherance of its measures, the secret of its impotence is disclosed. Even while it invokes their assistance, it is on the condition that they shall act exactly as much as the government chooses, and exactly in the manner it appoints. They are to take charge of the details, without aspiring to guide the system; they are to work in a dark and subordinate sphere, and only to judge the acts in which they have themselves co-operated, by their results. These, however, are not conditions on which the alliance of the human will is to be obtained; its carriage must be free, and its actions responsible, or (such is the constitution of man) the citizen had rather remain a passive spectator than a dependent actor in schemes with which he is unacquainted.

It is undeniable, that the want of those uniform regulations which control the conduct of every inhabitant of France is not unfrequently felt in the United States. Gross instances of social indifference and neglect are to be met with; and from time to time disgraceful blemishes are seen, in complete contrast with the surrounding civilisation. Useful undertakings, which cannot succeed without perpetual attention and rigorous exactitude, are very frequently abandoned in the end; for in America, as well as in other countries, the people is subject to sudden impulses and momentary exertions. The European who is accustomed to find a functionary always at hand to interfere with all he undertakes, has some difficulty in accustoming himself to the complex mechanism of the administration of the townships. In general it may be affirmed that the lesser details of the police, which render life easy and comfortable, are neglected in America; but that the essential guarantees of man in society are as strong there as elsewhere. In America the power which conducts the government is far less regular, less enlightened, and less learned, but a hundredfold more authoritative, than in Eu-

* China appears to me to present the most perfect instance of that species of well-being which a completely central administration may furnish to the nations among which it exists. Travellers assure us that the Chinese have peace without happiness, industry without improvement, stability without strength, and public order without public morality. The condition of society is always tolerable, never excellent. I am convinced that, when China is opened to European observation, it will be found to contain the most perfect model of a central administration which exists in the universe.

rope. In no country in the world do the citizens make such exertions for the common weal; and I am acquainted with no people which has established schools as numerous and as efficacious, places of public worship better suited to the wants of the inhabitants, or roads kept in better repair. Uniformity or permanence of design, the minute arrangement of details,* and the perfection of an ingenious administration, must not be sought for in the United States; but it will be easy to find, on the other hand, the symptoms of a power, which, if it is somewhat barbarous, is at least robust; and of an existence, which is checkered with accidents indeed, but cheered at the same time by animation and effort.

Granting for an instant that the villages and counties of the United States would be more usefully governed by a remote authority, which they had never seen, than by functionaries taken from the midst of them—admitting, for the sake of argument, that the country would be more secure, and the resources of society better employed, if the whole administration centred in a single arm, still the *political* advantages which the Americans derive from their system would induce me to prefer it to the contrary plan. It profits me but little, after all, that a vigilant authority protects the tranquillity of my pleasures, and constantly averts all danger

* A writer of talent, who, in the comparison which he has drawn between the finances of France and those of the United States, has proved that ingenuity cannot always supply the place of a knowledge of facts, very justly reproaches the Americans for the sort of confusion which exists in the accounts of the expenditure in the townships; and after giving the model of a departmental budget in France, he adds: "We are indebted to centralisation, that admirable invention of a great man, for the uniform order and method which prevail alike in all the municipal budgets, from the largest town to the humblest commune." Whatever may be my admiration of this result, when I see the communes of France, with their excellent system of accounts, plunged in the grossest ignorance of their true interests, and abandoned to so incorrigible an apathy that they seem to vegetate rather than to live; when, on the other hand, I observe the activity, the information, and the spirit of enterprise which keeps society in perpetual labor, in those American townships whose budgets are drawn up with small method and with still less uniformity, I am struck by the spectacle; for to my mind the end of a good government is to ensure the welfare of a people, and not to establish order and regularity in the midst of its misery and its distress. I am therefore led to suppose that the prosperity of the American townships and the apparent confusion of their accounts, the distress of the French communes and the perfection of their budget, may be attributable to the same cause. At any rate I am suspicious of a benefit which is united to so many evils, and I am not averse to an evil which is compensated by so many benefits.

from my path, without my care or my concern, if the same authority is the absolute mistress of my liberty and of my life, and if it so monopolises all the energy of existence, that when it languishes everything languishes around it, that when it sleeps everything must sleep, that when it dies the state itself must perish.

In certain countries of Europe the natives consider themselves as a kind of settlers, indifferent to the fate of the spot upon which they live. The greatest changes are effected without their concurrence and (unless chance may have apprised them of the event) without their knowledge; nay more, the citizen is unconcerned as to the condition of his village, the police of his street, the repairs of the church or the parsonage; for he looks upon all these things as unconnected with himself, and as the property of a powerful stranger whom he calls the government. He has only a life-interest in these possessions, and he entertains no notions of ownership or of improvement. This want of interest in his own affairs goes so far, that if his own safety or that of his children is endangered, instead of trying to avert the peril, he will fold his arms, and wait till the nation comes to his assistance. This same individual, who has so completely sacrificed his own free will, has no natural propensity to obedience; he cowers, it is true, before the pettiest officer; but he braves the law with the spirit of a conquered foe as soon as its superior force is removed: his oscillations between servitude and license are perpetual. When a nation has arrived at this state, it must either change its customs and its laws, or perish: the source of public virtue is dry; and though it may contain subjects, the race of citizens is extinct. Such communities are a natural prey to foreign conquest; and if they do not disappear from the scene of life, it is because they are surrounded by other nations similar or inferior to themselves; it is because the instinctive feeling of their country's claims still exists in their hearts; and because an involuntary pride in the name it bears, or the vage reminiscence of its by-gone fame, suffices to give them the impulse of self-preservation.

Nor can the prodigious exertions made by certain people in the defence of a country, in which they may almost be said to have lived as aliens, be adduced in favor of such a system; for it will be found that in these cases their main incitement was religion. The permanence, the glory, and the prosperity of the nation, were become parts of their faith; and in defending the country they inhabited, they defended that holy city of which they were all citizens. The Turkish tribes have never taken an active share in the conduct of the affairs of society, but they accomplished stupendous enterprises as long as the victories of the sultans were the triumphs of the Mohammedan faith. In the present age they are in rapid decay, because their religion is departing, and despotism only remains. Montesquieu, who attributed to absolute power an authority peculiar to itself, did it, as I conceive, undeserved honor; for despotism, taken by itself, can produce no durable results. On close inspection we shall find that religion, and not fear, has ever been the cause of the long-lived prosperity of absolute governments. Whatever exertions may be made, no true power can be founded among men which does not depend upon the free union of their inclinations; and patriotism and religion are the only two motives in the world which can permanently direct the whole of a body politic to one end.

Laws cannot succeed in rekindling the ardor of an extinguished faith; but men may be interested in the fate of their country by the laws. By this influence, the vague impulse of patriotism, which never abandons the human heart, may be directed and revived: and if it be connected with the thoughts, the passions and daily habits of life, it may be consolidated into a durable and rational sentiment. Let it not be said that the time for the experiment is already past; for the old age of nations is not like the old age of men, and every fresh generation is a new people ready for the care of the legislator.

It is not the *administrative*, but the *political* effects of the local system that I most admire in America. In the United States the interests of the country are everywhere kept in view; they are an object of solicitude to the people of the whole Union, and every citizen is as warmly attached to them as if they were his own. He takes pride in the glory of his nation; he boasts of his success, to which he conceives himself to have contributed; and he rejoices in the general prosperity by which he profits. The feeling he entertains toward the state is analogous to that which unites him to his family, and it is by a kind of egotism that he interests himself in the welfare of his country.

The European generally submits to a public officer because he represents a superior force; but to an American he represents a right. In America it may be said that no one renders obedience to man, but to justice and to law. If the opinion which the citizen entertains of himself is exaggerated, it is at least salutary; he unhesitatingly confides in his own powers, which appear to him to be all-sufficient. When a private individual meditates an undertaking, however directly connected it may be with the welfare of society, he never thinks of soliciting the co-operation of the government: but he publishes his plan, offers to execute it himself, courts the assistance of other individuals, and struggles manfully against all obstacles. Undoubtedly he is less successful than the state might have been in his position; but in the end, the sum of these private undertakings far exceeds all that the government could effect.

As the administrative authority is within the reach of the citizens, whom it in some degree represents, it excites neither their jealousy nor their hatred: as its resources are limited, every one feels that he must not rely solely on its assistance. Thus when the administration thinks fit to interfere, it is not abandoned to itself as in Europe; the duties of the private citizens are not supposed to have lapsed because the state assists in their fulfilment; but every one is ready, on the contrary, to guide and to support it. This action of individual exertions, joined to that of the public authorities, frequently performs what the most energetic central administration would be unable to execute. It would be easy to adduce several facts in proof of what I advance, but I had rather give only one, with which I am more thoroughly acquainted.* In America, the means which the authorities have at their disposal for the discovery of crimes and the arrest of criminals are few. A state police does not exist, and passports are unknown. The criminal police of the United States cannot be compared with that of France; the magistrates and public prosecutors are not numerous, and the examinations of prisoners are rapid and oral. Nevertheless in no country does crime more rarely elude punishment. The reason is that every one conceives himself to be interested in furnishing evidence of the act committed, and in stopping the delinquent. During my stay in the United States, I saw the spontaneous formation of committees for the pursuit and prosecution of a man who had committed a great crime in a certain county. In Europe a criminal is an unhappy being, who is struggling for his life against the ministers of justice, while the population is merely a spectator of the conflict: in America he is looked upon as an enemy of the human race, and the whole of mankind is against him.

* See Appendix I.

I believe that provincial institutions are useful to all nations, but nowhere do they appear to me to be more indispensable than among a democratic people. In an aristocracy, order can always be maintained in the midst of liberty; and as the rulers have a great deal to lose, order is to them a first-rate consideration. In like manner an aristocracy protects the people from the excesses of despotism, because it always possesses an organized power ready to resist a despot. But a democracy without provincial institutions has no security against these evils. How can a populace, unaccustomed to freedom in small concerns, learn to use it temperately in great affairs? What resistance can be offered to tyranny in a country where every private individual is impotent, and where the citizens are united by no common tie? Those who dread the license of the mob, and those who fear the rule of absolute power, ought alike to desire the progressive growth of provincial liberties.

On the other hand, I am convinced that democratic nations are most exposed to fall beneath the yoke of a central administration, for several reasons, among which is the following:—

The constant tendency of these nations is to concentrate all the strength of the government in the hands of the only power which directly represents the people: because, beyond the people nothing is to be perceived but a mass of equal individuals confounded together. But when the same power is already in possession of all the attributes of the government, it can scarcely refrain from penetrating into the details of the administration; and an opportunity of doing so is sure to present itself in the end, as was the case in France. In the French revolution there were two impulses in opposite directions, which must never be confounded; the one was favorable to liberty, the other to despotism. Under the ancient monarchy the king was the sole author of the laws; and below the power of the sovereign, certain vestiges of provincial institutions half-destroyed, were still distinguishable. These provincial institutions were incoherent, ill-compacted, and frequently absurd; in the hands of the aristocracy they had sometimes been converted into instruments of oppression. The revolution declared itself the enemy of royalty and of provincial institutions at the same time; it confounded all that had preceded it—despotic power and the checks to its abuses—in an indiscriminate hatred; and its tendency was at once to republicanism and to centralisation. This double character of the French revolution is a fact which has been adroitly handled by the friends of absolute power. Can they be accused of laboring in the cause of despotism, when they are defending of the revolution ?* In this manner popularity may be conciliated with hostility to the rights of the people, and the secret slave of tyranny may be the professed admirer of freedom.

I have visited the two nations in which the system of provincial liberty has been most perfectly established, and I have listened to the opinions of different parties in those countries. In America I met with men who secretly aspired to destroy the democratic institutions of the Union ; in England, I found others who attacked aristocracy openly ; but I know of no one who does not regard provincial independence as a great benefit. In both countries I have heard a thousand different causes assigned for the evils of the state ; but the local system was never mentioned among them. I have heard citizens attribute the power and prosperity of their country to a multitude of reasons : but they *all* placed the advantages of local institutions in the foremost rank.

Am I to suppose that when men who are naturally so divided on religious opinions, and on political theories, agree on one point (and that, one of which they have daily experience), they are all in error ? The only nations which deny the utility of provincial liberties are those which have fewest of them ; in other words, those who are unacquainted with the institution are the only persons who pass a censure upon it.

CHAPTER VI.

JUDICIAL POWER IN THE UNITED STATES, AND ITS INFLUENCE ON POLITICAL SOCIETY.

The Anglo-Americans have retained the Characteristics of judicial Power which are common to all Nations.—They have, however, made it a powerful political Organ.—How.—In what the judicial System of the Anglo-Americans differs from that of all other Nations.—Why the American Judges have the right of declaring the Laws to be Unconstitutional.—How they use this Right.—Precautions taken by the Legislator to prevent its abuse.

I HAVE thought it essential to devote a separate chapter to the judicial authorities of the United States, lest their great poli-

* See Appendix K.

tical importance should be lessened in the reader's eyes by a merely incidental mention of them. Confederations have existed in other countries beside America; and republics have not been established on the shores of the New World alone: the representative system of government has been adopted in several states of Europe; but I am not aware that any nation of the globe has hitherto organized a judicial power on the principle adopted by the Americans. The judicial organization of the United States is the institution which the stranger has the greatest difficulty in understanding. He hears the authority of a judge invoked in the political occurrences of every day, and he naturally concludes that in the United States the judges are important political functionaries: nevertheless, when he examines the nature of the tribunals, they offer nothing which is contrary to the usual habits and privileges of those bodies; and the magistrates seem to him to interfere in public affairs by chance, but by a chance which recurs every day.

When the Parliament of Paris remonstrated, or refused to enregister an edict, or when it summoned a functionary accused of malversation to its bar, its political influence as a judicial body was clearly visible; but nothing of the kind is to be seen in the United States. The Americans have retained all the ordinary characteristics of judicial authority, and have carefully restricted its action to the ordinary circle of its functions.

The first characteristic of judicial power in all nations is the duty of arbitration. But rights must be contested in order to warrant the interference of a tribunal; and an action must be brought to obtain the decision of a judge. As long, therefore, as a law is uncontested, the judicial authority is not called upon to discuss it, and it may exist without being perceived. When a judge in a given case attacks a law relating to that case, he extends the circle of his customary duties, without, however, stepping beyond it; since he is in some measure obliged to decide upon the law, in order to decide the case. But if he pronounces upon a law without resting upon a case, he clearly steps beyond his sphere, and invades that of the legislative authority.

The second characteristic of judicial power is, that it pronounces on special cases, and not upon general principles. If a judge, in deciding a particular point, destroys a general principle, by passing a judgment which tends to reject all the inferences from that principle, and consequently to annul it, he remains within the ordinary limits of his functions. But if he directly attacks a general principle without having a particular case in view, he leaves the circle in which all nations have agreed to confine his authority; he assumes a more important, and perhaps a more useful influence than that of the magistrate, but he ceases to represent the judicial power.

The third characteristic of the judicial power is its inability to act unless it is appealed to, or until it has taken cognizance of an affair. This characteristic is less general than the other two; but notwithstanding the exceptions, I think it may be regarded as essential. The judicial power is by its nature devoid of action; it must be put in motion in order to produce a result. When it is called upon to repress a crime, it punishes the criminal; when a wrong is to be redressed, it is ready to redress it; when an act requires interpretation, it is prepared to interpret it; but it does not pursue criminals, hunt out wrongs, or examine into evidence of its own accord. A judicial functionary who should open proceedings, and usurp the censorship of the laws, would in some measure do violence to the passive nature of his authority.

The Americans have retained these three distinguishing characteristics of the judicial power; an American judge can only pronounce a decision when litigation has arisen, he is only conversant with special cases, and he cannot act until the cause has been duly brought before the court. His position is therefore perfectly similar to that of the magistrate of other nations; and he is nevertheless invested with immense political power. If the sphere of his authority and his means of action are the same as those of other judges, it may be asked whence he derives a power which they do not possess. The cause of this difference lies in the simple fact that the Americans have acknowledged the right of the judges to found their decisions on the constitution, rather than on the laws. In other words, they have left them at liberty not to apply such laws as may appear to them to be unconstitutional.

I am aware that a similar right has been claimed—but claimed in vain—by courts of justice in other countries; but in America it is recognized by all the authorities; and not a party, nor so much as an individual, is found to contest it. This fact can only be explained by the principles of the American constitution. In France the constitution is (or at least is supposed to be) immutable; and the received theory is that no power has the right of changing any part of it. In England, the parliament has an acknowledged right to modify the constitution: as, therefore, the constitution may undergo perpetual changes, it does not in reality exist; the parliament is at once a legislative and a constituent assembly. The political theories of America are more simple and more rational. An American constitution is not supposed to be immutable as in France; nor is it susceptible of modification by the ordinary powers of society as in England. It constitutes a detached whole, which, as it represents the determination of the whole people, is no less binding on the legislator than on the private citizen, but which may be altered by the will of the people in predetermined cases, according to established rules. In America the constitution may, therefore, vary, but as long as it exists it is the origin of all authority, and the sole vehicle of the predominating force.*

It is easy to perceive in what manner these differences must act upon the position and the rights of the judicial bodies in the three countries I have cited. If in France the tribunals were authorized to disobey the laws on the ground of their being opposed to the constitution, the supreme power would in fact be placed in their hands, since they alone would have the right of interpreting a constitution, the clauses of which can be modified by no authority. They would, therefore, take the place of the nation, and exercise as absolute a sway over society as the inherent weakness of judicial power would allow them to do. Undoubtedly, as the French judges are incompetent to declare a law to be unconstitutional, the power of changing the constitution is indirectly given to the legislative body, since no legal barrier would oppose the alterations which it might prescribe. But it is better to grant the power of changing the constitution of the people to men who represent (however imperfectly) the will of the people, than to men who represent no one but themselves.

It would be still more unreasonable to invest the English judges with the right of resisting the decisions of the legislative body, since the parliament which makes the laws also makes the constitution; and consequently a law emanating from the three powers of the state can in no case be unconstitutional. But neither of these remarks is applicable to America.†

In the United States the constitution governs the legislator as much as the private citizen: as it is the first of laws, it cannot be modified by a law; and it is therefore just that the tribunals should obey the constitution in preference to any law. This condition is essential to the power of the judica-

* See Appendix L. † See Appendix M.

ture; for to select that legal obligation by which he is most strictly bound, is the natural right of every magistrate.

In France the constitution is also the first of laws, and the judges have the same right to take it as the ground of their decisions; but were they to exercise this right, they must perforce encroach on rights more sacred than their own, namely, on those of society, in whose name they are acting. In this case the state motive clearly prevails over the motives of an individual. In America, where the nation can always reduce its magistrates to obedience by changing its constitution, no danger of this kind is to be feared. Upon this point therefore the political and the logical reason agree, and the people as well as the judges preserve their privileges.

Whenever a law which the judge holds to be unconstitutional is argued in a tribunal of the United States, he may refuse to admit it as a rule; this power is the only one which is peculiar to the American magistrate, but it gives rise to immense political influence. Few laws can escape the searching analysis; for there are few which are not prejudicial to some private interest or other, and none which may not be brought before a court of justice by the choice of parties, or by the necessity of the case. But from the time that a judge has refused to apply any given law in a case, that law loses a portion of its moral sanction. The persons to whose interest it is prejudicial, learn that means exist of evading its authority; and similar suits are multiplied, until it becomes powerless. One of two alternatives must then be resorted to: the people must alter the constitution, or the legislature must repeal the law.

The political power which the Americans have intrusted to their courts of justice is therefore immense; but the evils of this power are considerably diminished, by the obligation which has been imposed of attacking the laws through the courts of justice alone. If the judge had been empowered to contest the laws on the ground of theoretical generalities; if he had been enabled to open an attack or to pass a censure on the legislator, he would have played a prominent part in the political sphere; and as the champion or the antagonist of a party, he would have arrayed the hostile passions of the nation in the conflict. But when a judge contests a law, applied to some particular case in an obscure proceeding, the importance of his attack is concealed from the public gaze; his decision bears upon the interest of an individual, and if the law is slighted, it is only collaterally. Moreover, although it be censured, it is not abolished; its moral force may be diminished, but its cogency is by no means suspended; and its final destruction can only be accomplished by the reiterated attacks of judicial functionaries. It will readily be understood that by connecting the censorship of the laws with the private interests of members of the community, and by intimately uniting the prosecution of the law with the prosecution of an individual, the legislation is protected from wanton assailants, and from the daily aggressions of party spirit. The errors of the legislator are exposed whenever their evil consequences are most felt; and it is always a positive and appreciable fact which serves as the basis of a prosecution.

I am inclined to believe this practice of the American courts to be at once the most favorable to liberty as well as to public order. If the judge could only attack the legislator openly and directly, he would sometimes be afraid to oppose any resistance to his will; and at other moments party spirit might encourage him to brave it every day. The laws would consequently be attacked when the power from which they emanate is weak, and obeyed when it is strong. That is to say, when it would be useful to respect them, they would be contested; and when it would be easy to convert them into an instrument of oppression, they would be respected. But the American judge is brought into the political arena independently of his own will. He only judges the law because he is obliged to judge a case. The political question which he is called upon to resolve is connected with the interest of the parties, and he cannot refuse to decide it without abdicating the duties of his post. He performs his functions as a citizen by fulfilling the strict duties which belong to his profession as a magistrate. It is true that upon this system the judicial censorship which is exercised by the courts of justice over the legislation cannot extend to all laws indiscriminately, inasmuch as some of them can never give rise to that precise species of contestation which is termed a lawsuit; and even when such a contestation is possible, it may happen that no one cares to bring it before a court of justice. The Americans have often felt this disadvantage, but they have left the remedy incomplete, lest they should give it efficacy which in some cases might prove dangerous. Within these limits, the power vested in the American courts of justice of pronouncing a statute to be unconstitutional, forms one of the most powerful barriers which have ever been devised against the tyranny of political assemblies.

OTHER POWERS GRANTED TO THE AMERICAN JUDGES.

In the United States all the Citizens have the Right of indicting the public Functionaries before the ordinary Tribunals.—How they use this Right.—Art. 75 of the An VIII.—The Americans and the English cannot understand the Purport of this Clause.

It is perfectly natural that in a free country like America all the citizens should have the right of indicting public functionaries before the ordinary tribunals, and that all the judges should have the power of punishing public offences. The right granted to the courts of justice, of judging the agents of the executive government, when they have violated the laws, is so natural a one that it cannot be looked upon as an extraordinary privilege. Nor do the springs of government appear to me to be weakened in the United States by the custom which renders all public officers responsible to the judges of the land. The Americans seem, on the contrary, to have increased by this means that respect which is due to the authorities, and at the same time to have rendered those who are in power more scrupulous of offending public opinion. I was struck by the small number of political trials which occur in the United States; but I have no difficulty in accounting for this circumstance. A lawsuit, of whatever nature it may be, is always a difficult and expensive undertaking. It is easy to attack a public man in a journal, but the motives which can warrant an action at law must be serious. A solid ground of complaint must therefore exist, to induce an individual to prosecute a public officer, and public officers are careful not to furnish these grounds of complaint, when they are afraid of being prosecuted.

This does not depend upon the republican form of the American institutions, for the same facts present themselves in England. These two nations do not regard the impeachment of the principal officers of state as a sufficient guarantee of their independence. But they hold that the right of minor prosecutions, which are within the reach of the whole community, is a better pledge of freedom than those great judicial actions which are rarely employed until it is too late.

In the middle ages, when it was very difficult to overtake offenders, the judges inflicted the most dreadful tortures on the few who were arrested, which by no means diminished the number of crimes. It has since been discovered tha when justice is more certain and more mild, it is at the same time more efficacious. The English and the Americans hold, that tyranny and oppression are to be treated like any other crime, by lessening the penalty and facilitating conviction.

In the year VIII. of the French republic, a constitution was drawn up in which the following clause was introduced: "Art. 75. All the agents of the government below the rank of ministers can only be prosecuted for offences relating to their several functions by virtue of a decree of the conseil d'etat; in which case the prosecution takes place before the ordinary tribunals." This clause survived the "Constitution de l'an VIII.," and it is still maintained in spite of the just complaints of the nation. I have always found the utmost difficulty in explaining its meaning to Englishmen or Americans. They were at once led to conclude that the conseil d'etat in France was a great tribunal, established in the centre of the kingdom, which exercised a preliminary and somewhat tyrannical jurisdiction in all political causes. But when I told them that the conseil d'etat was not a judicial body, in the common sense of the term, but an administrative council composed of men dependent on the crown—so that the king, after having ordered one of his servants, called a prefect, to commit an injustice, has the power of commanding another of his servants, called a councillor of state, to prevent the former from being punished—when I demonstrated to them that the citizen who had been injured by the order of the sovereign is obliged to solicit from the sovereign permission to obtain redress, they refused to credit so flagrant an abuse, and were tempted to accuse me of falsehood or of ignorance. It frequently happened before the revolution that a parliament issued a warrant against a public officer who had committed an offence; and sometimes the proceedings were annulled by the authority of the crown. Despotism then displayed itself openly, and obedience was extorted by force. We have then retrograded from the point which our forefathers had reached, since we allow things to pass under the color of justice and the sanction of the law, which violence alone could impose upon them.

CHAPTER VII.

POLITICAL JURISDICTION IN THE UNITED STATES.

Definition of political Jurisdiction.—What is understood by political Jurisdiction in France, in England, and in the United States.—In America the political Judge can only pass Sentence on public Officers.—He more frequently passes a Sentence of Removal from Office than a Penalty.—Political Jurisdiction, as it Exists in the United States, is, notwithstanding its Mildness, and perhaps in Consequence of that Mildness, a most powerful Instrument in the Hands of the Majority.

I UNDERSTAND, by political jurisdiction, that temporary right of pronouncing a legal decision with which a political body may be invested.

In absolute governments no utility can accrue from the introduction of extraordinary forms of procedure; the prince, in whose name an offender is prosecuted, is as much the sovereign of the courts of justice as of everything else, and the idea which is entertained of his power is of itself a sufficient security. The only thing he has to fear is, that the external formalities of justice may be neglected, and that his authority may be dishonored, from a wish to render it more absolute. But in most free countries, in which the majority can never exercise the same influence upon the tribunals as an absolute monarch, the judicial power has occasionally been vested for a time in the representatives of society. It has been thought better to introduce a temporary confusion between the functions of the different authorities, than to violate the necessary principle of the unity of government.

England, France, and the United States, have established this political jurisdiction in their laws; and it is curious to examine the different use which these three great nations have made of the principle. In England and in France the house of lords and the chambre des pairs constitute the highest criminal court of their respective nations; and although they do not habitually try all political offences, they are competent to try them all. Another political body enjoys the right of impeachment before the house of lords: the only difference which exists between the two countries in this respect is, that in England the commons may impeach whomsoever they please before the lords, while in France the deputies can only employ this mode of prosecution against the ministers of the crown.

In both countries the upper house make use of all the existing penal laws of the nation to punish the delinquents.

In the United States, as well as in Europe, one branch of the legislature is authorized to impeach, and another to judge: the house of representatives arraigns the offender, and the senate awards his sentence. But the senate can only try such persons as are brought before it by the house of representatives, and those persons must belong to the class of public functionaries. Thus the jurisdiction of the senate is less extensive than that of the peers of France, while the right of impeachment by the representatives is more general than that of the deputies. But the great difference which exists between Europe and America is, that in Europe political tribunals are empowered to inflict all the dispositions of the penal code, while in America, when they have deprived the offender of his official rank, and have declared him incapable of filling any political office for the future, their jurisdiction terminates and that of the ordinary tribunals begins.

Suppose, for instance, that the president of the United States has committed the crime of high treason; the house of representatives impeaches him, and the senate degrades him; he must then be tried by a jury, which alone can deprive him of his liberty or his life. This accurately illustrates the subject we are treating. The political jurisdiction which is established by the laws of Europe is intended to try great offenders, whatever may be their birth, their rank, or their powers in the state; and to this end all the privileges of the courts of justice are temporarily extended to a great political assembly. The legislator is then transformed into a magistrate: he is called upon to admit, to distinguish, and to punish the offence; and as he exercises all the authority of a judge, the law restricts him to the observance of all the duties of that high office, and of all the formalities of justice. When a public functionary is impeached before an English or a French political tribunal, and is found guilty, the sentence deprives him *ipso facto* of his functions, and it may pronounce him to be incapable of resuming them or any others for the future. But in this case the political interdict is a consequence of the sentence, and not the sentence itself. In Europe the sentence of a political tribunal is therefore to be regarded as a judicial verdict, rather than as an administrative measure. In the United States the contrary takes place; and although the decision of the senate is judicial in its form, since the senators are obliged to comply with the practices and formalities of a court of justice; although it is judicial in respect to the motives on which it is founded, since the senate is in general obliged to take an offence at common law as the basis of its sentence; nevertheless the object of the proceeding is purely administrative.

If it had been the intention of the American legislator to invest a political body with great judicial authority, its action would not have been limited to the circle of public functionaries, since the most dangerous enemies of the state may be in the possession of no functions at all; and this is especially true in republics, where party favor is the first of authorities, and where the strength of many a leader is increased by his exercising no legal power. If it had been the intention of the American legislator to give society the means of repressing state offences by exemplary punishment, according to the practice of ordinary judgment, the resources of the penal code would all have been placed at the disposal of the political tribunals. But the weapon with which they are intrusted is an imperfect one, and it can never reach the most dangerous offenders; since men who aim at the entire subversion of the laws are not likely to murmur at a political interdict.

The main object of the political jurisdiction which obtains in the United States is, therefore, to deprive the citizen of an authority which he has used amiss, and to prevent him from ever acquiring it again. This is evidently an administrative measure sanctioned by the formalities of judicial investigation. In this matter the Americans have created a mixed system: they have surrounded the act which removes a public functionary with the securities of a political trial; and they have deprived all political condemnations of their severest penalties. Every link of the system may easily be traced from this point; we at once perceive why the American constitutions subject all the civil functionaries to the jurisdiction of the senate, while the military, whose crimes are nevertheless more formidable, are exempt from that tribunal. In the civil service none of the American functionaries can be said to be removeable; the places which some of them occupy are inalienable, and the others derive their rights from a power which cannot be abrogated. It is therefore necessary to try them all in order to deprive them of their authority. But military officers are dependent on the chief magistrate of the state, who is himself a civil functionary; and the decision which condemns him is a blow upon them all.

If we now compare the American and European systems,

we shall meet with differences no less striking in the different effects which each of them produces or may produce. In France and in England the jurisdiction of political bodies is looked upon as an extraordinary resource, which is only to be employed in order to rescue society from unwonted dangers. It is not to be denied that these tribunals, as they are constituted in Europe, are apt to violate the conservative principle of the balance of power in the state, and to threaten incessantly the lives and liberties of the subject. The same political jurisdiction in the United States is only indirectly hostile to the balance of power; it cannot menace the lives of the citizens, and it does not hover, as in Europe, over the heads of the community, since those only who have beforehand submitted to its authority upon accepting office are exposed to its severity. It is at the same time less formidable and less efficacious; indeed, it has not been considered by the legislators of the United States as a remedy for the more violent evils of society, but as an ordinary means of conducting the government. In this respect it probably exercises more real influence on the social body in America than in Europe. We must not be misled by the apparent mildness of the American Legislation in all that relates to political jurisdiction. It is to be observed, in the first place, that in the United States the tribunal which passes sentence is composed of the same elements, and subject to the same influences, as the body which impeaches the offender, and that this uniformity gives an almost irresistible impulse to the vindictive passions of parties. If political judges in the United States cannot inflict such heavy penalties as those of Europe, there is the less chance of their acquitting a prisoner; and the conviction, if it is less formidable, is more certain. The principal object of the political tribunals of Europe is to punish the offender; the purpose of those in America is to deprive him of his authority. A political condemnation in the United States may, therefore, be looked upon as a preventive measure; and there is no reason for restricting the judges to the exact definitions of criminal law. Nothing can be more alarming than the excessive latitude with which political offences are described in the laws of America. Article II., section iv., of the constitution of the United States runs thus: "The president, vice-president, and all the civil officers of the United States shall be removed from office on impeachment for, and conviction of, treason, bribery, *or other high crimes and misdemeanors.*" Many of the constitutions of the states are even less explicit. "Public officers," says the constitution of Massachusetts,* "shall be impeached for misconduct or mal-administration." The constitution of Virginia declares that all the civil officers who shall have offended against the state by mal-administration corruption, or other high crimes, may be impeached by the house of delegates: in some constitutions no offences are specified, in order to subject the public functionaries to an unlimited responsibility.† But I will venture to affirm, that it is precisely their mildness which renders the American laws most formidable in this respect. We have shown that in Europe the removal of a functionary and his political interdiction are consequences of the penalty he is to undergo, and that in America they constitute the penalty itself. The result is, that in Europe political tribunals are invested with rights which they are afraid to use, and that the fear of punishing too much hinders them from punishing at all. But in America no one hesitates to inflict a penalty from which humanity does not recoil. To condemn a political opponent to death, in order to deprive him of his power, is to commit what all the world would execrate as a horrible assassination; but to declare that opponent unworthy to exercise that authority, to deprive him of it, and to leave him uninjured in life and liberty, may appear to be the fair issue of the struggle. But this sentence, which it is so easy to pronounce, is not the less fatally severe to the majority of those upon whom it is inflicted. Great criminals may undoubtedly brave its intangible rigor, but ordinary offenders will dread it as a condemnation which destroys their position in the world, casts a blight upon their honor, and condemns them to a shameful inactivity worse than death. The influence exercised in the United States upon the progress of society by the jurisdiction of political bodies may not appear to be formidable, but it is only the more immense. It does not act directly upon the governed, but it renders the majority more absolute over those who govern; it does not confer an unbounded authority on the legislator which can only be exerted at some momentous crisis, but it establishes a temperate and regular influence, which is at all times available. If the power is decreased, it can, on the other hand, be more conveniently employed, and more easily abused. By preventing political tribunals from inflicting judicial punishments, the Americans seem to have eluded the worst consequences of legislative

* Chapter I., sect. ii., § 8.
† See the constitutions of Illinois, Maine, Connecticut, and Georgia.

tyranny, rather than tyranny itself; and I am not sure that political jurisdiction, as it is constituted in the United States, is not the most formidable which has ever been placed in the rude grasp of a popular majority. When the American republics begin to degenerate, it will be easy to verify the truth of this observation, by remarking whether the number of political impeachments augments.*

CHAPTER VIII.

THE FEDERAL CONSTITUTION.

I HAVE hitherto considered each state as a separate whole, and I have explained the different springs which the people sets in motion, and the different means of action which it employs. But all the states which I have considered as independent are forced to submit, in certain cases, to the supreme authority of the Union. The time is now come for me to examine the partial sovereignty which has been conceded to the Union, and to cast a rapid glance over the federal constitution.†

HISTORY OF THE FEDERAL CONSTITUTION.

Origin of the first Union.—Its Weakness.—Congress appeals to the constituent Authority.—Interval of two Years between the Appeal and the Promulgation of the new Constitution.

THE thirteen colonies which simultaneously threw off the yoke of England toward the end of the last century, possessed, as I have already observed, the same religion, the same language, the same customs, and almost the same laws; they were struggling against a common enemy; and these reasons were sufficiently strong to unite them one to another, and to consolidate them into one nation. But as each of them had enjoyed a separate existence, and a government within its own control, the peculiar interests and customs which resulted from this system, were opposed to a compact and intimate

* See Appendix N.

† See the constitution of the United States

union, which would have absorbed the individual importance of each in the general importance of all. Hence arose two opposite tendencies, the one prompting the Anglo-Americans to unite, the other to divide their strength. As long as the war with the mother-country lasted, the principle of union was kept alive by necessity ; and although the laws which constituted it were defective, the common tie subsisted in spite of their imperfections.* But no sooner was peace concluded than the faults of the legislation became manifest, and the state seemed to be suddenly dissolved. Each colony became an independent republic, and assumed an absolute sovereignty. The federal government, condemned to impotence by its constitution, and no longer sustained by the presence of a common danger, saw the outrages offered to its flag by the great nations of Europe, while it was scarcely able to maintain its ground against the Indian tribes, and to pay the interest of the debt which had been contracted during the war of independence. It was already on the verge of destruction, when it officially proclaimed its inability to conduct the government, and appealed to the constituent authority of the nation.†

If America ever approached (for however brief a time) that lofty pinnacle of glory to which the proud fancy of its inhabitants is wont to point, it was at the solemn moment at which the power of the nation abdicated, as it were, the empire of the land. All ages have furnished the spectacle of a people struggling with energy to win its independence; and the efforts of the Americans in throwing off the English yoke have been considerably exaggerated. Separated from their enemies by three thousand miles of ocean, and backed by a powerful ally, the success of the United States may be more justly attributed to their geographical position, than to the valor of their armies or the patriotism of their citizens. It would be ridiculous to compare the American war to the wars of the French revolution, or the efforts of the Americans to those of the French, who, when they were attacked by the whole of Europe, without credit and without allies, were still capable of opposing a twentieth part of their population to their foes, and of bearing the torch of revolution beyond their frontiers while they stifled its devouring flame within the

* See the articles of the first confederation formed in 1778. This constitution was not adopted by all the states until 1781. See also the analysis given of this constitution in the Federalist, from No. 15 to No. 22 inclusive, and Story's " Commentary on the Constitution of the United States," pp. 85-115.

† Congress made this declaration on the 21st of February, 1787.

bosom of their country. But it is a novelty in the history of society to see a great people turn a calm and scrutinizing eye upon itself when apprised by the legislature that the wheels of government had stopped ; to see it carefully examine the extent of the evil, and patiently wait for two whole years until a remedy was discovered, which it voluntarily adopted without having wrung a tear or a drop of blood from mankind. At the time when the inadequacy of the first constitution was discovered, America possessed the double advantage of that calm which had succeeded the effervescence of the revolution, and of those great men who had led the revolution to a successful issue. The assembly which accepted the task of composing the second constitution was small ;* but George Washington was its president, and it contained the choicest talents and the noblest hearts which had ever appeared in the New World. This national commission, after long and mature deliberation, offered to the acceptance of the people the body of general laws which still rules the Union. All the states adopted it successively.† The new federal government commenced its functions in 1789, after an interregnum of two years. The revolution of America terminated when that of France began.

SUMMARY OF THE FEDERAL CONSTITUTION.

Division of Authority between the Federal Government and the States. —The Government of the States is the Rule: the Federal Government the Exception.

THE first question which awaited the Americans was intricate, and by no means easy of solution ; the object was so to divide the authority of the different states which composed the Union, that each of them should continue to govern itself in all that concerned its internal prosperity, while the entire nation, represented by the Union, should continue to form a compact body, and to provide for the exigencies of the people. It was as impossible to determine beforehand, with any degree of accuracy, the share of authority which each of the

* It consisted of fifty-five members: Washington, Madison, Hamilton, and the two Morrises, were among the number.

† It was not adopted by the legislative bodies, but representatives were elected by the people for this sole purpose ; and the new constitution was discussed at length in each of these assemblies.

two governments was to enjoy, as to foresee all the incidents in the existence of a nation.

The obligations and the claims of the federal government were simple and easily definable, because the Union had been formed with the express purpose of meeting the general exigencies of the people; but the claims and obligations of the states were, on the other hand, complicated and various, because those governments penetrated into all the details of social life. The attributes of the federal government were, therefore, carefully enumerated, and all that was not included among them was declared to constitute a part of the privileges of the several governments of the states. Thus the government of the states remained the rule, and that of the confederation became the exception.*

But as it was foreseen, that, in practice, questions might arise as to the exact limits of this exceptional authority, and that it would be dangerous to submit these questions to the decision of the ordinary courts of justice, established in the states by the states themselves, a high federal court was created,† which was destined, among other functions, to maintain the balance of power which had been established by the constitution between the two rival governments.‡

* See the amendment to the federal constitution; Federalist, No. 32. Story, p. 711. Kent's Commentaries, vol. i., p. 364.

It is to be observed, that whenever the ***exclusive*** right of regulating certain matters is not reserved to congress by the constitution, the states may take up the affair, until it is brought before the national assembly. For instance, congress has the right of making a general law of bankruptcy, which, however, it neglects to do. Each state is then at liberty to make a law for itself. This point, however, has been established by discussion in the law-courts, and may be said to belong more properly to jurisprudence.

† The action of this court is indirect, as we shall hereafter show.

‡ It is thus that the Federalist, No. 45, explains the division of supremacy between the union and the states: "The powers delegated by the constitution to the federal government are few and defined. Those which are to remain in the state governments are numerous and indefinite. The former will be exercised principally on external objects, as war, peace, negotiation, and foreign commerce. The powers reserved to the several states will extend to all the objects which, in the ordinary course of affairs, concern the internal order and prosperity of the state."

I shall often have occasion to quote the Federalist in this work. When the bill which has since become the constitution of the United States was submitted to the approval of the people, and the discussions were still pending, three men who had already acquired a portion of that celebrity which they have since enjoyed, John Jay, Hamilton, and Madison, formed an association with the intention of explaining to the nation the advantages of the measure which was proposed. With this view they published a series of articles in the shape of a

PREROGATIVE OF THE FEDERAL GOVERNMENT.

Power of declaring War, making Peace, and levying general Taxes vested in the Federal Government.—What Part of the internal Policy of the Country it may direct.—The Government of the Union in some respects more central than the King's Government in the old French monarchy.

THE external relations of a people may be compared to those of private individuals, and they cannot be advantageously maintained without the agency of the single head of a government. The exclusive right of making peace and war, of concluding treaties of commerce, of raising armies, and equipping fleets, was therefore granted to the Union.* The necessity of a national government was less imperiously felt in the conduct of the internal affairs of society; but there are certain general interests which can only be attended to with advantage by a general authority. The Union was invested with the power of controlling the monetary system, of directing the post-office, and of opening the great roads which were to establish communication between the different parts of the country.† The independence of the government of each state was formally recognized in its sphere; nevertheless the federal government was authorized to interfere in the internal affairs of the states‡ in a few predetermined cases, in which an indiscreet abuse of their independence might compromise the security of the Union at large. Thus, while the power of modifying and changing their legislation at pleasure was preserved in all the republics, they were forbidden to enact *ex post facto* laws, or to create a class of nobles in their community.§ Lastly, as it was necessary that the federal government should be able to fulfil its engagements, it was endowed with an unlimited power of levying taxes.||

journal, which now form a complete treatise. They entitled their journal, "The Federalist," a name which has been retained in the work. The Federalist is an excellent book, which ought to be familiar to the statesmen of all countries, although it especially concerns America.

* See constitution, sect. 8. Federalist, Nos. 41 and 42. Kent's Commentaries, vol. i., p. 207. Story, pp. 358–382; 409–426.

† Several other privileges of the same kind exist, such as that which empowers the Union to legislate on bankruptcy, to grant patents, and other matters in which its intervention is clearly necessary.

‡ Even in these cases its interference is indirect. The Union interferes by means of the tribunals, as will be hereafter shown.

§ Federal Constitution, sect. 10, art. 1.

|| Constitution, sect. 8, 9, and 10. Federalist, Nos. 30–36 inclusive,

In examining the balance of power as established by the federal constitution; in remarking on the one hand the portion of sovereignty which has been reserved to the several states, and on the other the share of power which the Union has assumed, it is evident that the federal legislators entertained the clearest and most accurate notions on the nature of the centralisation of government. The United States form not only a republic, but a confederation; nevertheless the authority of the nation is more central than it was in several of the monarchies of Europe when the American constitution was formed. Take, for instance, the two following examples:—

Thirteen supreme courts of justice existed in France, which, generally speaking, had the right of interpreting the law without appeal; and those provinces, styled *pays d'etats*, were authorized to refuse their assent to an impost which had been levied by the sovereign who represented the nation.

In the Union there is but one tribunal to interpret, as there is one legislature to make the laws; and an impost voted by the representatives of the nation is binding upon all the citizens.

In these two essential points, therefore, the Union exercises more central authority than the French monarchy possessed, although the Union is only an assemblage of confederate republics.

In Spain certain provinces had the right of establishing a system of customhouse duties peculiar to themselves, although that privilege belongs, by its very nature, to the national sovereignty. In America the congress alone has the right of regulating the commercial relations of the states. The government of the confederation is therefore more centralized in this respect than the kingdom of Spain. It is true that the power of the crown in France or in Spain was always able to obtain by force whatever the constitution of the country denied, and that the ultimate result was consequently the same; and I am here discussing the theory of the constitution.

FEDERAL POWERS.

AFTER having settled the limits within which the federal government was to act, the next point was to determine the powers which it was to exert.

and 41–44. Kent's Commentaries, vol. i., pp 207 and 381. Story, pp. 329 and 514.

LEGISLATIVE POWERS.

Division of the legislative Body into two Branches.—Difference in the Manner of forming the two Houses.—The Principle of the Independence of the States predominates in the Formation of the Senate.—The Principle of the Sovereignty of the Nation in the Composition of the House of Representatives.—Singular Effects of the Fact that a Constitution can only be Logical in the early Stages of a Nation

THE plan which had been laid down beforehand for the constitution of the several states was followed, in many points, in the organization of the powers of the Union. The federal legislature of the Union was composed of a senate and a house of Representatives. A spirit of conciliation prescribed the observance of distinct principles in the formation of each of these two assemblies. I have already shown that two contrary interests were opposed to each other in the establishment of the federal constitution. These two interests had given rise to two opinions. It was the wish of one party to convert the Union into a league of independent states, or a sort of congress, at which the representatives of he several peoples would meet to discuss certain points of their common interests. The other party desired to unite the inhabitants of the American colonies into one sole nation, and to establish a government, which should act as the sole representative of the nation, as far as the limited sphere of its authority would permit. The practical consequences of these two theories were exceedingly different.

The question was, whether a league was to be established instead of a national government; whether the majority of the states, instead of a majority of the inhabitants of the Union, was to give the law; for every state, the small as well as the great, then retained the character of an independent power, and entered the Union upon a footing of perfect equality. If, on the contrary, the inhabitants of the United States were to be considered as belonging to one and the same nation, it was natural that the majority of the citizens of the Union should prescribe the law. Of course the lesser states could not subscribe to the application of this doctrine without, in fact, abdicating their existence in relation to the sovereignty of the confederation; since they would have passed from the condition of a co-equal and co-legislative authority, to that of an insignificant fraction of a great people. The former system would have invested them with an excessive authority, the latter would have annulled their influence altogether. Under these circumstances, the result was, that the strict rules of logic were evaded, as is usually the case when interests are opposed to arguments. A middle course was hit upon by the legislators, which brought together by force two systems theoretically irreconcilable.

The principle of the independence of the states prevailed in the formation of the senate, and that of the sovereignty of the nation predominated in the composition of the house of representatives. It was decided that each state should send two senators to congress, and a number of representatives proportioned to its population.* It results from this arrangement that the state of New York has at the present day forty representatives, and only two senators; the state of Delaware has two senators, and only one representative; the state of Delaware is therefore equal to the state of New York in the senate, while the latter has forty times the influence of the former in the house of representatives. Thus, if the minority of the nation preponderates in the senate, it may paralyze the decisions of the majority represented in the other house, which is contrary to the spirit of constitutional government.

The facts show how rare and how difficult it is rationally and logically to combine all the several parts of legislation. In the course of time different interests arise, and different principles are sanctioned by the same people; and when a general constitution is to be established, these interests and principles are so many natural obstacles to the rigorous application of any political system, with all its consequences. The early stages of national existence are the only periods at which it is possible to maintain the complete logic of legislation; and when we perceive a nation in the enjoyment of this advantage, before we hasten to conclude that it is wise, we should do well to remember that it is young. When the federal constitution was formed, the interest of independence for the separate states, and the interest of union for the whole people, were

* Every ten years congress fixes anew the number of representatives which each state is to furnish. The total nnmber was 69 in 1789, and 240 in 1833. (See American Almanac, 1834, p. 194.)

The constitution decided that there should not be more than one representative for every 30,000 persons; but no minimum was fixed upon. The congress has not thought fit to augment the number of representatives in proportion to the increase of population. The first act which was passed on the subject (14th April, 1792: see Laws of the United States, by Story, vol. i., p. 235) decided that there should be one representative for every 33,000 inhabitants. The last act, which was passed in 1822, fixes the proportion at one for 48,000. The population represented is composed of all the freemen and of three-fifths of the slaves.

the only two conflicting interests which existed among the Anglo-Americans; and a compromise was necessarily made between them.

It is, however, just to acknowledge that this part of the constitution has not hitherto produced those evils which might have been feared. All the states are young and contiguous; their customs, their ideas, and their wants, are not dissimilar; and the differences which result from their size or inferiority do not suffice to set their interests at variance. The small states have consequently never been induced to league themselves together in the senate to oppose the designs of the larger ones; and indeed there is so irresistible an authority in the legitimate expression of the will of a people, that the senate could offer but a feeble opposition to the vote of the majority of the house of representatives.

It must not be forgotten, on the other hand, that it was not in the power of the American legislators to reduce to a single nation the people for whom they were making laws. The object of the federal constitution was not to destroy the independence of the states, but to restrain it. By acknowledging the real authority of these secondary communities (and it was impossible to deprive them of it), they disavowed beforehand the habitual use of constraint in enforcing the decisions of the majority. Upon this principle the introduction of the influence of the states into the mechanism of the federal government was by no means to be wondered at; since it only attested the existence of an acknowledged power, which was to be humored, and not forcibly checked.

A FARTHER DIFFERENCE BETWEEN THE SENATE AND THE HOUSE OF REPRESENTATIVES.

The Senate named by the provincial Legislature—the Representatives, by the People.—Double Election of the Former—Single Election of the Latter.—Term of the different Offices.—Peculiar Functions of each House.

THE senate not only differs from the other house in the principle which it represents, but also in the mode of its election, in the term for which it is chosen, and in the nature of its functions. The house of representatives is named by the people, the senate by the legislators of each state; the former is directly elected; the latter is elected by an elected body; the term for which the representatives are chosen is only two years, that of the senators is six. The functions of the house of representatives are purely legislative, and the only share it takes in the judicial power is in the impeachment of public officers. The senate co-operates in the work of legislation, and tries those political offences which the house of representatives submits to its decision. It also acts as the great executive council of the nation; the treaties which are concluded by the president must be ratified by the senate; and the appointments he may make must be definitively approved by the same body.*

THE EXECUTIVE POWER.†

Dependence of the President.—He is Elective and Responsible.—He is Free to act in his own Sphere under the Inspection, but not under the Direction, of the Senate.—His Salary fixed at his Entry into Office.—Suspensive Veto.

THE American legislators undertook a difficult task in attempting to create an executive power dependent on the majority of the people and nevertheless sufficiently strong to act without restraint in its own sphere. It was indispensable to the maintenance of the republican form of government that the representatives of the executive power should be subject to the will of the nation.

The president is an elective magistrate. His honor, his property, his liberty, and his life, are the securities which the people has for the temperate use of his power. But in the exercise of his authority he cannot be said to be perfectly independent; the senate takes cognizance of his relations with foreign powers, and of the distribution of public appointments, so that he can neither be bribed, nor can he employ the means of corruption. The legislators of the Union acknowledged that the executive power would be incompetent to fulfil its task with dignity and utility, unless it enjoyed a greater degree of stability and of strength than had been granted to it in the separate states.

The president is chosen for four years, and he may be reelected; so that the chances of a prolonged administration may inspire him with hopeful undertakings for the public good, and with the means of carrying them into execution. The president was made the sole representative of the executive power of the Union; and care was taken not to render

* See the Federalist, Nos. 52-66, inclusive. Story, pp. 199-314 Constitution of the United States, sections 2 and 3.

† See the Federalist, Nos. 67-77. Constitution of the United States, art. 2. Story, pp. 115; 515-780. Kent's Commentaries, p. 255

his decisions subordinate to the vote of a council—a dangerous measure, which tends at the same time to clog the action of the government and to diminish its responsibility. The senate has the right of annulling certain acts of the president; but it cannot compel him to take any steps, nor does it participate in the exercise of the executive power.

The action of the legislature on the executive power may be direct; and we have just shown that the Americans carefully obviated this influence; but it may, on the other hand, be indirect. Public assemblies which have the power of depriving an officer of state of his salary, encroach upon his independence; and as they are free to make the laws, it is to be feared lest they should gradually appropriate to themselves a portion of that authority which the constitution had vested in his hands. This dependence of the executive power is one of the defects inherent in republican constitutions. The Americans have not been able to counteract the tendency which legislative assemblies have to get possession of the government, but they have rendered this propensity less irresistible. The salary of the president is fixed, at the time of his entering upon office, for the whole period of his magistracy. The president is, moreover, provided with a suspensive veto, which allows him to oppose the passing of such laws as might destroy the portion of independence which the constitution awards him. The struggle between the president and the legislature must always be an unequal one, since the latter is certain of bearing down all resistance by persevering in its plans; but the suspensive veto forces it at least to reconsider the matter, and, if the motion be persisted in, it must then be backed by a majority of two-thirds of the whole house. The veto is, in fact, a sort of appeal to the people. The executive power, which, without this security, might have been secretly oppressed, adopts this means of pleading its cause and stating its motives. But if the legislature is certain of overpowering all resistance by persevering in its plans, I reply, that in the constitutions of all nations, of whatever kind they may be, a certain point exists at which the legislator is obliged to have recourse to the good sense and the virtue of his fellow-citizens. This point is more prominent and more discoverable in republics, while it is more remote and more carefully concealed in monarchies, but it always exists somewhere. There is no country in the world in which everything can be provided for by the laws, or in which political institutions can prove a substitute for common sense and public morality.

DIFFERENCE BETWEEN THE POSITION OF THE PRESIDENT OF THE UNITED STATES AND THAT OF A CONSTITUTIONAL KING OF FRANCE.

Executive Power in the United States as Limited and as Partial as the Supremacy which it Represents.—Executive Power in France as Universal as the Supremacy it Represents.—The King a Branch of the Legislature.—The President the mere Executor of the Law.—Other Differences resulting from the Duration of the two Powers.—The President checked in the Exercise of the executive Authority.—The King Independent in its Exercise.—Notwithstanding these Discrepancies, France is more akin to a Republic than the Union to a Monarchy.—Comparison of the Number of public Officers depending upon the executive Power in the two countries.

THE executive power has so important an influence on the destinies of nations that I am inclined to pause for an instant at this portion of my subject, in order more clearly to explain the part it sustains in America. In order to form an accurate idea of the position of the president of the United States, it may not be irrelevant to compare it to that of one of the constitutional kings of Europe. In this comparison I shall pay but little attention to the external signs of power, which are more apt to deceive the eye of the observer than to guide his researches. When a monarchy is being gradually transformed into a republic, the executive power retains the titles, the honors, the etiquette, and even the funds of royalty, long after its authority has disappeared. The English, after having cut off the head of one king, and expelled another from his throne, were accustomed to accost the successors of those princes upon their knees. On the other hand, when a republic falls under the sway of a single individual, the demeanor of the sovereign is simple and unpretending, as if his authority was not yet paramount. When the emperors exercised an unlimited control over the fortunes and the lives of their fellow-citizens, it was customary to call them Cesar in conversation, and they were in the habit of supping without formality at their friends' houses. It is therefore necessary to look below the surface.

The sovereignty of the United States is shared between the Union and the states, while in France it is undivided and compact: hence arises the first and the most notable difference which exists between the president of the United States and the king of France. In the United States the executive power is as limited and partial as the sovereignty of the Union in whose name it acts; in France it is as universal as the authority of the state. The Americans have a federal, and the French a national government.

The first cause of inferiority results from the nature of things, but it is not the only one; the second in importance is as follows: sovereignty may be defined to be the right of making laws: in France, the king really exercises a portion of the sovereign power, since the laws have no weight till he has given his assent to them; he is moreover the executor of all they ordain. The president is also the executor of the laws, but he does not really co-operate in their formation, since the refusal of his assent does not annul them. He is therefore merely to be considered as the agent of the sovereign power. But not only does the king of France exercise a portion of the sovereign power, he also contributes to the nomination of the legislature, which exercises the other portion. He has the privilege of appointing the members of one chamber, and of dissolving the other at his pleasure; whereas the president of the United States has no share in the formation of the legislative body, and cannot dissolve any part of it. The king has the same right of bringing forward measures as the chambers; a right which the president does not possess. The king is represented in each assembly by his ministers, who explain his intentions, support his opinions, and maintain the principles of the government. The president and his ministers are alike excluded from congress; so that his influence and his opinions can only penetrate indirectly into that great body. The king of France is therefore on an equal footing with the legislature, which can no more act without him, than he can without it. The president exercises an authority inferior to, and depending upon, that of the legislature.

Even in the exercise of the executive power, properly so called, the point upon which his position seems to be almost analogous to that of the king of France—the president labors under several causes of inferiority. The authority of the king, in France, has, in the first place, the advantage of duration over that of the president: and durability is one of the chief elements of strength; nothing is either loved or feared but what is likely to endure. The president of the United States is a magistrate elected for four years. The king, in France, is an hereditary sovereign.

In the exercise of the executive power the president of the United States is constantly subject to jealous scrutiny. He may make, but he cannot conclude a treaty; he may designate, but he cannot appoint, a public officer.* The king of France is absolute in the sphere of the executive power.

The president of the United States is responsible for his actions; but the person of the king is declared inviolable by the French charter.

Nevertheless, the supremacy of public opinion is no less above the head of one than of the other. This power is less definite, less evident, and less sanctioned by the laws in France than in America, but in fact exists. In America it acts by elections and decrees; in France it proceeds by revolutions; but notwithstanding the different constitutions of these two countries, public opinion is the predominant authority in both of them. The fundamental principle of legislation—a principle essentially republican—is the same in both countries, although its consequences may be different, and its results more or less extensive. Whence I am led to conclude, that France with its king is nearer akin to a republic, than the Union with its president is to a monarchy.

In what I have been saying I have only touched upon the main points of distinction; and if I could have entered into details, the contrast would have been rendered still more striking.

I have remarked that the authority of the president in the United States is only exercised within the limits of a partial sovereignty, while that of the king, in France, is undivided. I might have gone on to show that the power of the king's government in France exceeds its natural limits, however extensive they may be, and penetrates in a thousand different ways into the administration of private interests. Among the examples of this influence may be quoted that which results from the great number of public functionaries, who all derive their appointments from the government. This number now exceeds all previous limits; it amounts to 138,000† nominations, each of which may be considered as an element of power. The president of the United States has not the exclusive right

* The constitution had left it doubtful whether the president was obliged to consult the senate in the removal as well as in the appointment of federal officers. The Federalist (No. 77) seemed to establish the affirmative; but in 1789, congress formally decided that as the president was responsible for his actions, he ought not to be forced to employ agents who had forfeited his esteem. See Kent's Commentaries, vol. i., p. 289.

† The sums annually paid by the state to these officers amount to 200,000,000 francs (eight millions sterling).

of making any public appointments, and their whole number scarcely exceeds 12,000.*

[Those who are desirous of tracing the question respecting the power of the president to remove every executive officer of the government without the sanction of the senate, will find some light upon it by referring to 5th Marshall's Life of Washington, p. 196 : 5 Sergeant and Rawle's Reports (Pennsylvania), 451 : Elliot's Debates on the Federal Constitution, vol iv., p. 355, contains the debate in the House of Representatives, June 16, 1799, when the question was first mooted Report of a committee of the senate in 1822, in Niles's Register of 29th August in that year. It is certainly very extraordinary that such a vast power, and one so extensively affecting the whole administration of the government, should rest on such slight foundations, as an *inference* from an act of congress, providing that when the secretary of the treasury should be removed by the president, his assistant should discharge the duties of the office. How congress could confer the power, even by a direct act, is not perceived. It must be a necessary implication from the words of the constitution, or it does not exist. It has been repeatedly denied in and out of congress, and must be considered, as yet, an unsettled question.—*American Editor.*]

ACCIDENTAL CAUSES WHICH MAY INCREASE THE INFLUENCE OF THE EXECUTIVE.

External security of the Union.—Army of six thousand Men.—Few Ships.—The President has no Opportunity of exercising his great Prerogatives.—In the Prerogatives he exercises he is weak.

If the executive power is feebler in America than in France, the cause is more attributable to the circumstances than to the laws of the country.

It is chiefly in its foreign relations that the executive power of a nation is called upon to exert its skill and vigor. If the existence of the Union were perpetually threatened, and its chief interest were in daily connexion with those of other powerful nations, the executive government would assume an increased importance in proportion to the measures expected of it, and those which it would carry into effect. The president of the United States is the commander-in-chief of the army, but of an army composed of only six thousand men ; he com-

* This number is extracted from the "National Calendar," for 1833, The National Calendar is an American almanac which contains the names of all the federal officers.

It results from this comparison that the king of France has eleven times as many places at his disposal as the president, although the population of France is not much more than double that of the Union

mands the fleet, but the fleet reckons but few sail; he conducts the foreign relations of the Union, but the United States are a nation without neighbors. Separated from the rest of the world by the ocean, and too weak as yet to aim at the dominion of the seas, they have no enemies, and their interests rarely come into contact with those of any other nation of the globe.

The practical part of a government must not be judged by the theory of its constitution. The president of the United States is in the possession of almost royal prerogatives, which he has no opportunity of exercising; and those privileges which he can at present use are very circumscribed: the laws allow him to possess a degree of influence which circum stances do not permit him to employ.

On the other hand, the great strength of the royal prerogative in France arises from circumstances far more than from the laws. There the executive government is constantly struggling against prodigious obstacles, and exerting all its energies to repress them; so that it increases by the extent of its achievements, and by the importance of the events it controls, without, for that reason, modifying its constitution. If the laws had made it as feeble and as circumscribed as it is in the Union, its influence would very soon become much greater.

WHY THE PRESIDENT OF THE UNITED STATES DOES NOT REQUIRE THE MAJORITY OF THE TWO HOUSES IN ORDER TO CARRY ON THE GOVERNMENT.

It is an established axiom in Europe that a constitutional king cannot persevere in a system of government which is opposed by the two other branches of the legislature. But several presidents of the United States have been known to lose the majority in the legislative body, without being obliged to abandon the supreme power, and without inflicting a serious evil upon society. I have heard this fact quoted as an instance of the independence and power of executive government in America: a moment's reflection will convince us, on the contrary, that it is a proof of its extreme weakness.

A king in Europe requires the support of the legislature to enable him to perform the duties imposed upon him by the constitution, because those duties are enormous. A constitutional king in Europe is not merely the executor of the law, but the execution of its provisions devolves so completely upon him, that he has the power of paralyzing its influence if it opposes his designs. He requires the assistance of the legislative assemblies to make the law, but those assemblies stand in need of his aid to execute it: these two authorities cannot subsist without each other, and the mechanism of government is stopped as soon as they are at variance.

In America the president cannot prevent any law from being passed, nor can he evade the obligation of enforcing it. His sincere and zealous co-operation is no doubt useful, but it is not indispensable in the carrying on of public affairs. All his important acts are directly or indirectly submitted to the legislature; and where he is independent of it he can do but little. It is therefore his weakness, and not his power, which enables him to remain in opposition to congress. In Europe, harmony must reign between the crown and the other branches of the legislature, because a collision between them may prove serious; in America, this harmony is not indispensable, because such a collision is impossible.

ELECTION OF THE PRESIDENT.

Dangers of the elective System increase in Proportion to the Extent of the Prerogative.—This System possible in America because no powerful executive Authority is required.—What Circumstances are favorable to the elective System.—Why the Election of the President does not cause a Deviation from the Principles of the Government.—Influence of the Election of the President on secondary Functionaries.

The dangers of the system of election applied to the head of the executive government of a great people, have been sufficiently exemplified by experience and by history; and the remarks I am about to make refer to America alone. These dangers may be more or less formidable in proportion to the place which the executive power occupies, and to the importance it possesses in the state; and they may vary according to the mode of election, and the circumstances in which the electors are placed. The most weighty argument against the election of a chief-magistrate is, that it offers so splendid a lure to private ambition, and is so apt to inflame men in the pursuit of power, that when legitimate means are wanting, force may not unfrequently seize what right denies.

It is clear that the greater the privileges of the executive authority are, the greater is the temptation; the more the ambition of the candidates is excited, the more warmly are their interests espoused by a throng of partisans who hope to share the power when their patron has won the prize. The dangers of the elective system increase, therefore, in the exact ratio of the influence exercised by the executive power in the affairs of state. The revolutions of Poland are not solely attributable to the elective system in general, but to the fact that the elected magistrate was the head of a powerful monarchy. Before we can discuss the absolute advantages of the elective system, we must make preliminary inquiries as to whether the geographical position, the laws, the habits, the manners, and the opinions of the people among whom it is to be introduced, will admit of the establishment of a weak and dependent executive government; for to attempt to render the representative of the state a powerful sovereign, and at the same time elective, is, in my opinion, to entertain two incompatible designs. To reduce hereditary royalty to the condition of an elective authority, the only means that I am acquainted with are to circumscribe its sphere of action beforehand, gradually to diminish its prerogatives, and to accustom the people to live without its protection. Nothing, however, is farther from the designs of the republicans of Europe than this course: as many of them only owe their hatred of tyranny to the sufferings which they have personally undergone, the extent of the executive power does not excite their hostility, and they only attack its origin without perceiving how nearly the two things are connected.

Hitherto no citizen has shown any disposition to expose his honor and his life, in order to become the president of the United States; because the power of that office is temporary, limited, and subordinate. The prize of fortune must be great to encourage adventurers in so desperate a game. No candidate has as yet been able to arouse the dangerous enthusiasm or the passionate sympathies of the people in his favor, for the very simple reason, that when he is at the head of the government he has but little power, but little wealth, and but little glory to share among his friends; and his influence in the state is too small for the success or the ruin of a faction to depend upon the elevation of an individual to power.

The great advantage of hereditary monarchies is, that as the private interest of a family is always intimately connected with the interests of the state, the executive government is never suspended for a single instant; and if the affairs of a monarchy are not better conducted than those of a republic, at least there is always some one to conduct them, well or ill, according to his capacity. In elective states, on the contrary, the wheels of government cease to act, as it were of their own accord, at the approach of an election, and even for some time previous to that event. The laws may indeed accelerate the operation of the election, which may be conducted with such simplicity and rapidity that the seat of power will never be left vacant; but, notwithstanding these precautions, a break necessarily occurs in the minds of the people.

At the approach of an election the head of the executive government is wholly occupied by the coming struggle; his future plans are doubtful; he can undertake nothing new, and he will only prosecute with indifference those designs which another will perhaps terminate. "I am so near the time of my retirement from office," said President Jefferson on the 21st of January, 1809 (six weeks before the election), "that I feel no passion, I take no part, I express no sentiment. It appears to me just to leave to my successor the commencement of those measures which he will have to prosecute, and for which he will be responsible."

On the other hand, the eyes of the nation are centred on a single point; all are watching the gradual birth of so important an event. The wider the influence of the executive power extends, the greater and the more necessary is its constant action, the more fatal is the term of suspense; and a nation which is accustomed to the government, or, still more, one used to the administrative protection of a powerful executive authority, would be infallibly convulsed by an election of this kind. In the United States the action of the government may be slackened with impunity, because it is always weak and circumscribed.

One of the principal vices of the elective system is, that it always introduces a certain degree of instability into the internal and external policy of the state. But this disadvantage is less sensibly felt if the share of power vested in the elected magistrate is small. In Rome the principles of the government underwent no variation, although the consuls were changed every year, because the senate, which was an hereditary assembly, possessed the directing authority. If the elective system were adopted in Europe, the condition of most of the monarchical states would be changed at every new election. In America the president exercises a certain influence on state affairs, but he does not conduct them; the preponderating power is vested in the representatives of the whole nation. The political maxims of the country depend therefore on the mass of the people, not on the president alone; and consequently in America the elective system has no very prejudicial influence on the fixed principles of the government. But the want of fixed principles is an evil so inherent in the elective system, that it is still extremely perceptible in the narrow sphere to which the authority of the president extends.

The Americans have admitted that the head of the executive power, who has to bear the whole responsibility of the duties he is called upon to fulfil, ought to be empowered to choose his own agents, and to remove them at pleasure: the legislative bodies watch the conduct of the president more than they direct it. The consequence of this arrangement is, that at every new election the fate of all the federal public officers is in suspense. Mr. Quincy Adams, on his entry into office, discharged the majority of the individuals who had been appointed by his predecessor; and I am not aware that General Jackson allowed a single removeable functionary employed in the federal service to retain his place beyond the first year which succeeded his election. It is sometimes made a subject of complaint, that in the constitutional monarchies of Europe the fate of the humbler servants of an administration depends upon that of the ministers. But in elective governments this evil is far greater. In a constitutional monarchy successive ministers are rapidly formed; but as the principal representative of the executive power does not change, the spirit of innovation is kept within bounds; the changes which take place are in the details rather than in the principles of the administrative system; but to substitute one system for another, as is done in America every four years by law, is to cause a sort of revolution. As to the misfortunes which may fall upon individuals in consequence of this state of things, it must be allowed that the uncertain situation of the public officers is less fraught with evil consequences in America than elsewhere. It is so easy to acquire an independent position in the United States, that the public officer who loses his place may be deprived of the comforts of life, but not of the means of subsistence.

I remarked at the beginning of this chapter that the dangers of the elective system applied to the head of the state, are augmented or decreased by the peculiar circumstances of the people which adopts it. However the functions of the executive power may be restricted, it must always exercise a great influence upon the foreign policy of the country, for a negotiation cannot be opened or successfully carried on otherwise than by a single agent. The more precarious and the more perilous the position of a people becomes, the more absolute is the want of a fixed and consistent external policy, and the more dangerous does the elective system of the chief magistrate become. The policy of the Americans in relation to the whole world is exceedingly simple; and it may almost be said that no country stands in need of them, nor do they require the co-operation of any other people. Their independence is never threatened. In their present condition, therefore, the functions of the executive power are no less limited by circumstances, than by the laws; and the president may frequently change his line of policy without involving the state in difficulty or destruction.

Whatever the prerogatives of the executive power may be, the period which immediately precedes an election, and the moment of its duration, must always be considered as a national crisis, which is perilous in proportion to the internal embarrassments and the external dangers of the country. Few of the nations of Europe could escape the calamities of anarchy or of conquest, every time they might have to elect a new sovereign. In America society is so constituted that it can stand without assistance upon its own basis; nothing is to be feared from the pressure of external dangers; and the election of the president is a cause of agitation, but not of ruin.

MODE OF ELECTION.

Skill of the American Legislators shown in the Mode of Election adopted by them.—Creation of a special electoral Body.—Separate Votes of these Electors.—Case in which the House of Representatives is called upon to choose the President.—Results of the twelve Elections which have taken Place since the Constitution has been established.

Beside the dangers which are inherent in the system, many other difficulties may arise from the mode of election, which may be obviated by the precaution of the legislator. When a people met in arms on some public spot to choose its head, it was exposed to all the chances of civil war resulting from so martial a mode of proceeding, beside the dangers of the elective system in itself. The Polish laws, which subjected the election of the sovereign to the veto of a single individual, suggested the murder of that individual, or prepared the way to anarchy.

In the examination of the institutions, and the political as well as the social condition of the United States, we are struck by the admirable harmony of the gifts of fortune and the efforts of man. That nation possessed two of the main causes of internal peace; it was a new country, but it was inhabited by a people grown old in the exercise of freedom. America had no hostile neighbors to dread; and the American legislators, profiting by these favorable circumstances, created a weak and subordinate executive power, which could without danger be made elective.

It then only remained for them to choose the least dangerous of the various modes of election; and the rules which they laid down upon this point admirably complete the securities which the physical and political constitution of the country already afforded. Their object was to find the mode of election which would best express the choice of the people with the least possible excitement and suspense. It was admitted in the first place that the *simple* majority should be decisive; but the difficulty was to obtain this majority without an interval of delay which it was most important to avoid. It rarely happens that an individual can at once collect the majority of the suffrages of a great people; and this difficulty is enhanced in a republic of confederate states, where local influences are apt to preponderate. The means by which it was proposed to obviate this second obstacle was to delegate the electoral powers of the nation to a body of representatives. The mode of election rendered a majority more probable; for the fewer the electors are, the greater is the chance of their coming to a final decision. It also offered an additional probability of a judicious choice. It then remained to be decided whether this right of election was to be intrusted to the legislative body, the habitual representative assembly of the nation, or whether an electoral assembly should be formed for the express purpose of proceeding to the nomination of a president. The Americans chose the latter alternative, from a belief that the individuals who were returned to make the laws were incompetent to represent the wishes of the nation in the election of its chief magistrate; and that as they are chosen for more than a year, the constituency they represented might have changed its opinion in that time. It was thought that if the legislature was empowered to elect the head of the executive power, its members would, for some time before the election, be exposed to the manœuvres of corruption, and the tricks of intrigue; whereas, the special electors would, like a jury, remain mixed up with the crowd till the day of action, when they would appear for the sole purpose of giving their votes.

It was therefore established that every state should name a certain number of electors,* who in their turn should elect the president; and as it had been observed that the assemblies to which the choice of a chief magistrate had been intrusted in elective countries, inevitably became the centres of passion and of cabal; that they sometimes usurped an authority which did not belong to them: and that their proceedings, or the uncertainty which resulted from them, were sometimes prolonged so much as to endanger the welfare of the state, it was determined that the electors should all vote upon the same day, without being convoked to the same place.† This double election rendered a majority probable, though not certain; for it was possible that as many differences might exist between the electors as between their constituents. In this case it was necessary to have recourse to one of three measures; either to appoint new electors, or to consult a second time those already appointed, or to defer the election to another authority. The first two of these alternatives, independently of the uncertainty of their results, were likely to delay the final decision, and to perpetuate an agitation which must always be accompanied with danger. The third expedient was therefore adopted, and it was agreed that the votes should be transmitted sealed to the president of the senate, and that they should be opened and counted in the presence of the senate and the house of representatives. If none of the candidates has a majority, the house of representatives then proceeds immediately to elect the president; but with the condition that it must fix upon one of the three candidates who have the highest numbers.‡

* As many as it sends members to congress. The number of electors at the election of 1833 was 288. (See the National Calendar, 1833.)

† The electors of the same state assemble, but they transmit to the central government the list of their individual votes, and not the mere result of the vote of the majority.

‡ In this case it is the majority of the states, and not the majority of the members, which decides the question; so that New York has not more influence in the debate than Rhode Island. Thus the citizens of the Union are first consulted as members of one and the same community; and, if they cannot agree, recourse is had to the division of the states, each of which has a separate and independent vote. This is one of the singularities of the federal constitution which can only be explained by the jar of conflicting interests.

Thus it is only in case of an event which cannot often happen, and which can never be foreseen, that the election is intrusted to the ordinary representatives of the nation; and even then they are obliged to choose a citizen who has already been designated by a powerful minority of the special electors. It is by this happy expedient that the respect due to the popular voice is combined with the utmost celerity of execution and those precautions which the peace of the country demands. But the decision of the question by the house of representatives does not necessarily offer an immediate solution of the difficulty, for the majority of that assembly may still be doubtful, and in this case the constitution prescribes no remedy. Nevertheless, by restricting the number of candidates to three, and by referring the matter to the judgment of an enlightened public body, it has smoothed all the obstacles* which are not inherent in the elective system.

In the forty years which have elapsed since the promulgation of the federal constitution, the United States have twelve times chosen a president. Ten of these elections took place simultaneously by the votes of the special electors in the different states. The house of representatives has only twice exercised its conditional privilege of deciding in cases of uncertainty: the first time was at the election of Mr. Jefferson in 1801; the second was in 1825, when Mr. John Quincy Adams was chosen.

CRISIS OF THE ELECTION.

The election may be considered as a national Crisis.—Why?—Passions of the People.—Anxiety of the President.—Calm which succeeds the Agitation of the Election.

I HAVE shown what the circumstances are which favored the adoption of the elective system in the United States, and what precautions were taken by the legislators to obviate its dangers. The Americans are accustomed to all kinds of elections; and they know by experience the utmost degree of excitement which is compatible with security. The vast extent of the country, and the dissemination of the inhabitants, render a collision between parties less probable and less dangerous there than elsewhere. The political circumstances under

* Jefferson, in 1801, was not elected until the thirty-sixth time of balloting.

which the elections have hitherto been carried on, have presented no real embarrassments to the nation.

Nevertheless, the epoch of the election of a president of the United States may be considered as a crisis in the affairs of the nation. The influence which he exercises on public business is no doubt feeble and indirect; but the choice of the president, which is of small importance to each individual citizen, concerns the citizens collectively; and however trifling an interest may be, it assumes a great degree of importance as soon as it becomes general. The president possesses but few means of rewarding his supporters in comparison to the kings of Europe; but the places which are at his disposal are sufficiently numerous to interest, directly or indirectly, several thousand electors in his success. Moreover, political parties in the United States, as well as elsewhere, are led to rally around an individual, in order to acquire a more tangible shape in the eyes of the crowd, and the name of the candidate for the presidency is put forth as the symbol and personification of their theories. For these reasons parties are strongly interested in gaining the election, not so much with a view to the triumph of their principles under the auspices of the president elected, as to show, by the majority which returned him, the strength of the supporters of those principles.

For a long while before the appointed time is at hand, the election becomes the most important and the all-engrossing topic of discussion. The ardor of faction is redoubled; and all the artificial passions which the imagination can create in the bosom of a happy and peaceful land are agitated and brought to light. The president, on the other hand, is absorbed by the cares of self-defence. He no longer governs for the interest of the state, but for that of his re-election; he does homage to the majority, and instead of checking its passions, as his duty commands him to do, he frequently courts its worst caprices. As the election draws near, the activity of intrigue and the agitation of the populace increase; the citizens are divided into several camps, each of which assumes the name of its favorite candidate; the whole nation glows with feverish excitement; the election is the daily theme of the public papers, the subject of private conversation, the end of every thought and every action, the sole interest of the present. As soon as the choice is determined, this ardor is dispelled; and as a calmer season returns, the current of the state, which has nearly broken its banks, sinks to its usual level; but who can refrain from astonishment at the causes of the storm?

RE-ELECTION OF THE PRESIDENT.

When the Head of the executive Power is re-eligible, it is the State which is the Source of Intrigue and Corruption.—The desire of being re-elected, the chief Aim of a President of the United States.—Disadvantage of the System peculiar to America.—The natural Evil of Democracy is that it subordinates all Authority to the slightest Desires of the Majority.—The Re-election of the President encourages this Evil.

It may be asked whether the legislators of the United States did right or wrong in allowing the re-election of the president. It seems at first sight contrary to all reason to prevent the head of the executive power from being elected a second time. The influence which the talents and the character of a single individual may exercise upon the fate of a whole people, especially in critical circumstances or arduous times, is well known: a law preventing the re-election of the chief magistrate would deprive the citizens of the surest pledge of the prosperity and the security of the commonwealth; and, by a singular inconsistency, a man would be excluded from the government at the very time when he had shown his ability in conducting its affairs.

But if these arguments are strong, perhaps still more powerful reasons may be advanced against them. Intrigue and corruption are the natural defects of elective government; but when the head of the state can be re-elected, these evils rise to a great height, and compromise the very existence of the country. When a simple candidate seeks to rise by intrigue, his manœuvres must necessarily be limited to a narrow sphere; but when the chief magistrate enters the lists, he borrows the strength of the government for his own purposes. In the former case the feeble resources of an individual are in action; in the latter, the state itself, with all its immense influence, is busied in the work of corruption and cabal. The private citizen, who employs the most immoral practices to acquire power, can only act in a manner indirectly prejudicial to the public prosperity. But if the representative of the executive descends into the lists, the cares of government dwindle into second-rate importance, and the success of his election is his first concern. All laws and negotiations are then to him nothing more than electioneering schemes; places become the reward of services rendered, not to the nation, but to its chief; and the influence of the government, if not injurious to the country, is at least no longer beneficial to the community for which it was created.

It is impossible to consider the ordinary course of affairs in the United States without perceiving that the desire of being re-elected is the chief aim of the president; that his whole administration, and even his most indifferent measures, tend to this object; and that, as the crisis approaches, his personal interest takes the place of his interest in the public good. The principle of re-eligibility renders the corrupt influence of elective governments still more extensive and pernicious. It tends to degrade the political morality of the people, and to substitute adroitness for patriotism.

In America it exercises a still more fatal influence on the sources of national existence. Every government seems to be afflicted by some evil inherent in its nature, and the genius of the legislator is shown in eluding its attacks. A state may survive the influence of a host of bad laws, and the mischief they cause is frequently exaggerated; but a law which encourages the growth of the canker within must prove fatal in the end, although its bad consequences may not be immediately perceived.

The principle of destruction in absolute monarchies lies in the excessive and unreasonable extension of the prerogative of the crown; and a measure tending to remove the constitutional provisions which counterbalance this influence would be radically bad, even if its consequences should long appear to be imperceptible. By a parity of reasoning, in countries governed by a democracy, where the people is perpetually drawing all authority to itself, the laws which increase or accelerate its action are the direct assailants of the very principle of the government.

The greatest proof of the ability of the American legislators is, that they clearly discerned this truth, and that they had the courage to act up to it. They conceived that a certain authority above the body of the people was necessary, which should enjoy a degree of independence, without however being entirely beyond the popular control; an authority which would be forced to comply with the *permanent* determinations of the majority, but which would be able to resist its caprices, and to refuse its most dangerous demands. To this end they centred the whole executive power of the nation in a single arm; they granted extensive prerogatives to the president, and they armed him with the veto to resist the encroachments of the legislature.

But by introducing the principle of re-election, they partly destroyed their work; and they rendered the president but little inclined to exert the great power they had invested in his hands. If ineligible a second time, the president would be far from independent of the people, for his responsibility would not be lessened; but the favor of the people would not be so necessary to him as to induce him to court it by humoring its desires. If re-eligible (and this is more especially true at the present day, when political morality is relaxed, and when great men are rare), the president of the United States becomes an easy tool in the hands of the majority. He adopts its likings and its animosities, he hastens to anticipate its wishes, he forestalls its complaints, he yields to its idlest cravings, and instead of guiding it, as the legislature intended that he should do, he is ever ready to follow its bidding. Thus, in order not to deprive the state of the talents of an individual, those talents have been rendered almost useless, and to reserve an expedient for extraordinary perils the country has been exposed to daily dangers.

[The question of the propriety of leaving the president re-eligible, is one of that class which probably must for ever remain undecided The author himself, at page 125, gives a strong reason for re-eligibility, "so that the chance of a prolonged administration may inspire him with hopeful undertakings for the public good, and with the means of carrying them into execution,"—considerations of great weight. There is an important fact bearing upon this question, which should be stated in connexion with it. President Washington established the practice of declining a third election, and every one of his successors, either from a sense of its propriety or from apprehensions of the force of public opinion, has followed the example. So that it has become as much a part of the constitution, that no citizen can be a third time elected president, as if it were expressed in that instrument in words. This may perhaps be considered a fair adjustment of objections on either side. Those against a continued and perpetual re-eligibility are certainly met: while the arguments in favor of an opportunity to prolong an administration under circumstances that may justify it, are allowed their due weight. One effect of this practical interpolation of the constitution unquestionably is, to increase the chances of a president's being once re-elected; as men will be more disposed to acquiesce in a measure that thus practically excludes the individual from ever again entering the field of competition.—*American Editor.*]

FEDERAL COURTS.*

Political Importance of the Judiciary in the United States.—Difficulty of treating this Subject.—Utility of judicial Power in Confederations.—What Tribunals could be introduced into the Union.—Necessity of establishing federal Courts of Justice.—Organization of the national Judiciary.—The Supreme Court.—In what it differs from all known Tribunals.

I HAVE inquired into the legislative and executive power of the Union, and the judicial power now remains to be examined; but in this place I cannot conceal my fears from the reader. Judicial institutions exercise a great influence on the condition of the Anglo-Americans, and they occupy a prominent place among what are properly called political institutions: in this respect they are peculiarly deserving of our attention. But I am at a loss to explain the political action of the American tribunals without entering into some technical details on their constitution and their forms of proceeding; and I know not how to descend to these minutiæ without wearying the curiosity of the reader by the natural aridity of the subject, or without risking to fall into obscurity through a desire to be succinct. I can scarcely hope to escape these various evils; for if I appear too prolix to a man of the world, a lawyer may on the other hand complain of my brevity. But these are the natural disadvantages of my subject, and more especially of the point which I am about to discuss.

The great difficulty was, not to devise the constitution of the federal government, but to find out a method of enforcing its laws. Governments have in general but two means of overcoming the opposition of the people they govern, viz., the physical force which is at their own disposal, and the moral force which they derive from the decisions of the courts of justice.

A government which should have no other means of exacting obedience than open war, must be very near its ruin;

* See chapter vi., entitled, "Judicial Power in the United States." This chapter explains the general principles of the American theory of judicial institutions. See also the federal constitution, art. 3. See the Federalist, Nos. 78–83, inclusive: and a work entitled, "Constitutional Law, being a View of the Practice and Jurisdiction of the Courts of the United States," by Thomas Sergeant. See Story, pp 134, 162, 489, 511, 581, 668; and the organic law of the 24th September, 1789, in the collection of the laws of the United States, by Story, vol. i., p. 53.

for one of two alternatives would then probably occur: if its authority was small, and its character temperate, it would not resort to violence till the last extremity, and it would connive at a number of partial acts of insubordination, in which case the state would gradually fall into anarchy; if it was enterprising and powerful, it would perpetually have recourse to its physical strength, and would speedily degenerate into a military despotism. So that its activity would not be less prejudicial to the community than its inaction.

The great end of justice is to substitute the notion of right for that of violence; and to place a legal barrier between the power of the government and the use of physical force. The authority which is awarded to the intervention of a court of justice by the general opinion of mankind is so surprisingly great, that it clings to the mere formalities of justice, and gives a bodily influence to the shadow of the law. The moral force which courts of justice possess renders the introduction of physical force exceedingly rare, and it is very frequently substituted for it; but if the latter proves to be indispensable, its power is doubled by the association of the idea of law.

A federal government stands in greater need of the support of judicial institutions than any other, because it is naturally weak, and opposed to formidable opposition.* If it were always obliged to resort to violence in the first instance, it could not fulfil its task. The Union, therefore, required a national judiciary to enforce the obedience of the citizens to the laws, and to repel the attacks which might be directed against them. The question then remained what tribunals were to exercise these privileges; were they to be intrusted to the courts of justice which were already organized in every state? or was it necessary to create federal courts? It may easily be proved that the Union could not adapt the judicial power of the state to its wants. The separation of the judiciary from the administrative power of the state, no doubt affects the security of every citizen, and the liberty of all. But it is no less important to the existence of the nation that these several powers should have the same origin, should fol-

* Federal laws are those which most require courts of justice, and those at the same time which have most rarely established them. The reason is that confederations have usually been formed by independent states, which entertained no real intention of obeying the central government, and which very readily ceded the right of commanding to the federal executive, and very prudently reserved the right of non-compliance to themselves.

low the same principles, and act in the same sphere; in a word, that they should be correlative and homogeneous. No one, I presume, ever suggested the advantage of trying offences committed in France, by a foreign court of justice, in order to ensure the impartiality of the judges. The Americans form one people in relation to their federal government; but in the bosom of this people divers political bodies have been allowed to subsist, which are dependent on the national government in a few points, and independent in all the rest —which have all a distinct origin, maxims peculiar to themselves, and special means of carrying on their affairs. To intrust the execution of the laws of the Union to tribunals instituted by these political bodies, would be to allow foreign judges to preside over the nation. Nay more, not only is each state foreign to the Union at large, but it is in perpetual opposition to the common interests, since whatever authority the Union loses turns to the advantage of the states. Thus to enforce the laws of the Union by means of the tribunals of the states, would be to allow not only foreign, but partial judges to preside over the nation.

But the number, still more than the mere character, of the tribunals of the states rendered them unfit for the service of the nation. When the federal constitution was formed, there were already thirteen courts of justice in the United States which decided causes without appeal. That number is now increased to twenty-four. To suppose that a state can subsist, when its fundamental laws may be subjected to four-and-twenty different interpretations at the same time, is to advance a proposition alike contrary to reason and to experience.

The American legislators therefore agreed to create a federal judiciary power to apply the laws of the Union, and to determine certain questions affecting general interests, which were carefully determined beforehand. The entire judicial power of the Union was centred in one tribunal, which was denominated the supreme court of the United States. But, to facilitate the expedition of business, inferior courts were appended to it, which were empowered to decide causes of small importance without appeal, and with appeal causes of more magnitude. The members of the supreme court are named neither by the people nor the legislature, but by the president of the United States, acting with the advice of the senate. In order to render them independent of the other authorities, their office was made inalienable; and it was determined that their salary, when once fixed, should not be altered by the legislature.* It was easy to proclaim the principle of a federal judiciary, but difficulties multiplied when the extent of its jurisdiction was to be determined

---

MEANS OF DETERMINING THE JURISDICTION OF THE FEDERAL COURTS.

Difficulty of determining the Jurisdiction of separate courts of Justice in Confederation.—The Courts of the Union obtained the Right of fixing their own Jurisdiction.—In what Respect this Rule attacks the Portion of Sovereignty reserved to the several States.—The Sovereignty of these States restricted by the Laws, and the Interpretation of the Laws.—Consequently, the Danger of the several States is more apparent than real.

As the constitution of the United States recognized two distinct powers, in presence of each other, represented in a judicial point of view by two distinct classes of courts of justice, the utmost care which could be taken in defining their separate jurisdictions would have been insufficient to prevent frequent collisions between those tribunals. The question then arose, to whom the right of deciding the competency of each court was to be referred.

In nations which constitute a single body politic, when a question is debated between two courts relating to their mutual jurisdiction, a third tribunal is generally within reach to decide the difference; and this is effected without difficulty, because in these nations the questions of judicial competency have no connexion with the privileges of the national supre-

* The Union was divided into districts, in each of which a resident federal judge was appointed, and the court in which he presided was termed a "district court." Each of the judges of the supreme court annually visits a certain portion of the Republic, in order to try the most important causes upon the spot; the court presided over by this magistrate is styled a "circuit court." Lastly, all the most serious cases of litigation are brought before the supreme court, which holds a solemn session once a year, at which all the judges of the circuit courts must attend. The jury was introduced into the federal courts in the same manner, and in the same cases as into the courts of the states.

It will be observed that no analogy exists between the supreme court of the United States and the French cour de cassation, since the latter only hears appeals. The supreme court decides upon the evidence of the fact, as well as upon the law of the case, whereas the cour de cassation does not pronounce a decision of its own, but refers the cause to the arbitration of another tribunal. See the law of 24th September, 1789, laws of the United States, by Story, vol. i., p. 53.

macy. But it was impossible to create an arbiter between a superior court of the Union and the superior court of a separate state, which would not belong to one of these two classes. It was therefore necessary to allow one of these courts to judge its own cause, and to take or to retain cognizance of the point which was contested. To grant this privilege to the different courts of the states, would have been to destroy the sovereignty of the Union *de facto*, after having established it *de jure;* for the interpretation of the constitution would soon have restored that portion of independence to the states of which the terms of that act deprived them. The object of the creation of a federal tribunal was to prevent the courts of the states from deciding questions affecting the national interests in their own department, and so to form a uniform body of jurisprudence for the interpretation of the laws of the Union. This end would not have been accomplished if the courts of the several states had been competent to decide upon cases in their separate capacities, from which they were obliged to abstain as federal tribunals. The supreme court of the United States was therefore invested with the right of determining all questions of jurisdiction.*

This was a severe blow upon the independence of the states, which was thus restricted not only by the laws, but by the interpretation of them; by one limit which was known, and by another which was dubious; by a rule which was certain, and a rule which was arbitrary. It is true the constitution had laid down the precise limits of the federal supremacy, but whenever this supremacy is contested by one of the states, a federal tribunal decides the question. Nevertheless, the dangers with which the independence of the states was threatened by this mode of proceeding are less serious than they appear to be. We shall see hereafter that in America the real strength of the country is vested in the provincial far more than in the federal government. The federal judges are conscious of the relative weakness of the power in whose name they act, and they are more inclined to abandon a right of jurisdiction in cases where it is justly

* In order to diminish the number of these suits, it was decided that in a great many federal causes, the courts of the states should be empowered to decide conjointly with those of the Union, the losing party having then a right of appeal to the supreme court of the United States. The supreme court of Virginia contested the right of the supreme court of the United States to judge an appeal from its decisions, but unsuccessfully. See Kent's Commentaries, vol. i., pp. 300, 370, *et seq.;* Story's Commentaries, p. 646; and "The Organic Law of the United States," vol. i., p. 35.

their own, than to assert a privilege to which they have no legal claim.

DIFFERENT CASES OF JURISDICTION.

The Matter and the Party are the first Conditions of the federal Jurisdiction.—Suits in which Ambassadors are engaged.—Suits of the Union.—Of a separate State.—By whom tried.—Causes resulting from the Laws of the Union. Why judged by the federal Tribunal.—Causes relating to the Non-performance of Contracts tried by the federal Courts.—Consequences of this Arrangement.

After having appointed the means of fixing the competency of the federal courts, the legislators of the Union defined the cases which should come within their jurisdiction. It was established, on the one hand, that certain parties must always be brought before the federal courts, without any regard to the special nature of the cause; and, on the other, that certain causes must always be brought before the same courts, without any regard to the quality of the parties in the suit. These distinctions were therefore admitted to be the bases ot the federal jurisdiction.

Ambassadors are the representatives of nations in a state of amity with the Union, and whatever concerns these personages concerns in some degree the whole Union. When an ambassador is a party in a suit, that suit affects the welfare of the nation, and a federal tribunal is naturally called upon to decide it.

The Union itself may be involved in legal proceedings, and in this case it would be alike contrary to the customs of all nations, and to common sense, to appeal to a tribunal representing any other sovereignty than its own; the federal courts, therefore, take cognizance of these affairs.

When two parties belonging to two different states are engaged in a suit, the case cannot with propriety be brought before a court of either state. The surest expedient is to select a tribunal like that of the Union, which can excite the suspicions of neither party, and which offers the most natural as well as the most certain remedy.

When the two parties are not private individuals, but states, an important political consideration is added to the same motive of equity. The quality of the parties, in this case, gives a national importance to all their disputes; and the most trifling litigation of the states may be said to involve the peace of the whole Union.*

The nature of the cause frequently prescribes the rule of competency. Thus all the questions which concern maritime commerce evidently fall under the cognizance of the federal tribunals.† Almost all these questions are connected with the interpretation of the law of nations; and in this respect they essentially interest the Union in relation to foreign powers. Moreover, as the sea is not included within the limits of any peculiar jurisdiction, the national courts can only hear causes which originate in maritime affairs.

The constitution comprises under one head almost all the cases which by their very nature come within the limits of the federal courts. The rule which it lays down is simple, but pregnant with an entire system of ideas, and with a vast multitude of facts. It declares that the judicial power of the supreme court shall extend to all cases in law and equity *arising under the laws of the United States.*

Two examples will put the intentions of the legislator in the clearest light:—

The constitution prohibits the states from making laws on the value and circulation of money: if, notwithstanding this prohibition, a state passes a law of this kind, with which the interested parties refuse to comply because it is contrary to the constitution, the case must come before a federal court, because it arises under the laws of the United States. Again, if difficulties arise in the levying of import duties which have been voted by congress, the federal court must decide the case, because it arises under the interpretation of a law of the United States.

This rule is in perfect accordance with the fundamental principles of the federal constitution. The Union as it was established in 1789, possesses, it is true, a limited supremacy; but it was intended that within its limits it should form one

* The constitution also says that the federal courts shall decide "controversies between a state and the citizens of another state." And here a most important question of a constitutional nature arose, which was, whether the jurisdiction given by the constitution in cases in which a state is a party, extended to suits brought *against* a state as well as *by* it, or was exclusively confined to the latter. This question was most elaborately considered in the case of ***Chisholme*** v. ***Georgia,*** and was decided by the majority of the supreme court in the affirmative. The decision created general alarm among the states, and an amendment was proposed and ratified by which the power was entirely taken away so far as it regards suits brought *against* a state. See Story's Commentaries, p. 624, or in the large edition, § 1677.

† As, for instance, all cases of piracy.

and the same people.* Within those limits the Union is sovereign. When this point is established and admitted, the inference is easy; for if it be acknowledged that the United States constitute one and the same people within the bounds prescribed by their constitution, it is impossible to refuse them the rights which belong to other nations. But it has been allowed, from the origin of society, that every nation has the right of deciding by its own courts those questions which concern the execution of its own laws. To this it is answered, that the Union is in so singular a position, that in relation to some matters it constitutes a people, and that in relation to all the rest it is a nonentity. But the inference to be drawn is, that in the laws relating to these matters the Union possesses all the rights of absolute sovereignty. The difficulty is to know what these matters are; and when once it is resolved (and we have shown how it was resolved, in speaking of the means of determining the jurisdiction of the federal courts), no farther doubt can arise; for as soon as it is established that a suit is federal, that is to say, that it belongs to the share of sovereignty reserved by the constitution to the Union, the natural consequence is that it should come within the jurisdiction of a federal court.

Whenever the laws of the United States are attacked, or whenever they are resorted to in self-defence, the federal courts must be appealed to. Thus the jurisdiction of the tribunals of the Union extends and narrows its limits exactly in the same ratio as the sovereignty of the Union augments or decreases. We have shown that the principal aim of the legislators of 1789 was to divide the sovereign authority into two parts. In the one they placed the control of all the general interests of the Union, in the other the control of the special interest of its component states. Their chief solicitude was to arm the federal government with sufficient power to enable it to resist, within its sphere, the encroachments of the several states. As for these communities, the principle of independence within certain limits of their own was adopted in their behalf; and they were concealed from the inspection, and protected from the control, of the central government. In speaking of the division of the authority, I observed that this latter principle had not always been held sacred, since the

* This principle was in some measure restricted by the introduction of the several states as independent powers into the senate, and by allowing them to vote separately in the house of representatives when the president is elected by that body; but these are exceptions, and the contrary principle is the rule.

states are prevented from passing certain laws, which apparently belong to their own particular sphere of interest. When a state of the Union passes a law of this kind, the citizens who are injured by its execution can appeal to the federal courts.

[The remark of the author, that whenever the laws of the United States are attacked, or whenever they are resorted to in self-defence, the federal courts *must be* appealed to, which is more strongly expressed in the original, is erroneous and calculated to mislead on a point of some importance. By the grant of power to the courts of the United States to decide certain cases, the powers of the state courts are not suspended, but are exercised concurrently, subject to an appeal to the courts of the United States. But if the decision of the state court is *in favor* of the right, title, or privilege claimed under the constitution, a treaty, or under a law of congress, no appeal lies to the federal courts. The appeal is given only when the decision *is against* the claimant under the treaty or law. See 3d Cranch, 268. 1 Wheaton, 304.—*American Editor.*]

Thus the jurisdiction of the general courts extends not only to all the cases which arise under the laws of the Union, but also to those which arise under laws made by the several states in opposition to the constitution. The states are prohibited from making *ex-post-facto* laws in criminal cases; and any person condemned by virtue of a law of this kind can appeal to the judicial power of the Union. The states are likewise prohibited from making laws which may have a tendency to impair the obligations of contracts.* If a citizen thinks that an obligation of this kind is impaired by a law passed in his state, he may refuse to obey it, and may appeal to the federal courts.†

* It is perfectly clear, says Mr. Story (Commentaries, p. 503, or in the large edition, § 1379), that any law which enlarges, abridges, or in any manner changes the intention of the parties, resulting from the stipulations in the contract, necessarily impairs it. He gives in the same place a very long and careful definition of what is understood by a contract in federal jurisprudence. A grant made by the state to a private individual, and accepted by him, is a contract, and cannot be revoked by any future law. A charter granted by the state to a company is a contract, and equally binding to the state as to the grantee. The clause of the constitution here referred to ensures, therefore, the existence of a great part of acquired rights, but not of all. Property may legally be held, though it may not have passed into the possessor's hands by means of a contract; and its possession is an acquired right, not guarantied by the federal constitution.

† A remarkable instance of this is given by Mr. Story (p. 508, or in the large edition, § 1388). "Dartmouth college in New Hampshire had been founded by a charter granted to certain individuals before the American revolution, and its trustees formed a corporation under this

This provision appears to me to be the most serious attack upon the independence of the states. The rights awarded to the federal government for purposes of obvious national importance are definite and easily comprehensible; but those with which this last clause invests it are not either clearly appreciable or accurately defined. For there are vast numbers of political laws which influence the obligations of contracts, which may thus furnish an easy pretext for the aggressions of the central authority.

[The fears of the author respecting the danger to the independence of the states of that provision of the constitution, which gives to the federal courts the authority of deciding when a state law impairs the obligation of a contract, are deemed quite unfounded. The citizens of every state have a deep interest in preserving the obligation of the contracts entered into by them in other states: indeed without such a controlling power, "commerce among several states" could not exist. The existence of this common arbiter is of the last importance to the continuance of the Union itself, for if there were no peaceable means of enforcing the obligations of contracts, independent of all state authority, the states themselves would inevitably come in collision in their efforts to protect their respective citizens from the consequences of the legislation of another state.

M. De Tocqueville's observation, that the rights with which the clause in question invests the federal government "are not clearly appreciable or accurately defined," proceeds upon a mistaken view of the clause itself. It relates to the *obligation* of a contract, and forbids any act by which that obligation is impaired. To American lawyers, this seems to be as precise and definite as any rule can be made by human language. The distinction between the *right* to the fruits of a contract, and the time, tribunal, and manner, in which that right is to be enforced, seems very palpable. At all events, since the decision

charter. The legislature of New Hampshire had, without the consent of this corporation, passed an act changing the organization of the original provincial charter of the college, and transferring all the rights, privileges, and franchises, from the old charter trustees to new trustees appointed under the act. The constitutionality of the act was contested, and after solemn arguments, it was deliberately held by the supreme court that the provincial charter was a contract within the meaning of the constitution (art. i., sect. 10), and that the amendatory act was utterly void, as impairing the obligation of that charter. The college was deemed, like other colleges of private foundation, to be a private eleemosynary institution, endowed by its charter with a capacity to take property unconnected with the government. Its funds were bestowed upon the faith of the charter, and those funds consisted entirely of private donations. It is true that the uses were in some sense public, that is, for the general benefit, and not for the mere benefit of the corporators; but this did not make the corporation a public corporation. It was a private institution for general charity. It was not distinguishable in principle from a private donation, vested in private trustees, for a public charity, or for a particular purpose of beneficence. And the state itself, if it had bestowed funds upon a charity of the same nature, could not resume those funds."

of the supreme court of the United States in those cases in which this clause has been discussed, no difficulty is found, practically, in understanding the exact limits of the prohibition.

The next observation of the author, that "there are vast numbers of political laws which influence the obligations of contracts, which may thus furnish an easy pretext for the aggressions of the central authority," is rather obscure. Is it intended that political laws may be passed by the central authority, influencing the obligation of a contract, and thus the contracts themselves be destroyed? The answer to this would be, that the question would not arise under the clause forbidding laws impairing the obligation of contracts, for that clause applies only to the states and not to the federal government.

If it be intended, that the states may find it necessary to pass political laws, which affect contracts, and that under the pretence of vindicating the obligation of contracts, the central authority may make aggressions on the states and annul their political laws:—the answer is, that the motive to the adoption of the clause was to reach laws of every description, political as well as all others, and that it was the abuse by the states of what may be called political laws, viz.: acts confiscating demands of foreign creditors, that gave rise to the prohibition. The settled doctrine now is, that states may pass laws in respect to the making of contracts, may prescribe what contracts shall be made, and how, but that they cannot impair any that are already made.

The writer of this note is unwilling to dismiss the subject, without remarking upon what he must think a fundamental error of the author, which is exhibited in the passage commented on, as well as in other passages:—and that is, in supposing the judiciary of the United States, and particularly the supreme court, to be a part of the *political* federal government, and as the ready instrument to execute its designs upon the state authorities. Although the judges are in form commissioned by the United States, yet, in fact, they are appointed by the delegates of the state, in the senate of the United States, concurrently with, and acting upon, the nomination of the president. If the legislature of each state in the Union were to elect a judge of the supreme court, he would not be less a political officer of the United States than he now is. In truth, the judiciary have no political duties to perform; they are arbiters chosen by the federal and state governments, jointly, and when appointed, as independent of the one as of the other. They cannot be removed without the consent of the states represented in the senate, and they can be removed without the consent of the president, and against his wishes. Such is the theory of the constitution. And it has been felt practically, in the rejection by the senate of persons nominated as judges, by a president of the same political party with a majority of the senators. Two instances of this kind occurred during the administration of Mr. Jefferson.

If it be alleged that they are exposed to the influence of the executive of the United States, by the expectation of offices in his gift, the answer is, that judges of state courts are equally exposed to the same influence—that all state officers, from the highest to the lowest, are in the same predicament; and that this circumstance does not, therefore, deprive them of the character of impartial and independent arbiters.

These observations receive confirmation from every recent decision of the supreme court of the United States, in which certain laws of individual states have been sustained, in cases where, to say the least, it was very questionable whether they did not infringe the provisions of the constitution, and where a disposition to construe those provisions broadly and extensively, would have found very plausible grounds to indulge itself in annulling the state laws referred to. See the cases of *City of New York* vs. *Miln*, 11*th Peters*, 103; *Briscor* vs. *the Bank of the Commonwealth of Kentucky*, *ib.*, 257; *Charles River Bridge* vs. *Warren Bridge*, *ib.*, 420.—*American Ed.*]

PROCEDURE OF THE FEDERAL COURTS.

Natural Weakness of the judiciary Power in Confederations.—Legislators ought to strive as much as possible to bring private Individuals, and not States, before the federal Courts.—How the Americans have succeeded in this.—Direct Prosecutions of private Individuals in the federal Courts.—Indirect Prosecution in the States which violate the Laws of the Union.—The Decrees of the Supreme Court enervate but do not destroy the provincial Laws.

I HAVE shown what the privileges of the federal courts are, and it is no less important to point out the manner in which they are exercised. The irresistible authority of justice in countries in which the sovereignty is undivided, is derived from the fact that the tribunals of those countries represent the entire nation at issue with the individual against whom their decree is directed; and the idea of power is thus introduced to corroborate the idea of right. But this is not always the case in countries in which the sovereignty is divided: in them the judicial power is more frequently opposed to a fraction of the nation than to an isolated individual, and its moral authority and physical strength are consequently diminished. In federal states the power of the judge is naturally decreased, and that of the justiciable parties is augmented. The aim of the legislator in confederate states ought therefore to be, to render the position of the courts of justice analogous to that which they occupy in countries where the sovereignty is undivided; in other words, his efforts ought constantly to tend to maintain the judicial power of the confederation as the representative of the nation, and the justiciable party as the representative of an individual interest.

Every government, whatever may be its constitution, requires the means of constraining its subjects to discharge their obligations, and of protecting its privileges from their assaults. As far as the direct action of the government on the community is concerned, the constitution of the United States contrived, by a master-stroke of policy, that the federal courts, acting in the name of the laws, should only take cognizance of parties in an individual capacity. For, as it had been declared that the Union consisted of one and the same people within the limits laid down by the constitution, the inference was that the government created by this constitution, and acting within these limits, was invested with all the privileges of a national government, one of the principal of which is the right of transmitting its injunctions directly to the private citizen. When, for instance, the Union votes an impost, it does not apply to the states for the levying of it, bu to every American citizen, in proportion to his assessment. The supreme court, which is empowered to enforce the execution of this law of the Union, exerts its influence not upon a refractory state, but upon the private taxpayer; and, like the judicial power of other nations, it is opposed to the person of an individual. It is to be observed that the Union chose its own antagonist; and as that antagonist is feeble, he is naturally worsted.

But the difficulty increases when the proceedings are not brought forward *by* but *against* the Union. The constitution recognizes the legislative power of the state; and a law so enacted may impair the privileges of the Union, in which case a collision is unavoidable between that body and the state which had passed the law; and it only remains to select the least dangerous remedy, which is very clearly deducible from the general principles I have before established.*

It may be conceived that, in the case under consideration, the Union might have sued the state before a federal court, which would have annulled the act; and by this means it would have adopted a natural course of proceeding: but the judicial power would have been placed in open hostility to the state, and it was desirable to avoid this predicament as much as possible. The Americans hold that it is nearly impossible that a new law should not impair the interests of some private individuals by its provisions: these private interests are assumed by the American legislators as the ground of attack against such measures as may be prejudicial to the Union, and it is to these cases that the protection of the supreme court is extended.

Suppose a state vends a certain portion of its territory to a company, and that a year afterwards it passes a law by which the territory is otherwise disposed of, and that clause of the constitution, which prohibits laws impairing the obligation of contracts, is violated. When the purchaser under

* See chapter vi., on judicial power in America.

the second act appears to take possession, the possessor under the first act brings his action before the tribunals of the Union, and causes the title of the claimant to be pronounced null and void.* Thus, in point of fact, the judicial power of the Union is contesting the claims of the sovereignty of a state; but it only acts indirectly and upon a special application of detail: it attacks the law in its consequences, not in its principle, and it rather weakens than destroys it.

The last hypothesis that remained was that each state formed a corporation enjoying a separate existence and distinct civil rights, and that it could therefore sue or be sued before a tribunal. Thus a state could bring an action against another state. In this instance the Union was not called upon to contest a provincial law, but to try a suit in which a state was a party. This suit was perfectly similar to any other cause, except that the quality of the parties was different; and here the danger pointed out at the beginning of this chapter exists with less chance of being avoided. The inherent disadvantage of the very essence of federal constitutions is, that they engender parties in the bosom of the nation which present powerful obstacles to the free course of justice.

HIGH RANK OF THE SUPREME COURTS AMONG THE GREAT POWERS OF STATE.

No Nation ever constituted so great a judicial Power as the Americans. Extent of its Prerogative.—Its political Influence.—The Tranquillity and the very Existence of the Union depend on the Discretion of the seven federal Judges.

When we have successfully examined in detail the organization of the supreme court, and the entire prerogatives which it exercises, we shall readily admit that a more imposing judicial power was never constituted by any people. The supreme court is placed at the head of all known tribunals, both by the nature of its rights and the class of justiciable parties which it controls.

In all the civilized countries of Europe, the government has always shown the greatest repugnance to allow the cases to which it was itself a party to be decided by the ordinary course of justice. This repugnance naturally attains its

* See Kent's Commentaries, vol. i., p. 387.

utmost height in an absolute government; and, on the other hand, the privileges of the courts of justice are extended with the increasing liberties of the people; but no European nation has at present held that all judicial controversies, without regard to their origin, can be decided by the judges of common law.

In America this theory has been actually put in practice; and the supreme court of the United States is the sole tribunal of the nation. Its power extends to all the cases arising under laws and treaties made by the executive and legislative authorities, to all cases of admiralty and maritime jurisdiction, and in general to all points which affect the law of nations. It may even be affirmed that, although its constitution is essentially judicial, its prerogatives are almost entirely political. Its sole object is to enforce the execution of the laws of the Union; and the Union only regulates the relations of the government with the citizens, and of the nation with foreign powers: the relations of citizens among themselves are almost exclusively regulated by the sovereignty of the states.

A second and still greater cause of the preponderance of this court may be adduced. In the nations of Europe the courts of justice are only called upon to try the controversies of private individuals; but the supreme court of the United States summons sovereign powers to its bar. When the clerk of the court advances on the steps of the tribunal, and simply says, "The state of New York *versus* the state of Ohio," it is impossible not to feel that the court which he addresses is no ordinary body; and when it is recollected that one of these parties represents one million, and the other two millions of men, one is struck by the responsibility of the seven judges whose decision is about to satisfy or to disappoint so large a number of their fellow-citizens.

The peace, the prosperity, and the very existence of the Union, are invested in the hands of the seven judges. Without their active co-operation the constitution would be a dead letter: the executive appeals to them for assistance against the encroachments of the legislative powers; the legislature demands their protection from the designs of the executive; they defend the Union from the disobedience of the states, the states from the exaggerated claims of the Union, the public interest against the interests of private citizens, and the conservative spirit of order against the fleeting innovations of democracy. Their power is enormous, but it is clothed in the authority of public opinion. They are the all-powerful guardians of a people which respects law; but they would be impotent against popular neglect or popular contempt. The force of public opinion is the most intractable of agents, because its exact limits cannot be defined; and it is not less dangerous to exceed, than to remain below the boundary prescribed.

The federal judges must not only be good citizens, and men possessed of that information and integrity which are indispensable to magistrates, but they must be statesmen—politicians, not unread in the signs of the times, not afraid to brave the obstacles which can be subdued, nor slow to turn aside such encroaching elements as may threaten the supremacy of the Union and the obedience which is due to the laws.

The president, who exercises a limited power, may err without causing great mischief in the state. Congress may decide amiss without destroying the Union, because the electoral body in which congress originates may cause it to retract its decision by changing its members. But if the supreme court is ever composed of imprudent men or bad citizens, the Union may be plunged into anarchy or civil war.

The real cause of this danger, however, does not lie in the constitution of the tribunal, but in the very nature of federal governments. We have observed that in confederate peoples it is especially necessary to consolidate the judicial authority, because in no other nations do those independent persons who are able to cope with the social body, exist, in greater power or in a better condition to resist the physical strength of the government. But the more a power requires to be strengthened, the more extensive and independent it must be made; and the dangers which its abuse may create are heightened by its independence and its strength. The source of the evil is not, therefore, in the constitution of the power, but in the constitution of those states which renders its existence necessary.

IN WHAT RESPECTS THE FEDERAL CONSTITUTION IS SUPERIOR TO THAT OF THE STATES.

In what respects the Constitution of the Union can be compared to that of the States.—Superiority of the Constitution of the Union attributable to the Wisdom of the federal Legislators.—Legislature of the Union less dependent on the People than that of the States. —Executive Power more independent in its Sphere.—Judicial Power less subjected to the Inclinations of the Majority.—Practical Consequences of these Facts.—The Dangers inherent in a democratic Government eluded by the federal Legislators, and increased by the Legislators of the States.

The federal constitution differs essentially from that of the states in the ends which it is intended to accomplish; but in the means by which these ends are promoted, a greater analogy exists between them. The objects of the governments are different, but their forms are the same; and in this special point of view there is some advantage in comparing them together.

I am of opinion that the federal constitution is superior to all the constitutions of the states, for several reasons.

The present constitution of the Union was formed at a later period than those of the majority of the states, and it may have derived some melioration from past experience. But we shall be led to acknowledge that this is only a secondary cause of its superiority, when we recollect that eleven new states have been added to the American confederation since the promulgation of the federal constitution, and that these new republics have always rather exaggerated than avoided the defects which existed in the former constitutions.

The chief cause of the superiority of the federal constitution lay in the character of the legislators who composed it. At the time when it was formed the dangers of the confederation were imminent, and its ruin seemed inevitable. In this extremity the people chose the men who most deserved the esteem, rather than those who had gained the affections of the country. I have already observed, that distinguished as almost all the legislators of the Union were for their intelligence, they were still more so for their patriotism. They had all been nurtured at a time when the spirit of liberty was braced by a continual struggle against a powerful and predominant authority. When the contest was terminated, while the excited passions of the populace persisted in warring with dangers which had ceased to threaten them, these men stopped short in their career; they cast a calmer and more penetrating look upon the country which was now their own; they perceived that the war of independence was definitely ended, and that the only dangers which America had to fear were those which might result from the abuse of the freedom she had won. They had the courage to say what they believed to be true, because they were animated by a warm and sincere love of liberty; and they ventured to propose restrictions, because they were resolutely opposed to destruction.*

The greater number of the constitutions of the states assign one year for the duration of the house of representatives, and two years for that of the senate; so that members of the legislative body are constantly and narrowly tied down by the slightest desires of their constituents. The legislators of the Union were of opinion that this excessive dependence of the legislature tended to alter the nature of the main consequences of the representative system, since it vested the source not only of authority, but of government, in the peo-

* At this time Alexander Hamilton, who was one of the principal founders of the constitution, ventured to express the following sentiments in the Federalist, No. 71: "There are some who would be inclined to regard the servile pliancy of the executive to a prevailing current, either in the community or in the legislature, as its best recommendation. But such men entertain very crude notions, as well of the purpose for which government was instituted, as of the true means by which the public happiness may be promoted. The republican principle demands that the deliberative sense of the community should govern the conduct of those to whom they intrust the managements of their affairs; but it does not require an unqualified complaisance to every sudden breeze of passion, or to every transient impulse which the people may receive from the arts of men who flatter their prejudices to betray their interests It is a just observation that the people commonly *intend* the *public good*. This often applies to their very errors. But their good sense would despise the adulator who should pretend that they would always *reason right* about the *means* of promoting it. They know from experience that they sometimes err; and the wonder is that they so seldom err as they do, beset, as they continually are, by the wiles of parasites and sycophants; by the snares of the ambitious, the avaricious, the desperate; by the artifices of men who possess their confidence more than they deserve it; and of those who seek to possess rather than to deserve it. When occasions present themselves in which the interests of the people are at variance with their inclinations, it is the duty of persons whom they have appointed to be the guardians of those interests, to withstand the temporary delusion, in order to give them time and opportunity for more cool and sedate reflection. Instances might be cited in which a conduct of this kind has saved the people from very fatal consequences of their own mistakes, and has procured lasting monuments of their gratitude to the men who had courage and magnanimity enough to serve at the peril of their displeasure."

ple. They increased the length of the time for which the representatives were returned, in order to give them freer scope for the exercise of their own judgment.

The federal constitution, as well as the constitutions of the different states, divided the legislative body into two branches. But in the states these two branches were composed of the same elements and elected in the same manner. The consequence was that the passions and inclinations of the populace were as rapidly and as energetically represented in one chamber as in the other, and that laws were made with all the characteristics of violence and precipitation. By the federal constitution the two houses originate in like manner in the choice of the people; but the conditions of eligibility and the mode of election were changed, to the end that if, as is the case in certain nations, one branch of the legislature represents the same interests as the other, it may at least represent a superior degree of intelligence and discretion. A mature age was made one of the conditions of the senatorial dignity, and the upper house was chosen by an elected assembly of a limited number of members.

To concentrate the whole social force in the hands of the legislative body is the natural tendency of democracies; for as this is the power which emanates the most directly from the people, it is made to participate most fully in the preponderating authority of the multitude, and it is naturally led to monopolise every species of influence. This concentration is at once prejudicial to a well-conducted administration, and favorable to the despotism of the majority. The legislators of the states frequently yielded to these democratic propensities, which were invariably and courageously resisted by the founders of the Union.

In the states the executive power is vested in the hands of a magistrate, who is apparently placed upon a level with the legislature, but who is in reality nothing more than the blind agent and the passive instrument of its decisions. He can derive no influence from the duration of his functions, which terminate with the revolving year, or from the exercise of prerogatives which can scarcely be said to exist. The legislature can condemn him to inaction by intrusting the execution of the laws to special committees of its own members, and can annul his temporary dignity by depriving him of his salary. The federal constitution vests all the privileges and all the responsibility of the executive power in a single individual. The duration of the presidency is fixed at four years; the salary of the individual who fills that office cannot be altered during the term of his functions; he is protected by a body of official dependents, and armed with a suspensive veto. In short, every effort was made to confer a strong and independent position upon the executive authority, within the limits which had been prescribed to it.

In the constitution of all the states the judicial power is that which remains the most independent of the legislative authority: nevertheless, in all the states the legislature has reserved to itself the right of regulating the emoluments of the judges, a practice which necessarily subjects these magistrates to its immediate influence. In some states the judges are only temporarily appointed, which deprives them of a great portion of their power and their freedom. In others the legislative and judicial powers are entirely confounded: thus the senate of New York, for instance, constitutes in certain cases the superior court of the state. The federal constitution, on the other hand, carefully separates the judicial authority from all external influences: and it provides for the independence of the judges, by declaring that their salary shall not be altered, and that their functions shall be inalienable.

[It is not universally correct, as supposed by the author, that the state legislatures can deprive their governor of his salary at pleasure. In the constitution of New York it is provided, that the governor "shall receive for his services a compensation which shall neither be increased nor diminished during the term for which he shall have been elected;" and similar provisions are believed to exist in other states.

Nor is the remark strictly correct, that the federal constitution "provides for the independence of the judges, by declaring that their salary shall not be *altered*." The provision of the constitution is, that they shall, "at stated times, receive for their services a compensation which shall not be diminished during their continuance in office."—*American Editor*.]

The practical consequences of these different systems may easily be perceived. An attentive observer will soon remark that the business of the Union is incomparably better conducted than that of any individual state. The conduct of the federal government is more fair and more temperate than that of the states; its designs are more fraught with wisdom, its projects are more durable and more skilfully combined, its measures are put into execution with more vigor and consistency.

I recapitulate the substance of this chapter in a few words:—

The existence of democracies is threatened by two dangers,

viz.: the complete subjection of the legislative body to the caprices of the electoral body; and the concentration of all the powers of the government in the legislative authority.

The growth of these evils has been encouraged by the policy of the legislators of the states; but it has been resisted by the legislators of the Union by every means which lay within their control.

CHARACTERISTICS WHICH DISTINGUISH THE FEDERAL CONSTITUTION OF THE UNITED STATES OF AMERICA FROM ALL OTHER FEDERAL CONSTITUTIONS.

American Union appears to resemble all other Confederations.—Nevertheless its Effects are different.—Reason of this.—Distinctions between the Union and all other Confederations.—The American Government not a Federal, but an imperfect National Government.

THE United States of America do not afford either the first or the only instance of confederate states, several of which have existed in modern Europe, without adverting to those of antiquity. Switzerland, the Germanic empire, and the republic of the United Provinces, either have been or still are confederations. In studying the constitutions of these different countries, the politician is surprised to observe that the powers with which they invested the federal government are nearly identical with the privileges awarded by the American constitution to the government of the United States. They confer upon the central power the same rights of making peace and war, of raising money and troops, and of providing for the general exigencies and the common interests of the nation. Nevertheless the federal government of these different people has always been as remarkable for its weakness and inefficiency as that of the Union is for its vigorous and enterprising spirit. Again, the first American confederation perished through the excessive weakness of its government; and this weak government was, notwithstanding, in possession of rights even more extensive than those of the federal government of the present day. But the more recent constitution of the United States contains certain principles which exercise a most important influence, although they do not at once strike the observer.

This constitution, which may at first sight be confounded with the federal constitutions which preceded it, rests upon a novel theory, which may be considered as a great invention in modern political science. In all the confederations which had been formed before the American constitution of 1789, the allied states agreed to obey the injunctions of a federal government: but they reserved to themselves the right of ordaining and enforcing the execution of the laws of the Union. The American states which combined in 1789 agreed that the federal government should not only dictate the laws, but it should execute its own enactments. In both cases the right is the same, but the exercise of the right is different; and this alteration produced the most momentous consequences.

In all the confederations which have been formed before the American Union, the federal government demanded its supplies at the hands of the separate governments; and if the measure it prescribed was onerous to any one of those bodies, means were found to evade its claims: if the state was powerful, it had recourse to arms; if it was weak, it connived at the resistance which the law of the Union, its sovereign, met with, and resorted to inaction under the plea of inability. Under these circumstances one of two alternatives has invariably occurred: either the most preponderant of the allied peoples has assumed the privileges of the federal authority, and ruled all the other states in its name,* or the federal government has been abandoned by its natural supporters, anarchy has arisen between the confederates, and the Union has lost all power of action.†

In America the subjects of the Union are not states, but private citizens: the national government levies a tax, not upon the state of Massachusetts, but upon each inhabitant of Massachusetts. All former confederate governments presided over communities, but that of the Union rules individuals; its force is not borrowed, but self-derived; and it is served by its own civil and military officers, by its own army, and its own courts of justice. It cannot be doubted that the spirit of the nation, the passions of the multitude, and the provincial prejudices of each state, tend singularly to diminish the authority of a federal authority thus constituted, and to facilitate the means of resistance to its mandates; but the comparative

* This was the case in Greece, when Philip undertook to execute the decree of the Amphictyons; in the Low Countries, where the province of Holland always gave the law; and in our time in the Germanic confederation, in which Austria and Prussia assume a great degree of influence over the whole country, in the name of the Diet.

† Such has always been the situation of the Swiss confederation, which would have perished ages ago but for the mutual jealousies of its neighbors.

weakness of a restricted sovereignty is an evil inherent in the federal system. In America, each state has fewer opportunities of resistance, and fewer temptations to non-compliance; nor can such a design be put in execution (if indeed it be entertained), without an open violation of the laws of the Union, a direct interruption of the ordinary course of justice, and a bold declaration of revolt; in a word, without a decisive step, which men hesitate to adopt.

In all former confederations, the privileges of the Union furnished more elements of discord than of power, since they multiplied the claims of the nation without augmenting the means of enforcing them: and in accordance with this fact it may be remarked, that the real weakness of federal governments has almost always been in the exact ratio of their nominal power. Such is not the case with the American Union, in which, as in ordinary governments, the federal government has the means of enforcing all it is empowered to demand.

The human understanding more easily invents new things than new words, and we are thence constrained to employ a multitude of improper and inadequate expressions. When several nations form a permanent league, and establish a supreme authority, which, although it has not the same influence over the members of the community as a national government, acts upon each of the confederate states in a body, this government, which is so essentially different from all others, is denominated a federal one. Another form of society is afterward discovered, in which several peoples are fused into one and the same nation with regard to certain common interests, although they remain distinct, or at least only confederate, with regard to all their other concerns. In this case the central power acts directly upon those whom it governs, whom it rules, and whom it judges, in the same manner as, but in a more limited circle than, a national government. Here the term of federal government is clearly no longer applicable to a state of things which must be styled an incomplete national government: a form of government has been found out which is neither exactly national nor federal; but no farther progress has been made, and the new word which will one day designate this novel invention does not yet exist.

The absence of this new species of confederation has been the cause which has brought all unions to civil war, to subjection, or to a stagnant apathy; and the peoples which formed these leagues have been either too dull to discern, or too pusillanimous to apply this great remedy. The American confederation perished by the same defects.

But the confederate states of America had been long accustomed to form a portion of one empire before they had won their independence: they had not contracted the habit of governing themselves, and their national prejudices had not taken deep root in their minds. Superior to the rest of the world in political knowledge, and sharing that knowledge equally among themselves, they were little agitated by the passions which generally oppose the extension of federal authority in a nation, and those passions were checked by the wisdom of the chief citizens.

The Americans applied the remedy with prudent firmness as soon as they were conscious of the evil; they amended their laws, and they saved their country.

ADVANTAGES OF THE FEDERAL SYSTEM IN GENERAL, AND ITS SPECIAL UTILITY IN AMERICA.

Happiness and Freedom of small Nations.—Power of Great Nations.—Great Empires favorable to the Growth of Civilisation.—Strength often the first Element of national Prosperity.—Aim of the federal System to unite the twofold Advantages resulting from a small and from a large Territory.—Advantages derived by the United States from this System.—The Law adapts itself to the Exigencies of the Population; Population does not conform to the Exigencies of the Law.—Activity, Melioration, Love, and Enjoyment of Freedom in the American Communities.—Public Spirit of the Union the abstract of provincial Patriotism.—Principles and Things circulate freely over the Territory of the United States.—The Union is happy and free as a little Nation, and respected as a great Empire.

In small nations the scrutiny of society penetrates into every part, and the spirit of improvement enters into the most trifling details; as the ambition of the people is necessarily checked by its weakness, all the efforts and resources of the citizens are turned to the internal benefit of the community, and are not likely to evaporate in the fleeting breath of glory. The desires of every individual are limited, because extraordinary faculties are rarely to be met with. The gifts of an equal fortune render the various conditions of life uniform; and the manners of the inhabitants are orderly and simple. Thus, if we estimate the gradations of popular morality and enlightenment, we shall generally find that in small nations there are more persons in easy circumstances, a more numerous population, and a more tranquil state of society than in great empires.

When tyranny is established in the bosom of a small nation, it is more galling than elsewhere, because, as it acts within a narrow circle, every point of that circle is subject to its direct influence. It supplies the place of those great designs which it cannot entertain, by a violent or an exasperating interference in a multitude of minute details; and it leaves the political world to which it properly belongs, to meddle with the arrangements of domestic life. Tastes as well as actions are to be regulated at its pleasure; and the families of the citizens as well as the affairs of the state are to be governed by its decisions. This invasion of rights occurs, however, but seldom, and freedom is in truth the natural state of small communities. The temptations which the government offers to ambition are too weak, and the resources of private individuals are too slender, for the sovereign power easily to fall within the grasp of a single citizen: and should such an event have occurred, the subjects of the state can without difficulty overthrow the tyrant and his oppression by a simultaneous effort.

Small nations have therefore ever been the cradles of political liberty: and the fact that many of them have lost their immunities by extending their dominion, shows that the freedom they enjoyed was more a consequence of their inferior size than of the character of the people.

The history of the world affords no instance of a great nation retaining the form of a republican government for a long series of years,* and this had led to the conclusion that such a state of things is impracticable. For my own part, I cannot but censure the imprudence of attempting to limit the possible, and to judge the future, on the part of a being who is hourly deceived by the most palpable realities of life, and who is constantly taken by surprise in the circumstances with which he is most familiar. But it may be advanced with confidence that the existence of a great republic will always be exposed to far greater perils than that of a small one.

All the passions which are most fatal to republican institutions spread with an increasing territory, while the virtues which maintain their dignity do not augment in the same proportion. The ambition of the citizens increases with the

* I do not speak of a confederation of small republics, but of a great consolidated republic.

power of the state; the strength of parties, with the importance of the ends they have in view; but that devotion to the common weal, which is the surest check on destructive passions, is not stronger in a large than in a small republic. It might, indeed, be proved without difficulty that it is less powerful and less sincere. The arrogance of wealth and the dejection of wretchedness, capital cities of unwonted extent, a lax morality, a vulgar egotism, and a great confusion of interests, are the dangers which almost invariably arise from the magnitude of states. But several of these evils are scarcely prejudicial to a monarchy, and some of them contribute to maintain its existence. In monarchical states the strength of the government is its own; it may use, but it does not depend on, the community: and the authority of the prince is proportioned to the prosperity of the nation: but the only security which a republican government possesses against these evils lies in the support of the majority. This support is not, however, proportionably greater in a large republic than it is in a small one; and thus while the means of attack perpetually increase both in number and in influence, the power of resistance remains the same; or it may rather be said to diminish, since the propensities and interests of the people are diversified by the increase of the population, and the difficulty of forming a compact majority is constantly augmented. It has been observed, moreover, that the intensity of human passions is heightened, not only by the importance of the end which they propose to attain, but by the multitude of individuals who are animated by them at the same time. Every one has had occasion to remark that his emotions in the midst of a sympathizing crowd are far greater than those which he would have felt in solitude. In great republics the impetus of political passion is irresistible, not only because it aims at gigantic purposes, but because it is felt and shared by millions of men at the same time.

It may therefore be asserted as a general proposition, that nothing is more opposed to the well-being and the freedom of man than vast empires. Nevertheless it is important to acknowledge the peculiar advantages of great states. For the very reason which renders the desire of power more intense in these communities than among ordinary men, the love of glory is also more prominent in the hearts of a class of citizens, who regard the applause of a great people as a reward worthy of their exertions, and an elevating encouragement to man. If we would learn why it is that great nations contribute more powerfully to the spread of human improvement than small states, we shall discover an adequate cause in the rapid and energetic circulation of ideas, and in those great cities which are the intellectual centres where all the rays of human genius are reflected and combined. To this it may be added that most important discoveries demand a display of national power which the government of a small state is unable to make; in great nations the government entertains a greater number of general notions, and is more completely disengaged from the routine of precedent and the egotism of local prejudice; its designs are conceived with more talent, and executed with more boldness.

In time of peace the well-being of small nations is undoubtedly more general and more complete; but they are apt to suffer more acutely from the calamities of war than those great empires whose distant frontiers may for ages avert the presence of the danger from the mass of the people, which is more frequently afflicted than ruined by the evil.

But in this matter, as in many others, the argument derived from the necessity of the case predominates over all others. If none but small nations existed, I do not doubt that mankind would be more happy and more free; but the existence of great nations is unavoidable.

This consideration introduces the element of physical strength as a condition of national prosperity.

It profits a people but little to be affluent and free, if it is perpetually exposed to be pillaged or subjugated; the number of its manufactures and the extent of its commerce are of small advantage, if another nation has the empire of the seas and gives the law in all the markets of the globe. Small nations are often impoverished, not because they are small, but because they are weak; and great empires prosper less because they are great than because they are strong. Physical strength is therefore one of the first conditions of the happiness and even of the existence of nations. Hence it occurs, that unless very peculiar circumstances intervene, small nations are always united to large empires in the end, either by force or by their own consent; yet I am unacquainted with a more deplorable spectacle than that of a people unable either to defend or to maintain its independence.

The federal system was created with the intention of combining the different advantages which result from the greater and the lesser extent of nations; and a single glance over the United States of America suffices to discover the advantages which they have derived from its adoption.

In great centralized nations the legislator is obliged to impart a character of uniformity to the laws, which does not always suit the diversity of customs and of districts; as he takes no cognizance of special cases, he can only proceed upon general principles; and the population is obliged to conform to the exigencies of the legislation, since the legislation cannot adapt itself to the exigencies and customs of the population; which is the cause of endless trouble and misery. This disadvantage does not exist in confederations; congress regulates the principal measures of the national government, and all the details of the administration are reserved to the provincial legislatures. It is impossible to imagine how much this division of sovereignty contributes to the well-being of each of the states which compose the Union. In these small communities, which are never agitated by the desire of aggrandizement or the cares of self-defence, all public authority and private energy is employed in internal melioration. The central government of each state, which is in immediate juxtaposition to the citizens, is daily apprised of the wants which arise in society; and new projects are proposed every year, which are discussed either at town-meetings or by the legislature of the state, and which are transmitted by the press to stimulate the zeal and to excite the interest of the citizens. This spirit of melioration is constantly alive in the American republics, without compromising their tranquillity; the ambition of power yields to the less refined and less dangerous love of comfort. It is generally believed in America that the existence and the permanence of the republican form of government in the New World depend upon the existence and the permanence of the federal system; and it is not unusual to attribute a large share of the misfortunes which have befallen the new states of South America to the injudicious erection of great republics, instead of a divided and confederate sovereignty.

It is incontestably true that the love and the habits of republican government in the United States were engendered in the townships and in the provincial assemblies. In a small state, like that of Connecticut for instance, where cutting a canal or laying down a road is a momentous political question, where the state has no army to pay and no wars to carry on, and where much wealth and much honor cannot be bestowed upon the chief citizens, no form of government can be more natural or more appropriate than that of a republic. But it is this same republican spirit, it is these manners and customs of a free people, which are engendered and nurtured in the different states, to be afterward applied to the country at large. The public spirit of the Union is, so to speak, nothing more than an abstract of the patriotic zeal of the provinces. Every citizen of the United States transfuses his attachment to his little republic into the common store of American patriotism. In defending the Union, he defends the increasing prosperity of his own district, the right of conducting its affairs, and the hope of causing measures of improvement to be adopted which may be favorable to his own interests; and these are motives which are wont to stir men more readily than the general interests of the country and the glory of the nation.

On the other hand, if the temper and the manners of the inhabitants especially fitted them to promote the welfare of a great republic, the federal system smoothed the obstacles which they might have encountered. The confederation of all the American states presents none of the ordinary disadvantages resulting from great agglomerations of men. The Union is a great republic in extent, but the paucity of objects for which its government provides assimilates it to a small state. Its acts are important, but they are rare. As the sovereignty of the Union is limited and incomplete, its exercise is not incompatible with liberty; for it does not excite those insatiable desires of fame and power which have proved so fatal to great republics. As there is no common centre to the country, vast capital cities, colossal wealth, abject poverty, and sudden revolutions are alike unknown; and political passion, instead of spreading over the land like a torrent of desolation, spends its strength against the interests and the individual passions of every state.

Nevertheless, all commodities and ideas circulate throughout the Union as freely as in a country inhabited by one people. Nothing checks the spirit of enterprise. The government avails itself of the assistance of all who have talents or knowledge to serve it. Within the frontiers of the Union the profoundest peace prevails, as within the heart of some great empire; abroad, it ranks with the most powerful nations of the earth: two thousand miles of coast are open to the commerce of the world; and as it possesses the keys of the globe, its flag is respected in the most remote seas. The Union is as happy and as free as a small people, and as glorious and as strong as a great nation.

WHY THE FEDERAL SYSTEM IS NOT ADAPTED TO ALL PEOPLES, AND HOW THE ANGLO-AMERICANS WERE ENABLED TO ADOPT IT.

Every federal System contains defects which baffle the efforts of the Legislator.—The federal System is complex.—It demands a daily Exercise of Discretion on the Part of the Citizens.—Practical knowledge of the Government common among the Americans.—Relative weakness of the Government of the Union another defect inherent in the federal System.—The Americans have diminished without remedying it.—The Sovereignty of the separate States apparently weaker, but really stronger, than that of the Union.—Why.—Natural causes of Union must exist between confederate Peoples beside the Laws.—What these Causes are among the Anglo-Americans.—Maine and Georgia, separated by a Distance of a thousand Miles, more naturally united than Normandy and Britany.—War, the main Peril of Confederations.—This proved even by the Example of the United States.—The Union has no great Wars to fear.—Why.—Dangers to which Europeans would be exposed if they adopted the federal System of the Americans.

When a legislator succeeds, after persevering efforts, in exercising an indirect influence upon the destiny of nations, his genius is lauded by mankind, while in point of fact, the geographical position of the country which he is unable to change, a social condition which arose without his co-operation, manners and opinions which he cannot trace to their source, and an origin with which he is unacquainted, exercise so irresistible an influence over the courses of society, that he is himself borne away by the current, after an ineffectual resistance. Like the navigator, he may direct the vessel which bears him along, but he can neither change its structure, nor raise the winds, nor lull the waters which swell beneath him.

I have shown the advantages which the Americans derive from their federal system; it remains for me to point out the circumstances which render that system practicable, as its benefits are not to be enjoyed by all nations. The incidental defects of the federal system which originate in the laws may be corrected by the skill of the legislator, but there are farther evils inherent in the system which cannot be counteracted by the peoples which adopt it. These nations must therefore find the strength necessary to support the natural imperfections of the government.

The most prominent evil of all federal systems is the very complex nature of the means they employ. Two sovereignties are necessarily in the presence of each other. The legislator may simplify and equalize the action of these two sovereignties, by limiting each of them to a sphere of authority accurately defined; but he cannot combine them into one, or prevent them from running into collision at certain points. The federal system therefore rests upon a theory which is necessarily complicated, and which demands the daily exercise of a considerable share of discretion on the part of those it governs.

A proposition must be plain to be adopted by the understanding of a people. A false notion, which is clear and precise, will always meet with a greater number of adherents in the world than a true principle which is obscure or involved. Hence it arises that parties, which are like small communities in the heart of the nation, invariably adopt some principle or some name as a symbol, which very inadequately represents the end they have in view, and the means which are at their disposal, but without which they could neither act nor subsist. The governments which are founded upon a single principle or a single feeling which is easily defined, are perhaps not the best, but they are unquestionably the strongest and the most durable in the world.

In examining the constitution of the United States, which is the most perfect federal constitution that ever existed, one is startled, on the other hand, at the variety of information and the excellence of discretion which it presupposes in the people whom it is meant to govern. The government of the Union depends entirely upon legal fictions; the Union is an ideal notion which only exists in the mind, and whose limits and extent can only be discerned by the understanding.

When once the general theory is comprehended, numerous difficulties remain to be solved in its application; for the sovereignty of the Union is so involved in that of the states, that it is impossible to distinguish its boundaries at the first glance. The whole structure of the government is artificial and conventional; and it would be ill-adapted to a people which has not long been accustomed to conduct its own affairs, or to one in which the science of politics has not descended to the humblest classes of society. I have never been more struck by the good sense and the practical judgment of the Americans than in the ingenious devices by which they elude the numberless difficulties resulting from their federal constitution. I scarcely ever met with a plain American citizen who could not distinguish, with surprising facility, the obligations created by the laws of congress from those created by the laws of his own state; and who, after having discriminated between the matters which come under the cognizance of the Union, and those which the local legislature is competent to regulate, could not point out the exact limit of the several jurisdictions of the federal courts and the tribunals of the state.

The constitution of the United States is like those exquisite productions of human industry which ensure wealth and renown to their inventors, but which are profitless in any other hands. This truth is exemplified by the condition of Mexico at the present time. The Mexicans were desirous of establishing a federal system, and they took the federal constitution of their neighbors the Anglo-Americans as their model, and copied it with considerable accuracy.* But although they had borrowed the letter of the law, they were unable to create or to introduce the spirit and the sense which gave it life. They were involved in ceaseless embarrassments between the mechanism of their double government; the sovereignty of the states and that of the Union perpetually exceeded their respective privileges, and entered into collision; and to the present day Mexico is alternately the victim of anarchy and the slave of military despotism.

The second and the most fatal of all the defects I have alluded to, and that which I believe to be inherent in the federal system, is the relative weakness of the government of the Union. The principle upon which all confederations rest is that of a divided sovereignty. The legislator may render this partition less perceptible, he may even conceal it for a time from the public eye, but he cannot prevent it from existing; and a divided sovereignty must always be less powerful than an entire supremacy. The reader has seen in the remarks I have made on the constitution of the United States, that the Americans have displayed singular ingenuity in combining the restriction of the power of the Union within the narrow limits of the federal government, with the semblance, and to a certain extent with the force of a national government. By this means the legislators of the Union have succeeded in diminishing, though not in counteracting, the natural danger of confederations.

It has been remarked that the American government does not apply itself to the states, but that it immediately transmits its injunctions to the citizens, and compels them as isolated individuals to comply with its demands. But if the federal law were to clash with the interests and prejudices of a state, it might be feared that all the citizens of that

* See the Mexican constitution of 1824

state would conceive themselves to be interested in the cause of a single individual who should refuse to obey. If all the citizens of the state were aggrieved at the same time and in the same manner by the authority of the Union, the federal government would vainly attempt to subdue them individually; they would instinctively unite in the common defence, and they would derive a ready-prepared organization from the share of sovereignty which the institution of their state allows them to enjoy. Fiction would give way to reality, and an organized portion of the territory might then contest the central authority.

The same observation holds good with regard to the federal jurisdiction. If the courts of the Union violated an important law of a state in a private case, the real, if not the apparent contest would arise between the aggrieved state, represented by a citizen, and the Union, represented by its courts of justice.*

* For instance, the Union possesses by the constitution the right of selling unoccupied lands for its own profit. Supposing that the state of Ohio should claim the same right in behalf of certain territories lying within its boundaries, upon the plea that the constitution refers to those lands alone which do not belong to the jurisdiction of any particular state, and consequently should choose to dispose of them itself, the litigation would be carried on in the name of the purchasers from the state of Ohio, and the purchasers from the Union, and not in the names of Ohio and the Union. But what would become of this legal fiction if the federal purchaser was confirmed in his right by the courts of the Union, while the other competitor was ordered to retain possession by the tribunals of the state of Ohio?

[The difficulty supposed by the author in this note is imaginary. The question of title to the lands in the case put, must depend upon the constitution, treaties, and laws of the United States; and a decision in the state court adverse to the claim or title set up under those laws, must, by the very words of the constitution and of the judiciary act, be subject to review by the supreme court of the United States, whose decision is final.

The remarks in the text of this page upon the relative weakness of the government of the Union, are equally applicable to any form of republican or democratic government, and are not peculiar to a federal system. Under the circumstances supposed by the author, of all the citizens of a state, or a large majority of them, aggrieved at the same time and in the same manner, by the operation of any law, the same difficulty would arise in executing the laws of the state as those of the Union. Indeed, such instances of the total inefficacy of state laws are not wanting. The fact is, that all republics depend on the willingness of the people to execute the laws. If they will not enforce them, there is, so far, an end to the government, for it possesses no power adequate to the control of the physical power of the people.

Not only in theory, but in fact, a republican government must be

He would have but a partial knowledge of the world who should imagine that it is possible, by the aid of legal fictions, to prevent men from finding out and employing those means of gratifying their passions which have been left open to them; and it may be doubted whether the American legislators, when they rendered a collision between the two sovereignties less probable, destroyed the causes of such a misfortune. But it may even be affirmed that they were unable to ensure the preponderance of the federal element in a case of this kind. The Union is possessed of money and of troops, but the affections and the prejudices of the people are in the bosom of the states. The sovereignty of the Union is an abstract being, which is connected with but few external objects; the sovereignty of the states is hourly perceptible, easily understood, constantly active; and if the former is of recent creation, the latter is coeval with the people itself. The sovereignty of the Union is factitious, that of the states is natural, and derives its existence from its own simple influence, like the authority of a parent. The supreme power of the nation affects only a few of the chief interests of society; it represents an immense but remote country, and claims a feeling of patriotism which is vague and ill-defined; but the authority of the states controls every individual citizen at every hour and in all circumstances; it protects his property, his freedom, and his life; and when we recollect the traditions, the customs, the prejudices of local and familiar attachment with which it is connected, we cannot doubt the superiority of a power which is interwoven with every circumstance that renders the love of one's native country instinctive to the human heart.

Since legislators are unable to obviate such dangerous collisions as occur between the two sovereignties which co-exist in the federal system, their first object must be, not only to

administered by the people themselves. They, and they alone, must execute the laws. And hence, the first principles in such governments, that on which all others depend, and without which no other can exist, is and must be, obedience to the existing laws at all times and under all circumstances. It is the vital condition of the social compact. He who claims a dispensing power for himself, by which he suspends the operation of the law in his own case, is worse than a usurper, for he not only tramples under foot the constitution of his country, but violates the reciprocal pledge which he has given to his fellow-citizens, and has received from them, that he will abide by the laws constitutionally enacted; upon the strength of which pledge, his own personal rights and acquisitions are protected by the rest of the community.—*American Editor.*]

dissuade the confederate states from warfare, but to encourage such institutions as may promote the maintenance of peace. Hence it results that the federal compact cannot be lasting unless there exists in the communities which are leagued together, a certain number of inducements to union which render their common dependance agreeable, and the task of the government light; and that system cannot succeed without the presence of favorable circumstances added to the influence of good laws. All the people which have ever formed a confederation have been held together by a certain number of common interests, which served as the intellectual ties of association.

But the sentiments and the principles of man must be taken into consideration as well as his immediate interest. A certain uniformity of civilisation is not less necessary to the durability of a confederation, than a uniformity of interests in the states which compose it. In Switzerland the difference which exists between the canton of Uri and the canton of Vaud is equal to that between the fifteenth and nineteenth centuries; and, properly speaking, Switzerland has never possessed a federal government. The Union between these two cantons only subsists upon the map; and their discrepancies would soon be perceived if an attempt were made by a central authority to prescribe the same laws to the whole territory.

One of the circumstances which most powerfully contribute to support the federal government in America, is that the states have not only similar interests, a common origin, and a common tongue, but that they are also arrived at the same stage of civilisation; which almost always renders a union feasible. I do not know of any European nation, how small soever it may be, which does not present less uniformity in its different provinces than the American people, which occupies a territory as extensive as one half of Europe. The distance from the state of Maine to that of Georgia is reckoned at about one thousand miles; but the difference between the civilisation of Maine and that of Georgia is slighter than the difference between the habits of Normandy and those of Britany. Maine and Georgia, which are placed at the opposite extremities of a great empire, are consequently in the natural possession of more real inducements to form a confederation than Normandy and Britany, which are only separated by a bridge.

The geographical position of the country contributed to increase the facilities which the American legislators derived from the manners and customs of the inhabitants; and it is to this circumstance that the adoption and the maintenance of the federal system are mainly attributable.

The most important occurrence which can mark the annals of a people is the breaking out of a war. In war a people struggle with the energy of a single man against foreign nations, in the defence of its very existence. The skill of a government, the good sense of the community, and the natural fondness which men entertain for their country, may suffice to maintain peace in the interior of a district, and to favor its internal prosperity; but a nation can only carry on a great war at the cost of more numerous and more painful sacrifices; and to suppose that a great number of men will of their own accord comply with the exigencies of the state, is to betray an ignorance of mankind. All the peoples which have been obliged to sustain a long and serious warfare have consequently been led to augment the power of their government. Those which have not succeeded in this attempt have been subjugated. A long war almost always places nations in the wretched alternative of being abandoned to ruin by defeat, or to despotism by success. War therefore renders the symptoms of the weakness of a government most palpable and most alarming; and I have shown that the inherent defect of federal governments is that of being weak.

The federal system is not only deficient in every kind of centralized administration, but the central government itself is imperfectly organized, which is invariably an influential cause of inferiority when the nation is opposed to other countries which are themselves governed by a single authority. In the federal constitution of the United States, by which the central government possesses more real force, this evil is still extremely sensible. An example will illustrate the case to the reader.

The constitution confers upon congress the right of "calling forth militia to execute the laws of the Union, suppress insurrections, and repel invasions;" and another article declares that the president of the United States is the commander-in-chief of the militia. In the war of 1812, the president ordered the militia of the northern states to march to the frontiers; but Connecticut and Massachusetts, whose interests were impaired by the war, refused to obey the command. They argued that the constitution authorizes the federal government to call forth the militia in cases of insurrection or invasion, but that, in the present instance, there was neither invasion nor insurrection. They added, that the same constitution which conferred upon the Union the right of calling forth the militia, reserved to the states that of naming the officers; and that consequently (as they understood the clause) no officer of the Union had any right to command the militia, even during war, except the president in person: and in this case they were ordered to join an army commanded by another individual. These absurd and pernicious doctrines received the sanction not only of the governors and legislative bodies, but also of the courts of justice in both states; and the federal government was constrained to raise elsewhere the troops which it required.*

The only safeguard which the American Union, with all the relative perfection of its laws, possesses against the dissolution which would be produced by a great war, lies in its probable exemption from that calamity. Placed in the centre of an immense continent, which offers a boundless field for human industry, the Union is almost as much insulated from the world as if its frontiers were girt by the ocean. Canada contains only a million of inhabitants, and its population is divided into two inimical nations. The rigor of the climate limits the extension of its territory, and shuts up its ports during the six months of winter. From Canada to the Gulf of Mexico a few savage tribes are to be met with, which retire, perishing in their retreat, before six thousand soldiers. To the south, the Union has a point of contact with the empire of Mexico; and it is thence that serious hostilities may one day be expected to arise. But for a long while to come, the uncivilized state of the Mexican community, the depravity of its morals, and its extreme poverty, will prevent that country from ranking high among nations. As for the powers of Europe, they are too distant to be formidable.†

The great advantage of the United States does not, then, consist in a federal constitution which allows them to carry

* Kent's Commentaries, vol. i., p. 244. I have selected an example which relates to a time posterior to the promulgation of the present constitution. If I had gone back to the days of the confederation, I might have given still more striking instances. The whole nation was at that time in a state of enthusiastic excitement; the revolution was represented by a man who was the idol of the people; but at that very period congress had, to say the truth, no resources at all at its disposal. Troops and supplies were perpetually wanting. The best devised projects failed in the execution, and the Union, which was constantly on the verge of destruction, was saved by the weakness of its enemies far more than by its own strength.

† Appendix O.

on great wars, but in a geographical position, which renders such enterprises improbable.

No one can be more inclined than I am myself to appreciate the advantages of the federal system, which I hold to be one of the combinations most favorable to the prosperity and freedom of man. I envy the lot of those nations which have been enabled to adopt it; but I cannot believe that any confederate peoples could maintain a long or an equal contest with a nation of similar strength in which the government should be centralised. A people which should divide its sovereignty into fractional powers, in the presence of the great military monarchies of Europe, would, in my opinion, by that very act, abdicate its power, and perhaps its existence and its name. But such is the admirable position of the New World, that man has no other enemy than himself; and that in order to be happy and to be free, it suffices to seek the gifts of prosperity and the knowledge of freedom.

CHAPTER IX.

I HAVE hitherto examined the institutions of the United States; I have passed their legislation in review, and I have depicted the present characteristics of political society in that country. But a sovereign power exists above these institutions and beyond these characteristic features, which may destroy or modify them at its pleasure; I mean that of the people. It remains to be shown in what manner this power, which regulates the laws, acts: its propensities and its passions remain to be pointed out, as well as the secret springs which retard, accelerate, or direct its irresistible course; and the effects of its unbounded authority, with the destiny which is probably reserved for it.

WHY THE PEOPLE MAY STRICTLY BE SAID TO GOVERN IN THE UNITED STATES.

IN America the people appoints the legislative and the executive power, and furnishes the jurors who punish all offences against the laws. The American institutions are democratic, not only in their principle but in all their consequences; and the people elects its representatives *directly*, and for the most part *annually*, in order to ensure their dependence. The people is therefore the real directing power; and although the form of government is representative, it is evident that the opinions, the prejudices, the interests, and even the passions of the community are hindered by no durable obstacles from exercising a perpetual influence on society. In the United States the majority governs in the name of the people, as is the case in all the countries in which the people is supreme. This majority is principally composed of peaceable citizens, who, either by inclination or by interest, are sincerely desirous of the welfare of their country. But they are surrounded by the incessant agitation of parties, which attempt to gain their co-operation and to avail themselves of their support.

CHAPTER X.

PARTIES IN THE UNITED STATES.

Great Division to be made between Parties.—Parties which are to each other as rival Nations.—Parties properly so called.—Difference between great and small Parties.—Epochs which produce them.—Their Characteristics.—America has had great Parties.—They are extinct.—Federalists.—Republicans.—Defeat of the Federalists.—Difficulty of creating Parties in the United States.—What is done with this Intention.—Aristocratic and democratic Character to be met with in all Parties.—Struggle of General Jackson against the Bank.

A GREAT division must be made between parties. Some countries are so large that the different populations which inhabit them have contradictory interests, although they are the subjects of the same government; and they may thence be in a perpetual state of opposition. In this case the different fractions of the people may more properly be considered as distinct nations than as mere parties; and if a civil war breaks out, the struggle is carried off by rival peoples rather than by factions in the state.

But when the citizens entertain different opinions upon subjects which affect the whole country alike, such, for instance, as the principles upon which the government is to be conducted, then distinctions arise which may correctly be styled parties. Parties are a necessary evil in free governments; but they have not at all times the same character and the same propensities.

At certain periods a nation may be oppressed by such insupportable evils as to conceive the design of effecting a total change in its political constitution; at other times the mischief lies still deeper, and the existence of society itself is endangered. Such are the times of great revolutions and of great parties. But between these epochs of misery and of confusion there are periods during which human society seems to rest, and mankind to make a pause. This pause is, indeed, only apparent; for time does not stop its course for nations any more than for men; they are all advancing toward a goal with which they are unacquainted; and we only imagine them to be stationary when their progress escapes our observation; as men who are going at a foot pace seem to be standing still to those who run.

But however this may be, there are certain epochs at which the changes that take place in the social and political constitution of nations are so slow and so insensible, that men imagine their present condition to be a final state; and the human mind, believing itself to be firmly based upon certain foundations, does not extend its researches beyond the horizon which it descries. These are the times of small parties and of intrigue.

The political parties which I style great are those which cling to principles more than to consequences; to general, and not to especial cases; to ideas, and not to men. These parties are usually distinguished by a nobler character, by more generous passions, more genuine convictions, and a more bold and open conduct than the others. In them, private interest, which always plays the chief part in political passions, is more studiously veiled under the pretext of the public good; and it may even be sometimes concealed from the eyes of the very person whom it excites and impels.

Minor parties are, on the other hand, generally deficient in political faith. As they are not sustained or dignified by a lofty purpose, they ostensibly display the egotism of their character in their actions. They glow with a factitious zeal; their language is vehement, but their conduct is timid and irresolute. The means they employ are as wretched as the end at which they aim. Hence it arises that when a calm state of things succeeds a violent revolution, the leaders of society seem suddenly to disappear, and the powers of the human mind to lie concealed. Society is convulsed by great parties, by minor ones it is agitated; it is torn by the former, by the latter it is degraded; and if these sometimes save it by a salutary perturbation, those invariably disturb it to no good end.

America has already lost the great parties which once divided the nation; and if her happiness is considerably increased, her morality has suffered by their extinction. When the war of independence was terminated, and the foundations of the new government were to be laid down, the nation was divided between two opinions—two opinions which are as old as the world, and which are perpetually to be met with under all the forms and all the names which have ever obtained in free communities—the one tending to limit, the other to extend indefinitely, the power of the people. The conflict of these two opinions never assumed that degree of violence in America which it has frequently displayed elsewhere. Both parties of the Americans were in fact agreed upon the most essential points; and neither of them had to destroy a traditionary constitution, or to overthrow the structure of society, in order to insure its own triumph. In neither of them, consequently, were a great number of private interests affected by success or by defeat; but moral principles of a high order, such as the love of equality and of independence, were concerned in the struggle, and they sufficed to kindle violent passions.

The party which desired to limit the power of the people, endeavored to apply its doctrines more especially to the constitution of the Union, whence it derived its name of *federal*. The other party, which affected to be more exclusively attached to the cause of liberty, took that of *republican*. America is the land of democracy, and the federalists were always in a minority; but they reckoned on their side almost all the great men who had been called forth by the war of independence, and their moral influence was very considerable. Their cause was, moreover, favored by circumstances. The ruin of the confederation had impressed the people with a dread of anarchy, and the federalists did not fail to profit by this transient disposition of the multitude. For ten or twelve years they were at the head of affairs, and they were able to apply some, though not all, of their principles; for the hostile current was becoming from day to day too violent to be checked or stemmed. In 1801 the republicans got possession of the government: Thomas Jefferson was named president; and he increased the influence of their party by the weight of his celebrity, the greatness of his talents, and the immense extent of his popularity.

The means by which the federalists had maintained their position were artificial, and their resources were temporary: it was by the virtues or the talents of their leaders that they had risen to power. When the republicans attained to that lofty station, their opponents were overwhelmed by utter defeat. An immense majority declared itself against the retiring party, and the federalists found themselves in so small a minority, that they at once despaired of their future success. From that moment the republican or democratic party has proceeded from conquest to conquest, until it has acquired absolute supremacy in the country. The federalists, perceiving that they were vanquished without resource, and isolated in the midst of the nation, fell into two divisions, of which one joined the victorious republicans, and the other abandoned its rallying point and its name. Many years have already elapsed since they ceased to exist as a party.

The accession of the federalists to power was, in my opinion, one of the most fortunate incidents which accompanied the formation of the great American Union: they resisted the inevitable propensities of their age and of their country. But whether their theories were good or bad, they had the defect of being inapplicable, as a system, to the society which they professed to govern; and that which occurred under the auspices of Jefferson must therefore have taken place sooner or later. But their government gave the new republic time to acquire a certain stability, and afterward to support the rapid growth of the very doctrines which they had combated. A considerable number of their principles were in point of fact embodied in the political creed of their opponents; and the federal constitution, which subsists at the present day, is a lasting monument of their patriotism and their wisdom.

Great political parties are not, then, to be met with in the United States at the present time. Parties, indeed, may be found which threaten the future tranquillity of the Union; but there are none which seem to contest the present form of government, or the present course of society. The parties by which the Union is menaced do not rest upon abstract principles, but upon temporal interests. These interests, disseminated in the provinces of so vast an empire, may be said to constitute rival nations rather than parties. Thus, upon a recent occasion, the north contended for the system of commercial prohibition, and the south took up arms in favor of free trade, simply because the north is a manufacturing, and the south an agricultural district; and that the restrictive system which was profitable to the one, was prejudicial to the other.

In the absence of great parties, the United States abound with lesser controversies; and public opinion is divided into a thousand minute shades of difference upon questions of very little moment. The pains which are taken to create parties are inconceivable, and at the present day it is no easy task. In the United States there is no religious animosity, because all religion is respected, and no sect is predominant; there is no jealousy of rank, because the people is everything, and none can contest its authority; lastly, there is no public misery to serve as a means of agitation, because the physical position of the country opens so wide a field to industry, that man is able to accomplish the most surprising undertakings with his own native resources. Nevertheless, ambitious men are interested in the creation of parties, since it is difficult to eject a person from authority upon the mere ground that his place is coveted by others. The skill of the actors in the political world lies, therefore, in the art of creating parties. A political aspirant in the United States begins by discriminating his own interest, and by calculating upon those interests which may be collected around, and amalgamated with it; he then contrives to discover some doctrine or some principle which may suit the purposes of this new association, and which he adopts in order to bring forward his party and to secure its popularity: just as the *imprimatur* of a king was in former days incorporated with the volume which it authorized, but to which it nowise belonged. When these preliminaries are terminated, the new party is ushered into the political world.

All the domestic controversies of the Americans at first appear to a stranger to be so incomprehensible and so puerile, that he is at a loss whether to pity a people which takes such arrant trifles in good earnest, or to envy that happiness which enables it to discuss them. But when he comes to study the secret propensities which govern the factions of America, he easily perceives that the greater part of them are more or less connected with one or the other of these two divisions which have always existed in free communities. The deeper we penetrate into the workings of these parties, the more do we perceive that the object of the one is to limit, and that of the other to extend, the popular authority. I do not assert that the ostensible end, or even that the secret aim, of American parties is to promote the rule of aristocracy or democracy in the country, but I affirm that aristocratic or democratic pas-

12

sions may easily be detected at the bottom of all parties, and that, although they escape a superficial observation, they are the main point and the very soul of every faction in the United States.

To quote a recent example: when the president attacked the bank, the country was excited and parties were formed; the well-informed classes rallied round the bank, the common people round the president. But it must not be imagined that the people had formed a rational opinion upon a question which offers so many difficulties to the most experienced statesmen. The bank is a great establishment which enjoys an independent existence, and the people, accustomed to make and unmake whatsoever it pleases, is startled to meet with this obstacle to its authority. In the midst of the perpetual fluctuation of society, the community is irritated by so permanent an institution, and is led to attack it, in order to see whether it can be shaken and controlled, like all the other institutions of the country.

REMAINS OF THE ARISTOCRATIC PARTY IN THE UNITED STATES.

Secret Opposition of wealthy Individuals to Democracy.—Their retirement.—Their tastes for exclusive Pleasures and for Luxury at Home.—Their Simplicity Abroad.—Their affected Condescension toward the People.

It sometimes happens in a people among which various opinions prevail, that the balance of the several parties is lost, and one of them obtains an irresistible preponderance, overpowers all obstacles, harasses its opponents, and appropriates all the resources of society to its own purposes. The vanquished citizens despair of success, and they conceal their dissatisfaction in silence and in a general apathy. The nation seems to be governed by a single principle, and the prevailing party assumes the credit of having restored peace and unanimity to the country. But this apparent unanimity is merely a cloak to alarming dissensions and perpetual opposition.

This is precisely what occurred in America; when the democratic party got the upper hand, it took exclusive possession of the conduct of affairs, and from that time the laws and customs of society have been adapted to its caprices. At the present day the more affluent classes of society are so entirely removed from the direction of political affairs in the United States, that wealth, far from conferring a right to the exercise of power, is rather an obstacle than a means of attaining to it. The wealthy members of the community abandon the lists, through unwillingness to contend, and frequently to contend in vain, against the poorest classes of their fellow-citizens. They concentrate all their enjoyments in the privacy of their homes, where they occupy a rank which cannot be assumed in public; and they constitute a private society in the state, which has its own tastes and its own pleasures. They submit to this state of things as an irremediable evil, but they are careful not to show that they are galled by its continuance; it is even not uncommon to hear them laud the delights of a republican government, and the advantages of democratic institutions when they are in public. Next to hating their enemies, men are most inclined to flatter them.

Mark, for instance, that opulent citizen, who is as anxious as a Jew of the middle ages to conceal his wealth. His dress is plain, his demeanor unassuming; but the interior of his dwelling glitters with luxury, and none but a few chosen guests whom he haughtily styles his equals, are allowed to penetrate into this sanctuary. No European noble is more exclusive in his pleasures, or more jealous of the smallest advantages which his privileged station confers upon him. But the very same individual crosses the city to reach a dark counting-house in the centre of traffic, where every one may accost him who pleases. If he meets his cobbler upon the way, they stop and converse; the two citizens discuss the affairs of the state in which they have an equal interest, and they shake hands before they part.

But beneath this artificial enthusiasm, and these obsequious attentions to the preponderating power, it is easy to perceive that the wealthy members of the community entertain a hearty distaste to the democratic institutions of their country. The populace is at once the object of their scorn and of their fears. If the mal-administration of the democracy ever brings about a revolutionary crisis, and if monarchical institutions ever become practicable in the United States, the truth of what I advance will become obvious.

The two chief weapons which parties use in order to ensure success, are the *public press*, and the formation of *associations*.

CHAPTER XI.

LIBERTY OF THE PRESS IN THE UNITED STATES.

Difficulty of restraining the Liberty of the Press.—Particular reasons which some Nations have to cherish this Liberty.—The Liberty of the Press a necessary Consequence of the Sovereignty of the people as it is understood in America.—Violent Language of the periodical Press in the United States.—Propensities of the periodical Press.—Illustrated by the United States.—Opinion of the Americans upon the Repression of the Abuse of the Liberty of the Press by judicial Prosecutions.—Reasons for which the Press is less powerful in America than in France.

The influence of the liberty of the press does not affect political opinions alone, but it extends to all the opinions of men, and it modifies customs as well as laws. In another part of this work I shall attempt to determine the degree of influence which the liberty of the press has exercised upon civil society in the United States, and to point out the direction which it has given to the ideas, as well as the tone which it has imparted to the character and the feelings of the Anglo-Americans, but at present I purpose simply to examine the effects produced by the liberty of the press in the political world.

I confess that I do not entertain that firm and complete attachment to the liberty of the press, which things that are supremely good in their very nature are wont to excite in the mind; and I approve of it more from a recollection of the evils it prevents, than from a consideration of the advantages it ensures.

If any one can point out an intermediate, and yet a tenable position, between the complete independence and the entire subjection of the public expression of opinion, I should perhaps be inclined to adopt it; but the difficulty is to discover this position. If it is your intention to correct the abuses of unlicensed printing, and to restore the use of orderly language, you may in the first instance try the offender by a jury; but if the jury acquits him, the opinion which was that of a single individual becomes the opinion of the country at large. Too much and too little has therefore hitherto been done; if you proceed, you must bring the delinquent before permanent magistrates; but even here the cause must be heard before it can be decided; and the very principles which no book would have ventured to avow are blazoned forth in the pleadings, and what was obscurely hinted at in a single composition is then repeated in a multitude of other publications. The language in which a thought is embodied is the mere carcase of the thought, and not the idea itself; tribunals may condemn the form, but the sense and spirit of the work is too subtle for their authority: too much has still been done to recede, too little to attain your end: you must therefore proceed. If you establish a censorship of the press, the tongue of the public speaker will still make itself heard, and you have only increased the mischief. The powers of thought do not rely, like the powers of physical strength, upon the number of their mechanical agents, nor can a host of authors be reckoned like the troops which compose an army; on the contrary, the authority of a principle is often increased by the smallness of the number of men by whom it is expressed. The words of a strong-minded man, which penetrate amid the passions of a listening assembly, have more weight than the vociferations of a thousand orators; and if it be allowed to speak freely in any public place, the consequence is the same as if free speaking was allowed in every village. The liberty of discourse must therefore be destroyed as well as the liberty of the press; this is the necessary term of your efforts; but if your object was to repress the abuses of liberty, they have brought you to the feet of a despot. You have been led from the extreme of independence to the extreme of subjection, without meeting with a single tenable position for shelter or repose.

There are certain nations which have peculiar reasons for cherishing the press, independently of the general motives which I have just pointed out. For in certain countries which profess to enjoy the privileges of freedom, every individual agent of the government may violate the laws with impunity, since those whom he oppresses cannot prosecute him before the courts of justice. In this case the liberty of the press is not merely a guarantee, but it is the only guarantee of their liberty and their security which the citizens possess. If the rulers of these nations proposed to abolish the independence of the press, the people would be justified in saying: "Give us the right of prosecuting your offences before the ordinary tribunals, and perhaps we may then waive our right of appeal to the tribunal of public opinion."

But in the countries in which the doctrine of the sovereignty of the people ostensibly prevails, the censorship of the press is not only dangerous, but it is absurd. When the right of every citizen to co-operate in the government of society is acknowledged, every citizen must be presumed to possess the power of discriminating between the different opinions of his cotemporaries, and of appreciating the different facts from which inferences may be drawn. The sovereignty of the people and the liberty of the press may therefore be looked upon as correlative institutions; just as the censorship of the press and universal suffrage are two things which are irreconcileably opposed, and which cannot long be retained among the institutions of the same people. Not a single individual of the twelve millions who inhabit the territory of the United States has as yet dared to propose any restrictions to the liberty of the press. The first newspaper over which I cast my eyes, after my arrival in America, contained the following article:

"In all this affair, the language of Jackson has been that of a heartless despot, solely occupied with the preservation of his own authority. Ambition is his crime, and it will be his punishment too: intrigue is his native element, and intrigue will confound his tricks, and will deprive him of his power; he governs by means of corruption, and his immoral practices will redound to his shame and confusion. His conduct in the political arena has been that of a shameless and lawless gamester. He succeeded at the time, but the hour of retribution approaches, and he will be obliged to disgorge his winnings, to throw aside his false dice, and to end his days in some retirement where he may curse his madness at his leisure; for repentance is a virtue with which his heart is likely to remain for ever unacquainted."

It is not uncommonly imagined in France, that the virulence of the press originates in the uncertain social condition, in the political excitement, and the general sense of consequent evil which prevail in that country; and it is therefore supposed that as soon as society has resumed a certain degree of composure, the press will abandon its present vehemence. I am inclined to think that the above causes explain the reason of the extraordinary ascendency it has acquired over the nation, but that they do not exercise much influence upon the tone of its language. The periodical press appears to me to be actuated by passions and propensities independent of the circumstances in which it is placed; and the present position of America corroborates this opinion.

America is, perhaps, at this moment, the country of the whole world which contains the fewest germs of revolution; but the press is not less destructive in its principles than in France, and it displays the same violence without the same reasons for indignation. In America, as in France, it constitutes a singular power, so strangely composed of mingled good and evil, that it is at the same time indispensable to the existence of freedom, and nearly incompatible with the maintenance of public order. Its power is certainly much greater in France than in the United States; though nothing is more rare in the latter country than to hear of a prosecution having been instituted against it. The reason of this is perfectly simple; the Americans having once admitted the doctrine of sovereignty of the people, apply it with perfect consistency. It was never their intention to found a permanent state of things with elements which undergo daily modifications; and there is consequently nothing criminal in an attack upon the existing laws, provided it be not attended with a violent infraction of them. They are moreover of opinion that courts of justice are unable to check the abuses of the press; and that as the subtlety of human language perpetually eludes the severity of judicial analysis, offences of this nature are apt to escape the hand which attempts to apprehend them. They hold that to act with efficacy upon the press, it would be necessary to find a tribunal, not only devoted to the existing order of things, but capable of surmounting the influence of public opinion; a tribunal which should conduct its proceedings without publicity, which should pronounce its decrees without assigning its motives, and punish the intentions even more than the language of an author. Whosoever should have the power of creating and maintaining a tribunal of this kind, would waste his time in prosecuting the liberty of the press; for he would be the supreme master of the whole community, and he would be as free to rid himself of the authors as of their writings. In this question, therefore, there is no medium between servitude and extreme license; in order to enjoy the inestimable benefits which the liberty of the press ensures, it is necessary to submit to the inevitable evils which it engenders. To expect to acquire the former, and to escape the latter, is to cherish one of those illusions which commonly mislead nations in their times of sickness, when, tired with faction and exhausted by effort, they attempt to combine hostile opinions and contrary principles upon the same soil.

The small influence of the American journals is attributable to several reasons, among which are the following:—

The liberty of writing, like all other liberty, is most formidable when it is a novelty; for a people which has never been accustomed to co-operate in the conduct of state affairs, places implicit confidence in the first tribune who arouses its attention. The Anglo-Americans have enjoyed this liberty ever since the foundation of the settlements; moreover, the press cannot create human passions by its own power, however skilfully it may kindle them where they exist. In America politics are discussed with animation and a varied activity, but they rarely touch those deep passions which are excited whenever the positive interest of a part of the community is impaired: but in the United States the interests of the community are in a most prosperous condition. A single glance upon a French and an American newspaper is sufficient to show the difference which exists between the two nations on this head. In France the space allotted to commercial advertisements is very limited, and the intelligence is not considerable, but the most essential part of the journal is that which contains the discussion of the politics of the day. In America three quarters of the enormous sheet which is set before the reader are filled with advertisements, and the remainder is frequently occupied by political intelligence or trivial anecdotes: it is only from time to time that one finds a corner devoted to passionate discussions like those with which the journalists of France are wont to indulge their readers.

It has been demonstrated by observation, and discovered by the innate sagacity of the pettiest as well as the greatest of despots, that the influence of a power is increased in proportion as its direction is rendered more central. In France the press combines a twofold centralisation: almost all its power is centred in the same spot, and vested in the same hands, for its organs are far from numerous. The influence of a public press thus constituted, upon a sceptical nation, must be unbounded. It is an enemy with which a government may sign an occasional truce, but which it is difficult to resist for any length of time.

Neither of these kinds of centralisation exists in America. The United States have no metropolis; the intelligence as well as the power of the country is dispersed abroad, and instead of radiating from a point, they cross each other in every direction; the Americans have established no central control over the expression of opinion, any more than over the conduct of business. These are circumstances which do not depend on human foresight; but it is owing to the laws of the Union that there are no licenses to be granted to the printers, no securities demanded from editors, as in France, and no stamp duty as in France and England. The consequence of this is that nothing is easier than to set up a newspaper, and a small number of readers suffices to defray the expenses of the editor.

The number of periodical and occasional publications which appear in the United States actually surpasses belief.

The most enlightened Americans attribute the subordinate influence of the press to this excessive dissemination; and it is adopted as an axiom of political science in that country, that the only way to neutralise the effect of public journals is to multiply them indefinitely. I cannot conceive why a truth which is so self-evident has not already been more generally admitted in Europe; it is comprehensible that the persons who hope to bring about revolutions, by means of the press, should be desirous of confining its action to a few powerful organs; but it is perfectly incredible that the partisans of the existing state of things, and the natural supporters of the laws, should attempt to diminish the influence of the press by concentrating its authority. The governments of Europe seem to treat the press with the courtesy of the knights of old; they are anxious to furnish it with the same central power which they have found to be so trusty a weapon, in order to enhance the glory of their resistance to its attacks.

In America there is scarcely a hamlet which has not its own newspaper. It may readily be imagined that neither discipline nor unity of design can be communicated to so multifarious a host, and each one is constantly led to fight under his own standard. All the political journals of the United States are indeed arrayed on the side of the administration or against it; but they attack and defend it in a thousand different ways. They cannot succeed in forming those great currents of opinion which overwhelm the most solid obstacles. This division of the influence of the press produces a variety of other consequences which are scarcely less remarkable. The facility with which journals can be established induces a multitude of individuals to take a part in them; but as the extent of competition precludes the possibility of considerable profit, the most distinguished classes of society are rarely led to engage in these undertakings. But such is the number of the public prints, that even if they were a source of wealth, writers of ability could not be found to direct them all. The journalists of the United States are usually placed in a very humble position, with a scanty education, and a vulgar turn of mind. The will of the majority is the most general of laws, and it establishes certain habits which form the characteristics of each peculiar class of society; thus it dictates the etiquette practised at courts and the etiquette of the bar. The characteristics of the French journalist consist in a violent, but frequently an eloquent and lofty manner of discussing the politics of the day; and the exceptions to this habitual practice are only occasional. The characteristics of the American journalist consist in an open and coarse appeal to the passions of the populace; and he habitually abandons the principles of political science to assail the characters of individuals, to track them into private life, and disclose all their weaknesses and errors.

Nothing can be more deplorable than this abuse of the powers of thought; I shall have occasion to point out hereafter the influence of the newspapers upon the taste and the morality of the American people, but my present subject exclusively concerns the political world. It cannot be denied that the effects of this extreme license of the press tend indirectly to the maintenance of public order. The individuals who are already in possession of a high station in the esteem of their fellow-citizens, are afraid to write in the newspapers, and they are thus deprived of the most powerful instrument which they can use to excite the passions of the multitude to their own advantage.*

The personal opinions of the editors have no kind of weight in the eyes of the public: the only use of a journal is, that it imparts the knowledge of certain facts, and it is only by altering or distorting those facts, that a journalist can contribute to the support of his own views.

But although the press is limited to these resources, its influence in America is immense. It is the power which impels the circulation of political life through all the districts of that vast territory. Its eye is constantly open to detect the secret springs of political designs, and to summon the leaders of all parties to the bar of public opinion. It rallies the interests of the community round certain principles, and it draws up the creed which factions adopt; for it affords a means of intercourse between parties which hear, and which address each other, without ever having been in immediate contact. When a great number of the organs of the press adopt the same line of conduct, their influence becomes irresistible; and public opinion, when it is perpetually assailed from the same side, eventually yields to the attack. In the United States each separate journal exercises but little authority: but the power of the periodical press is only second to that of the people.†

* They only write in the papers when they choose to address the people in their own name; as, for instance, when they are called upon to repel calumnious imputations, and to correct a mis-statement of facts.

† See Appendix P.

The Opinions which are established in the United States under the Empire of the Liberty of the Press, are frequently more firmly rooted than those which are formed elsewhere under the Sanction of a Censor.

In the United States the democracy perpetually raises fresh individuals to the conduct of public affairs; and the measures of the administration are consequently seldom regulated by the strict rules of consistency or of order. But the general principles of the government are more stable, and the opinions most prevalent in society are generally more durable than in many other countries. When once the Americans have taken up an idea, whether it be well or ill-founded, nothing is more difficult than to eradicate it from their minds. The same tenacity of opinion has been observed in England, where, for the last century, greater freedom of conscience, and more invincible prejudices have existed, than in all the other countries of Europe. I attribute this consequence to a cause which may at first sight appear to have a very opposite tendency, namely, to the liberty of the press. The nations among which this liberty exists are as apt to cling to their opinions from pride as from conviction. They cherish them because they hold them to be just, and because they exercised their own free will in choosing them; and they maintain them, not only because they are true, but because they are their own. Several other reasons conduce to the same end.

It was remarked by a man of genius, that "ignorance lies at the two ends of knowledge." Perhaps it would have been more correct to say that absolute convictions are to be met with at the two extremities, and that doubt lies in the middle; for the human intellect may be considered in three distinct states, which frequently succeed one another.

A man believes implicitly, because he adopts a proposition without inquiry. He doubts as soon as he is assailed by the objections which his inquiries may have aroused. But he frequently succeeds in satisfying these doubts, and then he begins to believe afresh: he no longer lays hold on a truth in its most shadowy and uncertain form, but he sees it clearly before him, and he advances onward by the light it gives him.*

When the liberty of the press acts upon men who are in the first of these three states, it does not immediately disturb

* It may, however, be doubted whether this rational and self-guiding conviction arouses as much fervor or enthusiastic devotedness in men as their first dogmatical belief.

their habit of believing implicitly without investigation, but it constantly modifies the objects of their intuitive convictions. The human mind continues to discern but one point upon the whole intellectual horizon, and that point is in continual motion. Such are the symptoms of sudden revolutions, and of the misfortunes that are sure to befall those generations which abruptly adopt the unconditional freedom of the press.

The circle of novel ideas is, however, soon terminated; the torch of experience is upon them, and the doubt and mistrust which their uncertainty produces, become universal. We may rest assured that the majority of mankind will either believe they know not wherefore, or will not know what to believe. Few are the beings who can ever hope to attain that state of rational and independent conviction which true knowledge can beget, in defiance of the attacks of doubt.

It has been remarked that in times of great religious fervor, men sometimes change their religious opinions; whereas, in times of general scepticism, every one clings to his own persuasion. The same thing takes place in politics under the liberty of the press. In countries where all the theories of social science have been contested in their turn, the citizens who have adopted one of them, stick to it, not so much because they are assured of its excellence, as because they are not convinced of the superiority of any other. In the present age men are not very ready to die in defence of their opinions, but they are rarely inclined to change them; and there are fewer martyrs as well as fewer apostates.

Another still more valid reason may yet be adduced: when no abstract opinions are looked upon as certain, men cling to the mere propensities and external interest of their position, which are naturally more tangible and more permanent than any opinions in the world.

It is not a question of easy solution whether the aristocracy or the democracy is most fit to govern a country. But it is certain that democracy annoys one part of the community, and that aristocracy oppresses another part. When the question is reduced to the simple expression of the struggle between poverty and wealth, the tendency of each side of the dispute becomes perfectly evident without farther controversy.

CHAPTER XII.

POLITICAL ASSOCIATIONS IN THE UNITED STATES.

Daily use which the Anglo-Americans make of the Right of Association.—Three kinds of political Association.—In what Manner the Americans apply the representative System to Associations.—Dangers resulting to the State.—Great Convention of 1831 relative to the Tariff. Legislative character of this Convention.—Why the unlimited Exercise of the Right of Association is less dangerous in the United States than elsewhere.—Why it may be looked upon as necessary.—Utility of Associations in a democratic People.

In no country in the world has the principle of association been more successfully used, or more unsparingly applied to a multitude of different objects, than in America. Beside the permanent associations which are established by law under the names of townships, cities, and counties, a vast number of others are formed and maintained by the agency of private individuals.

The citizen of the United States is taught from his earliest infancy to rely upon his own exertions, in order to resist the evils and the difficulties of life; he looks upon the social authority with an eye of mistrust and anxiety, and he only claims its assistance when he is quite unable to shift without it. This habit may even be traced in the schools of the rising generation, where the children in their games are wont to submit to rules which they have themselves established, and to punish misdemeanors which they have themselves defined. The same spirit pervades every act of social life. If a stoppage occurs in a thoroughfare, and the circulation of the public is hindered, the neighbors immediately constitute a deliberative body; and this extemporaneous assembly gives rise to an executive power, which remedies the inconvenience, before anybody has thought of recurring to an authority superior to that of the persons immediately concerned. If the public pleasures are concerned, an association is formed to provide for the splendor and the regularity of the entertainment. Societies are formed to resist enemies which are exclusively of a moral nature, and to diminish the vice of intemperance: in the United States associations are established to promote public order, commerce, industry, morality, and religion; for there is no end which the human will, seconded by the collective exertions of individuals, despairs of attaining.

I shall hereafter have occasion to show the effects of association upon the course of society, and I must confine myself for the present to the political world. When once the right of association is recognized, the citizens may employ it in several different ways.

An association consists simply in the public assent which a number of individuals give to certain doctrines; and in the engagement which they contract to promote the spread of those doctrines by their exertions. The right of associating with these views is very analogous to the liberty of unlicensed writing; but societies thus formed possess more authority than the press. When an opinion is represented by a society, it necessarily assumes a more exact and explicit form. It numbers its partisans, and compromises their welfare in its cause; they, on the other hand, become acquainted with each other, and their zeal is increased by their number. An association unites the efforts of minds which have a tendency to diverge, in one single channel, and urges them vigorously toward one single end which it points out.

The second degree in the right of association is the power of meeting. When an association is allowed to establish centres of action at certain important points in the country, its activity is increased, and its influence extended. Men have the opportunity of seeing each other; means of execution are more readily combined; and opinions are maintained with a degree of warmth and energy which written language cannot approach.

Lastly, in the exercise of the right of political association, there is a third degree: the partisans of an opinion may unite in electoral bodies, and choose delegates to represent them in a central assembly. This is, properly speaking, the application of the representative system to a party.

Thus, in the first instance, a society is formed between individuals professing the same opinion, and the tie which keeps it together is of a purely intellectual nature: in the second case, small assemblies are formed which only represent a fraction of the party. Lastly, in the third case, they constitute a separate nation in the midst of the nation, a government within the government. Their delegates, like the real delegates of the majority, represent the entire collective force of their party; and they enjoy a certain degree of that national dignity and great influence which belong to the chosen representatives of the people. It is true that they have not the right of making the laws; but they have the power of attacking those which are in being, and of drawing up beforehand those which they may afterward cause to be adopted.

If, in a people which is imperfectly accustomed to the exercise of freedom, or which is exposed to violent political passions, a deliberating minority, which confines itself to the contemplation of future laws, be placed in juxtaposition to the legislative majority, I cannot but believe that public tranquillity incurs very great risks in that nation. There is doubtless a very wide difference between proving that one law is in itself better than another, and proving that the former ought to be substituted for the latter. But the imagination of the populace is very apt to overlook this difference, which is so apparent in the minds of thinking men. It sometimes happens that a nation is divided into two nearly equal parties, each of which affects to represent the majority. If, in immediate contiguity to the directing power, another power be established, which exercises almost as much moral authority as the former, it is not to be believed that it will long be content to speak without acting; or that it will always be restrained by the abstract consideration of the nature of associations, which are meant to direct, but not to enforce opinions, to suggest but not to make the laws.

The more we consider the independence of the press in its principal consequences, the more are we convinced that it is the chief, and, so to speak, the constitutive element of freedom in the modern world. A nation which is determined to remain free, is therefore right in demanding the unrestrained exercise of this independence. But the *unrestrained* liberty of political association cannot be entirely assimilated to the liberty of the press. The one is at the same time less necessary and more dangerous than the other. A nation may confine it within certain limits without forfeiting any part of its self-control; and it may sometimes be obliged to do so in order to maintain its own authority.

In America the liberty of association for political purposes is unbounded. An example will show in the clearest light to what an extent this privilege is tolerated.

The question of the Tariff, or of free trade, produced a great manifestation of party feeling in America; the tariff was not only a subject of debate as a matter of opinion, but it exercised a favorable or a prejudicial influence upon several very powerful interests of thestates. The north attributed a great portion of its prosperity, and the south all its sufferings, to this system. Insomuch, that for a long time the tariff was the sole source of the political animosities which agitated the Union.

In 1831, when the dispute was raging with the utmost virulence, a private citizen of Massachusetts proposed to all the enemies of the tariff, by means of the public prints, to send delegates to Philadelphia in order to consult together upon the means which were most fitted to promote the freedom of trade. This proposal circulated in a few days from Maine to New Orleans by the power of the printing press: the opponents of the tariff adopted it with enthusiasm; meetings were formed on all sides, and delegates were named. The majority of these individuals were well known, and some of them had earned a considerable degree of celebrity. South Carolina alone, which afterward took up arms in the same cause, sent sixty-three delegates. On the 1st October, 1831, this assembly, which, according to the American custom, had taken the name of a convention, met at Philadelphia; it consisted of more than two hundred members. Its debates were public, and they at once assumed a legislative character; the extent of the powers of congress, the theories of free trade, and the different clauses of the tariff, were discussed in turn. At the end of ten days' deliberation, the convention broke up, after having published an address to the American people, in which it is declared:

I. The congress had not the right of making a tariff, and that the existing tariff was unconstitutional.

II. That the prohibition of free trade was prejudicial to the interests of all nations, and to that of the American people in particular.

It must be acknowledged that the unrestrained liberty of political association has not hitherto produced, in the United States, those fatal consequences which might perhaps be expected from it elsewhere. The right of association was imported from England, and it has always existed in America. So that the exercise of this privilege is now amalgamated with the manners and customs of the people. At the present time, the liberty of association is become a necessary guarantee against the tyranny of the majority. In the United States, as soon as a party has become preponderant, all the public authority passes under its control; its private supporters occupy all the places, and have all the force of the administration at their disposal. As the most distinguished partisans of the other side of the question are unable to surmount the obstacles which exclude them from power, they require some means of establishing themselves upon their own basis, and of opposing the moral authority of the minority to the physical power which domineers over it. Thus, a dangerous expedient is used to obviate a still more formidable danger.

The omnipotence of the majority appears to me to present such extreme perils to the American republics, that the dangerous measure which is used to repress it, seems to be more advantageous than prejudicial. And here I am about to advance a proposition which may remind the reader of what I said before in speaking of municipal freedom. There are no countries in which associations are more needed, to prevent the despotism of faction, or the arbitrary power of a prince, than those which are democratically constituted. In aristocratic nations, the body of the nobles and the more opulent part of the community are in themselves natural associations, which act as checks upon the abuses of power. In countries in which those associations do not exist, if private individuals are unable to create an artificial and a temporary substitute for them, I can imagine no permanent protection against the most galling tyranny; and a great people may be oppressed by a small faction, or by a single individual, with impunity.

The meeting of a great political convention (for there are conventions of all kinds), which may frequently become a necessary measure, is always a serious occurrence, even in America, and one which is never looked forward to by the judicious friends of the country, without alarm. This was very perceptible in the convention of 1831, at which the exertions of all the most distinguished members of the assembly tended to moderate its language, and to restrain the subjects which it treated within certain limits. It is probable, in fact, that the convention of 1831 exercised a very great influence upon the minds of the malecontents, and prepared them for the open revolt against the commercial laws of the Union, which took place in 1832.

It cannot be denied that the unrestrained liberty of association for political purposes, is the privilege which a people is longest in learning how to exercise. If it does not throw the nation into anarchy, it perpetually augments the chances of that calamity. On one point, however, this perilous liberty offers a security against dangers of another kind; in countries where associations are free, secret societies are unknown. In America there are numerous factions, but no conspiracies.

Different ways in which the Right of Association is understood in Europe and in the United States. Different use which is made of it.

THE most natural privilege of man, next to the right of acting for himself, is that of combining his exertions with those of his fellow-creatures, and of acting in common with them. I am therefore led to conclude, that the right of association is almost as inalienable as the right of personal liberty. No legislator can attack it without impairing the very foundations of society. Nevertheless, if the liberty of association is a fruitful source of advantages and prosperity to some nations, it may be perverted or carried to excess by others, and the element of life may be changed into an element of destruction. A comparison of the different methods which associations pursue, in those countries in which they are managed with discretion, as well as in those where liberty degenerates into license, may perhaps be thought useful both to governments and to parties. The greater part of Europeans look upon an association as a weapon which is to be hastily fashioned, and immediately tried in the conflict. A society is to be formed for discussion, but the idea of impending action prevails in the minds of those who constitute it: it is, in fact, an army; and the time given to parley, serves to reckon up the strength and to animate the courage of the host, after which they direct the march against the enemy. Resources which lie within the bounds of the law may suggest themselves to the persons who compose it, as means, but never as the only means, of success.

Such, however, is not the manner in which the right of association is understood in the United States. In America, the citizens who form the minority associate, in order, in the first place, to show their numerical strength, and so to diminish the moral authority of the majority; and, in the second place, to stimulate competition, and to discover those arguments which are most fitted to act upon the majority; for they always entertain hopes of drawing over their opponents to their own side, and of afterward disposing of the supreme power in their name. Political associations in the United States are therefore peaceable in their intentions, and strictly legal in the means which they employ; and they assert with perfect truth, that they only aim at success by lawful expedients.

The difference which exists between the Americans and ourselves depends on several causes. In Europe there are numerous parties so diametrically opposed to the majority, that they can never hope to acquire its support, and at the same time they think that they are sufficiently strong in themselves to struggle and to defend their cause. When a party of this kind forms an association, its object is, not to conquer, but to fight. In America, the individuals who hold opinions very much opposed to those of the majority, are no sort of impediment to its power; and all other parties hope to win it over to their own principles in the end. The exercise of the right of association becomes dangerous in proportion to the impossibility which excludes great parties from acquiring the majority. In a country like the United States, in which the differences of opinion are mere differences of hue, the right of association may remain unrestrained without evil consequences. The inexperience of many of the European nations in the enjoyment of liberty, leads them only to look upon the liberty of association as a right of attacking the government. The first notion which presents itself to a party, as well as to an individual, when it has acquired a consciousness of its own strength, is that of violence: the notion of persuasion arises at a later period, and is only derived from experience. The English, who are divided into parties which differ most essentially from each other, rarely abuse the right of association, because they have long been accustomed to exercise it. In France, the passion for war is so intense that there is no undertaking so mad, or so injurious to the welfare of the state, that a man does not consider himself honored in defending it, at the risk of his life.

But perhaps the most powerful of the causes which tend to mitigate the excesses of political association in the United States is universal suffrage. In countries in which universal suffrage exists, the majority is never doubtful, because neither party can pretend to represent that portion of the community which has not voted. The associations which are formed are aware, as well as the nation at large, that they do not represent the majority; this is, indeed, a condition inseparable from their existence; for if they did represent the preponderating power, they would change the law instead of soliciting its reform. The consequence of this is, that the moral influence of the government which they attack is very much increased, and their own power is very much enfeebled.

In Europe there are few associations which do not affect to represent the majority, or which do not believe that they represent it. This conviction or this pretension tends to aug ment their force amazingly, and contributes no less to legalize their measures. Violence may seem to be excusable in defence of the cause of oppressed right. Thus it is, in the vast labyrinth of human laws, that extreme liberty sometimes corrects abuses of license, and that extreme democracy obviates the dangers of democratic government. In Europe, associations consider themselves, in some degree, as the legislative and executive councils of the people, which is unable to speak for itself. In America, where they only represent a minority of the nation, they argue and they petition.

The means which the associations of Europe employ, are in accordance with the end which they propose to obtain. As the principal aim of these bodies is to act, and not to debate, to fight rather than to persuade, they are naturally led to adopt a form of organization which differs from the ordinary customs of civil bodies, and which assumes the habits and the maxims of military life. They centralize the direction of their resources as much as possible, and they intrust the power of the whole party to a very small number of leaders. The members of these associations reply to a watchword, like soldiers on duty: they profess the doctrine of passive obedience; say rather, that in uniting together they at once abjure the exercise of their own judgment and free will; and the tyrannical control, which these societies exercise, is often far more insupportable than the authority possessed over society by the government which they attack. Their moral force is much diminished by these excesses, and they lose the powerful interest which is always excited by a struggle between oppressors and the oppressed. The man who in given cases consents to obey his fellows with servility, and who submits his activity, and even his opinions, to their control, can have no claim to rank as a free citizen.

The Americans have also established certain forms of government which are applied to their associations, but these are invariably borrowed from the forms of the civil administration. The independence of each individual is formally recognized; the tendency of the members of the association points, as it does in the body of the community, toward the same end, but they are not obliged to follow the same track. No one abjures the exercise of his reason and his free will; but every one exerts that reason and that will for the benefit of a common undertaking.

CHAPTER XIII.

GOVERNMENT OF THE DEMOCRACY IN AMERICA.

I AM well aware of the difficulties which attend this part of my subject, but although every expression which I am about to make use of may clash, upon some one point, with the feelings of the different parties which divide my country, I shall speak my opinion with the most perfect openness.

In Europe we are at a loss how to judge the true character and the more permanent propensities of democracy, because in Europe two conflicting principles exist, and we do not know what to attribute to the principles themselves, and what to refer to the passions which they bring into collision. Such, however, is not the case in America; there the people reigns without any obstacle, and it has no perils to dread, and no injuries to avenge. In America, democracy is swayed by its own free propensities; its course is natural, and its activity is unrestrained: the United States consequently afford the most favorable opportunity of studying its real character. And to no people can this inquiry be more vitally interesting than to the French nation, which is blindly driven onward by a daily and irresistible impulse, toward a state of things which may prove either despotic or republican, but which will assuredly be democratic.

UNIVERSAL SUFFRAGE.

I HAVE already observed that universal suffrage has been adopted in all the states of the Union: it consequently occurs among different populations which occupy very different positions in the scale of society. I have had opportunities of observing its effects in different localities, and among races of men who are nearly strangers to each other by their language, their religion, and their manner of life; in Louisiana as well as in New England, in Georgia and in Canada. I have remarked that universal suffrage is far from producing in America either all the good or all the evil consequences which are assigned to it in Europe, and that its effects differ very widely from those which are usually attributed to it.

CHOICE OF THE PEOPLE, AND INSTINCTIVE PREFERENCES OF THE AMERICAN DEMOCRACY.

In the United States the most talented Individuals are rarely placed at the Head of Affairs.—Reasons of this Peculiarity.—The Envy which prevails in the lower Orders of France against the higher Classes, is not a French, but a purely democratic Sentiment.—For what Reason the most distinguished Men in America frequently seclude themselves from public affairs.

Many people in Europe are apt to believe without saying it, or to say without believing it, that one of the great advantages of universal suffrage is, that it intrusts the direction of public affairs to men who are worthy of the public confidence. They admit that the people is unable to govern for itself, but they aver that it is always sincerely disposed to promote the welfare of the state, and that it instinctively designates those persons who are animated by the same good wishes, and who are the most fit to wield the supreme authority. I confess that the observations I made in America by no means coincide with these opinions. On my arrival in the United States I was surprised to find so much distinguished talent among the subjects, and so little among the heads of the government. It is a well-authenticated fact, that at the present day the most talented men in the United States are very rarely placed at the head of affairs; and it must be acknowledged that such has been the result, in proportion as democracy has outstepped all its former limits. The race of American statesmen has evidently dwindled most remarkably in the course of the last fifty years.

Several causes may be assigned to this phenomenon. It is impossible, notwithstanding the most strenuous exertions, to raise the intelligence of the people above a certain level. Whatever may be the facilities of acquiring information, whatever may be the profusion of easy methods and of cheap science, the human mind can never be instructed and educated without devoting a considerable space of time to those objects.

The greater or the lesser possibility of subsisting without labor is therefore the necessary boundary of intellectual improvement. This boundary is more remote in some countries, and more restricted in others; but it must exist somewhere as long as the people is constrained to work in order to procure the means of physical subsistence, that is to say, as long as it retains its popular character. It is therefore quite as difficult to imagine a state in which all the citizens should be very well-informed, as a state in which they should all be wealthy; these two difficulties may be looked upon as correlative. It may very readily be admitted that the mass of the citizens are sincerely disposed to promote the welfare of their country; nay more, it may even be allowed that the lower classes are less apt to be swayed by considerations of personal interest than the higher orders; but it is always more or less impossible for them to discern the best means of attaining the end, which they desire with sincerity. Long and patient observation, joined to a multitude of different notions, is required to form a just estimate of the character of a single individual; and can it be supposed that the vulgar have the power of succeeding in an inquiry which misleads the penetration of genius itself? The people has neither the time nor the means which are essential to the prosecution of an investigation of this kind; its conclusions are hastily formed from a superficial inspection of the more prominent features of a question. Hence it often assents to the clamor of a mountebank, who knows the secret of stimulating its tastes; while its truest friends frequently fail in their exertions.

Moreover, the democracy is not only deficient in that soundness of judgment which is necessary to select men really deserving of its confidence, but it has neither the desire nor the inclination to find them out. It cannot be denied that democratic institutions have a very strong tendency to promote the feeling of envy in the human heart; not so much because they afford to every one the means of rising to the level of any of his fellow-citizens, as because those means perpetually disappoint the persons who employ them. Democratic institutions awaken and foster a passion for equality which they can never entirely satisfy. This complete equality eludes the grasp of the people at the very moment when it thinks to hold it fast, and "flies," as Pascal says, "with eternal flight;" the people is excited in the pursuit of an advantage, which is the more precious because it is not sufficiently remote to be unknown, or sufficiently near to be enjoyed. The lower orders are agitated by the chance of success, they are irritated by its uncertainty; and they pass from the enthusiasm of pursuit to the exhaustion of ill-success, and lastly to the acrimony of disappointment. Whatever transcends their own limits appears to be an obstacle to their desires, and there is no kind of superiority, however legitimate it may be, which is not irksome in their sight.

It has been supposed that the secret instinct, which leads the lower orders to remove their superiors as much as possible from the direction of public affairs, is peculiar to France. This, however, is an error; the propensity to which I allude is not inherent in any particular nation, but in democratic institutions in general; and although it may have been heightened by peculiar political circumstances, it owes its origin to a higher cause.

In the United States, the people is not disposed to hate the superior class of society; but it is not very favorably inclined toward them, and it carefully excludes them from the exercise of authority. It does not entertain any dread of distinguished talents, but it is rarely captivated by them; and it awards its approbation very sparingly to such as have risen without the popular support.

While the natural propensities of democracy induce the people to reject the most distinguished citizens as its rulers, these individuals are no less apt to retire from a political career, in which it is almost impossible to retain their independence, or to advance without degrading themselves. This opinion has been very candidly set forth by Chancellor Kent, who says, in speaking with great eulogium of that part of the constitution which empowers the executive to nominate the judges: "It is indeed probable that the men who are best fitted to discharge the duties of this high office would have too much reserve in their manners, and too much austerity in their principles, for them to be returned by the majority at an election where universal suffrage is adopted." Such were the opinions which were printed without contradiction in America in the year 1830.

I hold it to be sufficiently demonstrated, that universal suffrage is by no means a guarantee of the wisdom of the popular choice; and that whatever its advantages may be, this is not one of them.

CAUSES WHICH MAY PARTLY CORRECT THESE TENDENCIES OF THE DEMOCRACY.

Contrary Effects produced on Peoples as well as on individuals by great Dangers.—Why so many distinguished Men stood at the Head of Affairs in America fifty Years ago.—Influence which the intelligence and the Manners of the People exercise upon its choice.—Example of New England.—States of the Southwest.—Influence of certain Laws upon the Choice of the People.—Election by an elected Body.—Its Effects upon the Composition of the Senate.

When a state is threatened by serious dangers, the people frequently succeed in selecting the citizens who are the most able to save it. It has been observed that man rarely retains his customary level in presence of very critical circumstances; he rises above, or he sinks below, his usual condition, and the same thing occurs in nations at large. Extreme perils sometimes quench the energy of a people instead of stimulating it; they excite without directing its passions; and instead of clearing, they confuse its powers of perception. The Jews deluged the smoking ruins of their temples with the carnage of the remnant of their host. But it is more common, both in the case of nations and in that of individuals, to find extraordinary virtues arising from the very imminence of the danger. Great characters are then thrown into relief, as the edifices which are concealed by the gloom of night, are illuminated by the glare of a conflagration. At those dangerous times genius no longer abstains from presenting itself in the arena; and the people, alarmed by the perils of its situation, buries its envious passions in a short oblivion. Great names may then be drawn from the urn of an election.

I have already observed that the American statesmen of the present day are very inferior to those who stood at the head of affairs fifty years ago. This is as much a consequence of the circumstances, as of the laws of the country. When America was struggling in the high cause of independence to throw off the yoke of another country, and when it was about to usher a new nation into the world, the spirits of its inhabitants were roused to the height which their great efforts required. In this general excitement, the most distinguished men were ready to forestall the wants of the community, and the people clung to them for support, and placed them at its head. But events of this magnitude are rare; and it is from an inspection of the ordinary course of affairs that our judgment must be formed.

If passing occurrences sometimes act as checks upon the passions of democracy, the intelligence and the manners of the community exercise an influence which is not less powerful, and far more permanent. This is extremely perceptible in the United States.

In New England the education and the liberties of the communities were engendered by the moral and religious principles of their founders. Where society has acquired a sufficient degree of stability to enable it to hold certain maxims and to retain fixed habits, the lower orders are accustomed to respect intellectual superiority, and to submit to it without complaint, although they set at naught all those privileges which wealth and birth have introduced among mankind. The democracy in New England consequently makes a more judicious choice than it does elsewhere.

But as we descend toward the south, to those states in which the constitution of society is more modern and less strong, where instruction is less general, and where the principles of morality, of religion, and of liberty, are less happily combined, we perceive that the talents and the virtues of those who are in authority become more and more rare.

Lastly, when we arrive at the new southwestern states, in which the constitution of society dates but from yesterday, and presents an agglomeration of adventurers and speculators, we are amazed at the persons who are invested with public authority, and we are led to ask by what force, independent of the legislation and of the men who direct it, the state can be protected, and society be made to flourish.

There are certain laws of a democratic nature which contribute, nevertheless, to correct, in some measure, the dangerous tendencies of democracy. On entering the house of representatives at Washington, one is struck by the vulgar demeanor of that great assembly. The eye frequently does not discover a man of celebrity within its walls. Its members are almost all obscure individuals, whose names present no associations to the mind: they are mostly village-lawyers, men in trade, or even persons belonging to the lower classes of society. In a country in which education is very general, it is said that the representatives of the people do not always know how to write correctly.

At a few yards distance from this spot is the door of the senate, which contains within a small space a large proportion of the celebrated men of America. Scarcely an individual is to be perceived in it who does not recall the idea of an active and illustrious career: the senate is composed of eloquent advocates, distinguished generals, wise magistrates, and statesmen of note, whose language would at all times do honor to the most remarkable parliamentary debates of Europe.

What then is the cause of this strange contrast, and why are the most able citizens to be found in one assembly rather than in the other? Why is the former body remarkable for its vulgarity and its poverty of talent, while the latter seems to enjoy a monopoly of intelligence and of sound judgment? Both of these assemblies emanate from the people; both of them are chosen by universal suffrage; and no voice has hitherto been heard to assert, in America, that the senate is hostile to the interests of the people. From what cause, then, does so startling a difference arise? The only reason which appears to me adequately to account for it is, that the house of representatives is elected by the populace directly, and that of the senate is elected by elected bodies. The whole body of the citizens names the legislature of each state, and the federal constitution converts these legislatures into so many electoral bodies, which return the members of the senate. The senators are elected by an indirect application of universal suffrage; for the legislatures which name them are not aristocratic or privileged bodies which exercise the electoral franchise in their own right; but they are chosen by the totality of the citizens; they are generally elected every year, and new members may constantly be chosen, who will employ their electoral rights in conformity with the wishes of the public. But this transmission of the popular authority through an assembly of chosen men, operates an important change in it, by refining its discretion and improving the forms which it adopts. Men who are chosen in this manner, accurately represent the majority of the nation which governs them; but they represent the elevated thoughts which are current in the community, the generous propensities which prompt its nobler actions, rather than the petty passions which disturb, or the vices which disgrace it.

The time may be already anticipated at which the American republics will be obliged to introduce the plan of election by an elected body more frequently into their system of representation, or they will incur no small risk of perishing miserably among the shoals of democracy.

And here I have no scruple in confessing that I look upon this peculiar system of election as the only means of bringing the exercise of political power to the level of all classes of the people. Those thinkers who regard this institution as the exclusive weapon of a party, and those who fear, on the other hand, to make use of it, seem to me to fall into as great an error in the one case as in the other.

INFLUENCE WHICH THE AMERICAN DEMOCRACY HAS EXERCISED ON THE LAWS RELATING TO ELECTIONS.

When Elections are rare, they expose the State to a violent Crisis.—When they are frequent, they keep up a degree of feverish Excitement.—The Americans have preferred the second of these two Evils.—Mutability of the Laws.—Opinions of Hamilton and Jefferson on this Subject.

When elections recur at long intervals, the state is exposed to violent agitation every time they take place. Parties exert themselves to the utmost in order to gain a prize which is so rarely within their reach; and as the evil is almost irremediable for the candidates who fail, the consequence of their disappointed ambition may prove most disastrous: if, on the other hand, the legal struggle can be repeated within a short space of time, the defeated parties take patience.

When elections occur frequently, this recurrence keeps society in a perpetual state of feverish excitement, and imparts a continual instability to public affairs.

Thus, on the one hand, the state is exposed to the perils of a revolution, on the other, to perpetual mutability; the former system threatens the very existence of the government, the latter is an obstacle to all steady and consistent policy. The Americans have preferred the second of these evils to the first; but they were led to this conclusion by their instinct much more than by their reason; for a taste for variety is one of the characteristic passions of democracy. An extraordinary mutability has, by this means, been introduced into their legislation.

Many of the Americans consider the instability of their laws as a necessary consequence of a system whose general results are beneficial. But no one in the United States affects to deny the fact of this instability, or to contend that it is not a great evil.

Hamilton, after having demonstrated the utility of a power which might prevent, or which might at least impede, the promulgation of bad laws, adds: "It may perhaps be said that the power of preventing bad laws includes that of preventing good ones, and may be used to the one purpose as well as to the other. But this objection will have but little weight with those who can properly estimate the mischiefs of that inconstancy and mutability in the laws which form the greatest blemish in the character and genius of our government.—(Federalist, No. 73.)

And again, in No. 62 of the same work, he observes: "The facility and excess of law-making seem to be the diseases to which our governments are most liable.******* The mischievous effects of the mutability in the public councils arising from a rapid succession of new members, would fill a volume; every new election in the states is found to change one half of the representatives. From this change of men must proceed a change of opinions and of measures which forfeits the respect and confidence of nations, poisons the blessings of liberty itself, and diminishes the attachment and reverence of the people toward a political system which betrays so many marks of infirmity."

Jefferson himself, the greatest democrat whom the democracy of America has as yet produced, pointed out the same evils.

"The instability of our laws," he said in a letter to Madison, "is really a very serious inconvenience. I think we ought to have obviated it by deciding that a whole year should always be allowed to elapse between the bringing in of a bill and the final passing of it. It should afterward be discussed and put to the vote without the possibility of making any alteration in it; and if the circumstances of the case required a more speedy decision, the question should not be decided by a simple majority, but by a majority of at least two thirds of both houses."

PUBLIC OFFICERS UNDER THE CONTROL OF THE DEMOCRACY OF AMERICA.

Simple Exterior of the American public Officers.—No official Costume.—All public Officers are remunerated.—Political Consequences of this System.—No public Career exists in America.—Result of this.

Public officers in the United States are commingled with the crowd of citizens; they have neither palaces, nor guards, nor ceremonial costumes. This simple exterior of the persons in authority is connected, not only with the peculiarities of the American character, but with the fundamental principles of that society. In the estimation of tne democracy, a government is not a benefit, but a necessary evil. A certain degree of power must be granted to public officers, for they would be of no use without it. But the ostensible semblance of authority is by no means indispensable to the conduct of affairs; and it is needlessly offensive to the susceptibility of the public. The public officers themselves are well aware that they only enjoy the superiority over their fellow-citizens, which they derive from their authority, upon condition of putting themselves on a level with the whole community by their manners. A public officer in the United States is uniformly civil, accessible to all the world, attentive to all requests, and obliging in all his replies. I was pleased by these characteristics of a democratic government; and I was struck by the manly independence of the citizens, who respect the office more than the officer, and who are less attached to the emblems of authority than to the man who bears them.

I am inclined to believe that the influence which costumes really exercise, in an age like that in which we live, has been a good deal exaggerated. I never perceived that a public officer in America was the less respected while he was in the discharge of his duties because his own merit was set off by no adventitious signs. On the other hand, it is very doubtful whether a peculiar dress contributes to the respect which public characters ought to have for their own position, at least when they are not otherwise inclined to respect it. When a magistrate (and in France such instances are not rare), indulges his trivial wit at the expense of a prisoner, or derides a predicament in which a culprit is placed, it would be well to deprive him of his robes of office, to see whether he would recall some portion of the natural dignity of man kind when he is reduced to the apparel of a private citizen.

A democracy may, however, allow a certain show of magisterial pomp, and clothe its officers in silks and gold, without seriously compromising its principles. Privileges of this kind are transitory; they belong to the place, and are distinct from the individual: but if public officers are not uniformly remunerated by the state, the public charges must be intrusted to men of opulence and independence, who constitute the basis of an aristocracy; and if the people still retains its right of election, that election can only be made from a certain class of citizens.

When a democratic republic renders offices which had formerly been remunerated, ·gratuitous, it may safely be believed that that state is advancing to monarchical institutions; and when a monarchy begins to remunerate such officers as had hitherto been unpaid, it is a sure sign that it is approaching toward a despotic or a republican form of government. The substitution of paid for unpaid functionaries is of itself, in my opinion, sufficient to constitute a serious revolution.

I look upon the entire absence of gratuitous functionaries in America as one of the most prominent signs of the absolute dominion which democracy exercises in that country. All public services, of whatsoever nature they may be, are paid; so that every one has not merely a right, but also the means of performing them. Although, in democratic states, all the citizens are qualified to occupy stations in the government, all are not tempted to try for them. The number and the capacities of the candidates are more apt to restrict the choice of electors than the conditions of the candidateship.

In nations in which the principle of election extends to every place in the state, no political career can, properly speaking, be said to exist. Men are promoted as if by chance to the rank which they enjoy, and they are by no means sure of retaining it. The consequence is that in tranquil times public functions offer but few lures to ambition. In the United States the persons who engage in the perplexities of political life are individuals of very moderate pretensions. The pursuit of wealth generally diverts men of great talents and of great passions from the pursuit of power; and it very frequently happens that a man does not undertake to direct the fortune of the state until he has discovered his incompetence to conduct his own affairs. The vast number of very ordinary men who occupy public stations is quite as attributable to these causes as to the bad choice of the democracy. In the United States, I am not sure that the people would return the men of superior abilities who might solicit its support, but it is certain that men of this description do not come forward.

ARBITRARY POWER OF MAGISTRATES* UNDER THE RULE OF AMERICAN DEMOCRACY.

For what Reason the arbitrary Power of Magistrates is greater in absolute Monarchies and in democratic Republics that it is in limited Monarchies.—Arbitrary Power of the Magistrates in New England.

In two different kinds of government the magistrates exercise a considerable degree of arbitrary power; namely, under the absolute government of a single individual, and under that of a democracy.

This identical result proceeds from causes which are nearly analogous.

In despotic states the fortune of no citizen is secure; and public officers are not more safe than private individuals. The sovereign, who has under his control the lives, the property, and sometimes the honor of the men whom he employs, does not scruple to allow them a great latitude of action, because he is convinced that they will not use it to his prejudice. In despotic states the sovereign is so attached to the exercise of his power, that he dislikes the constraint even of his own regulations; and he is well pleased that his agents should follow a somewhat fortuitous line of conduct, provided he be certain that their actions will never counteract his desires.

In democracies, as the majority has every year the right of depriving the officers whom it has appointed of their power, it has no reason to fear abuse of their authority. As the people is always able to signify its wishes to those who conduct the government, it prefers leaving them to make their own exertions, to prescribing an invariable rule of conduct which would at once fetter their activity and the popular authority.

It may even be observed, on attentive consideration, that under the rule of a democracy the arbitrary power of the magistrate must be still greater than in despotic states. In the latter, the sovereign has the power of punishing all the faults with which he becomes acquainted, but it would be vain for him to hope to become acquainted with all those which are committed. In the former the sovereign power is not only supreme, but it is universally present. The Ameri-

* I here use the word *magistrates* in the widest sense in which it can be taken; I apply it to all the officers to whom the execution of the laws is intrusted.

can functionaries are, in point of fact, much more independent in the sphere of action which the law traces out for them, than any public officer in Europe. Very frequently the object which they are to accomplish is simply pointed out to them, and the choice of the means is left to their own discretion.

In New England, for instance, the selectmen of each township are bound to draw up the list of persons who are to serve on the jury; the only rule which is laid down to guide them in their choice is that they are to select citizens possessing the elective franchise and enjoying a fair reputation.* In France the lives and liberties of the subjects would be thought to be in danger, if a public officer of any kind was intrusted with so formidable a right. In New England, the same magistrates are empowered to post the names of habitual drunkards in public houses, and to prohibit the inhabitants of a town from supplying them with liquor.† A censorial power of this excessive kind would be revolting to the population of the most absolute monarchies; here, however, it is submitted to without difficulty.

Nowhere has so much been left by the law to the arbitrary determination of the magistrates as in democratic republics, because this arbitrary power is unattended by any alarming consequences. It may even be asserted that the freedom of the magistrate increases as the elective franchise is extended, and as the duration of the time of office is shortened. Hence arises the great difficulty which attends the conversion of a democratic republic into a monarchy. The magistrate ceases to be elective, but he retains the rights and the habits of an elected officer, which lead directly to despotism.

It is only in limited monarchies that the law which prescribes the sphere in which public officers are to act, superintends all their measures. The cause of this may be easily detected. In limited monarchies the power is divided between the king and the people, both of whom are interested in the stability of the magistrate. The king does not venture to place the public officers under the control of the people, lest they should be tempted to betray his interests; on the other hand, the people fears lest the magistrates should serve to oppress the liberties of the country, if they were entirely dependent upon the crown: they cannot therefore be said to depend on either

* See the act 27th February, 1813. General Collection of the Laws of Massachusetts, vol. ii., p. 331. It should be added that the jurors are afterward drawn from these lists by lot.

† See the act of 28th February, 1787. General Collection of the Laws of Massachusetts, vol. i., p. 302,

the one or the other. The same cause which induces the king and the people to render public officers independent, suggests the necessity of such securities as may prevent their independence from encroaching upon the authority of the former and the liberties of the latter. They consequently agree as to the necessity of restricting the functionary to a line of conduct laid down beforehand, and they are interested in confining him by certain regulations which he cannot evade.

[The observations respecting the arbitrary powers of magistrates are practically among the most erroneous in the work. The author seems to have confounded the idea of magistrates being ***independent*** with their being arbitrary. Yet he had just before spoken of their dependance on popular election as a reason why there was no apprehension of the abuse of their authority. The independence, then, to which he alludes must be an immunity from responsibility to any other department. But it is a fundamental principle of our system, that all officers are liable to criminal prosecution "whenever they act partially or oppressively from a malicious or corrupt motive." See 15 Wendell's Reports, 278. That our magistrates are independent when they do not act partially or oppressively is very true, and, it is to be hoped, is equally true in every form of government. There would seem, therefore, not to be such a degree of independence as necessarily to produce arbitrariness. The author supposes that magistrates are more arbitrary in a despotism and in a democracy than in a limited monarchy. And yet, the limits of independence and of responsibility existing in the United States are borrowed from and identical with those established in England—the most prominent instance of a limited monarchy. See the authorities referred to in the case in Wendell's Reports, before quoted. Discretion in the execution of various ministerial duties, and in the awarding of punishment by judicial officers, is indispensable in every system of government, from the utter impossibility of "laying down beforehand a line of conduct" (as the author expresses it) in such cases. The very instances of discretionary power to which he refers, and which he considers ***arbitrary***, exist in England. There, the persons from whom juries are to be formed for the trial of causes, civil and criminal, are selected by the sheriffs, who are appointed by the crown—a power, certainly more liable to abuse in their hands, than in those of selectmen or other town-officers, chosen annually by the people. The other power referred to, that of posting the names of habitual drunkards, and forbidding their being supplied with liquor, is but a reiteration of the principles contained in the English statute of 32 Geo. III., ch. 45, respecting idle and disorderly persons. Indeed it may be said with great confidence, that there is not an instance of discretionary power being vested in American magistrates which does not find its prototype in the English laws. The whole argument of the author on this point, therefore, would seem to fail.—*American Editor.*]

INSTABILITY OF THE ADMINISTRATION IN THE UNITED STATES.

In America the public Acts of a Community frequently leave fewer Traces than the Occurrences of a Family.—Newspapers the only historical Remains.—Instability of the Administration prejudicial to the Art of Government.

THE authority which public men possess in America is so brief, and they are so soon commingled with the ever-changing population of the country, that the acts of a community frequently leave fewer traces than the occurrences of a private family. The public administration is, so to speak, oral and traditionary. But little is committed to writing, and that little is wafted away for ever, like the leaves of the sibyl, by the smallest breeze.

The only historical remains in the United States are the newspapers; but if a number be wanting, the chain of time is broken, and the present is severed from the past. I am convinced that in fifty years it will be more difficult to collect authentic documents concerning the social condition of the Americans at the present day, than it is to find remains of the administration of France during the middle ages; and if the United States were ever invaded by barbarians, it would be necessary to have recourse to the history of other nations, in order to learn anything of the people which now inhabits them.

The instability of the administration has penetrated into the habits of the people: it even appears to suit the general taste, and no one cares for what occurred before his time. No methodical system is pursued; no archives are formed; and no documents are brought together when it would be very easy to do so. Where they exist little store is set upon them; and I have among my papers several original public documents which were given to me in answer to some of my inquiries. In America society seems to live from hand to mouth, like an army in the field. Nevertheless, the art of administration may undoubtedly be ranked as a science, and no sciences can be improved, if the discoveries and observations of successive generations are not connected together in the order in which they occur. One man, in the short space of his life, remarks a fact; another conceives an idea; the former invents a means of execution, the latter reduces a truth to a fixed proposition; and mankind gathers the fruits of individual experience upon its way, and gradually forms the sciences. But the persons who conduct the administration in America can seldom afford any instruction to each other;

and when they assume the direction of society, they simply possess those attainments which are most widely disseminated in the community, and no experience peculiar to themselves. Democracy, carried to its farthest limits, is therefore prejudicial to the art of government; and for this reason it is better adapted to a people already versed in the conduct of an administration, than to a nation which is uninitiated in public affairs.

This remark, indeed, is not exclusively applicable to the science of administration. Although a democratic government is founded upon a very simple and natural principle, it always presupposes the existence of a high degree of culture and enlightenment in society.* At the first glance it may be imagined to belong to the earliest ages of the world; but maturer observation will convince us that it could only come last in the succession of human history.

[These remarks upon the "instability of administration" in America, are partly correct, but partly erroneous. It is certainly true that our public men are not educated to the business of government; even our diplomatists are selected with very little reference to their experience in that department. But the universal attention that is paid by the intelligent, to the measures of government and to the discussions to which they give rise, is in itself no slight preparation for the ordinary duties of legislation. And, indeed, this the author subsequently seems to admit. As to there being "no archives formed" of public documents, the author is certainly mistaken. The journals of congress, the journals of state legislatures, the public documents transmitted to and originating in those bodies, are carefully preserved and disseminated through the nation: and they furnish in themselves the materials of a full and accurate history. Our great defect, doubtless, is in the want of statistical information. Excepting the annual reports of the state of our commerce, made by the secretary of the treasury, under a law, and excepting the census which is taken every ten years under the authority of congress, and those taken by the states, we have no official statistics. It is supposed that the author had this species of information in his mind when he alluded to the general deficiency of our archives.—*American Editor.*]

* It is needless to observe, that I speak here of the democratic form of government as applied to a people, not merely to a tribe.

CHARGES LEVIED BY THE STATE UNDER THE RULE OF THE AMERICAN DEMOCRACY.

In all Communities Citizens divisible into three Classes.—Habits of each of these Classes in the Direction of public Finances.—Why public Expenditures must tend to increase when the People governs.—What renders the Extravagance of a Democracy less to be feared in America.—Public Expenditure under a Democracy.

Before we can affirm whether a democratic form of government is economical or not, we must establish a suitable standard of comparison. The question would be one of easy solution if we were to attempt to draw a parallel between a democratic republic and an absolute monarchy. The public expenditure would be found to be more considerable under the former than under the latter; such is the case with all free states compared to those which are not so. It is certain that despotism ruins individuals by preventing them from producing wealth, much more than by depriving them of the wealth they have produced: it dries up the source of riches, while it usually respects acquired property. Freedom, on the contrary, engenders far more benefits than it destroys; and the nations which are favored by free institutions, invariably find that their resources increase even more rapidly than their taxes.

My present object is to compare free nations to each other; and to point out the influence of democracy upon the finances of a state.

Communities, as well as organic bodies, are subject to certain fixed rules in their formation which they cannot evade. They are composed of certain elements which are common to them at all times and under all circumstances. The people may always be mentally divided into three distinct classes. The first of these classes consists of the wealthy; the second, of those who are in easy circumstances; and the third is composed of those who have little or no property, and who subsist more especially by the work which they perform for the two superior orders. The proportion of the individuals who are included in these three divisions may vary according to the condition of society; but the divisions themselves can never be obliterated.

It is evident that each of these classes will exercise an influence, peculiar to its own propensities, upon the administration of the finances of the state. If the first of the three exclusively possess the legislative power, it is probable that it will not be sparing of the public funds, because the taxes which are levied on a large fortune only tend to diminish the sum of superfluous enjoyment, and are, in point of fact, but little felt. If the second class has the power of making the laws, it will certainly not be lavish of taxes, because nothing is so onerous as a large impost which is levied upon a small income. The government of the middle classes appears to me to be the most economical, though perhaps not the most enlightened, and certainly not the most generous, of free governments.

But let us now suppose that the legislative authority is vested in the lowest orders: there are two striking reasons which show that the tendency of the expenditure will be to increase, not to diminish.

As the great majority of those who create the laws are possessed of no property upon which taxes can be imposed, all the money which is spent for the community appears to be spent to their advantage, at no cost of their own; and those who are possessed of some little property readily find means of regulating the taxes so that they are burthensome to the wealthy and profitable to the poor, although the rich are unable to take the same advantage when they are in possession of the government.

In countries in which the poor* should be exclusively invested with the power of making the laws, no great economy of public expenditure ought to be expected; that expenditure will always be considerable; either because the taxes do not weigh upon those who levy them, or because they are levied in such a manner as not to weigh upon those classes. In other words, the government of the democracy is the only one under which the power which lays on taxes escapes the payment of them.

It may be objected (but the argument has no real weight) that the true interest of the people is indissolubly connected with that of the wealthier portion of the community, since it cannot but suffer by the severe measures to which it resorts. But is it not the true interest of kings to render their subjects happy; and the true interest of nobles to admit recruits into their order on suitable grounds? If remote advantages had power to prevail over the passions and the exigencies of the

* The word *poor* is used here, and throughout the remainder of this chapter, in a relative and not in an absolute sense. Poor men in America would often appear rich in comparison with the poor of Europe: but they may with propriety be styled poor in comparison with their more affluent countrymen.

moment, no such thing as a tyrannical sovereign or an exclusive aristocracy could ever exist.

Again, it may be objected that the poor are never invested with the sole power of making the laws; but I reply, that wherever universal suffrage has been established, the majority of the community unquestionably exercises the legislative authority, and if it be proved that the poor always constitute the majority, it may be added, with perfect truth, that in the countries in which they possess the elective franchise, they possess the sole power of making laws. But it is certain that in all the nations of the world the greater number has always consisted of those persons who hold no property, or of those whose property is insufficient to exempt them from the necessity of working in order to procure an easy subsistence Universal suffrage does therefore in point of fact invest the poor with the government of society.

The disastrous influence which popular authority may sometimes exercise upon the finances of a state, was very clearly seen in some of the democratic republics of antiquity, in which the public treasure was exhausted in order to relieve indigent citizens, or to supply the games and theatrical amusements of the populace. It is true that the representative system was then very imperfectly known, and that, at the present time, the influence of popular passions is less felt in the conduct of public affairs; but it may be believed that the delegate will in the end conform to the principles of his constituents, and favor their propensities as much as their interests.

The extravagance of democracy is, however, less to be dreaded in proportion as the people acquires a share of property, because on the one hand the contributions of the rich are then less needed, and on the other, it is more difficult to lay on taxes which do not affect the interests of the lower classes. On this account universal suffrage would be less dangerous in France than in England, because in the latter country the property on which taxes may be levied is vested in fewer hands. America, where the great majority of the citizens is possessed of some fortune, is in a still more favorable position than France.

There are still farther causes which may increase the sum of public expenditures in democratic countries. When the aristocracy governs, the individuals who conduct the affairs of state are exempted, by their own station in society, from every kind of privation: they are contented with their position; power and renown are the objects for which they strive; and, as they are placed far above the obscurer throng of citizens, they do not always distinctly perceive how the wellbeing of the mass of the people ought to redound to their own honor. They are not, indeed, callous to the sufferings of the poor, but they cannot feel those miseries as acutely as if they were themselves partakers of them. Provided that the people appear to submit to its lot, the rulers are satisfied and they demand nothing farther from the government. An aristocracy is more intent upon the means of maintaining its influence, than upon the means of improving its condition.

When, on the contrary, the people is invested with the supreme authority, the perpetual sense of their own miseries impels the rulers of society to seek for perpetual meliorations. A thousand different objects are subjected to improvement; the most trivial details are sought out as susceptible of amendment; and those changes which are accompanied with considerable expense, are more especially advocated, since the object is to render the condition of the poor more tolerable, who cannot pay for themselves.

Moreover, all democratic communities are agitated by an ill-defined excitement, and by a kind of feverish impatience, that engenders a multitude of innovations, almost all of which are attended with expense.

In monarchies and aristocracies, the natural taste which the rulers have for power and for renown, is stimulated by the promptings of ambition, and they are frequently incited by these temptations to very costly undertakings. In democracies, where the rulers labor under privations, they can only be courted by such means as improve their wellbeing, and these improvements cannot take place without a sacrifice of money. When a people begins to reflect upon its situation, it discovers a multitude of wants, to which it had not before been subject, and to satisfy these exigencies, recourse must be had to the coffers of the state. Hence it arises, that the public charges increase in proportion as civilisation spreads, and that the imposts are augmented as knowledge pervades the community.

The last cause which frequently renders a democratic government dearer than any other is, that a democracy does not always succeed in moderating its expenditure, because it does not understand the art of being economical. As the designs which it entertains are frequently changed, and the agents of those designs are more frequently removed, its undertakings are often ill-conducted or left unfinished: in the former case the state spends sums out of all proportion to the end which it proposes to accomplish; in the second, the expense itself is unprofitable.

TENDENCIES OF THE AMERICAN DEMOCRACY AS REGARDS THE SALARIES OF PUBLIC OFFICERS.

In Democracies those who establish high Salaries have no Chance of profiting by them.—Tendency of the American Democracy to increase the Salaries of subordinate Officers, and to lower those of the more important functionaries.—Reason of this.—Comparative Statement of the Salaries of public Officers in the United States and in France.

THERE is a powerful reason which usually induces democracies to economise upon the salaries of public officers. As the number of citizens who dispense the remuneration is extremely large in democratic countries, so the number of persons who can hope to be benefited by the receipt of it is comparatively small. In aristocratic countries, on the contrary, the individuals who appoint high salaries, have almost always a vague hope of profiting by them. These appointments may be looked upon as a capital which they create for their own use, or at least, as a resource for their children.

It must, however, be allowed that a democratic state is most parsimonious toward its principal agents. In America the secondary officers are much better paid, and the dignitaries of the administration much worse than they are elsewhere.

These opposite effects result from the same cause: the people fixes the salaries of the public officers in both cases; and the scale of remuneration is determined by the consideration of its own wants. It is held to be fair that the servants of the public should be placed in the same easy circumstances as the public itself;* but when the question turns upon the salaries of the great officers of state, this rule fails, and chance alone can guide the popular decision. The poor have no adequate conceptions of the wants which the higher classes of society may feel. The sum which is scanty to the rich, appears enormous to the poor man, whose wants do not extend beyond the necessaries of life: and in his estimation the governor of a state, with his two or three hundred a year, is a very fortunate and enviable being.† If you undertake to

* The easy circumstances in which secondary functionaries are placed in the United States, result also from another cause, which is independent of the general tendencies of democracy: every kind of private business is very lucrative, and the state would not be served at all if it did not pay its servants. The country is in the position of a commercial undertaking, which is obliged to sustain an expensive competition, notwithstanding its taste for economy.

† The state of Ohio, which contains a million of inhabitants, gives its governor a salary of only $1,200 (260*l.*) a year.

convince him that the representative of a great people ought to be able to maintain some show of splendor in the eyes of foreign nations, he will perhaps assent to your meaning; but when he reflects on his own humble dwelling, and on the hard-earned produce of his wearisome toil, he remembers all that he could do with a salary which you say is insufficient, and he is startled or almost frightened at the sight of such uncommon wealth. Besides, the secondary public officer is almost on a level with the people, while the others are raised above it. The former may therefore excite his interest, but the latter begins to arouse his envy.

This is very clearly seen in the United States, where the salaries seem to decrease as the authority of those who receive them augments.*

Under the rule of an aristocracy it frequently happens, on the contrary, that while the high officers are receiving munificent salaries, the inferior ones have not more than enough to procure the necessaries of life. The reason of this fact is easily discoverable from causes very analogous to those to which I have just alluded. If a democracy is unable to conceive the pleasures of the rich, or to see them without envy, an aristocracy is slow to understand, or, to speak more correctly, is unacquainted with the privations of the poor. The poor man is not (if we use the term aright) the fellow of the rich one; but he is the being of another species. An aristocracy is therefore apt to care but little for the fate of its subordinate

* To render this assertion perfectly evident, it will suffice to examine the scale of salaries of the agents of the federal government. I have added the salaries attached to the corresponding officers in France, to complete the comparison:—

UNITED STATES. *Treasury Department.*			FRANCE. *Ministère des Finances.*	
Messenger . . .	$ 700	150*l.*	Huissier, 1,500 fr. . . .	60*l.*
Clerk with lowest salary	1,000	217	Clerk with lowest salary, 1,000 to 1,800 fr. . .	40 to 72
Clerk with highest salary	1,600	347	Clerk with highest salary, 3,200 to 3,600 fr.	128 to 144
Chief clerk . . .	2,000	434	Secretaire-general, 20,000 fr.	800
Secretary of state .	6,000	1,300	The minister, 80,000 fr. .	3,200
The President . .	25,000	5,400	The king, 12,000,000 fr.	480,000

I have perhaps done wrong in selecting France as my standard of comparison. In France the democratic tendencies of the nation exercise an ever-increasing influence upon the government, and the chambers show a disposition to raise the lowest salaries and to lower the principal ones. Thus the minister of finance, who received 160,000 fr. under the empire, receives 80,000 fr., in 1835; the directeurs-generaux of finance, who then received 50,000 fr., now receive only 20,000 fr.

agents: and their salaries are only raised when they refuse to perform their service for too scanty a remuneration.

It is the parsimonious conduct of democracy toward its principal officers, which has countenanced a supposition of far more economical propensities than any which it really possesses. It is true that it scarcely allows the means of honorable subsistence to the individuals who conduct its affairs; but enormous sums are lavished to meet the exigencies or to facilitate the enjoyments of the people.* The money raised by taxation may be better employed, but it is not saved. In general, democracy gives largely to the community, and very sparingly to those who govern it. The reverse is the case in the aristocratic countries, where the money of the state is expended to the profit of the persons who are at the head of affairs.

DIFFICULTY OF DISTINGUISHING THE CAUSES WHICH CONTRIBUTE TO THE ECONOMY OF THE AMERICAN GOVERNMENT.

We are liable to frequent errors in the research of those facts which exercise a serious influence upon the fate of mankind, since nothing is more difficult than to appreciate their real value. One people is naturally inconsistent and enthusiastic; another is sober and calculating; and these charaeteristics originate in their physical constitution, or in remote causes with which we are unacquainted.

There are nations which are fond of parade and the bustle of festivity, and which do not regret the costly gaieties of an hour. Others, on the contrary, are attached to more retiring pleasures, and seem almost ashamed of appearing to be pleased. In some countries the highest value is set upon the beauty of public edifices; in others the productions of art are treated with indifference, and everything which is unproductive is looked down upon with contempt. In some renown, in others money, is the ruling passion.

Independently of the laws, all these causes concur to exer-

* See the American budgets for the cost of indigent citizens and gratuitous instruction. In 1831, 50,000*l.* were spent in the state of New York for the maintenance of the poor; and at least 200,000*l.* were devoted to gratuitous instruction. (Williams's New York Annual Register, 1832, pp. 205, 243.) The state of New York contained only 1,900,000 inhabitants in the year 1830; which is not more than double the amount of population in the department du Nord in France.

cise a very powerful influence upon the conduct of the finances of the state. If the Americans never spend the money of the people in galas, it is not only because the imposition of taxes is under the control of the people, but because the people takes no delight in public rejoicings. If they repudiate all ornament from their architecture, and set no store on any but the more practical and homely advantages, it is not only because they live under democratic institutions, but because they are a commercial nation. The habits of private life are continued in public; and we ought carefully to distinguish that economy which depends upon their institutions, from that which is the natural result of their manners and customs.

WHETHER THE EXPENDITURE OF THE UNITED STATES CAN BE COMPARED TO THAT OF FRANCE.

Two Points to be established in order to estimate the Extent of the public Charges, viz.: the national Wealth, and the Rate of Taxation. The Wealth and the Charges of France not accurately known.—Why the Wealth and Charges of the Union cannot be accurately known. Researches of the Author with a View to discover the Amount of Taxation in Pennsylvania.—General Symptoms which may serve to indicate the Amount of the public Charges in a given Nation.—Result of this Investigation for the Union.

Many attempts have recently been made in France to compare the public expenditure of that country with the expenditure of the United States; all these attempts have, however, been unattended by success; and a few words will suffice to show that they could not have had a satisfactory result.

In order to estimate the amount of the public charges of a people, two preliminaries are indispensable; it is necessary, in the first place, to know the wealth of that people; and in the second, to learn what portion of that wealth is devoted to the expenditure of the state. To show the amount of taxation without showing the resources which are destined to meet the demand, is to undertake a futile labor; for it is not the expenditure, but the relation of the expenditure to the revenue, which it is desirable to know.

The same rate of taxation which may easily be supported by a wealthy contributor, will reduce a poor one to extreme misery. The wealth of nations is composed of several distinct elements, of which population is the first, real property the second, and personal property the third. The first of these three elements may be discovered without difficulty.

Among civilized nations it is easy to obtain an accurate census of the inhabitants; but the two others cannot be determined with so much facility. It is difficult to take an exact account of all the lands in a country which are under cultivation, with their natural or their acquired value; and it is still more impossible to estimate the entire personal property which is at the disposal of the nation, and which eludes the strictest analysis by the diversity and number of shapes under which it may occur. And, indeed, we find that the most ancient civilized nations of Europe, including even those in which the administration is most central, have not succeeded, as yet, in determining the exact condition of their wealth.

In America the attempt has never been made; for how would such an investigation be possible in a country where society has not yet settled into habits of regularity and tranquillity; where the national government is not assisted by a multitude of agents whose exertions it can command, and direct to one sole end; and where statistics are not studied, because no one is able to collect the necessary documents, or can find time to peruse them? Thus the primary elements of the calculations which have been made in France, cannot be obtained in the Union; the relative wealth of the two countries is unknown: the property of the former is not accurately determined, and no means exist of computing that of the latter.

I consent, therefore, for the sake of the discussion, to abandon this necessary term of the comparison, and I confine myself to a computation of the actual amount of taxation, without investigating the relation which subsists between the taxation and the revenue. But the reader will perceive that my task has not been facilitated by the limits which I here lay down for my researches.

It cannot be doubted that the central administration of France, assisted by all the public officers who are at its disposal, might determine with exactitude the amount of the direct and indirect taxes levied upon the citizens. But this investigation, which no private individual can undertake, has not hitherto been completed by the French government, or, at least, its results have not been made public. We are acquainted with the sum total of the state; we know the amount of the departmental expenditure; but the expenses of the communal divisions have not been computed, and the amount of the public expenses of France is unknown.

If we now turn to America, we shall perceive that the difficulties are multiplied and enhanced. The Union publishes an exact return of the amount of its expenditure; the budgets of the four-and-twenty states furnish similar returns of their revenues; but the expenses incident to the affairs of the counties and the townships are unknown.*

The authority of the federal government cannot oblige the provincial governments to throw any light upon this point; and even if these governments were inclined to afford their simultaneous co-operation, it may be doubted whether they possess the means of procuring a satisfactory answer. Independently of the natural difficulties of the task, the political organization of the country would act as a hindrance to the success of their efforts. The county and town magistrates are not appointed by the authorities of the state, and they are not subjected to their control. It is therefore very allowable to suppose, that if the state was desirous of obtaining the returns which we require, its designs would be counteracted by the neglect of those subordinate officers whom it would be obliged to employ.† It is, in point of fact, useless to inquire

* The Americans, as we have seen, have four separate budgets; the Union, the states, the counties, and the townships, having each severally their own. During my stay in America I made every endeavor to discover the amount of the public expenditure in the townships and counties of the principal states of the Union, and I readily obtained the budget of the larger townships, but I found it quite impossible to procure that of the smaller ones. I possess, however, some documents relating to county expenses, which, although incomplete, are still curious. I have to thank Mr. Richards, mayor of Philadelphia, for the budgets of thirteen of the counties of Pennsylvania, viz.: Lebanon, Centre, Franklin, Fayette, Montgomery, Luzerne, Dauphin, Butler, Allegany, Columbia, Northampton, Northumberland, and Philadelphia, for the year 1830. Their population at that time consisted of 495,207 inhabitants. On looking at the map of Pennsylvania, it will be seen that these thirteen counties are scattered in every direction, and so generally affected by the causes which usually influence the condition of a country, that they may easily be supposed to furnish a correct average of the financial state of the counties of Pennsylvania in general; and thus, upon reckoning that the expenses of these counties amounted in the year 1830 to about 72,330*l.*, or nearly 3*s.* for each inhabitant, and calculating that each of them contributed in the same year about 10*s.* 2*d.* toward the Union, and about 3*s.* to the state of Pennsylvania, it appears that they each contributed as their share of all the public expenses (except those of the townships), the sum of 16*s.* 2*d.* This calculation is doubly incomplete, as it applies only to a single year and to one part of the public charges; but it has at least the merit of not being conjectural.

† Those who have attempted to draw a comparison between the expenses of France and America, have at once perceived that no such comparison could be drawn between the total expenditures of the two countries; but they have endeavored to contrast detached portions of this expenditure. It may readily be shown that this second system is not at all less defective than the first.

what the Americans might do to forward this inquiry, since it is certain that they have hitherto done nothing at all. There does not exist a single individual at the present day, in America or in Europe, who can inform us what each citizen of the Union annually contributes to the public charges of the nation.*

If I attempt to compare the French budget with the budget of the Union, it must be remembered that the latter embraces much fewer objects than the central government of the former country, and that the expenditure must consequently be much smaller. If I contrast the budgets of the departments to those of the states which constitute the Union, it must be observed, that as the power and control exercised by the states is much greater than that which is exercised by the departments, their expenditure is also more considerable. As for the budgets of the counties, nothing of the kind occurs in the French system of finance; and it is, again, doubtful whether the corresponding expenses should be referred to the budget of the state or to those of the municipal divisions.

Municipal expenses exist in both countries, but they are not always analogous. In America the townships discharge a variety of offices which are reserved in France to the departments or the state. It may, moreover, be asked, what is to be understood by the municipal expenses of America. The organization of the municipal bodies or townships differs in the several states: Are we to be guided by what occurs in New England or in Georgia, in Pennsylvania or the state of Illinois?

A kind of analogy may very readily be perceived between certain budgets in the two countries: but as the elements of which they are composed always differ more or less, no fair comparison can be instituted between them.

* Even if we knew the exact pecuniary contributions of every French and American citizen to the coffers of the state, we should only come at a portion of the truth. Governments not only demand supplies of money, but they call for personal services, which may be looked upon as equivalent to a given sum. When a state raises an army, beside the pay of the troops which is furnished by the entire nation, each soldier must give up his time, the value of which depends on the use he might make of it if he were not in the service. The same remark applies to the militia: the citizen who is in the militia devotes a certain portion of valuable time to the maintenance of the public peace, and he does in reality surrender to the state those earnings which he is prevented from gaining. Many other instances might be cited in addition to these. The governments of France and America both levy taxes of this kind, which weigh upon the citizens; but who can estimate with accuracy their relative amount in the two countries?

This, however, is not the last of the difficulties which prevent us from comparing the expenditure of the Union with that of France. The French government contracts certain obligations which do not exist in America, and *vice versâ*. The French government pays the clergy; in America, the voluntary principle prevails. In America, there is a legal provision for the poor; in France they are abandoned to the charity of the public. The French public officers are paid by a fixed salary: in America they are allowed certain perquisites. In France, contributions in kind take place on very few roads; in America upon almost all the thoroughfares: in the former country the

Hence we must conclude, that it is no less difficult to compare the social expenditure, than it is to estimate the relative wealth of France and of America. I will even add, that it would be dangerous to attempt this comparison; for when statistics are not founded upon computations which are strictly accurate, they mislead instead of guiding aright. The mind is easily imposed upon by the false affectation of exactitude which prevails even in the mis-statements of the science, and adopts with confidence the errors which are apparelled in the forms of mathematical truth.

We abandon, therefore, our numerical investigation, with the hope of meeting with data of another kind. In the absence of positive documents, we may form an opinion as to the proportion which the taxation of a people bears to its real prosperity, by observing whether its external appearance is flourishing; whether, after having discharged the calls of the state, the poor man retains the means of subsistence, and the rich the means of enjoyment; and whether both classes are contented with their position, seeking however to meliorate it by perpetual exertions, so that industry is never in want of capital, nor capital unemployed by industry. The observer who draws his inferences from these signs will, undoubtedly, be led to the conclusion, that the American of the United States contributes a much smaller portion of his income to the state than the citizen of France. Nor, indeed, can the result be otherwise.

A portion of the French debt is the consequence of two successive invasions; and the Union has no similar calamity to fear. A nation placed upon the continent of Europe is obliged to maintain a large standing army; the isolated position of the Union enables it to have only 6,000 soldiers. The French have a fleet of 300 sail; the Americans have 52 vessels.* How, then, can the inhabitant of the Union be called upon to contribute as largely as the inhabitant of France? No parallel can be drawn between the finances of two countries so differently situated.

It is by examining what actually takes place in the Union, and not by comparing the Union with France, that we may

roads are free to all travellers: in the latter turnpikes abound. All these differences in manner in which contributions are levied in the two countries, enhance the difficulty of comparing their expenditure; for there are certain expenses which the citizens would not be subjected to, or which would at any rate be much less considerable, if the state did not take upon itself to act in the name of the public.

* See the details in the budget of the French minister of marine; and for America, the National Calendar of 1833, p. 228.

discover whether the American government is really economical. On casting my eyes over the different republics which form the confederation, I perceive that their governments lack perseverance in their undertakings, and that they exercise no steady control over the men whom they employ. Whence I naturally infer, that they must often spend the money of the people to no purpose, or consume more of it than is really necessary to their undertakings. Great efforts are made, in accordance with the democratic origin of society, to satisfy the exigencies of the lower orders, to open the career of power to their endeavors, and to diffuse knowledge and comfort among them. The poor are maintained, immense sums are annually devoted to public instruction, all services whatsoever are remunerated, and the most subordinate agents are liberally paid. If this kind of government appears to me to be useful and rational, I am nevertheless constrained to admit that it is expensive.

Wherever the poor direct public affairs and dispose of the national resources, it appears certain, that as they profit by the expenditure of the state, they are apt to augment that expenditure.

I conclude therefore, without having recourse to inaccurate computations, and without hazarding a comparison which might prove incorrect, that the democratic government of the Americans is not a cheap government, as is sometimes asserted; and I have no hesitation in predicting, that if the people of the United States is ever involved in serious difficulties, its taxation will speedily be increased to the rate of that which prevails in the greater part of the aristocracies and the monarchies of Europe.

CORRUPTION AND VICES OF THE RULERS IN A DEMOCRACY, AND CONSEQUENT EFFECTS UPON PUBLIC MORALITY.

In Aristocracies Rulers sometimes endeavor to corrupt the People.—In Democracies Rulers frequently show themselves to be corrupt.—In the former their Vices are directly prejudicial to the Morality of the People.—In the latter their indirect Influence is still more pernicious.

A DISTINCTION must be made, when the aristocratic and the democratic principles mutually inveigh against each other, as tending to facilitate corruption. In aristocratic governments the individuals who are placed at the head of affairs are rich men, who are solely desirous of power. In democracies statesmen are poor, and they have their fortunes to make. The consequence is, that in aristocratic states the rulers are rarely accessible to corruption, and have very little craving for money; while the reverse is the case in democratic nations.

But in aristocracies, as those who are desirous of arriving at the head of affairs are possessed of considerable wealth, and as the number of persons by whose assistance they may rise is comparatively small, the government is, if I may use the expression, put up to a sort of auction. In democracies, on the contrary, those who are covetous of power are very seldom wealthy, and the number of citizens who confer that power is extremely great. Perhaps in democracies the number of men who might be bought is by no means smaller, but buyers are rarely to be met with; and, besides, it would be necessary to buy so many persons at once, that the attempt is rendered nugatory.

Many of the men who have been in the administration in France during the last forty years, have been accused of making their fortunes at the expense of the state or of its allies; a reproach which was rarely addressed to the public characters of the ancient monarchy. But in France the practice of bribing electors is almost unknown, while it is notoriously and publicly carried on in England. In the United States I never heard a man accused of spending his wealth in corrupting the populace; but I have often heard the probity of public officers questioned; still more frequently have I heard their success attributed to low intrigues and immoral practices.

If, then, the men who conduct the government of an aristocracy sometimes endeavor to corrupt the people, the heads of a democracy are themselves corrupt. In the former case the morality of the people is directly assailed; in the latter, an indirect influence is exercised upon the people, which is still more to be dreaded.

As the rulers of democratic nations are almost always exposed to the suspicion of dishonorable conduct, they in some measure lend the authority of the government to the base practices of which they are accused. They thus afford an example which must prove discouraging to the struggles of virtuous independence, and must foster the secret calculations of a vicious ambition. If it be asserted that evil passions are displayed in all ranks of society; that they ascend the throne by hereditary right; and that despicable characters are to be met with at the head of aristocratic nations as well as in the sphere of a democracy; this objection has but little weight in my estimation. The corruption of men who have casually risen to power has a coarse and vulgar infection in it, which renders it contagious to the multitude. On the contrary, there is a kind of aristocratic refinement, and an air of grandeur, in the depravity of the great, which frequently prevents it from spreading abroad.

The people can never penetrate the perplexing labyrinth of court intrigue, and it will always have difficulty in detecting the turpitude which lurks under elegant manners, refined tastes, and graceful language. But to pillage the public purse, and to vend the favors of the state, are arts which the meanest villain may comprehend, and hope to practise in his turn.

In reality it is far less prejudicial to be a witness to the immorality of the great, than to that immorality which leads to greatness. In a democracy, private citizens see a man of their own rank in life, who rises from that obscure position, and who becomes possessed of riches and of power in a few years: the spectacle excites their surprise and their envy: and they are led to inquire how the person who was yesterday their equal, is to-day their ruler. To attribute his rise to his talents or his virtues is unpleasant; for it is tacitly to acknowledge that they are themselves less virtuous and less talented than he was. They are therefore led (and not unfrequently their conjecture is a correct one) to impute his success mainly to some of his defects; and an odious mixture is thus formed of the ideas of turpitude and power, unworthiness and success, utility and dishonor.

EFFORTS OF WHICH A DEMOCRACY IS CAPABLE.

The Union has only had one struggle hitherto for its Existence.—Enthusiasm at the Commencement of the War.—Indifference toward its Close.—Difficulty of establishing a military Conscription or impressment of Seamen in America.—Why a democratic People is less capable of sustained Effort than another.

I HERE warn the reader that I speak of a government which implicitly follows the real desires of the people, and not of a government which simply commands in its name. Nothing is so irresistible as a tyrannical power commanding in the name of the people, because, while it exercises that moral influence which belongs to the decisions of the majority, it acts at the same time with the promptitude and the tenacity of a single man.

It is difficult to say what degree of exertion a democratic government may be capable of making, at a crisis in the history of the nation. But no great democratic republic has hitherto existed in the world. To style the oligarchy which ruled over France in 1793, by that name, would be to offer an insult to the republican form of government. The United States afford the first example of the kind.

The American Union has now subsisted for half a century, in the course of which time its existence has only once been attacked, namely, during the war of independence. At the commencement of that long war, various occurrences took place which betokened an extraordinary zeal for the service of the country.* But as the contest was prolonged, symptoms of private egotism began to show themselves. No money was poured into the public treasury; few recruits could be raised to join the army; the people wished to acquire independence, but was very ill disposed to undergo the privations by which alone it could be obtained. "Tax laws," says Hamilton in the Federalist (No. 12), "have in vain been multiplied; new methods to enforce the collection have in vain been tried; the public expectation has been uniformly disappointed; and the treasuries of the states have remained empty. The popular system of administration inherent in the nature of popular government, coinciding with the real scarcity of money incident to a languid and mutilated state of trade, has hitherto defeated every experiment for extensive collections, and has at length taught the different legislatures the folly of attempting them."

The United States have not had any serious war to carry on since that period. In order, therefore, to appreciate the sacrifices which democratic nations may impose upon themselves, we must wait until the American people is obliged to put half its entire income at the disposal of the government, as was done by the English; or until it sends forth a twentieth part of its population to the field of battle, as was done by France.

In America the use of conscription is unknown, and men

* One of the most singular of these occurrences was the resolution which the Americans took of temporarily abandoning the use of tea. Those who know that men usually cling more to their habits than to their life, will doubtless admire this great and obscure sacrifice which was made by a whole people.

are induced to enlist by bounties. The notions and habits of the people of the United States are so opposed to compulsory enlistments, that I do not imagine that it can ever be sanctioned by the laws. What is termed the conscription in France is assuredly the heaviest tax upon the population of that country; yet how could a great continental war be carried on without it? The Americans have not adopted the British impressment of seamen, and they have nothing which corresponds to the French system of maritime conscription; the navy, as well as the merchant service, is supplied by voluntary engagement. But it is not easy to conceive how a people can sustain a great maritime war, without having recourse to one or the other of these two systems. Indeed, the Union, which has fought with some honor upon the seas, has never possessed a very numerous fleet, and the equipment of the small number of American vessels has always been excessively expensive.

[The remark that "in America the use of conscription is unknown, and men are induced to enlist by bounties," is not exactly correct. During the last war with Great Britain, the state of New York, in October, 1814 (see the laws of that session, p. 15), passed an act to raise troops for the defence of the state, in which the whole body of the militia were directed to be classed, and each class to furnish one soldier, so as to make up the whole number of 12,000 directed to be raised. In case of the refusal of a class to furnish a man, one was to be detached from them by ballot, and was compelled to procure a substitute or serve personally. The intervention of peace rendered proceedings under the act unnecessary, and we have not, therefore, the light of experience to form an opinion whether such a plan of raising a military force is practicable. Other states passed similar laws. The system of classing was borrowed from the practice of the revolution. —*American Editor.*]

I have heard American statesmen confess that the Union will have great difficulty in maintaining its rank on the seas, without adopting the system of impressment or of maritime conscription; but the difficulty is to induce the people, which exercises the supreme authority, to submit to impressment or any compulsory system.

It is incontestable, that in times of danger a free people displays far more energy than one which is not so. But I incline to believe, that this is more especially the case in those free nations in which the democratic element preponderates. Democracy appears to me to be much better adapted for the peaceful conduct of society, or for an occasional effort of remarkable vigor, than for the hardy and prolonged endurance of the storms which beset the political existence of nations. The reason is very evident; it is enthusiasm which prompts men to expose themselves to dangers and privations; but they will not support them long without reflection. There is more calculation, even in the impulses of bravery, than is generally attributed to them; and although the first efforts are suggested by passion, perseverance is maintained by a distinct regard of the purpose in view. A portion of what we value is exposed, in order to save the remainder.

But it is this distinct perception of the future, founded upon a sound judgment and an enlightened experience, which is most frequently wanting in democracies. The populace is more apt to feel than to reason; and if its present sufferings are great, it is to be feared that the still greater sufferings attendant upon defeat will be forgotten.

Another cause tends to render the efforts of a democratic government less persevering than those of an aristocracy. Not only are the lower classes less awakened than the higher orders to the good or evil chances of the future, but they are liable to suffer far more acutely from present privations. The noble exposes his life, indeed, but the chance of glory is equal to the chance of harm. If he sacrifices a large portion of his income to the state, he deprives himself for a time of the pleasure of affluence; but to the poor man death is embellished by no pomp or renown; and the imposts which are irksome to the rich are fatal to him.

This relative impotence of democratic republics is, perhaps, the greatest obstacle to the foundation of a republic of this kind in Europe. In order that such a state should subsist in one country of the Old World, it would be necessary that similar institutions should be introduced into all the other nations.

I am of opinion that a democratic government tends in the end to increase the real strength of society; but it can never combine, upon a single point and at a given time, so much power as an aristocracy or a monarchy. If a democratic country remained during a whole century subject to a republican government, it would probably at the end of that period be more populous and more prosperous than the neighboring despotic states. But it would have incurred the risk of being conquered much oftener than they would in that lapse of years.

SELF-CONTROL OF THE AMERICAN DEMOCRACY.

The American People acquiesces slowly, or frequently does not acquiesce in what is beneficial to its Interests.—The faults of the American Democracy are for the most part reparable.

THE difficulty which a democracy has in conquering the passions, and in subduing the exigencies of the moment, with a view to the future, is conspicuous in the most trivial occurrences in the United States. The people which is surrounded by flatterers, has great difficulty in surmounting its inclinations; and whenever it is solicited to undergo a privation or any kind of inconvenience, even to attain an end which is sanctioned by its own rational conviction, it almost always refuses to comply at first. The deference of the Americans to the laws has been very justly applauded; but it must be added, that in America the legislation is made by the people and for the people. Consequently, in the United States, the law favors those classes which are most interested in evading it elsewhere. It may therefore be supposed that an offensive law, which should not be acknowledged to be one of immedite utility, would either not be enacted or would not be obeyed.

In America there is no law against fraudulent bankruptcies; not because they are few, but because there are a great number of bankruptcies. The dread of being prosecuted as a bankrupt acts with more intensity upon the mind of the majority of the people, than the fear of being involved in losses or ruin by the failure of other parties; and a sort of guilty tolerance is extended by the public conscience, to an offence which every one condemns in his individual capacity. In the new states of the southwest, the citizens generally take justice into their own hands, and murders are of very frequent occurrence. This arises from the rude manners and the ignorance of the inhabitants of those deserts, who do not perceive the utility of investing the law with adequate force, and who prefer duels to prosecutions.

Some one observed to me one day, in Philadelphia, that almost all crimes in America are caused by the abuse of intoxicating liquors, which the lower classes can procure in great abundance from their excessive cheapness.—"How comes it," said I, "that you do not put a duty upon brandy?" —"Our legislators," rejoined my informant, "have frequently thought of this expedient; but the task of putting it in operation is a difficult one: a revolt might be apprehended;

and the members who should vote for a law of this kind would be sure of losing their seats."—"Whence I am to infer," I replied, "that the drinking population constitutes the majority in your country and that temperance is somewhat unpopular."

When these things are pointed out to the American statesmen, they content themselves with assuring you that time will operate the necessary change, and that the experience of evil will teach the people its true interests. This is frequently true; although a democracy is more liable to error than a monarch or a body of nobles, the chances of its regaining the right path, when once it has acknowledged its mistake, are greater also; because it is rarely embarrassed by internal interests, which conflict with those of the majority, and resist the authority of reason. But a democracy can only obtain truth as the result of experience; and many nations may forfeit their existence, while they are awaiting the consequences of their errors.

The great privilege of the Americans does not simply consist in their being more enlightened than other nations, but in their being able to repair the faults they may commit. To which it must be added, that a democracy cannot derive substantial benefit from past experience, unless it be arrived at a certain pitch of knowledge and civilisation. There are tribes and peoples whose education has been so vicious, and whose character presents so strange a mixture of passion, of ignorance, and of erroneous notions upon all subjects, that they are unable to discern the cause of their own wretchedness, and they fall a sacrifice to ills with which they are unacquainted.

I have crossed vast tracts of country that were formerly inhabited by powerful Indian nations which are now extinct; I have myself passed some time in the midst of mutilated tribes, which see the daily decline of their numerical strength, and of the glory of their independence; and I have heard these Indians themselves anticipate the impending doom of their race. Every European can perceive means which would rescue these unfortunate beings from inevitable destruction. They alone are insensible to the expedient; they feel the wo which year after year heaps upon their heads, but they will perish to a man without accepting the remedy. It would be necessary to employ force to induce them to submit to the protection and the constraint of civilisation.

The incessant revolutions which have convulsed the South American provinces for the last quarter of a century have frequently been adverted to with astonishment, and expectations have been expressed that those nations would speedily return to their *natural state*. But can it be affirmed that the turmoil of revolution is not actually the most natural state of the South American Spaniards at the present time? In that country society is plunged into difficulties from which all its efforts are insufficient to rescue it. The inhabitants of that fair portion of the western hemisphere seem obstinately bent on pursuing the work of inward havoc. If they fall into a momentary repose from the effects of exhaustion, that repose prepares them for a fresh state of phrensy. When I consider their condition, which alternates between misery and crime, I should be inclined to believe that despotism itself would be a benefit to them, if it were possible that the words despotism and benefit could ever be united in my mind.

CONDUCT OF FOREIGN AFFAIRS BY THE AMERICAN DEMOCRACY.

Direction given to the foreign Policy of the United States by Washington and Jefferson.—Almost all the defects inherent in democratic Institutions are brought to light in the Conduct of foreign Affairs.—Their advantages are less perceptible.

We have seen that the federal constitution intrusts the permanent direction of the external interests of the nation to the president and the senate;* which tends in some degree to detach the general foreign policy of the Union from the control of the people. It cannot therefore be asserted, with truth, that the external affairs of state are conducted by the democracy.

The policy of America owes its rise to Washington, and after him to Jefferson, who established those principles which it observes at the present day. Washington said, in the admirable letter which he addressed to his fellow-citizens, and which may be looked upon as his political bequest to the country:—

"The great rule of conduct for us in regard to foreign nations is, extending our commercial relations, to have with them as little *political* connexion as possible. So far as we

* "The president," says the constitution, art. ii., sect. 2, § 2, "shall have power, by and with the advice and consent of the senate, to make treaties, provided two-thirds of the senators present concur." The reader is reminded that the senators are returned for a term of six years, nd that they are chosen by the legislature of each state.

have already formed engagements, let them be fulfilled with perfect good faith. Here let us stop.

"Europe has a set of primary interests, which to us have none, or a very remote relation. Hence, she must be engaged in frequent controversies, the causes of which are essentially foreign to our concerns. Hence, therefore, it must be unwise in us to implicate ourselves, by artificial ties, in the ordinary vicissitudes of her politics, or the ordinary combinations and collisions of her friendships or enmities.

"Our detached and distant situation invites and enables us to pursue a different course. If we remain one people, under an efficient government, the period is not far off when we may defy material injury from external annoyance; when we may take such an attitude as will cause the neutrality we may at any time resolve upon to be scrupulously respected; when belligerent nations, under the impossibility of making acquisitions upon us, will not lightly hazard the giving us provocation; when we may choose peace or war, as our interest, guided by justice, shall counsel.

"Why forego the advantages of so peculiar a situation? Why quit our own to stand upon foreign ground? Why, by interweaving our destiny with that of any part of Europe, entangle our peace and prosperity in the toils of European ambition, rivalship, interest, humor, or caprice?

"It is our true policy to steer clear of permanent alliances with any portion of the foreign world; so far, I mean, as we are now at liberty to do it; for let me not be understood as capable of patronising infidelity to existing engagements. I hold the maxim no less applicable to public than to private affairs, that honesty is always the best policy. I repeat it, therefore, let those engagements be observed in their genuine sense; but in my opinion it is unnecessary, and would be unwise, to extend them.

"Taking care always to keep ourselves, by suitable establishments, in a respectable defensive posture, we may safely trust to temporary alliances for extraordinary emergencies."

In a previous part of the same letter, Washington makes the following admirable and just remark: "The nation which indulges toward another an habitual hatred, or an habitual fondness, is, in some degree, a slave. It is a slave to its animosity or its affection, either of which is sufficient to lead it astray from its duty and its interest."

The political conduct of Washington was always guided by these maxims. He succeeded in maintaining his country in a state of peace, while all the other nations of the globe were at war; and he laid it down as a fundamental doctrine, that the true interest of the Americans consisted in a perfect neutrality with regard to the internal dissensions of the European powers.

Jefferson went still farther, and introduced a maxim into the policy of the Union, which affirms, that "the Americans ought never to solicit any privileges from foreign nations, in order not to be obliged to grant similar privileges themselves."

These two principles, which were so plain and so just as to be adapted to the capacity of the populace, have greatly simplified the foreign policy of the United States. As the Union takes no part in the affairs of Europe, it has, properly speaking, no foreign interests to discuss, since it has at present no powerful neighbors on the American continent. The country is as much removed from the passions of the Old World by its position, as by the line of policy which it has chosen; and it is neither called upon to repudiate nor to espouse the conflicting interests of Europe; while the dissensions of the New World are still concealed within the bosom of the future.

The Union is free from all pre-existing obligations; and it is consequently enabled to profit by the experience of the old nations of Europe, without being obliged, as they are, to make the best of the past, and to adapt it to their present circumstances; or to accept that immense inheritance which they derive from their forefathers—an inheritance of glory mingled with calamities, and of alliances conflicting with national antipathies. The foreign policy of the United States is reduced by its very nature to await the chances of the future history of the nation; and for the present it consists more in abstaining from interference than in exerting its activity.

It is therefore very difficult to ascertain, at present, what degree of sagacity the American democracy will display in the conduct of the foreign policy of the country; and upon this point its adversaries, as well as its advocates, must suspend their judgment. As for myself, I have no hesitation in avowing my conviction, that it is most especially in the conduct of foreign relations, that democratic governments appear to me to be decidedly inferior to governments carried on upon different principles. Experience, instruction, and habit, may almost always succeed in creating a species of practical discretion in democracies, and that science of the daily occurrences of life which is called good sense. Good sense may suffice to direct the ordinary course of society;

and among a people whose education has been provided for, the advantages of democratic liberty in the internal affairs of the country may more than compensate for the evils inherent in a democratic government. But such is not always the case in the mutual relations of foreign nations.

Foreign politics demand scarcely any of those qualities which a democracy possesses; and they require, on the contrary, the perfect use of almost all those faculties in which it is deficient. Democracy is favorable to the increase of the internal resources of a state; it tends to diffuse a moderate independence; it promotes the growth of public spirit, and fortifies the respect which is entertained for law in all classes of society: and these are advantages which only exercise an indirect influence over the relations which one people bears to another. But a democracy is unable to regulate the details of an important undertaking, to persevere in a design, and to work out its execution in the presence of serious obstacles. It cannot combine its measures with secrecy, and will not await their consequences with patience. These are qualities which more especially belong to an individual or to an aristocracy; and they are precisely the means by which an individual people attains a predominant position.

If, on the contrary, we observe the natural defects of aristocracy, we shall find that their influence is comparatively innoxious in the direction of the external affairs of a state. The capital fault of which aristocratic bodies may be accused, is that they are more apt to contrive their own advantage than that of the mass of the people. In foreign politics it is rare for the interest of the aristocracy to be in any way distinct from that of the people.

The propensity which democracies have to obey the impulse of passion rather than the suggestions of prudence, and to abandon a mature design for the gratification of a momentary caprice, was very clearly seen in America on the breaking out of the French revolution. It was then as evident to the simplest capacity as it is at the present time, that the interests of the Americans forbade them to take any part in the contest which was about to deluge Europe with blood, but which could by no means injure the welfare of their own country. Nevertheless the sympathies of the people declared themselves with so much violence in behalf of France, that nothing but the inflexible character of Washington, and the immense popularity which he enjoyed, could have prevented the Americans from declaring war against England. And even then, the exertions, which the austere reason of that great man made to repress the generous but imprudent passions of his fellow-citizens, very nearly deprived him of the sole recompense which he had ever claimed—that of his country's love. The majority then reprobated the line of policy which he adopted, and which has since been unanimously approved by the nation.*

If the constitution and the favor of the public had not intrusted the direction of the foreign affairs of the country to Washington, it is certain that the American nation would at that time have taken the very measures which it now condemns.

Almost all the nations which have exercised a powerful influence upon the destinies of the world, by conceiving, following up, and executing vast designs—from the Romans to the English—have been governed by aristocratic institutions. Nor will this be a subject of wonder when we recollect that nothing in the world has so absolute a fixity of purpose as an aristocracy. The mass of the people may be led astray by ignorance or passion; the mind of a king may be biased, and his perseverance in his designs may be shaken—beside which a king is not immortal; but an aristocratic body is too numerous to be led astray by the blandishments of intrigue, and yet not numerous enough to yield readily to the intoxicating influence of unreflecting passion: it has the energy of a firm and enlightened individual, added to the power which it derives from its perpetuity.

* See the fifth volume of Marshall's Life of Washington. "In a government constituted like that of the United States," he says, "it is impossible for the chief magistrate, however firm he may be, to oppose for any length of time the torrents of popular opinion; and the prevalent opinion of that day seemed to incline to war. In fact, in the session of congress held at the time, it was frequently seen that Washington had lost the majority in the house of representatives." The violence of the language used against him in public was extreme, and in a political meeting they did not scruple to compare him indirectly to the treacherous Arnold. "By the opposition," says Marshall, "the friends of the administration were declared to be an aristocratic and corrupt faction, who, from a desire to introduce monarchy, were hostile to France, and under the influence of Britain; that they were a paper nobility, whose extreme sensibility at every measure which threatened the funds, induced a tame submission to injuries and insults, which the interests and honor of the nation required them to resist."

CHAPTER XIV.

WHAT THE REAL ADVANTAGES ARE WHICH AMERICAN SOCIETY DERIVES FROM THE GOVERNMENT OF THE DEMOCRACY.

Before I enter upon the subject of the present chapter, I am induced to remind the reader of what I have more than once adverted to in the course of this book. The political institutions of the United States appear to me to be one of the forms of government which a democracy may adopt but I do not regard the American constitution as the best, or as the only one which a democratic people may establish. In showing the advantages which the Americans derive from the government of democracy, I am therefore very far from meaning, or from believing, that similar advantages can be obtained only from the same laws.

GENERAL TENDENCY OF THE LAWS UNDER THE RULE OF THE AMERICAN DEMOCRACY, AND HABITS OF THOSE WHO APPLY THEM.

Defects of a democratic Government easy to be discovered.—Its advantages only to be discerned by long Observation.—Democracy in America often inexpert, but the general Tendency of the Laws advantageous.—In the American Democracy public Officers have no permanent Interests distinct from those of the Majority.—Result of this State of Things.

The defects and the weaknesses of a democratic government may very readily be discovered; they are demonstrated by the most flagrant instances, while its beneficial influence is less perceptibly exercised. A single glance suffices to detect its evil consequences, but its good qualities can only be discerned by long observation. The laws of the American democracy are frequently defective or incomplete; they sometimes attack vested rights, or give a sanction to others which are dangerous to the community; but even if they were good, the frequent changes which they undergo would be an evil. How comes it, then, that the American republics prosper, and maintain their position?

In the consideration of laws, a distinction must be carefully observed between the end at which they aim, and the means by which they are directed to that end; between their absolute and their relative excellence. If it be the intention of the legislator to favor the interests of the minority at the expense of the majority, and if the measures he takes are so combined as to accomplish the object he has in view with the least possible expense of time and exertion, the law may be well drawn up, although its purpose be bad; and the more efficacious it is, the greater is the mischief which it causes.

Democratic laws generally tend to promote the welfare of the greatest possible number; for they emanate from a majority of the citizens, who are subject to error, but who cannot have an interest opposed to their own advantage. The laws of an aristocracy tend, on the contrary, to concentrate wealth and power in the hands of the minority, because an aristocracy, by its very nature, constitutes a minority. It may therefore be asserted, as a general proposition, that the purpose of a democracy, in the conduct of its legislation, is useful to a greater number of citizens than that of an aristocracy. This is, however, the sum total of its advantages.

Aristocracies are infinitely more expert in the science of legislation than democracies ever can be. They are possessed of a self-control which protects them from the errors of a temporary excitement; and they form lasting designs which they mature with the assistance of favorable opportunities. Aristocratic government proceeds with the dexterity of art; it understands how to make the collective force of all its laws converge at the same time to a given point. Such is not the case with democracies, whose laws are almost always ineffective, or inopportune. The means of democracy are therefore more imperfect than those of aristocracy, and the measures which it unwittingly adopts are frequently opposed to its own cause; but the object it has in view is more useful.

Let us now imagine a community so organized by nature, or by its constitution, that it can support the transitory action of bad laws, and it can await, without destruction, the general tendency of the legislation: we shall then be able to conceive that a democratic government, notwithstanding its defects, will be most fitted to conduce to the prosperity of this community. This is precisely what has occurred in the United States; and I repeat, what I have before remarked, that the great advantage of the Americans consists in their being able to commit faults which they may afterward repair.

An analogous observation may be made respecting public

officers. It is easy to perceive that the American democracy frequently errs in the choice of the individuals to whom it intrusts the power of the administration; but it is more difficult to say why the state prospers under their rule. In the first place it is to be remarked, that if in a democratic state the governors have less honesty and less capacity than elsewhere, the governed on the other hand are more enlightened and more attentive to their interests. As the people in democracies is more incessantly vigilant in its affairs, and more jealous of its rights, it prevents its representatives from abandoning that general line of conduct which its own interest prescribes. In the second place, it must be remembered that if the democratic magistrate is more apt to misuse his power, he possesses it for a shorter period of time. But there is yet another reason which is still more general and conclusive. It is no doubt of importance to the welfare of nations that they should be governed by men of talents and virtue; but it is perhaps still more important that the interests of those men should not differ from the interests of the community at large; for if such were the case, virtues of a high order might become useless, and talents might be turned to a bad account.

I say that it is important that the interests of the persons in authority should not conflict with or oppose the interests of the community at large; but I do not insist upon their having the same interests as the *whole* population, because I am not aware that such a state of things ever existed in any country.

No political form has hitherto been discovered, which is equally favorable to the prosperity and the development of all the classes into which society is divided. These classes continue to form, as it were, a certain number of distinct nations in the same nation; and experience has shown that it is no less dangerous to place the fate of these classes exclusively in the hands of any one of them, than it is to make one people the arbiter of the destiny of another. When the rich alone govern, the interest of the poor is always endangered; and when the poor make the laws, that of the rich incurs very serious risks. The advantage of democracy does not consist, therefore, as has been sometimes asserted, in favoring the prosperity of all, but simply in contributing to the well-being of the greatest possible number.

The men who are entrusted with the direction of public affairs in the United States, are frequently inferior, both in point of capacity and of morality, to those whom aristocratic nstitutions would raise to power. But their interest is identified and confounded with that of the majority of their fellow-citizens. They may frequently be faithless, and frequently mistake; but they will never systematically adopt a line of conduct opposed to the will of the majority; and it is impossible that they should give a dangerous or an exclusive tendency to the government.

The mal-administration of a democratic magistrate is a mere isolated fact, which only occurs during the short period for which he is elected. Corruption and incapacity do not act as common interests, which may connect men permanently with one another. A corrupt or an incapable magistrate will concert his measures with another magistrate, simply because that individual is as corrupt and as incapable as himself; and these two men will never unite their endeavors to promote the corruption and inaptitude of their remote posterity. The ambition and manœuvres of the one will serve, on the contrary, to unmask the other. The vices of a magistrate, in democratic states, are usually peculiar to his own person.

But under aristocratic governments public men are swayed by the interests of their order, which, if it is sometimes confounded with the interests of the majority, is very frequently distinct from them. This interest is the common and lasting bond which unites them together; it induces them to coalesce, and to combine their efforts in order to attain an end which does not always ensure the greatest happiness of the greatest number; and it serves not only to connect the persons in authority, but to unite them to a considerable portion of the community, since a numerous body of citizens belongs to the aristocracy, without being invested with official functions. The aristocratic magistrate is therefore constantly supported by a portion of the community, as well as by the government of which he is a member.

The common purpose which connects the interest of the magistrates in aristocracies, with that of a portion of their contemporaries, identifies it with that of future generations; their influence belongs to the future as much as to the present. The aristocratic magistrate is urged at the same time toward the same point, by the passions of the community, by his own, and I may almost add, by those of his posterity. Is it, then, wonderful that he does not resist such repeated impulses? And, indeed, aristocracies are often carried away by the spirit of their order without being corrupted by it; and they unconsciously fashion society to their own ends, and prepare it for their own descendants.

The English aristocracy is perhaps the most liberal which ever existed, and no body of men has ever, uninterruptedly, furnished so many honorable and enlightened individuals to the government of a country. It cannot, however, escape observation, that in the legislation of England the good of the poor has been sacrificed to the advantage of the rich, and the rights of the majority to the privileges of the few. The consequence is, that England, at the present day, combines the extremes of fortune in the bosom of her society; and her perils and calamities are almost equal to her power and her renown.

In the United States, where the public officers have no interests to promote connected with their caste, the general and constant influence of the government is beneficial, although the individuals who conduct it are frequently unskilful and sometimes contemptible. There is, indeed, a secret tendency in democratic institutions to render the exertions of the citizens subservient to the prosperity of the community, notwithstanding their private vices and mistakes; while in aristocratic institutions there is a secret propensity, which, notwithstanding the talents and the virtues of those who conduct the government, leads them to contribute to the evils which oppress their fellow-creatures. In aristocratic governments public men may frequently do injuries which they do not intend; and in democratic states they produce advantages which they never thought of.

PUBLIC SPIRIT IN THE UNITED STATES.

Patriotism of Instinct.—Patriotism of Reflection.—Their different Characteristics.—Nations ought to strive to acquire the second when the first has disappeared.—Efforts of the Americans to acquire it.—Interest of the Individual intimately connected with that of the Country.

THERE is one sort of patriotic attachment which principally arises from that instinctive, disinterested, and undefinable feeling which connects the affections of man with his birthplace. This natural fondness is united to a taste for ancient customs, and to a reverence for ancestral traditions of the past; those who cherish it love their country as they love the mansion of their fathers. They enjoy the tranquillity which it affords them; they cling to the peaceful habits which they have contracted within its bosom; they are attached to the reminiscences which it awakens, and they are even pleased by the state of obedience in which they are placed. This patriotism is sometimes stimulated by religious enthusiasm, and then it is capable of making the most prodigious efforts. It is in itself a kind of religion; it does not reason, but it acts from the impulse of faith and of sentiment. By some nations the monarch has been regarded as a personification of the country; and the fervor of patriotism being converted into the fervor of loyalty, they took a sympathetic pride in his conquests, and gloried in his power. At one time, under the ancient monarchy, the French felt a sort of satisfaction in the sense of their dependence upon the arbitrary pleasure of their king, and they were wont to say with pride: "We are the subjects of the most powerful king in the world."

But, like all instinctive passions, this kind of patriotism is more apt to prompt transient exertion than to supply the motives of continuous endeavor. It may save the state in critical circumstances, but it will not unfrequently allow the nation to decline in the midst of peace. While the manners of a people are simple, and its faith unshaken, while society is steadily based upon traditional institutions, whose legitimacy has never been contested, this instinctive patriotism is wont to endure.

But there is another species of attachment to a country which is more rational than the one we have been describing. It is perhaps less generous and less ardent, but it is more fruitful and more lasting; it is coeval with the spread of knowledge, it is nurtured by the laws, it grows by the exercise of civil rights, and in the end, it is confounded with the personal interest of the citizen. A man comprehends the influence which the prosperity of his country has upon his own welfare; he is aware that the laws authorize him to contribute his assistance to that prosperity, and he labors to promote it as a portion of his interest in the first place, and as a portion of his right in the second.

But epochs sometimes occur, in the course of the existence of a nation, at which the ancient customs of a people are changed, public morality destroyed, religious belief disturbed, and the spell of tradition broken, while the diffusion of knowledge is yet imperfect, and the civil rights of the community are ill secured, or confined within very narrow limits. The country then assumes a dim and dubious shape in the eyes of the citizens; they no longer behold it in the soil which they inhabit, for that soil is to them a dull inanimate clod; nor in the usages of their forefathers, which they have been taught to look upon as a debasing yoke; nor in religion, for of that they doubt; nor in the laws, which do not originate in their own authority; nor in the legislator, whom they fear and despise. The country is lost to their senses, they can neither discover it under its own, nor under borrowed features, and they intrench themselves within the dull precincts of a narrow egotism. They are emancipated from prejudice, without having acknowledged the empire of reason; they are animated neither by the instinctive patriotism of monarchical subjects, nor by the thinking patriotism of republican citizens; but they have stopped half-way between the two, in the midst of confusion and of distress.

In this predicament, to retreat is impossible; for a people cannot restore the vivacity of its earlier times, any more than a man can return to the innocence and the bloom of childhood: such things may be regretted, but they cannot be renewed. The only thing, then, which remains to be done, is to proceed, and to accelerate the union of private with public interests, since the period of disinterested patriotism is gone by for ever.

I am certainly very far from averring, that, in order to obtain this result, the exercise of political rights should be immediately granted to all the members of the community. But I maintain that the most powerful, and perhaps the only means of interesting men in the welfare of their country, which we still possess, is to make them partakers in the government. At the present time civic zeal seems to me to be inseparable from the exercise of political rights; and I hold that the number of citizens will be found to augment or decrease in Europe in proportion as those rights are extended.

In the United States, the inhabitants were thrown but as yesterday upon the soil which they now occupy, and they brought neither customs nor traditions with them there; they meet each other for the first time with no previous acquaintance; in short, the instinctive love of their country can scarcely exist in their minds; but every one takes as zealous an interest in the affairs of his township, his country, and of the whole state, as if they were his own, because every one, in his sphere, takes an active part in the government of society.

The lower orders in the United States are alive to the perception of the influence exercised by the general prosperity upon their own welfare; and simple as this observation is, it is one which is but too rarely made by the people. But in America the people regard this prosperity as the result of its own exertions; the citizen looks upon the fortune of the public as his private interest, and he co-operates in its success, not so much from a sense of pride or of duty, as from what I shall venture to term cupidity.

It is unnecessary to study the institutions and the history of the Americans in order to discover the truth of this remark, for their manners render it sufficiently evident. As the American participates in all that is done in his country, he thinks himself obliged to defend whatever may be censured; for it is not only his country which is attacked upon these occasions, but it is himself. The consequence is that his national pride resorts to a thousand artifices, and to all the petty tricks of individual vanity.

Nothing is more embarrassing in the ordinary intercourse of life than this irritable patriotism of the Americans. A stranger may be well inclined to praise many of the institutions of their country, but he begs permission to blame some of the peculiarities which he observes—a permission which is however inexorably refused. America is therefore a free country, in which, lest anybody should be hurt by your remarks, you are not allowed to speak freely of private individuals or of the state; of the citizens or of the authorities; of public or of private undertakings; or, in short, of anything at all, except it be of the climate and the soil; and even then Americans will be found ready to defend either the one or the other, as if they had been contrived by the inhabitants of the country.

In our times, option must be made between the patriotism of all and the government of a few; for the force and activity which the first confers, are irreconcilable with the guarantees of tranquillity which the second furnishes.

NOTION OF RIGHTS IN THE UNITED STATES.

No great People without a Notion of Rights.—How the Notion of Rights can be given to a People.—Respect of Rights in the United States.—Whence it arises.

After the idea of virtue, I am acquainted with no higher principle than that of right; or, to speak more accurately, these two ideas are commingled in one. The idea of right is simply that of virtue introduced into the political world. It is the idea of right which enabled men to define anarchy and tyranny; and which taught them to remain independent without arrogance, as well as to obey without servility. The man who submits to violence is debased by his compliance; but when he obeys the mandate of one who possesses that right of authority which he acknowledges in a fellow-creature, he rises in some measure above the person who delivers the command. There are no great men without virtue, and there are no great nations—it may also be added that there would be no society—without the notion of rights; for what is the condition of a mass of rational and intelligent beings who are only united together by the bond of force?

I am persuaded that the only means which we possess at the present time of inculcating the notion of rights, and of rendering it, as it were, palpable to the senses, is to invest all the members of the community with the peaceful exercise of certain rights: this is very clearly seen in children, who are men without the strength and the experience of manhood. When a child begins to move in the midst of the objects which surround him, he is instinctively led to turn everything which he can lay his hands upon to his own purpose; he has no notion of the property of others; but as he gradually learns the value of things, and begins to perceive that he may in his turn be deprived of his possessions, he becomes more circumspect, and he observes those rights in others which he wishes to have respected in himself. The principle which the child derives from the possession of his toys, is taught to the man by the objects which he may call his own. In America those complaints against property in general, which are so frequent in Europe, are never heard, because in America there are no paupers; and as every one has property of his own to defend, every one recognizes the principle upon which he holds it.

The same thing occurs in the political world. In America the lowest classes have conceived a very high notion of political rights, because they exercise those rights; and they refrain from attacking those of other people, in order to ensure their own from attack. While in Europe the same classes sometimes recalcitrate even against the supreme power, the American submits without a murmur to the authority of the pettiest magistrate.

This truth is exemplified by the most trivial details of national peculiarities. In France very few pleasures are exclusively reserved for the higher classes; the poor are admitted wherever the rich are received; and they consequently behave with propriety, and respect whatever contributes to the enjoyments in which they themselves participate. In England, where wealth has a monopoly of amusement as well as of power, complaints are made that whenever the poor happen to steal into the enclosures which are reserved for the pleasures of the rich, they commit acts of wanton mischief: can this be wondered at, since care has been taken that they should have nothing to lose?

The government of the democracy brings the notion of political rights to the level of the humblest citizens, just as the dissemination of wealth brings the notion of property within the reach of all the members of the community; and I confess that, to my mind, this is one of its greatest advantages. I do not assert that it is easy to teach men to exercise political rights; but I maintain that when it is possible, the effects which result from it are highly important: and I add that if there ever was a time at which such an attempt ought to be made, that time is our own. It is clear that the influence of religious belief is shaken, and that the notion of divine rights is declining; it is evident that public morality is vitiated, and the notion of moral rights is also disappearing: these are general symptoms of the substitution of argument for faith, and of calculation for the impulses of sentiment. If, in the midst of this general disruption, you do not succeed in connecting the notion of rights with that of personal interest, which is the only immutable point in the human heart, what means will you have of governing the world except by fear? When I am told that since the laws are weak and the populace is wild, since passions are excited and the authority of virtue is paralyzed, no measures must be taken to increase the rights of the democracy; I reply that it is for these very reasons that some measures of the kind must be taken; and I am persuaded that governments are still more interested in taking them than society at large, because governments are liable to be destroyed, and society cannot perish.

I am not, however, inclined to exaggerate the example which America furnishes. In those states the people was invested with political rights at a time when they could scarcely be abused, for the citizens were few in number and simple in their manners. As they have increased, the Americans have not augmented the power of the democracy, but they have, if I may use the expression, extended its dominions.

It cannot be doubted that the moment at which political

rights are granted to a people that had before been without them, is a very critical, though it be a very necessary one. A child may kill before he is aware of the value of life; and he may deprive another person of his property before he is aware that his own may be taken away from him. The lower orders, when first they are invested with political rights, stand in relation to those rights, in the same position as a child does to the whole of nature, and the celebrated adage may then be applied to them, *Homo, puer robustus*. This truth may even be perceived in America. The states in which the citizens have enjoyed their rights longest are those in which they make the best use of them.

It cannot be repeated too often that nothing is more fertile in prodigies than the art of being free; but there is nothing more arduous than the apprenticeship of liberty. Such is not the case with despotic institutions; despotism often promises to make amends for a thousand previous ills; it supports the right, it protects the oppressed, and it maintains public order. The nation is lulled by the temporary prosperity which accrues to it, until it is roused to a sense of its own misery. Liberty, on the contrary, is generally established in the midst of agitation, it is perfected by civil discord, and its benefits cannot be appreciated until it is already old.

RESPECT FOR THE LAW IN THE UNITED STATES.

Respect of the Americans for the Law.—Parental Affection which they entertain for it.—Personal Interest of every one to increase the Authority of the Law.

It is not always feasible to consult the whole people, either directly or indirectly, in the formation of the law; but it cannot be denied that when such a measure is possible, the authority of the law is very much augmented. This popular origin, which impairs the excellence and the wisdom of legislation, contributes prodigiously to increase its power. There is an amazing strength in the expression of the determination of a whole people; and when it declares itself, the imagination of those who are most inclined to contest it, is overawed by its authority. The truth of this fact is very well known by parties; and they consequently strive to make out a majority whenever they can. If they have not the greater number of voters on their side, they assert that the true majority abstained from voting; and if they are foiled even there, they have recourse to the body of those persons who had no votes to give.

In the United States, except slaves, servants, and paupers in the receipt of relief from the townships, there is no class of persons who do not exercise the elective franchise, and who do not contribute indirectly to make the laws. Those who design to attack the laws must consequently either modify the opinion of the nation or trample upon its decision.

A second reason, which is still more weighty, may be farther adduced : in the United States every one is personally interested in enforcing the obedience of the whole community to the law ; for as the minority may shortly rally the majority to its principles, it is interested in professing that respect for the decrees of the legislator, which it may soon have occasion to claim for its own. However irksome an enactment may be, the citizen of the United States complies with it, not only because it is the work of the majority, but because it originates in his own authority ; and he regards it as a contract to which he is himself a party.

In the United States, then, that numerous and turbulent multitude does not exist, which always looks upon the law as its natural enemy, and accordingly surveys it with fear and with distrust. It is impossible, on the other hand, not to perceive that all classes display the utmost reliance upon the legislation of their country, and that they are attached to it by a kind of parental affection.

I am wrong, however, in saying all classes; for as in America the European scale of authority is inverted, the wealthy are there placed in a position analogous to that of the poor in the Old World, and it is the opulent classes which frequently look upon the law with suspicion. I have already observed that the advantage of democracy is not, as has been sometimes asserted, that it protects the interests of the whole community, but simply that it protects those of the majority. In the United States, where the poor rule, the rich have always some reason to dread the abuses of their power. This natural anxiety of the rich may produce a sullen dissatisfaction, but society is not disturbed by it; for the same reason which induces the rich to withhold their confidence in the legislative authority, makes them obey its mandates ; their wealth, which prevents them from making the law, prevents them from withstanding it. Among civilized nations revolts are rarely excited except by such persons as have nothing to lose by them ; and if the laws of a democracy are not always worthy of respect, at least they always obtain it ; for those who usually infringe the laws have no excuse for not complying with the enactments they have themselves made, and by which they are themselves benefited, while the citizens whose interests might be promoted by the infraction of them, are induced, by their character and their station, to submit to the decisions of the legislature, whatever they may be. Beside which, the people in America obeys the law not only because it emanates from the popular authority, but because that authority may modify it in any points which may prove vexatory; a law is observed because it is a self-imposed evil in the first place, and an evil of transient duration in the second.

ACTIVITY WHICH PERVADES ALL THE BRANCHES OF THE BODY POLITIC IN THE UNITED STATES; INFLUENCE WHICH IT EXERCISES UPON SOCIETY.

More difficult to conceive the political Activity which pervades the United States than the Freedom and Equality which reign here.—The great activity which perpetually agitates the legislative Bodies is only an Episode to the general Activity.—Difficult for an American to confine himself to his own Business.—Political Agitation extends to all social intercourse.—Commercial Activity of the Americans partly attributable to this cause.—Indirect Advantages which Society derives from a democratic Government.

On passing from a country in which free institutions are established to one where they do not exist, the traveller is struck by the change; in the former all is bustle and activity, in the latter everything is calm and motionless. In the one, melioration and progress are the general topics of inquiry; in the other, it seems as if the community only aspired to repose in the enjoyment of the advantages which it has acquired. Nevertheless, the country which exerts itself so strenuously to promote its welfare is generally more wealthy and more prosperous than that which appears to be so contented with its lot; and when we compare them together, we can scarcely conceive how so many new wants are daily felt in the former, while so few seem to occur in the latter.

If this remark is applicable to those free countries in which monarchical and aristocratic institutions subsist, it is still more striking with regard to democratic republics. In these states it is not only a portion of the people which is busied with the melioration of its social condition, but the whole community is engaged in the task; and it is not the exigencies and the convenience of a single class for which a provision is to be made, but the exigencies and the convenience of all ranks of life.

It is not impossible to conceive the surpassing liberty which the Americans enjoy; some idea may likewise be formed of the extreme equality which subsists among them; but the political activity which pervades the United States must be seen in order to be understood. No sooner do you set foot upon the American soil than you are stunned by a kind of tumult; a confused clamor is heard on every side; and a thousand simultaneous voices demand the immediate satisfaction of their social wants. Everything is in motion around you; here, the people of one quarter of a town are met to decide upon the building of a church; there, the election of a representative is going on; a little further, the delegates of a district are posting to the town in order to consult upon some local improvements; or, in another place, the laborers of a village quit their ploughs to deliberate upon the project of a road or a public school. Meetings are called for the sole purpose of declaring their disapprobation of the line of conduct pursued by the government; while in other assemblies the citizens salute the authorities of the day as the fathers of their country. Societies are formed, which regard drunkenness as the principal cause of the evils under which the state labors, and which solemnly bind themselves to give a constant example of temperance.*

The great political agitation of the American legislative bodies, which is the only kind of excitement that attracts the attention of foreign countries, is a mere episode or a sort of continuation of that universal movement which originates in the lowest classes of the people and extends successively to all the ranks of society. It is impossible to spend more efforts in the pursuit of enjoyment.

The cares of political life engross a most prominent place in the occupation of a citizen in the United States; and almost the only pleasure of which an American has any idea, is to take a part in the government, and to discuss the part he has taken. This feeling pervades the most trifling habits of life; even the women frequently attend public meetings, and listen to political harangues as a recreation after their

* At the time of my stay in the United States the temperance societies already consisted of more than 270,000 members; and their effect had been to diminish the consumption of fermented liquors by 500,000 gallons per annum in the state of Pennsylvania alone.

household labors. Debating clubs are to a certain extent a substitute for theatrical entertainments: an American cannot converse, but he can discuss; and when he attempts to talk he falls into a dissertation. He speaks to you as if he were addressing a meeting; and if he should warm in the course of the discussion, he will infallibly say "gentlemen," to the person with whom he is conversing.

In some countries the inhabitants display a certain repugnance to avail themselves of the political privileges with which the law invests them; it would seem that they set too high a value upon their time to spend it on the interests of the community; and they prefer to withdraw within the exact limits of a wholesome egotism, marked out by four sunk fences and a quickset hedge. But if an American were condemned to confine his activity to his own affairs, he would be robbed of one half of his existence; he would feel an immense void in the life which he is accustomed to lead, and his wretchedness would be unbearable.* I am persuaded that if ever a despotic government is established in America, it will find it more difficult to surmount the habits which free institutions have engendered, than to conquer the attachment of the citizens to freedom.

This ceaseless agitation which democratic government has introduced into the political world, influences all social intercourse. I am not sure that upon the whole this is not the greatest advantage of democracy; and I am much less inclined to applaud it for what it does, than for what it causes to be done.

It is incontestable that the people frequently conducts public business very ill; but it is impossible that the lower orders should take a part in public business without extending the circle of their ideas, and without quitting the ordinary routine of their mental acquirements. The humblest individual who is called upon to co-operate in the government of society, acquires a certain degree of self-respect; and as he possesses authority, he can command the services of minds much more enlightened than his own. He is canvassed by a multitude of applicants, who seek to deceive him in a thousand different ways, but who instruct him by their deceit. He takes a part in political undertakings which did not originate in his own conception, but which give him a taste for undertakings of

* The same remark was made at Rome under the first Cesars. Montesquieu somewhere alludes to the excessive despondency of certain Roman citizens who, after the excitement of political life, were all at once flung back into the stagnation of private life.

the kind. New meliorations are daily pointed out in the property which he holds in common with others, and this gives him the desire of improving that property which is more peculiarly his own. He is perhaps neither happier nor better than those who came before him, but he is better informed and more active. I have no doubt that the democratic institutions of the United States, joined to the physical constitution of the country, are the cause (not the direct, as is so often asserted, but the indirect cause) of the prodigious commercial activity of the inhabitants. It is not engendered by the laws, but the people learns how to promote it by the experience derived from legislation.

When the opponents of democracy assert that a single individual performs the duties which he undertakes much better than the government of the community, it appears to me that they are perfectly right. The government of an individual, supposing an equality of instruction on either side, is more consistent, more persevering, and more accurate than that of a multitude, and it is much better qualified judiciously to discriminate the characters of the men it employs. If any deny what I advance, they have certainly never seen a democratic government, or have formed their opinion upon very partial evidence. It is true that even when local circumstances and the disposition of the people allow democratic institutions to subsist, they never display a regular and methodical system of government. Democratic liberty is far from accomplishing all the projects it undertakes, with the skill of an adroit despotism. It frequently abandons them before they have borne their fruits, or risks them when the consequences may prove dangerous; but in the end it produces more than any absolute government, and if it do fewer things well, it does a great number of things. Under its sway, the transactions of the public administration are not nearly so important as what is done by private exertion. Democracy does not confer the most skilful kind of government upon the people, but it produces that which the most skilful governments are frequently unable to awaken, namely, an all-pervading and restless activity, a superabundant force, and an energy which is inseparable from it, and which may, under favorable circumstances, beget the most amazing benefits. These are the true advantages of democracy.

In the present age, when the destinies of Christendom seem to be in suspense, some hasten to assail democracy as its foe while it is yet in its early growth; and others are ready with their vows of adoration for this new duty which is springing forth from chaos: but both parties are very imperfectly acquainted with the object of their hatred or of their desires; they strike in the dark, and distribute their blows by mere chance.

We must first understand what the purport of society and the aim of government are held to be. If it be your intention to confer a certain elevation upon the human mind, and to teach it to regard the things of this world with generous feelings; to inspire men with a scorn of mere temporal advantage; to give birth to living convictions, and to keep alive the spirit of honorable devotedness; if you hold it to be a good thing to refine the habits, to embellish the manners, to cultivate the arts of a nation, and to promote the love of poetry, of beauty, and of renown; if you would constitute a people not unfitted to act with power upon all other nations; nor unprepared for those high enterprises, which, whatever be the result of its efforts, will leave a name for ever famous in time—if you believe such to be the principal object of society, you must avoid the government of democracy, which would be a very uncertain guide to the end you have in view.

But if you hold it to be expedient to divert the moral and intellectual activity of man to the production of comfort, and to the acquirement of the necessaries of life; if a clear understanding be more profitable to men than genius; if your object be not to stimulate the virtues of heroism, but to create habits of peace; if you had rather behold vices than crimes, and are content to meet with fewer noble deeds, provided offences be diminished in the same proportion; if, instead of living in the midst of a brilliant state of society, you are contented to have prosperity around you; if, in short, you are of opinion that the principal object of a government is not to confer the greatest possible share of power and of glory upon the body of the nation, but to ensure the greatest degree of enjoyment, and the least degree of misery, to each of the individuals who compose it—if such be your desires, you can have no surer means of satisfying them than by equalizing the condition of men, and establishing democratic institutions.

But if the time be past at which such a choice was possible, and if some superhuman power impel us toward one or the other of these two governments without consulting our wishes, let us at least endeavor to make the best of that which is allotted to us: and let us so inquire into its good and its evil propensities as to be able to foster the former, and repress the latter to the utmost.

CHAPTER XV.

UNLIMITED POWER OF THE MAJORITY IN THE UNITED STATES AND ITS CONSEQUENCES.

Natural Strength of the Majority in Democracies.—Most of the American Constitutions have increased this Strength by artificial Means.—How this has been done.—Pledged Delegates.—Moral Power of the Majority.—Opinions as to its Infallibility.—Respect for its Rights, how augmented in the United States.

THE very essence of democratic government consists in the absolute sovereignty of the majority: for there is nothing in democratic states which is capable of resisting it. Most of the American constitutions have sought to increase this natural strength of the majority by artificial means.*

The legislature is, of all political institutions, the one which is most easily swayed by the wishes of the majority. The Americans determined that the members of the legislature should be elected by the people immediately, and for a very brief term, in order to subject them not only to the general convictions, but even to the daily passions of their constituents. The members of both houses are taken from the same class in society, and are nominated in the same manner; so that the modifications of the legislative bodies are almost as rapid and quite as irresistible as those of a single assembly. It is to a legislature thus constituted, that almost all the authority of the government has been intrusted.

But while the law increased the strength of those authorities which of themselves were strong, it enfeebled more and more those which were naturally weak. It deprived the representatives of the executive of all stability and independence; and by subjecting them completely to the caprices of the legislature, it robbed them completely of the slender influence which the nature of a democratic government might have allowed them to retain. In several states the judicial power was also submitted to the elective discretion of the ma-

* We observed in examining the federal constitution that the efforts of the legislators of the Union had been diametrically opposed to the present tendency. The consequence has been that the federal government is more independent in its sphere than that of the states. But the federal government scarcely ever interferes in any but external affairs; and the governments of the states are in reality the authorities which direct society in America.

jority; and in all of them its existence was made to depend on the pleasure of the legislative authority, since the representatives were empowered annually to regulate the stipend of the judges.

Custom, however, has done even more than law. A proceeding which will in the end set all the guarantees of representative government at naught, is becoming more and more general in the United States: it frequently happens that the electors, who choose a delegate, point out a certain line of conduct to him, and impose upon him a certain number of positive obligations which he is pledged to fulfil. With the exception of the tumult, this comes to the same thing as if the majority of the populace held its deliberations in the market-place.

Several other circumstances concur in rendering the power of the majority in America, not only preponderant, but irresistible. The moral authority of the majority is partly based upon the notion, that there is more intelligence and more wisdom in a great number of men collected together than in a single individual, and that the quantity of legislators is more important than their quality. The theory of equality is in fact applied to the intellect of man; and human pride is thus assailed in its last retreat, by a doctrine which the minority hesitate to admit, and in which they very slowly concur. Like all other powers, and perhaps more than all other powers, the authority of the many requires the sanction of time; at first it enforces obedience by constraint; but its laws are not respected until they have long been maintained.

The right of governing society, which the majority supposes itself to derive from its superior intelligence, was introduced into the United States by the first settlers; and this idea, which would be sufficient of itself to create a free nation, has now been amalgamated with the manners of the people, and the minor incidents of social intercourse.

The French, under the old monarchy, held it for a maxim (which is still a fundamental principle of the English constitution), that the king could do no wrong; and if he did wrong, the blame was imputed to his advisers. This notion was highly favorable to habits of obedience; and it enabled the subject to complain of the law, without ceasing to love and honor the lawgiver. The Americans entertain the same opinion with respect to the majority.

The moral power of the majority is founded upon yet another principle, which is, that the interests of the many are to be preferred to those of the few. It will readily be perceived that the respect here professed for the rights of the majority must naturally increase or diminish according to the state of parties. When a nation is divided into several irreconcilable factions, the privilege of the majority is often overlooked, because it is intolerable to comply with its demands

If there existed in America a class of citizens whom the legislating majority sought to deprive of exclusive privileges, which they had possessed for ages, and to bring down from an elevated station to the level of the ranks of the multitude, it is probable that the minority would be less ready to comply with its laws. But as the United States were colonized by men holding an equal rank among themselves, there is as yet no natural or permanent source of dissension between the interests of its different inhabitants.

There are certain communities in which the persons who constitute the minority can never hope to draw over the majority to their side, because they must then give up the very point which is at issue between them. Thus, an aristocracy can never become a majority while it retains its exclusive privileges, and it cannot cede its privileges without ceasing to be an aristocracy.

In the United States, political questions cannot be taken up in so general and absolute a manner; and all parties are willing to recognize the rights of the majority, because they all hope to turn those rights to their own advantage at some future time. The majority therefore in that country exercises a prodigious actual authority, and a moral influence which is scarcely less preponderant; no obstacles exist which can impede, or so much as retard its progress, or which can induce it to heed the complaints of those whom it crushes upon its path. This state of things is fatal in itself and dangerous for the future.

HOW THE UNLIMITED POWER OF THE MAJORITY INCREASES, IN AMERICA, THE INSTABILITY OF LEGISLATION AND THE ADMINISTRATION INHERENT IN DEMOCRACY.

The Americans increase the mutability of the Laws which is inherent in Democracy by changing the Legislature every Year, and by vesting it with unbounded Authority.—The same Effect is produced upon the Administration.—In America social Melioration is conducted more energeticallv, but less perseveringly than in Europe.

I HAVE already spoken of the natural defects of democratic institutions, and they all of them increase in the exact ratio of the power of the majority. To begin with the most evident of them all; the mutability of the laws is an evil inherent in democratic government, because it is natural to democracies to raise men to power in very rapid succession. But this evil is more or less sensible in proportion to the authority and the means of action which the legislature possesses.

In America the authority exercised by the legislative bodies is supreme; nothing prevents them from accomplishing their wishes with celerity, and with irresistible power, while they are supplied by new representatives every year. That is to say, the circumstances which contribute most powerfully to democratic instability, and which admit of the free application of caprice to every object in the state, are here in full operation. In conformity with this principle, America is, at the present day, the country in the world where laws last the shortest time. Almost all the American constitutions have been amended within the course of thirty years: there is, therefore, not a single American state which has not modified the principles of its legislation in that lapse of time. As for the laws themselves, a single glance upon the archives of the different states of the Union suffices to convince one, that in America the activity of the legislator never slackens. Not that the American democracy is naturally less stable than any other, but that it is allowed to follow its capricious propensities in the formation of the laws.*

The omnipotence of the majority and the rapid as well as absolute manner in which its decisions are executed in the United States, have not only the effect of rendering the law unstable, but they exercise the same influence upon the execution of the law and the conduct of the public administration. As the majority is the only power which it is important to court, all its projects are taken up with the greatest ardor; but no sooner is its attention distracted, than all this ardor ceases; while in the free states of Europe, the administration is at once independent and secure, so that the pro-

* The legislative acts promulgated by the state of Massachusetts alone, from the year 1780 to the present time, already fill three stout volumes: and it must not be forgotten that the collection to which I allude was published in 1823, when many old laws which had fallen into disuse were omitted. The state of Massachusetts, which is not more populous than a department of France, may be considered as the most stable, the most consistent, and the most sagacious in its undertakings of the whole Union.

jects of the legislature are put into execution, although its immediate attention may be directed to other objects.

In America certain meliorations are undertaken with much more zeal and activity than elsewhere; in Europe the same ends are promoted by much less social effort, more continuously applied.

Some years ago several pious individuals undertook to meliorate the condition of the prisons. The public was excited by the statements which they put forward, and the regeneration of criminals became a very popular undertaking. New prisons were built; and, for the first time, the idea of reforming as well as of punishing the delinquent, formed a part of prison discipline. But this happy alteration, in which the public had taken so hearty an interest, and which the exertions of the citizens had irresistibly accelerated, could not be completed in a moment. While the new penitentiaries were being erected (and it was the pleasure of the majority they should be terminated with all possible celerity), the old prisons existed, which still contained a great number of offenders. These jails became more unwholesome and more corrupt in proportion as the new establishments were beautified and improved, forming a contrast which may readily be understood. The majority was so eagerly employed in founding the new prisons, that those which already existed were forgotten; and as the general attention was diverted to a novel object, the care which had hitherto been bestowed upon the others ceased. The salutary regulations of discipline were first relaxed, and afterward broken; so that in the immediate neighborhood of a prison which bore witness to the mild and enlightened spirit of our time, dungeons might be met with, which reminded the visitor of the barbarity of the middle ages.

TYRANNY OF THE MAJORITY.

How the Principle of the Sovereignty of the People is to be understood.—Impossibility of conceiving a mixed Government.—The sovereign Power must centre somewhere.—Precautions to be taken to control its Action.—These Precautions have not been taken in the United States.—Consequences.

I HOLD it to be an impious and an execrable maxim that, politically speaking, a people has a right to do whatsoever it pleases; and yet I have asserted that all authority originates in the will of the majority. Am I, then, in contradiction with myself?

A general law—which bears the name of justice—has been made and sanctioned, not only by a majority of this or that people, but by a majority of mankind. The rights of every people are consequently confined within the limits of what is just. A nation may be considered in the light of a jury which is empowered to represent society at large, and to apply the great and general law of justice. Ought such a jury, which represents society, to have more power than the society in which the laws it applies originate?

When I refuse to obey an unjust law, I do not contest the right which the majority has of commanding, but I simply appeal from the sovereignty of the people to the sovereignty of mankind. It has been asserted that a people can never entirely outstep the boundaries of justice and of reason in those affairs which are more peculiarly its own; and that consequently full power may fearlessly be given to the majority by which it is represented. But this language is that of a slave.

A majority taken collectively may be regarded as a being whose opinions, and most frequently whose interests, are opposed to those of another being, which is styled a minority. If it be admitted that a man, possessing absolute power, may misuse that power by wronging his adversaries, why should a majority not be liable to the same reproach? Men are not apt to change their characters by agglomeration; nor does their patience in the presence of obstacles increase with the consciousness of their strength.* And for these reasons I can never willingly invest any number of my fellow-creatures with that unlimited authority which I should refuse to any one of them.

I do not think it is possible to combine several principles in the same government, so as at the same time to maintain freedom, and really to oppose them to one another. The form of government which is usually termed *mixed* has always appeared to me to be a mere chimera. Accurately speaking, there is no such thing as a mixed government (with the meaning usually given to that word), because in all communities some one principle of action may be discovered, which

* No one will assert that a people cannot forcibly wrong another people: but parties may be looked upon as lesser nations within a greater one, and they are aliens to each other: if therefore it be admitted that a nation can act tyrannically toward another nation, it cannot be denied that a party may do the same toward another party.

preponderates over the others. England in the last century, which has been more especially cited as an example of this form of government, was in point of fact an essentially aristocratic state, although it comprised very powerful elements of democracy: for the laws and customs of the country were such, that the aristocracy could not but preponderate in the end, and subject the direction of public affairs to its own will. The error arose from too much attention being paid to the actual struggle which was going on between the nobles and the people, without considering the probable issue of the contest, which was in reality the important point. When a community really has a mixed government, that is to say, when it is equally divided between two adverse principles, it must either pass through a revolution, or fall into complete dissolution.

I am therefore of opinion that some one social power must always be made to predominate over the others; but I think that liberty is endangered when this power is checked by no obstacles which may retard its course, and force it to moderate its own vehemence.

Unlimited power is in itself a bad and dangerous thing; human beings are not competent to exercise it with discretion; and God alone can be omnipotent, because his wisdom and his justice are always equal to his power. But no power upon earth is so worthy of honor for itself, or of reverential obedience to the rights which it represents, that I would consent to admit its uncontrolled and all-predominate authority. When I see that the right and the means of absolute command are conferred on a people or upon a king, upon an aristocracy or a democracy, a monarchy or a republic, I recognize the germ of tyranny, and I journey onward to a land of more hopeful institutions.

In my opinion the main evil of the present democratic institutions of the United States does not arise, as is often asserted in Europe, from their weakness, but from their overpowering strength; and I am not so much alarmed at the excessive liberty which reigns in that country, as at the very inadequate securities which exist against tyranny.

When an individual or a party is wronged in the United States, to whom can he apply for redress? If to public opinion, public opinion constitutes the majority; if to the legislature, it represents the majority, and implicitly obeys its instructions: if to the executive power, it is appointed by the majority and is a passive tool in its hands; the public troops consist of the majority under arms; the jury is the majority invested with the right of hearing judicial cases; and in certain states even the judges are elected by the majority. However iniquitous or absurd the evil of which you complain may be, you must submit to it as well as you can.*

If, on the other hand, a legislative power could be so constituted as to represent the majority without necessarily being the slave of its passions; an executive, so as to retain a certain degree of uncontrolled authority; and a judiciary, so as to remain independent of the two other powers; a government would be formed which would still be democratic, without incurring any risk of tyrannical abuse.

I do not say that tyrannical abuses frequently occur in America at the present day; but I maintain that no sure barrier is established against them, and that the causes which

* A striking instance of the excesses which may be occasioned by the despotism of the majority occurred at Baltimore in the year 1812. At that time the war was very popular in Baltimore. A journal which had taken the other side of the question excited the indignation of the inhabitants by its opposition. The populace assembled, broke the printing-presses, and attacked the houses of the newspaper editors. The militia was called out, but no one obeyed the call; and the only means of saving the poor wretches who were threatened by the phrensy of the mob, was to throw them into prison as common malefactors. But even this precaution was ineffectual; the mob collected again during the night; the magistrates again made a vain attempt to call out the militia; the prison was forced, one of the newspaper editors was killed upon the spot, and the others were left for dead: the guilty parties were acquitted by the jury when they were brought to trial.

I said one day to an inhabitant of Pennsylvania: "Be so good as to explain to me how it happens, that in a state founded by quakers, and celebrated for its toleration, freed blacks are not allowed to exercise civil rights. They pay the taxes: is it not fair that they should have a vote."

"You insult us," replied my informant, "if you imagine that our legislators could have committed so gross an act of injustice and intolerance."

"What, then, the blacks possess the right of voting in this country?"

"Without the smallest doubt."

"How comes it then, that at the polling-booth this morning I did not perceive a single negro in the whole meeting?"

"This is not the fault of the law; the negroes have the undisputed right of voting; but they voluntarily abstain from making their appearance."

"A very pretty piece of modesty on their parts," rejoined I.

"Why, the truth is, that they are not disinclined to vote, but they are afraid of being maltreated; in this country the law is sometimes unable to maintain its authority without the support of the majority. But in this case the majority entertains very strong prejudices against the blacks, and the magistrates are unable to protect them in the exercise of their legal privileges."

"What, then, the majority claims the right not only of making the laws, but of breaking the laws it has made?"

mitigate the government are to be found in the circumstances and the manners of the country more than its laws.

EFFECTS OF THE UNLIMITED POWER OF THE MAJORITY UPON THE ARBITRARY AUTHORITY OF THE AMERICAN PUBLIC OFFICERS.

Liberty left by the American Laws to public Officers within a certain Sphere.—Their Power.

A DISTINCTION must be drawn between tyranny and arbitrary power. Tyranny may be exercised by means of the law, and in that case it is not arbitrary; arbitrary power may be exercised for the good of the community at large, in which case it is not tyrannical. Tyranny usually employs arbitrary means, but, if necessary, it can rule without them.

In the United States the unbounded power of the majority, which is favorable to the legal despotism of the legislature, is likewise favorable to the arbitrary authority of the magistrates. The majority has an entire control over the law when it is made and when it is executed; and as it possesses an equal authority over those who are in power, and the community at large, it considers public officers as its passive agents, and readily confides the task of serving its designs to their vigilance. The details of their office and the privileges which they are to enjoy are rarely defined beforehand; but the majority treats them as a master does his servants, when they are always at work in his sight, and he has the power of directing or reprimanding them at every instant.

In general the American functionaries are far more independent than the French civil officers, within the sphere which is prescribed to them. Sometimes, even, they are allowed by the popular authority to exceed those bounds; and as they are protected by the opinion, and backed by the co-operation of the majority, they venture upon such manifestations of their power as astonish a European. By this means habits are formed in the heart of a free country which may some day prove fatal to its liberties.

POWER EXERCISED BY THE MAJORITY IN AMERICA UPON OPINION.

In America, when the Majority has once irrevocably decided a Question, all Discussion ceases.—Reason of this.—Moral Power exercised by the Majority upon Opinion.—Democratic Republics have deprived Despotism of its physical Instruments —Their Despotism sways the Minds of Men.

It is in the examination of the display of public opinion in the United States, that we clearly perceive how far the power of the majority surpasses all the powers with which we are acquainted in Europe. Intellectual principles exercise an influence which is so invisible and often so inappreciable, that they baffle the toils of oppression. At the present time the most absolute monarchs in Europe are unable to prevent certain notions, which are opposed to their authority, from circulating in secret throughout their dominions, and even in their courts. Such is not the case in America; so long as the majority is still undecided, discussion is carried on; but as soon as its decision is irrevocably pronounced, a submissive silence is observed; and the friends, as well as the opponents of the measure, unite in assenting to its propriety. The reason of this is perfectly clear: no monarch is so absolute as to combine all the powers of society in his own hands, and to conquer all opposition, with the energy of a majority, which is invested with the right of making and of executing the laws.

The authority of a king is purely physical, and it controls the actions of the subject without subduing his private will; but the majority possesses a power which is physical and moral at the same time; it acts upon the will as well as upon the actions of men, and it represses not only all contest, but all controversy.

I know no country in which there is so little true independence of mind and freedom of discussion as in America. In any constitutional state in Europe every sort of religious and political theory may be advocated and propagated abroad; for there is no country in Europe so subdued by any single authority, as not to contain citizens who are ready to protect the man who raises his voice in the cause of truth, from the consequences of his hardihood. If he is unfortunate enough to live under an absolute government, the people is upon his side; if he inhabits a free country, he may find a shelter behind the authority of the throne, if he require one. The aristocratic part of society supports him in some countries, and the democracy in others. But in a nation where democratic institutions exist, organized like those of the United States, there is but one sole authority, one single element of strength and success, with nothing beyond it.

In America, the majority raises very formidable barriers to the liberty of opinion: within these barriers an author may write whatever he pleases, but he will repent it if he ever step beyond them. Not that he is exposed to the terrors of an auto-da-fé, but he is tormented by the slights and persecutions of daily obloquy. His political career is closed for ever, since he has offended the only authority which is able to promote his success. Every sort of compensation, even that of celebrity, is refused to him. Before he published his opinions, he imagined that he held them in common with many others; but no sooner has he declared them openly, than he is loudly censured by his overbearing opponents, while those who think, without having the courage to speak, like him, abandon him in silence. He yields at length, oppressed by the daily efforts he has been making, and he subsides into silence as if he was tormented by remorse for having spoken the truth.

Fetters and headsmen were the coarse instruments which tyranny formerly employed; but the civilisation of our age has refined the arts of despotism, which seemed however to have been sufficiently perfected before. The excesses of monarchical power had devised a variety of political means of oppression; the democratic republics of the present day have rendered it as entirely an affair of the mind, as that will which it is intended to coerce. Under the absolute sway of an individual despot, the body was attacked in order to subdue the soul; and the soul escaped the blows which were directed against it, and rose superior to the attempt; but such is not the course adopted by tyranny in democratic republics; there the body is left free, and the soul is enslaved. The sovereign can no longer say, "You shall think as I do on pain of death;" but he says, "You are free to think differently from me, and to retain your life, your property, and all that you possess; but if such be your determination, you are henceforth an alien among your people. You may retain your civil rights, but they will be useless to you, for you will never be chosen by your fellow-citizens, if you solicit their suffrages; and they will affect to scorn you, if you solicit their esteem. You will remain among men, but you will be deprived of the rights of mankind. Your fellow-creatures will shun you like an impure being; and those who are most persuaded of your innocence will abandon you too, lest they should be shunned in their turn. Go in peace! I have given you your life, but it is an existence incomparably worse than death."

Absolute monarchies have thrown an odium upon despotism; let us beware lest democratic republics should restore oppression, and should render it less odious and less degrading in the eyes of the many, by making it still more onerous to the few.

Works have been published in the proudest nations of the Old World, expressly intended to censure the vices and deride the follies of the time; Labruyère inhabited the palace of Louis XIV. when he composed his chapter upon the Great, and Molière criticised the courtiers in the very pieces which were acted before the court. But the ruling power in the United States is not to be made game of; the smallest reproach irritates its sensibility, and the slightest joke which has any foundation in truth, renders it indignant; from the style of its language to the more solid virtues of its character, everything must be made the subject of encomium. No writer, whatever be his eminence, can escape from this tribute of adulation to his fellow-citizens. The majority lives in the perpetual exercise of self-applause; and there are certain truths which the Americans can only learn from strangers or from experience.

If great writers have not at present existed in America, the reason is very simply given in these facts; there can be no literary genius without freedom of opinion, and freedom of opinion does not exist in America. The inquisition has never been able to prevent a vast number of anti-religious books from circulating in Spain. The empire of the majority succeeds much better in the United States, since it actually removes the wish of publishing them. Unbelievers are to be met with in America, but, to say the truth, there is no public organ of infidelity. Attempts have been made by some governments to protect the morality of nations by prohibiting licentious books. In the United States no one is punished for this sort of works, but no one is induced to write them; not because all the citizens are immaculate in their manners, but because the majority of the community is decent and orderly.

In these cases the advantages derived from the exercise of this power are unquestionable; and I am simply discussing the nature of the power itself. This irresistible authority is a constant fact, and its beneficent exercise is an accidental occurrence.

EFFECTS OF THE TYRANNY OF THE MAJORITY UPON THE NATIONAL CHARACTER IN THE AMERICANS.

Effects of the Tyranny of the Majority more sensibly felt hitherto in the Manners than in the Conduct of Society.—They check the development of leading Characters.—Democratic Republics, organized like the United States, bring the Practice of courting favor within the reach of the many.—Proofs of this Spirit in the United States.—Why there is more Patriotism in the People than in those who govern in its name.

The tendencies which I have just alluded to are as yet very slightly perceptible in political society; but they already begin to exercise an unfavorable influence upon the national character of the Americans. I am inclined to attribute the paucity of distinguished political characters to the ever-increasing activity of the despotism of the majority in the United States.

When the American revolution broke out, they arose in great numbers; for public opinion then served, not to tyrannize over, but to direct the exertions of individuals. Those celebrated men took a full part in the general agitation of mind common at that period, and they attained a high degree of personal fame, which was reflected back upon the nation, but which was by no means borrowed from it.

In absolute governments, the great nobles who are nearest to the throne flatter the passions of the sovereign, and voluntarily truckle to his caprices. But the mass of the nation does not degrade itself by servitude; it often submits from weakness, from habit, or from ignorance, and sometimes from loyalty. Some nations have been known to sacrifice their own desires to those of the sovereign with pleasure and with pride; thus exhibiting a sort of independence in the very act of submission. These peoples are miserable, but they are not degraded. There is a great difference between doing what one does not approve, and feigning to approve what one does; the one is the necessary case of a weak person, the other befits the temper of a lacquey.

In free countries, where every one is more or less called upon to give his opinions in the affairs of state; in democratic republics, where public life is incessantly commingled with domestic affairs, where the sovereign authority is accessible on every side, and where its attention can almost always be attracted by vociferation, more persons are to be met with who speculate upon its foibles, and live at the cost of its passions, than in absolute monarchies. Not because men are naturally worse in these states than elsewhere, but the temptation is stronger, and of easier access at the same time. The result is a far more extensive debasement of the characters of citizens.

Democratic republics extend the practice of currying favor with the many, and they introduce it into a great number of classes at once: this is one of the most serious reproaches that can be addressed to them. In democratic states organized on the principles of the American republics, this is more especially the case, where the authority of the majority is so absolute and so irresistible, that a man must give up his rights as a citizen, and almost abjure his quality as a human being, if he intends to stray from the track which it lays down.

In that immense crowd which throngs the avenues to power in the United States, I found very few men who displayed any of that manly candor, and that masculine independence of opinion, which frequently distinguished the Americans in former times, and which constitute the leading feature in distinguished characters wheresoever they may be found. It seems, at first sight, as if all the minds of the Americans were formed upon one model, so accurately do they correspond in their manner of judging. A stranger does, indeed, sometimes meet with Americans who dissent from these rigorous formularies; with men who deplore the defects of the laws, the mutability and the ignorance of democracy; who even go so far as to observe the evil tendencies which impair the national character, and to point out such remedies as it might be possible to apply; but no one is there to hear these things besides yourself, and you, to whom these secret reflections are confided, are a stranger and a bird of passage. They are very ready to communicate truths which are useless to you, but they continue to hold a different language in public.

If ever these lines are read in America, I am well assured of two things: in the first place, that all who peruse them will raise their voices to condemn me; and in the second place, that very many of them will acquit me at the bottom of their conscience.

[The author's views upon what he terms the tyranny of the majority, the despotism of public opinion in the United States, have already excited some remarks in this country, and will probably give occasion to more. As stated in the preface to this edition, the editor does not conceive himself called upon to discuss the speculative opinions of the author, and supposes he will best discharge his duty by confining his observations to what he deems errors of fact or law. But in reference to this particular subject, it seems due to the author to remark, that he visited the United States at a particular time, when a successful political chieftain had succeeded in establishing his party in power, as it seemed, firmly and permanently; when the preponderance of that party was immense, and when there seemed little prospect of any change. He may have met with men, who sank under the astonishing popularity of General Jackson, who despaired of the republic, and who therefore shrank from the expression of their opinions. It must be confessed, however, that the author is obnoxious to the charge which has been made, of the want of perspicuity and distinctness in this part of his work. He does not mean that the press was silent, for he has himself not only noticed, but furnished proof of the great freedom, not to say licentiousness, with which it assailed the character of the president, and the measures of his administration.

He does not mean to represent the opponents of the dominant party as having thrown down their weapons of warfare, for his book shows throughout his knowledge of the existence of an active and able party, constantly opposing and harassing the administration.

But, after a careful perusal of the chapters on this subject, the editor is inclined to the opinion, that M. De Tocqueville intends to speak of the *tyranny of the party* in excluding from public employment all those who do not adopt the *Shibboleth* of the majority. The language at pp. 266, 267, which he puts in the mouth of a majority, and his observations immediately preceding this note, seem to furnish the key to his meaning; although it must be admitted that there are other passages to which a wider construction may be given. Perhaps they may be reconciled by the idea that the author considers the acts and opinions of the dominant party as the just and true expression of public opinion. And hence, when he speaks of the intolerance of public opinion, he means the exclusiveness of the party, which, for the time being, may be predominant. He had seen men of acknowledged competency removed from office, or excluded from it, wholly on the ground of their entertaining opinions hostile to those of the dominant party, or majority. And he had seen this system extended to the very lowest officers of the government, and applied by the electors in their choice of all officers of all descriptions; and this he deemed persecution—tyranny—despotism. But he surely is mistaken in representing the effect of this system of terror as stifling all complaint, silencing all opposition, and inducing "enemies and friends to yoke themselves alike to the triumphant car of the majority." He mistook a temporary state of parties for a permanent and ordinary result, and he was carried away by the immense majority that then supported the administration, to the belief of a universal acquiescence. Without intending here to speak of the merits or demerits of those who represented that majority, it is proper to remark, that the great change which has taken place since the period when the author wrote, in the political condition of the very persons who he supposed then wielded the terrors of disfranchisement against their opponents, in itself furnishes a full and complete demonstration of the error of his opinions respecting the "true independence of mind and freedom of discussion" in America. For without such discussion to enlighten the minds of the people, and without a stern independence of the rewards and threats of those in power, the change alluded to could not have occurred.

There is reason to complain not only of the ambiguity, but of the style of exaggeration which pervades all the remarks of the author on this subject—so different from the well considered and nicely adjusted language employed by him on all other topics. Thus, p. 262, he implies that there is no means of redress afforded even by the judiciary, for a wrong committed by the majority. His error is, *first*, in supposing the jury to constitute the judicial power; *second*, overlooking what he has himself elsewhere so well described, the independence of the judiciary, and its means of controlling the action of a majority in a state or in the federal government; and *thirdly*, in omitting the proper consideration of the frequent changes of popular sentiment by which the majority of yesterday becomes the minority of to-day, and its acts of injustice are reversed.

Certain it is that the instances which he cites at this page, do not establish his position respecting the disposition of the majority. The riot at Baltimore was, like other riots in England and in France, the result of popular phrensy excited to madness by conduct of the most provoking character. The majority in the state of Maryland and throughout the United States, highly disapproved the acts of violence committed on the occasion. The acquittal by a jury of those arraigned for the murder of General Lingan, proves only that there was not sufficient evidence to identify the accused, or that the jury was governed by passion. It is not perceived how the majority of the people are answerable for the verdicts rendered. The guilty have often been erroneously acquitted in all countries, and in France particularly, recent instances are not wanting of acquittals especially in prosecutions for political offences, against clear and indisputable testimony. And it was entirely fortuitous that the jury was composed of men whose sympathies were with the rioters and murderers, if the fact was so. It not unfrequently happens that a jury taken from lists furnished years perhaps, and always a long time, before the trial, are decidedly hostile to the temporary prevailing sentiments of their city, county, or state.

As in the other instance, if the inhabitant of Pennsylvania intended to intimate to our author, that a colored voter would be in personal jeopardy for venturing to appear at the polls to exercise his right, it must be said in truth, that the incident was local and peculiar, and contrary to what is annually seen throughout the states where colored persons are permitted to vote, who exercise that privilege with as full immunity from injury or oppression, as any white citizen. And, after all, it is believed that the state of feeling intimated by the informant of our author, is but an indication of dislike to a *caste* degraded by servitude and ignorance; and it is not perceived how it proves the despotism of a majority over the freedom and independence of opinion. If it be true, it proves a detestable tyranny over *acts*, over the exercise of an acknowledged right. The apprehensions of a mob committing violence deterred the colored voters from approaching the polls. Are instances unknown in England or even in France, of peaceable subjects being prevented by mobs or the fear of them, from the exercise of a right, from the discharge of a duty? And are they evidences of the despotism of a majority in those countries?—*American Editor.*]

I have heard of patriotism in the United States, and it is a virtue which may be found among the people, but never among the leaders of the people. This may be explained by analogy; despotism debases the oppressed, much more than the oppressor; in absolute monarchies the king has often great virtues, but the courtiers are invariably servile. It is true that the American courtiers do not say, "sire," or "your majesty"—a distinction without a difference. They are for ever talking of the natural intelligence of the populace they serve; they do not debate the question as to which of the virtues of their master are pre-eminently worthy of admiration; for they assure him that he possesses all the virtues under heaven without having acquired them, or without caring to acquire them: they do not give him their daughters and their wives to be raised at his pleasure to the rank of his concubines, but, by sacrificing their opinions, they prostitute themselves. Moralists and philosophers in America are not obliged to conceal their opinions under the veil of allegory; but, before they venture upon a harsh truth, they say: "We are aware that the people which we are addressing is too superior to all the weaknesses of human nature to lose the command of its temper for an instant; and we should not hold this language if we were not speaking to men, whom their virtues and their intelligence render more worthy of freedom than all the rest of the world."

It would have been impossible for the sycophants of Louis XIV. to flatter more dexterously. For my part, I am persuaded that in all governments, whatever their nature may be, servility will cower to force, and adulation will cling to power. The only means of preventing men from degrading themselves, is to invest no one with that unlimited authority which is the surest method of debasing them.

THE GREATEST DANGERS OF THE AMERICAN REPUBLICS PROCEED FROM THE UNLIMITED POWER OF THE MAJORITY.

Democratic Republics liable to perish from a misuse of their Power, and not by Impotence.—The Governments of the American Republics are more Centralized and more Energetic than those of the Monarchies of Europe.—Dangers resulting from this.—Opinions of Hamilton and Jefferson upon this Point

GOVERNMENTS usually fall a sacrifice to impotence or to tyranny. In the former case their power escapes from them: it is wrested from their grasp in the latter. Many observers who have noticed the anarchy of domestic states, have imagined that the government of those states was naturally weak and impotent. The truth is, that when once hostilities are begun between parties, the government loses its control over society. But I do not think that a democratic power is naturally without resources: say rather, that it is almost always by the abuse of its force, and the misemployment of its resources, that a democratic government fails. Anarchy is almost always produced by its tyranny o· its mistakes, but not by its want of strength.

It is important not to confound stability with force, or the greatness of a thing with its duration. In democratic republics, the power which directs* society is not stable; for it often changes hands and assumes a new direction. But whichever way it turns, its force is almost irresistible. The governments of the American republics appear to me to be as much centralized as those of the absolute monarchies of Europe, and more energetic than they are. I do not, therefore, imagine that they will perish from weakness.†

If ever the free institutions of America are destroyed, that event may be attributed to the unlimited authority of the majority, which may at some future time urge the minorities to desperation, and oblige them to have recourse to physical force. Anarchy will then be the result, but it will have been brought about by despotism.

Mr. Hamilton expresses the same opinion in the Federalist, No. 51. "It is of great importance in a republic not only to guard the society against the oppression of its rulers, but to guard one part of the society against the injustice of the other part. Justice is the end of government. It is the end of civil society. It ever has been, and ever will be pursued until it be obtained, or until liberty be lost in the pursuit. In a society, under the forms of which the stronger faction can readily unite and oppress the weaker, anarchy may as truly be said to reign as in a state of nature, where the weaker individual is not secured against the violence of the stronger: and as in the latter state even the stronger individuals are prompted by the uncertainty of their condition to submit to a government which may protect the weak as well as themselves, so in the former state will the more powerful factions be gradually induced by a like motive to wish for a government which will protect all parties, the weaker as well as the more powerful. It can be little doubted, that if the state of

* This power may be centred in an assembly, in which case it will be strong without being stable; or it may be centred in an individual, in which case it will be less strong, but more stable.

† I presume that it is scarcely necessary to remind the reader here, as well as throughout the remainder of this chapter, that I am speaking not of the federal government, but of the several governments of each state which the majority controls at its pleasure.

Rhode Island was separated from the confederacy and left to itself, the insecurity of rights under the popular form of government within such narrow limits, would be displayed by such reiterated oppression of the factious majorities, that some power altogether independent of the people would soon be called for by the voice of the very factions whose misrule had proved the necessity of it."

Jefferson has also expressed himself in a letter to Madison:* "The executive power in our government is not the only, perhaps not even the principal object of my solicitude. The tyranny of the legislature is really the danger most to be feared, and will continue to be so for many years to come. The tyranny of the executive power will come in its turn, but at a more distant period."

I am glad to cite the opinion of Jefferson upon this subject rather than that of another, because I consider him to be the most powerful advocate democracy has ever sent forth.

CHAPTER XVI.

CAUSES WHICH MITIGATE THE TYRANNY OF THE MAJORITY IN THE UNITED STATES.

ABSENCE OF CENTRAL ADMINISTRATION.

The national Majority does not pretend to conduct all Business.—Is obliged to employ the town and county Magistrates to execute its supreme Decisions.

I HAVE already pointed out the distinction which is to be made between a centralized government and a centralized administration. The former exists in America, but the latter is nearly unknown there. If the directing power of the American communities had both these instruments of government at its disposal, and united the habit of executing its own commands to the right of commanding; if, after having established the general principles of government, it descended to the details of public business; and if, having regulated the great interests of the country, it would penetrate into the privacy of indi-

* 15th March, 1789.

vidual interest, freedom would soon be banished from the New World.

But in the United States the majority, which so frequently displays the tastes and the propensities of a despot, is still destitute of the more perfect instruments of tyranny.

In the American republics the activity of the central government has never as yet been extended beyond a limited number of objects sufficiently prominent to call forth its attention. The secondary affairs of society have never been regulated by its authority; and nothing has hitherto betrayed its desire of interfering in them. The majority is become more and more absolute, but it has not increased the prerogatives of the central government; those great prerogatives have been confined to a certain sphere; and although the despotism of the majority may be galling upon one point, it cannot be said to extend to all. However the predominant party of the nation may be carried away by its passions; however ardent it may be in the pursuit of its projects, it cannot oblige all the citizens to comply with its desire in the same manner, and at the same time, throughout the country. When the central government which represents that majority has issued a decree, it must intrust the execution of its will to agents, over whom it frequently has no control, and whom it cannot perpetually direct. The townships, municipal bodies, and counties, may therefore be looked upon as concealed breakwaters, which check or part the tide of popular excitement. If an oppressive law were passed, the liberties of the people would still be protected by the means by which that law would be put in execution: the majority cannot descend to the details, and (as I will venture to style them) the puerilities of administrative tyranny. Nor does the people entertain that full consciousness of its authority, which would prompt it to interfere in these matters; it knows the extent of its natural powers, but it is unacquainted with the increased resources which the art of government might furnish.

This point deserves attention; for if a democratic republic, similar to that of the United States, were ever founded in a country where the power of a single individual had previously subsisted, and the effects of a centralized administration had sunk deep into the habits and the laws of the people, I do not hesitate to assert, that in that country a more insufferable despotism would prevail than any which now exists in the absolute monarchies of Europe; or indeed than any which could be found on this side the confines of Asia.

THE PROFESSION OF THE LAW IN THE UNITED STATES SERVES TO COUNTERPOISE THE DEMOCRACY.

Utility of discriminating the natural Propensities of the Members of the legal Profession.—These Men called upon to act a prominent Part in future Society.—In what Manner the peculiar Pursuits of Lawyers give an aristocratic turn to their Ideas.—Accidental Causes which may check this Tendency.—Ease with which the Aristocracy coalesces with legal Men.—Use of Lawyers to a Despot.—The Profession of the Law constitutes the only aristocratic Element with which the natural Elements of Democracy will combine.—Peculiar Causes which tend to give an aristocratic turn of Mind to the English and American Lawyer.—The Aristocracy of America is on the Bench and at the Bar.—Influence of Lawyers upon American Society.—Their peculiar magisterial Habits affect the Legislature, the Administration, and even the People.

In visiting the Americans and in studying their laws, we perceive that the authority they have intrusted to members of the legal profession, and the influence which these individuals exercise in the government, is the most powerful existing security against the excesses of democracy.

This effect seems to me to result from a general cause which it is useful to investigate, since it may produce analogous consequences elsewhere.

The members of the legal profession have taken an important part in all the vicissitudes of political society in Europe during the last five hundred years. At one time they have been the instruments of those who are invested with political authority, and at another they have succeeded in converting political authorities into their instrument. In the middle ages they afforded a powerful support to the crown; and since that period they have exerted themselves to the utmost to limit the royal prerogative. In England they have contracted a close alliance with the aristocracy; in France they have proved to be the most dangerous enemies of that class. It is my object to inquire whether, under all these circumstances, the members of the legal profession have been swayed by sudden and momentary impulses; or whether they have been impelled by principles which are inherent in their pursuits, and which will always recur in history. I am incited to this investigation by reflecting that this particular class of men will most likely play a prominent part in that order of things to which the events of our time are giving birth.

Men who have more especially devoted themselves to legal pursuits, derive from those occupations certain habits of order, a taste for formalities, and a kind of instinctive regard for the regular connexion of ideas, which naturally render them very hostile to the revolutionary spirit and the unreflecting passions of the multitude.

The special information which lawyers derive from their studies, ensures them a separate station in society: and they constitute a sort of privileged body in the scale of intelligence. This notion of their superiority perpetually recurs to them in the practice of their profession: they are the masters of a science which is necessary, but which is not very generally known: they serve as arbiters between the citizens; and the habit of directing the blind passions of parties in litigation to their purpose, inspires them with a certain contempt for the judgment of the multitude. To this it may be added, that they naturally constitute *a body;* not by any previous understanding, or by any agreement which directs them to a common end; but the analogy of their studies and the uniformity of their proceedings connect their minds together, as much as a common interest would combine their endeavors.

A portion of the tastes and of the habits of the aristocracy may consequently be discovered in the characters of men in the profession of the law. They participate in the same instinctive love of order and of formalities; and they entertain the same repugnance to the actions of the multitude, and the same secret contempt of the government of the people. I do not mean to say that the natural propensities of lawyers are sufficiently strong to sway them irresistibly; for they, like most other men, are governed by their private interests and the advantages of the moment.

In a state of society in which the members of the legal profession are prevented from holding that rank in the political world which they enjoy in private life, we may rest assured that they will be the foremost agents of revolution. But it must then be inquired whether the cause which induces them to innovate and to destroy is accidental, or whether it belongs to some lasting purpose which they entertain. It is true that lawyers mainly contributed to the overthrow of the French monarchy in 1789; but it remains to be seen whether they acted thus because they had studied the laws, or because they were prohibited from co-operating in the work of legislation.

Five hundred years ago the English nobles headed the people, and spoke in its name; at the present time, the aristocracy supports the throne, and defends the royal prerogative. But aristocracy has, notwithstanding this, its peculiar instincts and propensities. We must be careful not to confound isolated members of a body with the body itself. In all free governments, of whatsoever form they may be, members of the legal profession may be found at the head of all parties. The same remark is also applicable to the aristocracy; for almost all the democratic convulsions which have agitated the world have been directed by nobles.

A privileged body can never satisfy the ambition of all its members; it has always more talents and more passions than it can find places to content and to employ; so that a considerable number of individuals are usually to be met with, who are inclined to attack those very privileges, which they find it impossible to turn to their own account.

I do not, then, assert that *all* the members of the legal profession are at *all* times the friends of order and the opponents of innovation, but merely that most of them usually are so. In a community in which lawyers are allowed to occupy, without opposition, that high station which naturally belongs to them, their general spirit will be eminently conservative and anti-democratic. When an aristocracy excludes the leaders of that profession from its ranks, it excites enemies which are the more formidable to its security as they are independent of the nobility by their industrious pursuits; and they feel themselves to be its equal in point of intelligence, although they enjoy less opulence and less power. But whenever an aristocracy consents to impart some of its privileges to these same individuals, the two classes coalesce very readily, and assume, as it were, the consistency of a single order of family interests.

I am, in like manner, inclined to believe that a monarch will always be able to convert legal practitioners into the most serviceable instruments of his authority. There is a far greater affinity between this class of individuals and the executive power, than there is between them and the people; just as there is a greater natural affinity between the nobles and monarch, than between the nobles and the people, although the higher orders of society have occasionally resisted the prerogative of the crown in concert with the lower classes.

Lawyers are attached to public order beyond every other consideration, and the best security of public order is authority. It must not be forgotten, that if they prize the free institutions of their country much, they nevertheless value the legality of those institutions far more; they are less afraid of tyranny than of arbitrary power; and provided that the legislature takes upon itself to deprive men of their independence, they are not dissatisfied. (*a*)

I am therefore convinced that the prince who, in presence of an encroaching democracy, should endeavor to impair the judicial authority in his dominions, and to diminish the political influence of lawyers, would commit a great mistake. He would let slip the substance of authority to grasp at the shadow. He would act more wisely in introducing men connected with the law into the government; and if he intrusted them with the conduct of a despotic power, bearing some marks of violence, that power would most likely assume the external features of justice and of legality in their hands.

The government of democracy is favorable to the political power of lawyers; for when the wealthy, the noble, and the prince, are excluded from the government, they are sure to occupy the highest stations in their own right, as it were, since they are the only men of information and sagacity, beyond the sphere of the people, who can be the object of the popular choice. If, then, they are led by their tastes to combine with the aristocracy, and to support the crown, they are naturally brought into contact with the people by their interests. They like the government of democracy, without participating in its propensities, and without imitating its weaknesses; whence they derive a twofold authority from it and over it. The people in democratic states does not mistrust the members of the legal profession, because it is well known that they are interested in serving the popular cause; and it listens to them without irritation, because it does not attribute to them any sinister designs. The object of lawyers is not, indeed, to overthrow the institutions of democracy, but they constantly endeavor to give it an impulse which diverts it from its real tendency, by means which are foreign to its nature. Lawyers belong to the people by birth and interest, to the aristocracy by habit and by taste, and they may be looked upon as the natural bond and connecting link of the two great classes of society.

The profession of the law is the only aristocratic element

(*a*) This translation does not accurately convey the meaning of M. de Tocqueville's expression. He says: "Ils craignent moins la tyrannie que l'arbitraire, et pourvu que le législateur se charge lui-même d'enlever aux hommes leur indépendance, ils sont à peu près content."

The more correct rendering would be: They fear tyranny less than arbitrary sway, and provided it is the legislator himself who undertakes to deprive men of their independence, they are almost content." —*Reviser*.

which can be amalgamated without violence with the natural elements of democracy, and which can be advantageously and permanently combined with them. I am not unacquainted with the defects which are inherent in the character of that body of men; but without this admixture of lawyer-like sobriety with the democratic principle, I question whether democratic institutions could long be maintained; and I cannot believe that a republic could subsist at the present time, if the influence of lawyers in public business did not increase in proportion to the power of the people.

This aristocratic character, which I hold to be common to the legal profession, is much more distinctly marked in the United States and in England than in any other country. This proceeds not only from the legal studies of the English and American lawyers, but from the nature of the legislation, and the position which those persons occupy, in the two countries. The English and the Americans have retained the law of precedents; that is to say, they continue to found their legal opinions and the decisions of their courts upon the opinions and decisions of their forefathers. In the mind of an English or an American lawyer, a taste and a reverence for what is old are almost always united to a love of regular and lawful proceedings.

This predisposition has another effect upon the character of the legal profession and upon the general course of society. The English and American lawyers investigate what has been done; the French advocate inquires what should have been done: the former produces precedents; the latter reasons. A French observer is surprised to hear how often an English or American lawyer quotes the opinions of others, and how little he alludes to his own; while the reverse occurs in France. There, the most trifling litigation is never conducted without the introduction of an entire system of ideas peculiar to the counsel employed; and the fundamental principles of law are discussed in order to obtain a perch of land by the decision of the court. This abnegation of his own opinion, and this implicit deference to the opinion of his forefathers, which are common to the English and American lawyer, this subjection of thought which he is obliged to profess, necessarily give him more timid habits and more sluggish inclinations in England and America than in France.

The French codes are often difficult of comprehension, but they can be read by every one; nothing, on the other hand, can be more impenetrable to the uninitiated than a legislation founded upon precedents. The indispensable want of legal assistance which is felt in England and in the United States, and the high opinion which is generally entertained of the ability of the legal profession, tend to separate it more and more from the people, and to place it in a distinct class. The French lawyer is simply a man extensively acquainted with the statutes of his country; but the English or American lawyer resembles the hierophants of Egypt, for, like them, he is the sole interpreter of an occult science.

[The remark that English and American lawyers found their opinions and their decisions upon those of their forefathers, is calculated to excite surprise in an American reader, who supposes that *law*, as a prescribed rule of action, can only be ascertained in cases where the statutes are silent, by reference to the decisions of courts. On the continent, and particularly in France, as the writer of this note learned from the conversation of M. De Tocqueville, the judicial tribunals do not deem themselves bound by any precedents, or by any decisions of their predecessors or of the appellate tribunals. They respect such decisions as the opinions of distinguished men, and they pay no higher regard to their own previous adjudications of any case. It is not easy to perceive how the law can acquire any stability under such a system, or how any individual can ascertain his rights, without a lawsuit. This note should not be concluded without a single remark upon what the author calls an implicit deference to the opinions of our forefathers, and abnegation of our own opinions. The common law consists of principles founded on the common sense of mankind, and adapted to the circumstances of man in civilized society. When these principles are once settled by competent authority, or rather *declared* by such authority, they are supposed to express the common sense and the common justice of the community; and it requires but a moderate share of modesty for any one entertaining a different view of them, to consider that the disinterested and intelligent judges who have declared them, are more likely to be right than he is. Perfection, even in the law, he does not consider attainable by human beings, and the greatest approximation to it is all he expects or desires. Besides, there are very few cases of positive and abstract rule, where it is of any consequence which, of any two or more modifications of it, should be adopted. The great point is, that there should be *a rule* by which conduct may be regulated. Thus, whether in mercantile transactions notice of a default by a principal shall be given to an endorser, or a guarantor, and when and how such notice shall be given, are not so important in themselves, as it is that there should be some rule to which merchants may adapt themselves and their transactions. Statutes cannot or at least do not, prescribe the rules in a large majority of cases. If then they are not drawn from the decision of courts, they will not exist, and men will be wholly at a loss for a guide in the most important transactions of business. Hence the deference paid to legal decisions. But this is not implicit, as the author supposes. The course of reasoning by which the courts have come to their conclusions, is often assailed by the advocate and shown to be fallacious, and the instances are not unfrequent of courts disregarding prior decisions and overruling them when not fairly deducible from sound reason.

Again, the principles of the common law are flexible, and adapt themselves to changes in society, and a well-known maxim in our system, that when the reason of the law ceases, the law itself ceases, has overthrown many an antiquated rule. Within these limits, it is conceived that there is range enough for the exercise of all the reason of the advocate and the judge, without unsettling everything and depriving the conduct of human affairs of all guidance from human authority;—and the talent of our lawyers and courts finds sufficient exercise in applying the principles of one case to facts of another.—*American Editor.*]

The station which lawyers occupy in England and America exercises no less an influence upon their habits and their opinions. The English aristocracy, which has taken care to attract to its sphere whatever is at all analogous to itself, has conferred a high degree of importance and of authority upon the members of the legal profession. In English society lawyers do not occupy the first rank, but they are contented with the station assigned to them; they constitute, as it were, the younger branch of the English aristocracy, and they are attached to their elder brothers, although they do not enjoy all their privileges. The English lawyers consequently mingle the tastes and the ideas of the aristocratic circles in which they move, with the aristocratic interest of their profession.

And indeed the lawyer-like character which I am endeavoring to depict, is most distinctly to be met with in England: there laws are esteemed not so much because they are good, as because they are old; and if it be necessary to modify them in any respect, or to adapt them to the changes which time operates in society, recourse is had to the most inconceivable contrivances in order to uphold the traditionary fabric, and to maintain that nothing has been done which does not square with the intentions, and complete the labors, of former generations. The very individuals who conduct these changes disclaim all intention of innovation, and they had rather resort to absurd expedients than plead guilty of so great a crime. This spirit more especially appertains to the English lawyers; they seem indifferent to the real meaning of what they treat, and they direct all their attention to the letter, seeming inclined to infringe the rules of common sense and of humanity, rather than to swerve one tittle from the law. The English legislation may be compared to the stock of an old tree, upon which lawyers have engrafted the most various shoots, with the hope, that, although their fruits may differ, their foliage at least will be confounded with the venerable trunk which supports them all.

In America there are no nobles or literary men, and the people is apt to mistrust the wealthy; lawyers consequently form the highest political class, and the most cultivated circle of society. They have therefore nothing to gain by innovation, which adds a conservative interest to their natural taste for public order. If I were asked where I place the American aristocracy, I should reply without hesitation, that it is not composed of the rich, who are united together by no common tie, but that it occupies the judicial bench and the bar.

The more we reflect upon all that occurs in the United States, the more shall we be persuaded that the lawyers, as a body, form the most powerful, if not the only counterpoise to the democratic element. In that country we perceive how eminently the legal profession is qualified by its powers, and even by its defects, to neutralize the vices which are inherent in popular government. When the American people is intoxicated by passion, or carried away by the impetuosity of its ideas, it is checked and stopped by the almost invisible influence of its legal counsellors, who secretly oppose their aristocratic propensities to its democratic instincts, their superstitious attachment to what is antique to its love of novelty, their narrow views to its immense designs, and their habitual procrastination to its ardent impatience.

The courts of justice are the most visible organs by which the legal profession is enabled to control the democracy. The judge is a lawyer, who, independently of the taste for regularity and order which he has contracted in the study of legislation, derives an additional love of stability from his own inalienable functions. His legal attainments have already raised him to a distinguished rank among his fellow-citizens; his political power completes the distinction of his station, and gives him the inclinations natural to privileged classes.

Armed with the power of declaring the laws to be unconstitutional,* the American magistrate perpetually interferes in political affairs. He cannot force the people to make laws, but at least he can oblige it not to disobey its own enactments, or to act inconsistently with its own principles. I am aware that a secret tendency to diminish the judicial power exists in the United States; and by most of the constitutions of the several states, the government can, upon the demand of the two houses of the legislature, remove the judges from their station. By some other constitutions the members of the tribunals are elected, and they are even subjected to frequent

* See chapter vi., p. 94, on the judicial power in the United States.

re-elections. I venture to predict that these innovations will sooner or later be attended with fatal consequences; and that it will be found out at some future period, that the attack which is made upon the judicial power has affected the democratic republic itself.

It must not, however, be supposed that the legal spirit of which I have been speaking has been confined in the United States to the courts of justice; it extends far beyond them. As the lawyers constitute the only enlightened class which the people does not mistrust, they are naturally called upon to occupy most of the public stations. They fill the legislative assemblies, and they conduct the administration; they consequently exercise a powerful influence upon the formation of the law, and upon its execution. The lawyers are, however, obliged to yield to the current of public opinion, which is too strong for them to resist it; but it is easy to find indications of what their conduct would be, if they were free to act as they chose. The Americans who have made such copious innovations in their political legislation, have introduced very sparing alterations in their civil laws, and that with great difficulty, although those laws are frequently repugnant to their social condition. The reason of this is, that in matters of civil law the majority is obliged to defer to the authority of the legal profession, and that the American lawyers are disinclined to innovate when they are left to their own choice.

It is curious for a Frenchman, accustomed to a very different state of things, to hear the perpetual complaints which are made in the United States, against the stationary propensities of legal men, and their prejudices in favor of existing institutions.

The influence of the legal habits which are common in America extends beyond the limits I have just pointed out. Scarcely any question arises in the United States which does not become, sooner or later, a subject of judicial debate; hence all parties are obliged to borrow the ideas, and even the language, usual in judicial proceedings, in their daily controversies. As most public men are, or have been, legal practitioners, they introduce the customs and technicalities of their profession into the affairs of the country. The jury extends this habitude to all classes. The language of the law thus becomes, in some measure, a vulgar tongue; the spirit of the law, which is produced in the schools and courts of justice, gradually penetrates beyond their walls into the bosom of society, where it descends to the lowest classes, so that the whole people contracts the habits and the tastes of the magistrate. The lawyers of the United States form a party which is but little feared and scarcely perceived, which has no badge peculiar to itself, which adapts itself with great flexibility to the exigencies of the time, and accommodates itself to all the movements of the social body: but this party extends over the whole community, and it penetrates into all classes of society; it acts upon the country imperceptibly, but it finally fashions it to suit its purposes.

TRIAL BY JURY IN THE UNITED STATES CONSIDERED AS A POLITICAL INSTITUTION.

Trial by Jury, which is one of the Instruments of the Sovereignty of the People, deserves to be compared with the other Laws which establish that sovereignty.—Composition of the Jury in the United States.—Effect of Trial by Jury upon the national Character.—It educates the People.—It tends to establish the Authority of the Magistrates, and to extend a knowledge of Law among the People.

SINCE I have been led by my subject to recur to the administration of justice in the United States, I will not pass over this point without adverting to the institution of the jury. Trial by jury may be considered in two separate points of view: as a judicial, and as a political institution. If it entered into my present purpose to inquire how far trial by jury (more especially in civil cases) contributes to ensure the best administration of justice, I admit that its utility might be contested. As the jury was first introduced at a time when society was in an uncivilized state, and when courts of justice were merely called upon to decide on the evidence of facts, it is not an easy task to adapt it to the wants of a highly civilized community, when the mutual relations of men are multiplied to a surprising extent, and have assumed the enlightened and intellectual character of the age.*

* The investigation of trial by jury as a judicial institution, and the appreciation of its effects in the United States, together with the advantages the Americans have derived from it, would suffice to form a book, and a book upon a very useful and curious subject. The state of Louisiana would in particular afford the curious phenomenon of a French and English legislation, as well as a French and English population, which are generally combining with each other. See the "Digeste des Lois de la Louisiane," in two volumes; and the "Traité sur les Regles des Actions civiles," printed in French and English at New Orleans in 1830.

My present object is to consider the jury as a political institution; and any other course would divert me from my subject. Of trial by jury, considered as a judicial institution, I shall here say but very few words. When the English adopted trial by jury they were a semi-barbarous people; they are become, in course of time, one of the most enlightened nations of the earth; and their attachment to this institution seems to have increased with their increasing cultivation. They soon spread beyond their insular boundaries to every corner of the habitable globe; some have formed colonies, others independent states; the mother-country has maintained its monarchical constitution; many of its offspring have founded powerful republics; but wherever the English have been, they have boasted of the privilege of trial by jury.* They have established it, or hastened to re-establish it, in all their settlements. A judicial institution which obtains the suffrages of a great people for so long a series of ages, which is zealously renewed at every epoch of civilisation, in all the climates of the earth, and under every form of human government, cannot be contrary to the spirit of justice.†

* All the English and American jurists are unanimous upon this head. Mr. Story, judge of the supreme court of the United States, speaks, in his treatise on the federal constitution, of the advantages of trial by jury in civil cases: "The inestimable privilege of a trial by jury in civil cases—a privilege scarcely inferior to that in criminal cases, which is counted by all persons to be essential to political and civil liberty"........(Story, book iii., ch. xxxviii.)

† If it were our province to point out the utility of the jury as a judicial institution in this place, much might be said, and the following arguments might be brought forward among others:—

By introducing the jury into the business of the courts, you are enabled to diminish the number of judges; which is a very great advantage. When judges are very numerous, death is perpetually thinning the ranks of the judicial functionaries, and laying places vacant for new comers. The ambition of the magistrates is therefore continually excited, and they are naturally made dependant upon the will of the majority, or the individual who fills up vacant appointments: the officers of the courts then rise like the officers of an army. This state of things is entirely contrary to the sound administration of justice, and to the intentions of the legislator. The office of a judge is made inalienable in order that he may remain independent; but of what advantage is it that his independence is protected, if he be tempted to sacrifice it of his own accord? When judges are very numerous, many of them must necessarily be incapable of performing their important duties; for a great magistrate is a man of no common powers: and I am inclined to believe that a half enlightened tribunal is the worst of all instruments for obtaining those objects which it is the purpose of courts of justice to accomplish. For my own part, I had rather submit the decision of a case to ignorant jurors directed by a skilful judge, than to judges, a

I turn, however, from this part of the subject. To look upon the jury as a mere judicial institution, is to confine our attention to a very narrow view of it; for, however great its influence may be upon the decisions of the law-courts, that influence is very subordinate to the powerful effects which it produces on the destinies of the community at large. The jury is above all a political institution, and it must be regarded in this light in order to be duly appreciated.

By the jury, I mean a certain number of citizens chosen indiscriminately, and invested with a temporary right of judging. Trial by jury, as applied to the repression of crime, appears to me to introduce an eminently republican element into the government, upon the following grounds:—

The institution of the jury may be aristocratic or democratic, according to the class of society from which the jurors are selected; but it always preserves its republican character, inasmuch as it places the real direction of society in the hands of the governed, or of a portion of the governed, instead of leaving it under the authority of the government. Force is never more than a transient element of success; and after force comes the notion of right. A government which should only be able to crush its enemies upon a field of battle, would very soon be destroyed. The true sanction of political laws is to be found in penal legislation, and if that sanction be wanting, the law will sooner or later lose its cogency. He who punishes infractions of the law is therefore the real master of society. Now, the institution of the jury raises the people itself, or at least a class of citizens, to the bench of judicial authority. The institution of the jury consequently invests the people, or that class of citizens, with the direction of society.*

majority of whom are imperfectly acquainted with jurisprudence and with the laws.

[I venture to remind the reader, lest this note should appear somewhat redundant to an English eye, that the jury is an institution which has only been naturalized in France within the present century; that it is even now exclusively applied to those criminal causes which come before the courts of assize, or to the prosecutions of the public press; and that the judges and counsellors of the numerous local tribunals of France—forming a body of many thousand judicial functionaries—try all civil causes, appeals from criminal causes, and minor offences, without the jury.—*Translator's Note.*]

* An important remark must however be made. Trial by jury does unquestionably invest the people with a general control over the actions of citizens, but it does not furnish means of exercising this control in all cases, or with an absolute authority. When an absolute monarch has the right of trying offences by his representatives, the fate of the

In England the jury is returned from the aristocratic portion of the nation,* the aristocracy makes the laws, applies the laws, and punishes all infractions of the laws; everything is established upon a consistent footing, and England may with truth be said to constitute an aristocratic republic. In the United States the same system is applied to the whole people. Every American citizen is qualified to be an elector, a juror, and is eligible to office.† The system of the jury, as it is understood in America, appears to me to be as direct and as extreme a consequence of the sovereignty of the people, as universal suffrage. These institutions are two instruments of equal power, which contribute to the supremacy of the majority. All the sovereigns who have chosen to govern by their own authority, and to direct society instead of obeying its direction, have destroyed or enfeebled the institution of the jury. The monarchs of the house of Tudor sent to prison jurors who refused to convict, and Napoleon caused them to be returned by his agents.

However clear most of these truths may seem to be, they do not command universal assent, and in France, at least, the institution of trial by jury is still very imperfectly understood. If the question arise as to the proper qualification of jurors, it is confined to a discussion of the intelligence and knowledge of the citizens who may be returned, as if the jury was merely a judicial institution. This appears to me to be the least part of the subject. The jury is pre-eminently a political institution; it must be regarded as one form of the sovereignty of the people; when that sovereignty is repudiated, it must be rejected; or it must be adapted to the laws by

prisoner is, as it were, decided beforehand. But even if the people were predisposed to convict, the composition and the non-responsibility of the jury would still afford some chances favorable to the protection of innocence.

* [In France, the qualification of the jurors is the same as the electoral qualification, namely, the payment of 200 francs per annum in direct taxes: they are chosen by lot. In England they are returned by the sheriff; the qualifications of jurors were raised to 10*l.* per annum in England, and 6*l.* in Wales, of freehold land or copyhold, by the statute W. and M., c. 24: leaseholders for a time determinable upon life or lives, of the clear yearly value of 20*l.* per annum over and above the rent reserved, are qualified to serve on juries; and jurors in the courts of Westminster and city of London must be householders, and possessed of real and personal estates of the value of 100*l.* The qualifications, however, prescribed in different statutes, vary according to the object for which the jury is impannelled. See Blackstone's Commentaries, b. iii., c. 23.—*Translator's Note.*]

† See Appendix Q.

which that sovereignty is established. The jury is that portion of the nation to which the execution of the laws is intrusted, as the houses of parliament constitute that part of the nation which makes the laws; and in order that society may be governed with consistency and uniformity, the list of citizens qualified to serve on juries must increase and diminish with the list of electors. This I hold to be the point of view most worthy of the attention of the legislator; and all that remains is merely accessary.

I am so entirely convinced that the jury is pre-eminently a political institution, that I still consider it in this light when it is applied in civil causes. Laws are always unstable unless they are founded upon the manners of a nation: manners are the only durable and resisting power in a people. When the jury is reserved for criminal offences, the people only sees its occasional action in certain particular cases; the ordinary course of life goes on without its interference, and it is considered as an instrument, but not as the only instrument, of obtaining justice. This is true *à fortiori* when the jury is only applied to certain criminal causes.

When, on the contrary, the influence of the jury is extended to civil causes, its application is constantly palpable; it affects all the interests of the community; every one co-operates in its work: it thus penetrates into all the usages of life, it fashions the human mind to its peculiar forms, and is gradually associated with the idea of justice itself.

The institution of the jury, if confined to criminal causes, is always in danger; but when once it is introduced into civil proceedings, it defies the aggressions of time and of man. If it had been as easy to remove the jury from the manners as from the laws of England, it would have perished under Henry VIII. and Elizabeth; and the civil jury did in reality, at that period, save the liberties of the country. In whatever manner the jury be applied, it cannot fail to exercise a powerful influence upon the national character; but this influence is prodigiously increased when it is introduced into civil causes. The jury, and more especially the civil jury, serves to communicate the spirit of the judges to the minds of all the citizens; and this spirit, with the habits which attend it, is the soundest preparation for free institutions. It imbues all classes with a respect for the thing judged, and with the notion of right. If these two elements be removed, the love of independence is reduced to a mere destructive passion. It teaches men to practise equity; every man learns to judge his neighbor as he would himself be judged: and this is especially true of the jury in civil causes; for, while the number of persons who have reason to apprehend a criminal prosecution is small, every one is liable to have a civil action brought against him. The jury teaches every man not to recoil before the responsibility of his own actions, and impresses him with that manly confidence without which political virtue cannot exist. It invests each citizen with a kind of magistracy; it makes them all feel the duties which they are bound to discharge toward society; and the part which they take in the government. By obliging men to turn their attention to affairs which are not exclusively their own, it rubs off that individual egotism which is the rust of society.

The jury contributes most powerfully to form the judgment, and to increase the natural intelligence of a people; and this is, in my opinion, its greatest advantage. It may be regarded as a gratuitous public school ever open, in which every juror learns to exercise his rights, enters into daily communication with the most learned and enlightened members of the upper classes, and becomes practically acquainted with the laws of his country, which are brought within the reach of his capacity by the efforts of the bar, the advice of the judge, and even by the passions of the parties. I think that the practical intelligence and political good sense of the Americans are mainly attributable to the long use which they have made of the jury in civil causes.

I do not know whether the jury is useful to those who are in litigation; but I am certain it is highly beneficial to those who decide the litigation: and I look upon it as one of the most efficacious means for the education of the people, which society can employ.

What I have hitherto said, applies to all nations; but the remark I am now about to make, is peculiar to the Americans and to democratic peoples. I have already observed that in democracies the members of the legal profession, and the magistrates, constitute the only aristocratic body which can check the irregularities of the people. This aristocracy is invested with no physical power; but it exercises its conservative influence upon the minds of men: and the most abundant source of its authority is the institution of the civil jury. In criminal causes, when society is armed against a single individual, the jury is apt to look upon the judge as the passive instrument of social power, and to mistrust his advice. Moreover, criminal causes are entirely founded upon the evidence of facts which common sense can readily appreciate; upon this ground the judge and the jury are equal. Such, however, is not the case in civil causes; then the judge appears as a disinterested arbiter between the conflicting passions of the parties. The jurors look up to him with confidence, and listen to him with respect, for in this instance their intelligence is completely under the control of his learning. It is the judge who sums up the various arguments with which their memory has been wearied out, and who guides them through the devious course of the proceedings; he points their attention to the exact question of fact, which they are called upon to solve, and he puts the answer to the question of law into their mouths. His influence upon their verdict is almost unlimited.

If I am called upon to explain why I am but little moved by the arguments derived from the ignorance of jurors in civil causes, I reply, that in these proceedings, whenever the question to be solved is not a mere question of fact, the jury has only the semblance of a judicial body. The jury sanctions the decisions of the judge; they, by the authority of society which they represent, and he, by that of reason and of law.*

In England and in America the judges exercise an influence upon criminal trials which the French judges have never possessed. The reason of this difference may easily be discovered; the English and American magistrates establish their authority in civil causes, and only transfer it afterward to tribunals of another kind, where that authority was not acquired. In some cases (and they are frequently the most important ones), the American judges have the right of deciding causes alone.† Upon these occasions they are, accidentally, placed in the position which the French judges habitually occupy: but they are still surrounded by the reminiscence of the jury, and their judgment has almost as much authority as the voice of the community at large, represented by that institution. Their influence extends beyond the limits of the courts; in the recreations of private life, as well as in the turmoil of public business, abroad and in the legislative assemblies, the American judge is constantly surrounded by men who are accustomed to regard his intelligence as superior to their own; and after having exercised his power in the decision of causes, he continues to influence the habits of thought, and the character of the individuals who took a part in his judgment.

* See Appendix R.

† The federal judges decide upon their own authority almost all the questions most important to the country.

[The remark in the text, that " in some cases, and they are frequently the most important ones, the American judges have the right of deciding causes alone," and the author's note, that " the federal judges decide, upon their own authority, almost all the questions most important to the country," seem to require explanation in consequence of their connexion with the context in which the author is speaking of the trial by jury. They seem to imply that there are some cases which ought to be tried by jury, that are decided by the judges. It is believed that the learned author, although a distinguished advocate in France, never thoroughly comprehended the grand divisions of our complicated system of law, in civil cases. *First*, is the distinction between cases in equity and those in which the rules of the common law govern.—Those in equity are always decided by the judge or judges, who *may*, however, send questions of fact to be tried in the common law courts by a jury. But as a general rule this is entirely in the discretion of the equity judge. *Second*, in cases at common law, there are questions of fact and questions of law :—the former are invariably tried by a jury, the latter, whether presented in the course of a jury trial, or by pleading, in which the facts are admitted, are always decided by the judges.

Third, cases of admiralty jurisdiction, and proceedings *in rem* of an analogous nature, are decided by the judges without the intervention of a jury. The cases in this last class fall within the peculiar jurisdiction of the federal courts, and, with this exception, the federal judges do not decide upon their own authority any questions, which, if presented in the state courts, would not also be decided by the judges of those courts. The supreme court of the United States, from the nature of its institution as almost wholly an appellant court, is called on to decide merely questions of law, and in no case can that court decide a question of fact, unless it arises in suits peculiar to equity or admiralty jurisdiction. Indeed the author's original note is more correct than the translation. It is as follows : " Les juges fédéraux tranchent presque toujours seuls les questions qui touchent de plus près au *gouvernement* du pays." And it is very true that the supreme court of the United States, in particular, decides those questions which most nearly affect the *government* of the country, because those are the very questions which arise upon the constitutionality of the laws of congress and of the several states, the final and conclusive determination of which is vested in that tribunal.—*American Editor.*]

The jury, then, which seems to restrict the rights of magistracy, does in reality consolidate its power; and in no country are the judges so powerful as there where the people partakes their privileges. It is more especially by means of the jury in civil causes that the American magistrates imbue all classes of society with the spirit of their profession. Thus the jury, which is the most energetic means of making the people rule, is also the most efficacious means of teaching it to rule well.

CHAPTER XVII.

PRINCIPAL CAUSES WHICH TEND TO MAINTAIN THE DEMOCRATIC REPUBLIC IN THE UNITED STATES.

A DEMOCRATIC republic subsists in the United States; and the principal object of this book has been to account for the fact of its existence. Several of the causes which contribute to maintain the institutions of America have been voluntarily passed by, or only hinted at, as I was borne along by my subject. Others I have been unable to discuss; and those on which I have dwelt most, are, as it were, buried in the details of the former part of this work.

I think, therefore, that before I proceed to speak of the future, I cannot do better than collect within a small compass the reasons which best explain the present. In this retrospective chapter I shall be succinct; for I shall take care to remind the reader very summarily of what he already knows; and I shall only select the most prominent of those facts which I have not yet pointed out.

All the causes which contribute to the maintenance of the democratic republic in the United States are reducible to three heads:

I. The peculiar and accidental situation in which Providence has placed the Americans.

II. The laws.

III. The manners and customs of the people.

ACCIDENTAL OR PROVIDENTIAL CAUSES WHICH CONTRIBUTE TO THE MAINTENANCE OF THE DEMOCRATIC REPUBLIC IN THE UNITED STATES.

The Union has no Neighbors.—No Metropolis.—The Americans have had the Chances of Birth in their favor.—America an empty country.—How this circumstance contributes powerfully to the Maintenance of the democratic Republic in America.—How the American Wilds are Peopled.—Avidity of the Anglo-Americans in taking Possession of the Solitudes of the New World.—Influence of physical Prosperity upon the political Opinions of the Americans.

A THOUSAND circumstances, independent of the will of man, concur to facilitate the maintenance of a democratic republic in the United States. Some of these peculiarities are known, the others may easily be pointed out; but I shall confine myself to the most prominent among them.

The Americans have no neighbors, and consequently they have no great wars, or financial crises, or inroads, or conquests to dread; they require neither great taxes, nor great armies, nor great generals; and they have nothing to fear from a scourge which is more formidable to republics than all these evils combined, namely, military glory. It is impossible to deny the inconceivable influence which military glory exercises upon the spirit of a nation. General Jackson, whom the Americans have twice elected to be the head of their government, is a man of violent temper and mediocre talents; no one circumstance in the whole course of his career ever proved that he is qualified to govern a free people; and indeed the majority of the enlightened classes of the Union has always been opposed to him. But he was raised to the presidency, and has been maintained in that lofty station, solely by the recollection of a victory which he gained, twenty years ago, under the walls of New Orleans; a victory which was, however, a very ordinary achievement, and which could only be remembered in a country where battles are rare. Now the people who are thus carried away by the illusions of glory, are unquestionably the most cold and calculating, the most unmilitary (if I may use the expression), and the most prosaic of all the peoples of the earth.

America has no great capital city,* whose influence is di-

* The United States have no metropolis; but they already contain several very large cities. Philadelphia reckoned 161,000 inhabitants, and New York 202,000, in the year 1830. The lower orders which inhabit these cities constitute a rabble even more formidable than the populace of European towns. They consist of freed blacks in the first place, who are condemned by the laws and by public opinion, to an hereditary state of misery and degradation. They also contain a multitude of Europeans who have been driven to the shores of the New World by their misfortunes or their misconduct; and these men inoculate the United States with all our vices, without bringing with them any of those interests which counteract their baneful influence. As inhabitants of a country where they have no civil rights, they are ready to turn all the passions which agitate the community to their own advantage; thus, within the last few months serious riots have broken out in Philadelphia and in New York. Disturbances of this kind are unknown in the rest of the country, which is nowise alarmed by them, because the population of the cities has hitherto exercised neither power nor influence over the rural districts.

Nevertheless, I look upon the size of certain American cities, and especially on the nature of their population, as a real danger which threatens the future security of the democratic republics of the New World: and I venture to predict that they will perish from this cir-

rectly or indirectly felt over the whole extent of the country, which I hold to be one of the first causes of the maintenance of republican institutions in the United States. In cities, men cannot be prevented from concerting together, and from awakening a mutual excitement which prompts sudden and passionate resolutions. Cities may be looked upon as large assemblies, of which all the inhabitants are members; their populace exercises a prodigious influence upon the magistrates, and frequently executes its own wishes without their intervention.

To subject the provinces to the metropolis, is therefore not only to place the destiny of the empire in the hands of a portion of the community, which may be reprobated as unjust, but to place it in the hands of a populace acting under its own impulses, which must be avoided as dangerous. The preponderance of capital cities is therefore a serious blow upon the representative system; and it exposes modern republics to the same defect as the republics of antiquity, which all perished from not being acquainted with that system.

It would be easy for me to adduce a great number of secondary causes which have contributed to establish, and which concur to maintain, the democratic republic of the United States. But I discern two principal circumstances among these favorable elements, which I hasten to point out. I have already observed that the origin of the American settlements may be looked upon as the first and most efficacious cause to which the present prosperity of the United States may be attributed. The Americans had the chances of birth in their favor; and their forefathers imported that equality of conditions into the country, whence the democratic republic has very naturally taken its rise. Nor was this all they did; for besides this republican condition of society, the early settlers bequeathed to their descendants those customs, manners, and opinions, which contribute most to the success of a republican form of government. When I reflect upon the consequences of this primary circumstance, methinks I see the destiny of America embodied in the first puritan who landed on those shores, just as the human race was represented by the first man.

The chief circumstance which has favored the establishment and the maintenance of a democratic republic in the

cumstance, unless the government succeed in creating an armed force, which, while it remains under the control of the majority of the nation, will be independent of the town population, and able to repress its excesses.

the United States, is the nature of the territory which the Americans inhabit. Their ancestors gave them the love of equality and of freedom: but God himself gave them the means of remaining equal and free, by placing them upon a boundless continent, which is open to their exertions. General prosperity is favorable to the stability of all governments, but more particularly of a democratic constitution, which depends upon the disposition of the majority, and more particularly of that portion of the community which is most exposed to feel the pressure of want. When the people rules, it must be rendered happy, or it will overturn the state: and misery is apt to stimulate it to those excesses to which ambition rouses kings. The physical causes, independent of the laws, which contribute to promote general prosperity, are more numerous in America than they have ever been in any other country in the world, at any other period of history. In the United States, not only is legislation democratic, but nature herself favors the cause of the people.

In what part of human tradition can be found anything at all similar to that which is occurring under our eyes in North America? The celebrated communities of antiquity were all founded in the midst of hostile nations, which they were obliged to subjugate before they could flourish in their place. Even the moderns have found, in some parts of South America, vast regions inhabited by a people of inferior civilisation, but which occupied and cultivated the soil. To found their new states, it was necessary to extirpate or to subdue a numerous population, until civilisation has been made to blush for their success. But North America was only inhabited by wandering tribes, who took no thought of the natural riches of the soil: and that vast country was still, properly speaking, an empty continent, a desert land awaiting its inhabitants.

Everything is extraordinary in America, the social condition of the inhabitants, as well as the laws; but the soil upon which these institutions are founded is more extraordinary than all the rest. When man was first placed upon the earth by the Creator, that earth was inexhaustible in its youth; but man was weak and ignorant: and when he had learned to explore the treasures which it contained, hosts of his fellow-creatures covered its surface, and he was obliged to earn an asylum for repose and for freedom by the sword. At that same period North America was discovered, as if it had been kept in reserve by the Deity, and had just risen from beneath the waters of the deluge.

That continent still presents, as it did in the primeval time, rivers which rise from never-failing sources, green and moist solitudes, and fields which the ploughshare of the husbandman has never turned. In this state it is offered to man, not in the barbarous and isolated condition of the early ages, but to a being who is already in possession of the most potent secrets of the natural world, who is united to his fellow-men, and instructed by the experience of fifty centuries. At this very time thirteen millions of civilized Europeans are peaceably spreading over those fertile plains, with whose resources and whose extent they are not yet accurately acquainted. Three or four thousand soldiers drive the wandering races of the aborigines before them; these are followed by the pioneers, who pierce the woods, scare off the beasts of prey, explore the courses of the inland streams, and make ready the triumphal procession of civilisation across the waste.

The favorable influence of the temporal prosperity of America upon the institutions of that country has been so often described by others, and adverted to by myself, that I shall not enlarge upon it beyond the addition of a few facts. An erroneous notion is generally entertained, that the deserts of America are peopled by European emigrants, who annually disembark upon the coasts of the New World, while the American population increases and multiplies upon the soil which its forefathers tilled. The European settler, however, usually arrives in the United States without friends, and sometimes without resources; in order to subsist he is obliged to work for hire, and he rarely proceeds beyond that belt of industrious population which adjoins the ocean. The desert cannot be explored without capital or credit, and the body must be accustomed to the rigors of a new climate before it can be exposed to the chances of forest life. It is the Americans themselves who daily quit the spots which gave them birth, to acquire extensive domains in a remote country. Thus the European leaves his country for the transatlantic shores; and the American, who is born on that very coast, plunges into the wilds of central America. This double emigration is incessant: it begins in the remotest parts of Europe, it crosses the Atlantic ocean, and it advances over the solitudes of the New World. Millions of men are marching at once toward the same horizon; their language, their religion, their manners differ, their object is the same. The gifts of fortune are promised in the west, and to the west they bend their course.

No event can be compared with this continuous removal

of the human race, except perhaps those irruptions which preceded the fall of the Roman Empire. Then, as well as now, generations of men were impelled forward in the same direction to meet and struggle on the same spot; but the designs of Providence were not the same; then, every new comer was the harbinger of destruction and of death; now, every adventurer brings with him the elements of prosperity and of life. The future still conceals from us the ulterior consequences of this emigration of the American toward the west; but we can hardly apprehend its more immediate results. As a portion of the inhabitants annually leave the states in which they were born, the population of these states increases very slowly, although they have long been established: thus in Connecticut, which only contains 59 inhabitants to the square mile, the population has not been increased by more than one quarter in forty years, while that of England has been augmented by one third in the lapse of the same period. The European emigrant always lands, therefore, in a country which is but half full, and where hands are in request: he becomes a workman in easy circumstances; his son goes to seek his fortune in unpeopled regions, and he becomes a rich landowner. The former amasses the capital which the latter invests, and the stranger as well as the native is unacquainted with want.

The laws of the United States are extremely favorable to the division of property; but a cause which is more powerful than the laws prevents property from being divided to excess.* This is very perceptible in the states which are beginning to be thickly peopled; Massachusetts is the most populous part of the Union, but it contains only 80 inhabitants to the square mile, which is much less than in France, where 162 are reckoned to the same extent of country. But in Massachusetts estates are very rarely divided; the eldest son takes the land, and the others go to seek their fortune in the desert. The law has abolished the right of primogeniture, but circumstances have concurred to re-establish it under a form of which none can complain, and by which no just rights are impaired.

A single fact will suffice to show the prodigious number of individuals who leave New England, in this manner, to settle themselves in the wilds. We were assured in 1830, that thirty-six of the members of congress were born in the little

* In New England the estates are exceedingly small, but they are rarely subjected to farther division.

state of Connecticut. The population of Connecticut, which constitutes only one forty-third part of that of the United States, thus furnished one-eighth of the whole body of representatives. The state of Connecticut, however, only sends five delegates to congress; and the thirty-one others sit for the new western states. If these thirty-one individuals had remained in Connecticut, it is probable that instead of becoming rich landowners they would have remained humble laborers, that they would have lived in obscurity without being able to rise into public life, and that, far from becoming useful members of the legislature, they might have been unruly citizens.

These reflections do not escape the observation of the Americans any more than of ourselves. "It cannot be doubted," says Chancellor Kent in his Treatise on American Law, "that the division of landed estates must produce great evils when it is carried to such excess that each parcel of land is insufficient to support a family; but these disadvantages have never been felt in the United States, and many generations must elapse before they can be felt. The extent of our inhabited territory, the abundance of adjacent land, and the continual stream of emigration flowing from the shores of the Atlantic toward the interior of the country, suffice as yet, and will long suffice, to prevent the parcelling out of estates."

It is difficult to describe the rapacity with which the American rushes forward to secure the immense booty which fortune proffers to him. In the pursuit he fearlessly braves the arrow of the Indian and the distempers of the forest; he is unimpressed by the silence of the woods; the approach of beasts of prey does not disturb him; for he is goaded onward by a passion more intense than the love of life. Before him lies a boundless continent, and he urges onward as if time pressed, and he was afraid of finding no room for his exertions. I have spoken of the emigration from the older states, but how shall I describe that which takes place from the more recent ones? Fifty years have scarcely elapsed since that of Ohio was founded; the greater part of its inhabitants were not born within its confines; its capital has only been built thirty years, and its territory is still covered by an immense extent of uncultivated fields; nevertheless, the population of Ohio is already proceeding westward, and most of the settlers who descend to the fertile savannahs of Illinois are citizens of Ohio. These men left their first country to improve their condition; they quit their resting-place to meliorate it still more; fortune awaits them everywhere, but happiness they cannot attain. The desire of prosperity has become an ardent and restless passion in their minds, which grows by what it gains. They early broke the ties which bound them to their natal earth, and they have contracted no fresh ones on their way. Emigration was at first necessary to them as a means of subsistence; and it soon becomes a sort of game of chance, which they pursue for the emotions it excites, as much as for the gain it procures.

Sometimes the progress of man is so rapid that the desert reappears behind him. The woods stoop to give him a passage, and spring up again when he has passed. It is not uncommon in crossing the new states of the west to meet with deserted dwellings in the midst of the wilds; the traveller frequently discovers the vestiges of a log-house in the most solitary retreats, which bear witness to the power, and no less to the inconstancy of man. In these abandoned fields, and over those ruins of a day, the primeval forest soon scatters a fresh vegetation; the beasts resume the haunts which were once their own; and nature covers the traces of man's path with branches and with flowers, which obliterate his evanescent track.

I remember that in crossing one of the woodland districts which still cover the state of New York, I reached the shore of a lake, which was embosomed with forests coeval with the world. A small island, covered with woods, whose thick foliage concealed its banks, rose from the centre of the waters. Upon the shores of the lake no object attested the presence of man, except a column of smoke which might be seen on the horizon rising from the tops of the trees to the clouds, and seeming to hang from heaven rather than to be mounting to the sky. An Indian shallop was hauled up on the sand, which tempted me to visit the islet that had at first attracted my attention, and in a few minutes I set foot upon its banks. The whole island formed one of those delicious solitudes of the New World, which almost lead civilized man to regret the haunts of the savage. A luxuriant vegetation bore witness to the incomparable fruitfulness of the soil. The deep silence, which is common to the wilds of North America, was only broken by the hoarse cooing of the wood-pigeon and the tapping of the woodpecker upon the bark of trees. I was far from supposing that this spot had ever been inhabited, so completely did nature seem to be left to her own caprices; but when I reached the centre of the isle I thought that I discovered some traces of man. I then proceeded to examine the surrounding objects with care, and I soon perceived that an European had undoubtedly been led to seek a refuge in this retreat. Yet what changes had taken place in the scene of his labors! The logs which he had hastily hewn to build himself a shed had sprouted afresh; the very props were intertwined with living verdure, and his cabin was transformed into a bower In the midst of these shrubs a few stones were to be seen, blackened with fire and sprinkled with thin ashes; here the hearth had no doubt been, and the chimney in falling had covered it with rubbish. I stood for some time in silent admiration of the exuberance of nature and the littleness of man; and when I was obliged to leave that enchanting solitude, I exclaimed with melancholy, "Are ruins, then, already here?"

In Europe we are wont to look upon a restless disposition, an unbounded desire of riches, and an excessive love of independence, as propensities very formidable to society. Yet these are the very elements which ensure a long and peaceful duration to the republics of America. Without these unquiet passions the population would collect in certain spots, and would soon be subject to wants like those of the Old World, which it is difficult to satisfy; for such is the present good fortune of the New World, that the vices of its inhabitants are scarcely less favorable to society than their virtues. These circumstances exercise a great influence on the estimation in which human actions are held in the two hemispheres. The Americans frequently term what we should call cupidity a laudable industry; and they blame as faint-heartedness what we consider to be the virtue of moderate desires.

In France simple tastes, orderly manners, domestic affections, and the attachment which men feel to the place of their birth, are looked upon as great guarantees of the tranquillity and happiness of the state. But in America nothing seems to be more prejudicial to society than these virtues. The French Canadians, who have faithfully preserved the traditions of their pristine manners, are already embarrassed for room upon their small territory; and this little community, which has so recently begun to exist, will shortly be a prey to the calamities incident to old nations. In Canada the most enlightened, patriotic, and humane inhabitants, make extraordinary efforts to render the people dissatisfied with those simple enjoyments which still content it. There the seductions of wealth are vaunted with as much zeal, as the charms of an honest but limited income in the Old World; and more exertions are made to excite the passions of the citizens there than to calm them elsewhere. If we listen to the eulogies, we shall hear that nothing is more praiseworthy than to exchange the pure and homely pleasures which even the poor man tastes in his own country, for the dull delights of prosperity under a foreign sky; to leave the patrimonial hearth, and the turf beneath which his forefathers sleep; in short, to abandon the living and the dead in quest of fortune.

At the present time America presents a field for human effort, far more extensive than any sum of labor which can be applied to work it. In America, too much knowledge cannot be diffused; for all knowledge, while it may serve him who possesses it, turns also to the advantage of those who are without it. New wants are not to be feared, since they can be satisfied without difficulty; the growth of human passions need not be dreaded, since all passions may find an easy and a legitimate object: nor can men be put in possession of too much freedom, since they are scarcely ever tempted to misuse their liberties.

The American republics of the present day are like companies of adventurers, formed to explore in common the waste lands of the New World, and busied in a flourishing trade. The passions which agitate the Americans most deeply, are not their political, but their commercial passions; or, to speak more correctly, they introduce the habits they contract in business into their political life. They love order, without which affairs do not prosper; and they set an especial value upon a regular conduct, which is the foundation of a solid business; they prefer the good sense which amasses large fortunes, to that enterprising spirit which frequently dissipates them; general ideas alarm their minds, which are accustomed to positive calculations; and they hold practice in more honor than theory.

It is in America that one learns to understand the influence which physical prosperity exercises over political actions, and even over opinions which ought to acknowledge no sway but that of reason; and it is more especially among strangers that this truth is perceptible. Most of the European emigrants to the New World carry with them that wild love of independence and of change, which our calamities are apt to engender. I sometimes met with Europeans, in the United States, who had been obliged to leave their own country on account of their political opinions. They all astonished me by the language they held; but one of them surprised me more than all the rest. As I was crossing one of the most remote districts of Pennsylvania, I was benighted, and obliged to beg for hospitality at the gate of a wealthy planter, who was a Frenchman by birth. He bade me sit down beside his fire, and we began to talk with that freedom which befits persons who meet in the backwoods, two thousand leagues from their native country. I was aware that my host had been a great leveller and an ardent demagogue, forty years ago, and that his name was not unknown to fame. I was therefore not a little surprised to hear him discuss the rights of property as an economist or a landowner might have done: he spoke of the necessary gradations which fortune established among men, of obedience to established laws, of the influence of good morals in commonwealths, and of the support which religious opinions give to order and to freedom; he even went so far as to quote an evangelical authority in corroboration of one of his political tenets.

I listened, and marvelled at the feebleness of human reason. A proposition is true or false, but no art can prove it to be one or the other, in the midst of the uncertainties of science and the conflicting lessons of experience, until a new incident disperses the clouds of doubt; I was poor, I become rich; and I am not to expect that prosperity will act upon my conduct, and leave my judgment free: my opinions change with my fortune, and the happy circumstances which I turn to my advantage, furnish me with that decisive argument which was before wanting.

[The sentence beginning "I was poor, I become rich," &c., struck the editor, on perusal, as obscure, if not contradictory. The original seems more explicit, and justice to the author seems to require that it should be presented to the reader. "J'étais pauvre, me voici riche; du moins, si le bien-être, en agissant sur ma conduite, laissait mon jugement en liberté! Mais non, mes opinions sont en effet changées avec ma fortune, et, dans l'événement heureux dont je profite, j'ai réellement découvert la raison déterminante qui jusque-là m'avait manqué."—*American Editor.*]

The influence of prosperity acts still more freely upon the American than upon strangers. The American has always seen the connexion of public order and public prosperity, intimately united as they are, go on before his eyes; he does not conceive that one can subsist without the other; he has therefore nothing to forget: nor has he, like so many Europeans, to unlearn the lessons of his early education.

INFLUENCE OF THE LAWS UPON THE MAINTENANCE OF THE DEMOCRATIC REPUBLIC IN THE UNITED STATES.

Three principal Causes of the Maintenance of the democratic Republic.— Federal Constitutions.— Municipal Institutions.— Judicial Power.

THE principal aim of this book has been to make known the laws of the United States; if this purpose has been accomplished, the reader is already enabled to judge for himself which are the laws that really tend to maintain the democratic republic, and which endanger its existence. If I have not succeeded in explaining this in the whole course of my work, I cannot hope to do so within the limits of a single chapter. It is not my intention to retrace the path I have already pursued; and a very few lines will suffice to recapitulate what I have previously explained.

Three circumstances seem to me to contribute most powerfully to the maintenance of the democratic republic in the United States.

The first is that federal form of government which the Americans have adopted, and which enables the Union to combine the power of a great empire with the security of a small state;—

The second consists in those municipal institutions which limit the despotism of the majority, and at the same time impart a taste for freedom, and a knowledge of the art of being free, to the people;—

The third is to be met with in the constitution of the judicial power. I have shown in what manner the courts of justice serve to repress the excesses of democracy; and how they check and direct the impulses of the majority, without stopping its activity.

INFLUENCE OF MANNERS UPON THE MAINTENANCE OF THE DEMOCRATIC REPUBLIC IN THE UNITED STATES.

I HAVE previously remarked that the manners of the people may be considered as one of the general causes to which the maintenance of a democratic republic in the United States is attributable. I here use the word *manners*, with the meaning which the ancients attached to the word *mores;* for I apply it not only to manners, in their proper sense of what constitutes the character of social intercourse, but I extend it to the various notions and opinions current among men, and to the mass of those ideas which constitute their character of mind. I comprise, therefore, under this term the whole moral and intellectual condition of a people. My intention is not to draw a picture of American manners, but simply to point out such features of them as are favorable to the maintenance of political institutions.

RELIGION CONSIDERED AS A POLITICAL INSTITUTION, WHICH POWERFULLY CONTRIBUTES TO THE MAINTENANCE OF THE DEMOCRATIC REPUBLIC AMONG THE AMERICANS.

North America peopled by Men who professed a democratic and republican Christianity.—Arrival of the Catholics.—For what Reason the Catholics form the most democratic and the most republican Class at the present Time.

Every religion is to be found in juxtaposition to a political opinion, which is connected with it by affinity. If the human mind be left to follow its own bent, it will regulate the temporal and spiritual institutions of society upon one uniform principle; and man will endeavor, if I may use the expression, to harmonize the state in which he lives upon earth, with the state he believes to await him in heaven.

The greatest part of British America was peopled by men who, after having shaken off the authority of the pope, acknowledged no other religious supremacy: they brought with them into the New World a form of Christianity, which I cannot better describe, than by styling it a democratic and republican religion. This sect contributed powerfully to the establishment of a democracy and a republic; and from the earliest settlement of the emigrants, politics and religion contracted an alliance which has never been dissolved.

About fifty years ago Ireland began to pour a catholic population into the United States; on the other hand, the catholics of America made proselytes, and at the present moment more than a million of Christians, professing the truths of the church of Rome, are to be met with in the Union. These catholics are faithful to the observances of their religion; they are fervent and zealous in the support and belief of their doctrines. Nevertheless they constitute the most republican and the most democratic class of citizens which exists in the United States; and although this fact may surprise the observer at first, the cause by which it is occasioned may easily be discovered upon reflection.

I think that the catholic religion has erroneously been looked upon as the natural enemy of democracy. Among the various sects of Christians, catholicism seems to me, on the contrary, to be one of those which are most favorable to the equality of conditions. In the catholic church, the religious community is composed of only two elements; the priest and the people. The priest alone rises above the rank of his flock, and all below him are equal.

On doctrinal points the catholic faith places all human capacities upon the same level; it subjects the wise and the ignorant, the man of genius and the vulgar crowd, to the details of the same creed; it imposes the same observances upon the rich and needy, it inflicts the same austerities upon the strong and the weak, it listens to no compromises with mortal man, but reducing all the human race to the same standard, it confounds all the distinctions of society at the foot of the same altar, even as they are confounded in the sight of God. If catholicism predisposes the faithful to obedience, it certainly does not prepare them for inequality; but the contrary may be said of protestantism, which generally tends to make men independent, more than to render them equal.

Catholicism is like an absolute monarchy; if the sovereign be removed, all the other classes of society are more equal than they are in republics. It has not unfrequently occurred that the catholic priest has left the service of the altar to mix with the governing powers of society, and to make his place among the civil gradations of men. This religious influence has sometimes been used to secure the interests of that political state of things to which he belonged. At other times catholics have taken the side of aristocracy from a spirit of religion.

But no sooner is the priesthood entirely separated from the government, as is the case in the United States, than it is found that no class of men are more naturally disposed than the catholics to transfuse the doctrine of the equality of conditions into the political world. If, then, the catholic citizens of the United States are not forcibly led by the nature of their tenets to adopt democratic and republican principles, at least they are not necessarily opposed to them; and their social position, as well as their limited number, obliges them to adopt these opinions. Most of the catholics are poor, and they have no chance of taking a part in the government un less it be open to all the citizens. They constitute a minority, and all rights must be respected in order to ensure to them the free exercise of their own privileges. These two causes induce them, unconsciously, to adopt political doctrines which they would perhaps support with less zeal if they were rich and preponderant.

The catholic clergy of the United States has never attempted to oppose this political tendency; but it seeks rather to justify its results. The priests in America have divided the intellectual world into two parts: in the one they place the doctrines of revealed religion, which command their assent; in the other they leave those truths, which they believe to have been freely left open to the researches of political inquiry. Thus the catholics of the United States are at the same time the most faithful believers and the most zealous citizens.

It may be asserted that in the United States no religious doctrine displays the slightest hostility to democratic and republican institutions. The clergy of all the different sects holds the same language; their opinions are consonant to the laws, and the human intellect flows onward in one sole current.

I happened to be staying in one of the largest towns in the Union, when I was invited to attend a public meeting which had been called for the purpose of assisting the Poles, and of sending them supplies of arms and money. I found two or three thousand persons collected in a vast hall which had been prepared to receive them. In a short time a priest in his ecclesiastical robes advanced to the front of the hustings: the spectators rose, and stood uncovered, while he spoke in the following terms:—

"Almighty God! the God of armies! Thou who didst strengthen the hearts and guide the arms of our fathers when they were fighting for the sacred rights of national independence; thou who didst make them triumph over a hateful oppression, and hast granted to our people the benefits of liberty and peace; turn, O Lord, a favorable eye upon the other hemisphere; pitifully look down upon that heroic nation which is even now struggling as we did in the former time, and for the same rights which we defended with our blood. Thou, who didst create man in the likeness of the same image, let no tyranny mar thy work, and establish inequality upon the earth. Almighty God! do thou watch over the destiny of the Poles, and render them worthy to be free. May thy wisdom direct their councils, and may thy strength sustain their arms! Shed forth thy terror over their enemies; scatter the powers which take counsel against them; and vouchsafe that the injustice which the world has beheld for fifty years, be not consummated in our time. O Lord, who holdest alike the hearts of nations and of men in thy powerful hand, raise up allies to the sacred cause of right; arouse the French nation from the apathy in which its rulers retain it, that it go forth again to fight for the liberties of the world.

"Lord, turn not thou thy face from us, and grant that we may always be the most religious as well as the freest people of the earth. Almighty God, hear our supplications this day. Save the Poles, we beseech thee, in the name of thy well-beloved Son, our Lord Jesus Christ, who died upon the cross for the salvation of men. Amen."

The whole meeting responded "Amen!" with devotion.

INDIRECT INFLUENCE OF RELIGIOUS OPINIONS UPON POLITICAL SOCIETY IN THE UNITED STATES.

Christian Morality common to all Sects.—Influence of Religion upon the Manners of the Americans.—Respect for the marriage Tie.—In what manner Religion confines the Imagination of the Americans within certain Limits, and checks the Passion of Innovation.—Opinion of the Americans on the political Utility of Religion.—Their Exertions to extend and secure its Predominance.

I HAVE just shown what the direct influence of religion upon politics is in the United States; but its indirect influence appears to me to be still more considerable, and it never instructs the Americans more fully in the art of being free than when it says nothing of freedom.

The sects which exist in the United States are innumerable. They all differ in respect to the worship which is due from man to his Creator; but they all agree in respect to the duties which are due from man to man. Each sect adores the Deity in its own peculiar manner; but all the sects preach the same moral law in the name of God. If it be of the slightest importance to man, as an individual, that his religion should be true, the case of society is not the same. Society has no future life to hope for or to fear; and provided the citizens profess a religion, the peculiar tenets of that religion are of very little importance to its interests. Moreover, almost all the sects of the United States are comprised within the great unity of Christianity, and Christian morality is everywhere the same.

It may be believed without unfairness, that a certain number of Americans pursue a peculiar form of worship,, from habit more than from conviction. In the United States the sovereign authority is religious, and consequently hypocrisy must be common; but there is no country in the whole world in which the Christian religion retains a greater influence over the souls of men than in America; and there can be no greater proof of its utility, and of its conformity to human nature, than that its influence is most powerfully felt over the most enlightened and free nation of the earth.

I have remarked that the members of the American clergy in general, without even excepting those who do not admit religious liberty, are all in favor of civil freedom; but they do not support any particular political system. They keep aloof from parties, and from public affairs. In the United States religion exercises but little influence upon the laws, and upon the details of public opinion; but it directs the manners of the community, and by regulating domestic life, it regulates the state.

I do not question that the great austerity of manners which is observable in the United States, arises, in the first instance, from religious faith. Religion is often unable to restrain man from the numberless temptations of fortune; nor can it check that passion for gain which every incident of his life contributes to arouse; but its influence over the mind of women is supreme, and women are the protectors of morals. There is certainly no country in the world where the tie of marriage is so much respected as in America, or where conjugal happiness is more highly or worthily appreciated. In Europe almost all the disturbances of society arise from the irregularities of domestic life. To despise the natural bonds and legitimate pleasures of home, is to contract a taste for excesses, a restlessness of heart, and the evil of fluctuating desires. Agitated by the tumultuous passions which frequently disturb his dwelling, the European is galled by the obedience which the legislative powers of the state exact. But when the American retires from the turmoil of public life to the bosom of his family, he finds in it the image of order and of peace. There his pleasures are simple and natural, his joys are innocent and calm; and as he finds that an orderly life is the surest path to happiness, he accustoms himself without difficulty to moderate his opinions as well as his tastes. While the European endeavors to forget his domestic troubles by agitating society, the American derives from his own home that love of order, which he afterward carries with him into public affairs.

In the United States the influence of religion is not confined to the manners, but it extends to the intelligence of the people. Among the Anglo-Americans, there are some who profess the doctrines of Christianity from a sincere belief in them, and others who do the same because they are afraid to be suspected of unbelief. Christianity, therefore, reigns without any obstacle, by universal consent; the consequence is, as I have before observed, that every principle of the moral world is fixed and determinate, although the political world is abandoned to the debates and the experiments of men. Thus the human mind is never left to wander across a boundless field; and, whatever may be its pretensions, it is checked from time to time by barriers which it cannot surmount. Before it can perpetrate innovation, certain primal and immutable principles are laid down, and the boldest conceptions of human device are subjected to certain forms which retard and stop their completion.

The imagination of the Americans, even in its greatest flights, is circumspect and undecided; its impulses are checked, and its works unfinished. These habits of restraint recur in political society, and are singularly favorable both to the tranquillity of the people and the durability of the institutions it has established. Nature and circumstances concurred to make the inhabitants of the United States bold men, as is sufficiently attested by the enterprising spirit with which they seek for fortune. If the minds of the Americans were free from all trammels, they would very shortly become the most daring innovators and the most implacable disputants in the world. But the revolutionists of America are obliged to profess an ostensible respect for Christian morality and equity, which does not easily permit them to violate the laws that oppose their designs; nor would they find it easy to surmount the scruples of their partisans, even if they were able to get over their own. Hitherto no one, in the United States, has dared to advance the maxim, that everything is permissible with a view to the interests of society; an impious adage, which seems to have been invented in an age of freedom, to shelter all the tyrants of future ages. Thus while the law permits the Americans to do what they please, religion prevents them from conceiving, and forbids them to commit, what is rash and unjust.

Religion in America takes no direct part in the government of society, but it must nevertheless be regarded as the foremost of the political institutions of that country; for if it does not impart a taste for freedom, it facilitates the use of free institutions. Indeed, it is in this same point of view that the inhabitants of the United States themselves look upon religious belief. I do not know whether all the Americans have a sincere faith in their religion; for who can search the human heart? but I am certain that they hold it to be indispensable to the maintenance of republican institutions. This opinion is not peculiar to a class of citizens or to a party, but it belongs to the whole nation, and to every rank of society.

In the United States, if a political character attacks a sect, this may not prevent even the partisans of that very sect, from supporting him; but if he attacks all the sects together, every one abandons him, and he remains alone.

While I was in America, a witness, who happened to be called at the assizes of the county of Chester (state of New York), declared that he did not believe in the existence of God or in the immortality of the soul. The judge refused to admit his evidence, on the ground that the witness had destroyed beforehand all the confidence of the court in what he was about to say.* The newspapers related the fact without any farther comment.

* The New York Spectator of August 23d, 1831, relates the fact in the following terms: "The court of common pleas of Chester county (New York), a few days since rejected a witness who declared his disbelief in the existence of God. The presiding judge remarked, that he had not before been aware that there was a man living who did not believe in the existence of God; that this belief constituted the sanction of all testimony in a court of justice; and that he knew of no cause in a Christian country, where a witness had been permitted to testify without such belief.

[The instance given by the author, of a person offered as a witness having been rejected on the ground that he did not believe in the existence of a God, seems to be adduced to prove either his assertion that the Americans hold religion to be indispensable to the maintenance of republican institutions—or his assertion, that if a man attacks all the sects together, every one abandons him and he remains alone. But it is questionable how far the fact quoted proves either of these positions. The rule which prescribes as a qualification for a witness the belief in a Supreme Being who will punish falsehood, without which he is deemed wholly incompetent to testify, is established for the protection of personal rights, and not to compel the adoption of any system of religious belief. It came with all our fundamental principles from England as a part of the common law which the colonists brought with them. It is supposed to prevail in every country in Christendom, whatever may be the form of its government; and the only doubt that arises respecting its existence in France, is created by our author's apparent surprise at finding such a rule in America.—*American Editor.*]

The Americans combine the notions of Christianity and of liberty so intimately in their minds, that it is impossible to make them conceive the one without the other; and with them this conviction does not spring from that barren traditionary faith which seems to vegetate in the soul rather than to live.

I have known of societies formed by the Americans to send out ministers of the gospel into the new western states, to found schools and churches there, lest religion should be suffered to die away in those remote settlements, and the rising states be less fitted to enjoy free institutions than the people from which they emanated. I met with wealthy New Englanders who abandoned the country in which they were born, in order to lay the foundations of Christianity and of freedom on the banks of the Missouri or in the prairies of Illinois. Thus religious zeal is perpetually stimulated in the United States by the duties of patriotism. These men do not act from an exclusive consideration of the promises of a future life; eternity is only one motive of their devotion to the cause; and if you converse with these missionaries of Christian civilisation, you will be surprised to find how much value they set upon the goods of this world, and that you meet with a politician where you expected to find a priest. They will tell you that "all the American republics are collectively involved with each other; if the republics of the west were to fall into anarchy, or to be mastered by a despot, the republican institutions which now flourish upon the shores of the Atlantic ocean would be in great peril. It is therefore our interest that the new states should be religious, in order to maintain our liberties."

Such are the opinions of the Americans; and if any hold that the religious spirit which I admire is the very thing most amiss in America, and that the only element wanting to the freedom and happiness of the human race is to believe in some blind cosmogony, or to assert with Cabanis the secretion of thought by the brain, I can only reply, that those who hold this language have never been in America, and that they have never seen a religious or a free nation. When they return from their expedition, we shall hear what they have to say.

There are persons in France who look upon republican institutions as a temporary means of power, of wealth and distinction; men who are the *condottieri* of liberty, and who fight for their own advantage, whatever be the colors they wear: it is not to these that I address myself. But there are others who look forward to the republican form of government as a tranquil and lasting state, toward which modern society is daily impelled by the ideas and manners of the time, and who sincerely desire to prepare men to be free. When these men attack religious opinions, they obey the dictates of their passions to the prejudice of their interests. Despotism may govern without faith, but liberty cannot. Religion is much more necessary in the republic which they set forth in glowing colors, than in the monarchy which they attack; and it is more needed in democratic republics than in any others. How is it possible that society should escape destruction if the moral tie be not strengthened in proportion as the political tie is relaxed? and what can be done with a people which is its own master, if it be not submissive to the Divinity?

PRINCIPAL CAUSES WHICH RENDER RELIGION POWERFUL IN AMERICA.

Care taken by the Americans to separate the Church from the State.—The Laws, public Opinion, and even the Exertions of the Clergy concur to promote this end.—Influence of Religion upon the Mind, in the United States, attributable to this Cause.—Reason of this.—What is the natural State of Men with regard to Religion at the present time.—What are the peculiar and incidental Causes which prevent Men, in certain Countries, from arriving at this State.

THE philosophers of the eighteenth century explained the gradual decay of religious faith in a very simple manner. Religious zeal, said they, must necessarily fail, the more generally liberty is established and knowledge diffused. Unfortunately, facts are by no means in accordance with their theory. There are certain populations in Europe whose unbelief is only equalled by their ignorance and their debasement, while in America one of the freest and most enlightened nations in the world fulfils all the outward duties of religion with fervor.

Upon my arrival in the United States, the religious aspect of the country was the first thing that struck my attention; and the longer I stayed there, the more did I perceive the great political consequences resulting from this state of things, to which I was unaccustomed. In France I had almost always seen the spirit of religion and the spirit of freedom pursuing courses diametrically opposed to each other; but in

America I found that they were intimately united, and that they reigned in common over the same country. My desire to discover the causes of this phenomenon increased from day to day. In order to satisfy it, I questioned the members of all the different sects; and I more especially sought the society of the clergy, who are the depositaries of the different persuasions, and who are more especially interested in their duration. As a member of the Roman catholic church I was more particularly brought into contact with several of its priests, with whom I became intimately acquainted. To each of these men I expressed my astonishment and I explained my doubts: I found that they differed upon matters of detail alone; and that they mainly attributed the peaceable dominion of religion in their country, to the separation of church and state. I do not hesitate to affirm that during my stay in America, I did not meet with a single individual, of the clergy or of the laity, who was not of the same opinion upon this point.

This led me to examine more attentively than I had hitherto done, the station which the American clergy occupy in political society. I learned with surprise that they fill no public appointments;* not one of them is to be met with in the administration, and they are not even represented in the legislative assemblies. In several states† the law excludes them from political life; public opinion in all. And when I came to inquire into the prevailing spirit of the clergy, I found that most of its members seemed to retire of their own accord from the exercise of power, and that they made it the pride of their profession to abstain from politics.

I heard them inveigh against ambition and deceit, under whatever political opinions these vices might chance to lurk; but I learned from their discourses that men are not guilty in the eye of God for any opinions concerning political government, which they may profess with sincerity, any more than

* Unless this term be applied to the functions which many of them fill in the schools. Almost all education is intrusted to the clergy.

† See the constitution of New York, art. 7, § 4:—

"And whereas, the ministers of the gospel are, by their profession, dedicated to the service of God and the care of souls, and ought not to be diverted from the great duties of their functions; therefore no minister of the gospel, or priest of any denomination whatsoever, shall, at any time hereafter, under any pretence or description whatever, be eligible to, or capable of holding any civil or military office or place within this state."

See also the constitutions of North Carolina, art. 31. Virginia. South Carolina, art. 1, § 23. Kentucky, art. 2, § 26. Tennessee, art. 8, § 1. Louisiana, art. 2, § 22.

they are for their mistakes in building a house or in driving a furrow. I perceived that these ministers of the gospel eschewed all parties, with the anxiety attendant upon personal interest. These facts convinced me that what I had been told was true; and it then became my object to investigate their causes, and to inquire how it happened that the real authority of religion was increased by a state of things which diminished its apparent force: these causes did not long escape my researches.

The short space of threescore years can never content the imagination of man; nor can the imperfect joys of this world satisfy his heart. Man alone, of all created beings, displays a natural contempt of existence, and yet a boundless desire to exist; he scorns life, but he dreads annihilation. These different feelings incessantly urge his soul to the contemplation of a future state, and religion directs his musings thither. Religion, then, is simply another form of hope; and it is no less natural to the human heart than hope itself. Men cannot abandon their religious faith without a kind of aberration of intellect, and a sort of violent distortion of their true natures; but they are invincibly brought back to more pious sentiments; for unbelief is an accident, and faith is the only permanent state of mankind. If we only consider religious institutions in a purely human point of view, they may be said to derive an inexhaustible element of strength from man himself, since they belong to one of the constituent principles of human nature.

I am aware that at certain times religion may strengthen this influence, which originates in itself, by the artificial power of the laws, and by the support of those temporal institutions which direct society. Religions, intimately united to the governments of the earth, have been known to exercise a sovereign authority derived from the twofold source of terror and of faith; but when a religion contracts an alliance of this nature, I do not hesitate to affirm that it commits the same error, as a man who should sacrifice his future to his present welfare; and in obtaining a power to which it has no claim, it risks that authority which is rightfully its own. When a religion founds its empire upon the desire of immortality which lives in every human heart, it may aspire to universal dominion: but when it connects itself with a government, it must necessarily adopt maxims which are only applicable to certain nations. Thus, in forming an alliance with a political power, religion augments its authority over a few, and forfeits the hope of reigning over all.

As long as a religion rests upon those sentiments which are the consolation of all affliction, it may attract the affections of mankind. But if it be mixed up with the bitter passions of the world, it may be constrained to defend allies whom its interests, and not the principle of love, have given to it; or to repel as antagonists men who are still attached to its own spirit, however opposed they may be to the powers to which it is allied. The church cannot share the temporal power of the state, without being the object of a portion of that animosity which the latter excites.

The political powers which seem to be most firmly established have frequently no better guarantee for their duration, than the opinions of a generation, the interests of the time, or the life of an individual. A law may modify the social condition which seems to be most fixed and determinate; and with the social condition everything else must change. The powers of society are more or less fugitive, like the years which we spend upon the earth; they succeed each other with rapidity like the fleeting cares of life; and no government has ever yet been founded upon an invariable disposition of the human heart, or upon an imperishable interest.

As long as religion is sustained by those feelings, propensities, and passions, which are found to occur under the same forms at all the different periods of history, it may defy the efforts of time; or at least it can only be destroyed by another religion. But when religion clings to the interests of the world, it becomes almost as fragile a thing as the powers of the earth. It is the only one of them all which can hope for immortality; but if it be connected with their ephemeral authority, it shares their fortunes, and may fall with those transient passions which supported them for a day. The alliance which religion contracts with political powers must needs be onerous to itself; since it does not require their assistance to live, and by giving them its assistance it may be exposed to decay.

The danger which I have just pointed out always exists, but it is not always equally visible. In some ages governments seem to be imperishable, in others the existence of society appears to be more precarious than the life of man. Some constitutions plunge the citizens into a lethargic somnolence, and others rouse them to feverish excitement. When government appears to be so strong, and laws so stable, men do not perceive the dangers which may accrue from a union of church and state. When governments display so much inconstancy, the danger is self-evident, but it is no longer possible to avoid it; to be effectual, measures must be taken to discover its approach.

In proportion as a nation assumes a democratic condition of society, and as communities display democratic propensities, it becomes more and more dangerous to connect religion with political institutions; for the time is coming when authority will be bandied from hand to hand, when political theories will succeed each other, and when men, laws and constitutions, will disappear or be modified from day to day, and this not for a season only, but unceasingly. Agitation and mutability are inherent in the nature of democratic republics, just as stagnation and inertness are the law of absolute monarchies.

If the Americans, who change the head of the government once in four years, who elect new legislators every two years, and renew the provincial officers every twelvemonth; if the Americans, who have abandoned the political world to the attempts of innovators, had not placed religion beyond their reach, where could it abide in the ebb and flow of human opinions? where would that respect which belongs to it be paid, amid the struggles of faction? and what would become of its immortality in the midst of perpetual decay? The American clergy were the first to perceive this truth, and to act in conformity with it. They saw that they must renounce their religious influence, if they were to strive for political power; and they chose to give up the support of the state, rather than to share in its vicissitudes.

In America, religion is perhaps less powerful than it has been at certain periods in the history of certain peoples; but its influence is more lasting. It restricts itself to its own resources, but of those none can deprive it: its circle is limited to certain principles, but those principles are entirely its own, and under its undisputed control.

On every side in Europe we hear voices complaining of the absence of religious faith, and inquiring the means of restoring to religion some remnant of its pristine authority. It seems to me that we must first attentively consider what ought to be *the natural state* of men with regard to religion, at the present time; and when we know what we have to hope and to fear, we may discern the end to which our efforts ought to be directed.

The two great dangers which threaten the existence of religions are schism and indifference. In ages of fervent devotion, men sometimes abandon their religion, but they only shake it off in order to adopt another. Their faith changes the objects to which it is directed, but it suffers no decline. The old religion, then, excites enthusiastic attachment or bitter enmity in either party; some leave it with anger, others cling to it with increased devotedness, and although persuasions differ, irreligion is unknown. Such, however, is not the case when a religious belief is secretly undermined by doctrines which may be termed negative, since they deny the truth of one religion without affirming that of any other. Prodigious revolutions then take place in the human mind, without the apparent co-operation of the passions of man, and almost without his knowledge. Men lose the object of their fondest hopes, as if through forgetfulness. They are carried away by an imperceptible current which they have not the courage to stem, but which they follow with regret, since it bears them from a faith they love, to a scepticism that plunges them into despair.

In ages which answer to this description, men desert their religious opinions from lukewarmness rather than from dislike; they do not reject them, but the sentiments by which they were once fostered disappear. But if the unbeliever does not admit religion to be true, he still considers it useful. Regarding religious institutions in a human point of view, he acknowledges their influence upon manners and legislation. He admits that they may serve to make men live in peace with one another and to prepare them gently for the hour of death. He regrets the faith which he has lost; and as he is deprived of a treasure which he has learned to estimate at its full value, he scruples to take it from those who still possess it.

On the other hand, those who continue to believe, are not afraid openly to avow their faith. They look upon those who do not share their persuasion as more worthy of pity than of opposition; and they are aware, that to acquire the esteem of the unbelieving, they are not obliged to follow their example. They are hostile to no one in the world; and as they do not consider the society in which they live as an arena in which religion is bound to face its thousand deadly foes, they love their contemporaries, while they condemn their weaknesses, and lament their errors.

As those who do notbelieve, conceal their incredulity; and as those who believe, display their faith, public opinion pronounces itself in favor of religion: love, support, and honor, are bestowed upon it, and it is only by searching the human soul, that we can detect the wounds which it has received. The mass of mankind, who are never without the feeling of religion, do not perceive anything at variance with the established faith. The instinctive desire of a future life brings the crowd about the altar, and opens the hearts of men to the precepts and consolations of religion.

But this picture is not applicable to us; for there are men among us who have ceased to believe in Christianity, without adopting any other religion; others who are in the perplexities of doubt, and who already affect not to believe; and others, again, who are afraid to avow that Christian faith which they still cherish in secret.

Amid these lukewarm partisans and ardent antagonists, a small number of believers exist, who are ready to brave all obstacles, and to scorn all dangers in defence of their faith. They have done violence to human weakness, in order to rise superior to public opinion. Excited by the effort they have made, they scarcely know where to stop; and as they know that the first use which the French made of independence, was to attack religion, they look upon their contemporaries with dread, and they recoil in alarm from the liberty which their fellow-citizens are seeking to obtain. As unbelief appears to them to be a novelty, they comprise all that is new in one indiscriminate animosity. They are at war with their age and country, and they look upon every opinion which is put forth there as the necessary enemy of the faith.

Such is not the natural state of men with regard to religion at the present day; and some extraordinary or incidental cause must be at work in France, to prevent the human mind from following its original propensities, and to drive it beyond the limits at which it ought naturally to stop.

I am intimately convinced that this extraordinary and incidental cause is the close connexion of politics and religion. The unbelievers of Europe attack the Christians as their political opponents, rather than as their religious adversaries; they hate the Christian religion as the opinion of a party, much more than as an error of belief; and they reject the clergy less because they are the representatives of the Divinity, than because they are the allies of authority.

In Europe, Christianity has been intimately united to the powers of the earth. Those powers are now in decay, and it is, as it were, buried under their ruins. The living body of religion has been bound down to the dead corpse of superannuated polity; cut the bonds which restrain it, and that which is alive will rise once more. I know not what could restore the Christian church of Europe to the energy of its earlier days; that power belongs to God alone; but it may be the effect of human policy to leave the faith in all the full exercise of the strength which it still retains.

HOW THE INSTRUCTION, THE HABITS, AND THE PRACTICAL EXPERIENCE OF THE AMERICANS PROMOTE THE SUCCESS OF THEIR DEMOCRATIC INSTITUTIONS.

What is to be understood by the instruction of the American People.—The human Mind is more superficially instructed in the United States than in Europe.—No one completely uninstructed.—Reason of this Rapidity with which Opinions are diffused even in the uncultivated States of the West.—Practical Experience more serviceable to the Americans than Book-learning.

I HAVE but little to add to what I have already said, concerning the influence which the instruction and the habits of the Americans exercise upon the maintenance of their political institutions.

America has hitherto produced very few writers of distinction; it possesses no great historians, and not a single eminent poet. The inhabitants of that country look upon what are properly styled literary pursuits with a kind of disapprobation; and there are towns of very second rate importance in Europe, in which more literary works are annually published, than in the twenty-four states of the Union put together. The spirit of the Americans is averse to general ideas; and it does not seek theoretical discoveries. Neither politics nor manufactures direct them to these occupations; and although new laws are perpetually enacted in the United States, no great writers have hitherto inquired into the principles of their legislation. The Americans have lawyers and commentators, but no jurists; and they furnish examples rather than lessons to the world. The same observation applies to the mechanical arts. In America, the inventions of Europe are adopted with sagacity; they are perfected, and adapted with admirable skill to the wants of the country. Manufactures exist, but the science of manufacture is not cultivated; and they have good workmen, but very few inventors. Fulton was obliged to proffer his services to foreign nations for a long time before he was able to devote them to his own country.

[The remark that in America "there are very good workmen but very few inventors," will excite surprise in this country. The inventive character of Fulton he seems to admit, but would apparently deprive us of the credit of his name, by the remark that he was obliged to proffer his services to foreign nations for a long time. He might have added, that those proffers were disregarded and neglected, and that it was finally in his own country that he found the aid necessary to put in execution his great project. If there be patronage extended by the citizens of the United States to any one thing in preference to another, it is to the results of inventive genius. Surely Franklin, Rittenhouse, and Perkins, have been heard of by our author; and he must have heard something of that wonderful invention, the cotton-gin of Whitney, and of the machines for making cards to comb wool. The original machines of Fulton for the application of steam have been constantly improving, so that there is scarcely a vestige of them remaining. But to sum up the whole in one word, can it be possible that our author did not visit the patent office at Washington? Whatever may be said of the *utility* of nine-tenths of the inventions of which the descriptions and models are there deposited, no one who has ever seen that depository, or who has read a description of its contents, can doubt that they furnish the most incontestible evidence of extraordinary inventive genius—a genius that has excited the astonishment of other European travellers.—*American Editor.*]

The observer who is desirous of forming an opinion on the state of instruction among the Anglo-Americans, must consider the same object from two different points of view. If he only singles out the learned, he will be astonished to find how rare they are; but if he counts the ignorant, the American people will appear to be the most enlightened community in the world. The whole population, as I observed in another place, is situated between these two extremes.

In New England, every citizen receives the elementary notions of human knowledge; he is moreover taught the doctrines and the evidences of his religion, the history of his country, and the leading features of its constitution. In the states of Connecticut and Massachusetts, it is extremely rare to find a man imperfectly acquainted with all these things, and a person wholly ignorant of them is a sort of phenomenon.

When I compare the Greek and Roman republics with these American states; the manuscript libraries of the former, and their rude population, with the innumerable journals and the enlightened people of the latter; when I remember all the attempts which are made to judge the modern republics by the assistance of those of antiquity, and to infer what will happen in our time from what took place two thousand years ago, I am tempted to burn my books, in order to apply none but novel ideas to so novel a condition of society.

What I have said of New England must not, however, be applied indiscriminately to the whole Union: as we advance towards the west or the south, the instruction of the people diminishes. In the states which are adjacent to the Gulf of Mexico, a certain number of individuals may be found, as in our own countries, who are devoid of the rudiments of instruction. But there is not a single district in the United States sunk in complete ignorance; and for a very simple reason; the peoples of Europe started from the darkness of a barbarous condition to advance toward the light of civilisation; their progress has been unequal; some of them have improved apace, while others have loitered in their course, and some have stopped, and are still sleeping upon the way.

Such has not been the case in the United States. The Anglo-Americans settled in a state of civilisation, upon that territory which their descendants occupy; they had not to begin to learn, and it was sufficient not to forget. Now the children of these same Americans are the persons who, year by year, transport their dwellings into the wilds: and with their dwellings their acquired information and their esteem for knowledge. Education has taught them the utility of instruction, and has enabled them to transmit that instruction to their posterity. In the United States society has no infancy, but it is born in man's estate.

The Americans never use the word "peasant," because they have no idea of the peculiar class which that term denotes; the ignorance of more remote ages, the simplicity of rural life, and the rusticity of the villager, have not been preserved among them; and they are alike unacquainted with the virtues, the vices, the coarse habits, and the simple graces of an early stage of civilisation. At the extreme borders of the confederate states, upon the confines of society and of the wilderness, a population of bold adventurers have taken up their abode, who pierce the solitudes of the American woods, and seek a country there, in order to escape that poverty which awaited them in their native provinces. As soon as the pioneer arrives upon the spot which is to serve him for a retreat, he fells a few trees and builds a log-house. Nothing can offer a more miserable aspect than these isolated dwellings. The traveller who approaches one of them toward night-fall, sees the flicker of the hearth-flame through the chinks in the walls; and at night, if the wind rises, he hears the roof of boughs shake to and fro in the midst of the great forest trees. Who would not suppose that this poor hut is the asylum of rudeness and ignorance? Yet no sort of comparison can be drawn between the pioneer and the dwelling which shelters him. Everything about him is primitive and unformed, but he is himself the result of the labor and the experience of eighteen centuries. He wears the dress, and he speaks the language of cities; he is acquainted with the past, curious of the future, and ready for argument upon the present; he is, in short, a highly civilized being, who consents, for a time, to inhabit the back-woods, and who penetrates into the wilds of a New World with the Bible, an axe, and a file of newspapers.

It is difficult to imagine the incredible rapidity with which public opinion circulates in the midst of these deserts.* I do not think that so much intellectual intercourse takes place in the most enlightened and populous districts of France.† It cannot be doubted that in the United States, the instruction of the people powerfully contributes to the support of a democratic republic; and such must always be the case, I believe, where instruction, which awakens the understanding, is not separated from moral education which amends the heart. But I by no means exaggerate this benefit, and I am still farther from thinking, as so many people do think in Europe, that men can be instantaneously made citizens by teaching them to read and write. True information is mainly derived from experience, and if the Americans had not been gradually accustomed to govern themselves, their book-learning would not assist them much at the present day.

I have lived a great deal with the people in the United States, and I cannot express how much I admire their experience and their good sense. An American should never be allowed to speak of Europe; for he will then probably display a vast deal of presumption and very foolish pride. He will

* I travelled along a portion of the frontier of the United States in a sort of cart which was termed the mail. We passed, day and night, with great rapidity along roads which were scarcely marked out, through immense forests: when the gloom of the woods became impenetrable, the coachman lighted branches of fir and we journied along by the light they cast. From time to time we came to a hut in the midst of the forest, which was a postoffice. The mail dropped an enormous bundle of letters at the door of this isolated dwelling, and we pursued our way at full gallop, leaving the inhabitants of the neighboring log-houses to send for their share of the treasure.

† In 1832, each inhabitant of Michigan paid a sum equivalent to 1 franc, 22 centimes (French money) to the postoffice revenue; and each inhabitant of the Floridas paid 1 fr. 5 cent (See National Calendar, 1833, p. 244.) In the same year each inhabitant of the department du Nord, paid 1 fr. 4 cent. to the revenue of the French postoffice. (See the Compte rendu de l'Administration des Finances, 1833, p. 623.) Now the state of Michigan only contained at that time 7 inhabitants per square league; and Florida only 5; the instruction and the commercial activity of these districts are inferior to those of most of the states in the Union; while the department du Nord, which contains 3,400 inhabitants per square league, is one of the most enlightened and manufacturing parts of France.

take up with those crude and vague notions which are so useful to the ignorant all over the world. But if you question him respecting his own country, the cloud which dimmed his intelligence will immediately disperse; his language will become as clear and as precise as his thoughts. He will inform you what his rights are, and by what means he exercises them; he will be able to point out the customs which obtain in the political world. You will find that he is well acquainted with the rules of the administration, and that he is familiar with the mechanism of the laws. The citizen of the United States does not acquire his practical science and his positive notions from books; the instruction he has acquired may have prepared him for receiving those ideas, but it did not furnish them. The American learns to know the laws by participating in the act of legislation; and he takes a lesson in the forms of government, from governing. The great work of society is ever going on beneath his eyes, and, as it were, under his hands.

In the United States politics are the end and aim of education; in Europe its principal object is to fit men for private life. The interference of the citizens in public affairs is too rare an occurrence for it to be anticipated beforehand. Upon casting a glance over society in the two hemispheres, these differences are indicated even by its external aspect.

In Europe, we frequently introduce the ideas and the habits of private life into public affairs; and as we pass at once from the domestic circle to the government of the state, we may frequently be heard to discuss the great interests of society in the same manner in which we converse with our friends. The Americans, on the other hand, transfuse the habits of public life into their manners in private; and in their country the jury is introduced into the games of schoolboys, and parliamentary forms are observed in the order of a feast.

THE LAWS CONTRIBUTE MORE TO THE MAINTENANCE OF THE DEMOCRATIC REPUBLIC IN THE UNITED STATES THAN THE PHYSICAL CIRCUMSTANCES OF THE COUNTRY, AND THE MANNERS MORE THAN THE LAWS.

All the Nations of America have a democratic State of Society.—Yet democratic Institutions subsist only among the Anglo-Americans.—The Spaniards of South America, equally favored by physical Causes as the Anglo-Americans, unable to maintain a democratic Republic.—Mexico, which has adopted the Constitution of the United States, in the same Predicament.—The Anglo-Americans of the West less able to maintain it than those of the East.—Reason of these different Results.

I HAVE remarked that the maintenance of democratic institutions in the United States is attributable to the circumstances, the laws, and the manners of that country.* Most Europeans are only acquainted with the first of these three causes, and they are apt to give it a preponderating importance which it does not really possess.

It is true that the Anglo-Americans settled in the New World in a state of social equality; the low-born and the noble were not to be found among them; and professional prejudices were always as entirely unknown as the prejudices of birth. Thus, as the condition of society was democratic, the empire of democracy was established without difficulty. But this circumstance is by no means peculiar to the United States; almost all the transatlantic colonies were founded by men equal among themselves, or who became so by inhabiting them. In no one part of the New World have Europeans been able to create an aristocracy. Nevertheless democratic institutions prosper nowhere but in the United States.

The American Union has no enemies to contend with; it stands in the wilds like an island in the ocean. But the Spaniards of South America were no less isolated by nature; yet their position has not relieved them from the charge of standing armies. They make war upon each other when they have no foreign enemies to oppose; and the Anglo-American democracy is the only one which has hitherto been able to maintain itself in peace.

The territory of the Union presents a boundless field to human activity, and inexhaustible materials for industry and

* I remind the reader of the general signification which I give to the word *manners*, namely, the moral and intellectual characteristics of social man taken collectively.

labor. The passion of wealth takes the place of ambition, and the warmth of faction is mitigated by a sense of prosperity. But in what portion of the globe shall we meet with more fertile plains, with mightier rivers, or with more unexplored and inexhaustible riches, than in South America?

Nevertheless South America has been unable to maintain democratic institutions. If the welfare of nations depended on their being placed in a remote position, with an unbounded space of habitable territory before them, the Spaniards of South America would have no reason to complain of their fate. And although they might enjoy less prosperity than the inhabitants of the United States, their lot might still be such as to excite the envy of some nations in Europe. There are, however, no nations upon the face of the earth more miserable than those of South America.

Thus, not only are physical causes inadequate to produce results analogous to those which occur in North America, but they are unable to raise the population of South America above the level of European states, where they act in a contrary direction. Physical causes do not therefore affect the destiny of nations so much as has been supposed.

I have met with men in New England who were on the point of leaving a country, where they might have remained in easy circumstances, to go to seek their fortunes in the wilds. Not far from that district I found a French population in Canada, which was closely crowded on a narrow territory, although the same wilds were at hand; and while the emigrant from the United States purchased an extensive estate with the earnings of a short term of labor, the Canadian paid as much for land as he would have done in France. Nature offers the solitudes of the New World to Europeans; but they are not always acquainted with the means of turning her gifts to account. Other peoples of America have the same physical conditions of prosperity as the Anglo-Americans, but without their laws and their manners; and these peoples are wretched. The laws and manners of the Anglo-Americans are therefore that cause of their greatness which is the object of my inquiry.

I am far from supposing that the American laws are preeminently good in themselves; I do not hold them to be applicable to all democratic peoples; and several of them seem to me to be dangerous, even in the United States. Nevertheless, it cannot be denied that the American legislation, taken collectively, is extremely well adapted to the genius of the people and the nature of the country which it is intended to govern. The American laws are therefore good, and to them must be attributed a large portion of the success which attends the government of democracy in America: but I do not believe them to be the principal cause of that success; and if they seem to me to have more influence upon the social happiness of the Americans than the nature of the country, on the other hand there is reason to believe that their effect is still inferior to that produced by the manners of the people.

The federal laws undoubtedly constitute the most important part of the legislation of the United States. Mexico, which is not less fortunately situated than the Anglo-American Union, has adopted these same laws, but is unable to accustom itself to the government of democracy. Some other cause is therefore at work independently of those physical circumstances and peculiar laws which enable the democracy to rule in the United States.

Another still more striking proof may be adduced. Almost all the inhabitants of the territory of the Union are the descendants of a common stock; they speak the same language, they worship God in the same manner, they are affected by the same physical causes, and they obey the same laws. Whence, then, do their characteristic differences arise? Why, in the eastern states of the Union, does the republican government display vigor and regularity, and proceed with mature deliberation? Whence does it derive the wisdom and durability which mark its acts, while in the western states, on the contrary, society seems to be ruled by the powers of chance? There, public business is conducted with an irregularity, and a passionate and feverish excitement, which does not announce a long or sure duration.

I am no longer comparing the Anglo-American states to foreign nations; but I am contrasting them with each other, and endeavoring to discover why they are so unlike. The arguments which are derived from the nature of the country and the difference of legislation, are here all set aside. Recourse must be had to some other cause; and what other cause can there be except the manners of the people?

It is in the eastern states that the Anglo-Americans have been longest accustomed to the government of democracy, and that they have adopted the habits and conceived the notions most favorable to its maintenance. Democracy has gradually penetrated into their customs, their opinions, and the forms of social intercourse; it is to be found in all the details of daily life equally as in the laws. In the eastern states the instruction and practical education of the people have been most perfected, and religion has been most thoroughly amalgamated with liberty. Now these habits, opinions, customs, and convictions, are precisely the constituent elements of that which I have denominated manners.

In the western states, on the contrary, a portion of the same advantages is still wanting. Many of the Americans of the west were born in the woods, and they mix the ideas and the customs of savage life with the civilisation of their parents. Their passions are more intense; their religious morality less authoritative; and their convictions are less secure. The inhabitants exercise no sort of control over their fellow-citizens, for they are scarcely acquainted with each other. The nations of the west display, to a certain extent, the inexperience and the rude habits of a people in its infancy; for although they are composed of old elements, their assemblage is of recent date.

The manners of the Americans of the United States are, then, the real cause which renders that people the only one of the American nations that is able to support a democratic government; and it is the influence of manners which produces the different degrees of order and of prosperity, that may be distinguished in the several Anglo-American democracies. Thus the effect which the geographical position of a country may have upon the duration of democratic institutions is exaggerated in Europe. Too much importance is attributed to legislation, too little to manners. These three great causes serve, no doubt, to regulate and direct the American democracy; but if they were to be classed in their proper order, I should say that the physical circumstances are less efficient than the laws, and the laws very subordinate to the manners of the people. I am convinced that the most advantageous situation and the best possible laws cannot maintain a constitution in spite of the manners of a country: while the latter may turn the most unfavorable positions and the worst laws to some advantage. The importance of manners is a common truth to which study and experience incessantly direct our attention. It may be regarded as a central point in the range of human observation, and the common termination of all inquiry. So seriously do I insist upon this head, that if I have hitherto failed in making the reader feel the important influence which I attribute to the practical experience, the habits, the opinions, in short, to the manners of the Americans, upon the maintenance of their institutions, I have failed in the principal object of my work.

WHETHER LAWS AND MANNERS ARE SUFFICIENT TO MAINTAIN DEMOCRATIC INSTITUTIONS IN OTHER COUNTRIES BESIDE AMERICA.

The Anglo-Americans, if transported into Europe, would be obliged to modify their Laws.—Distinction to be made between democratic Institutions and American Institutions.—Democratic Laws may be conceived better than, or at least different from, those which the American Democracy has adopted.—The Example of America only proves that it is possible to regulate Democracy by the assistance of Manners and Legislation.

I HAVE asserted that the success of democratic institutions in the United States is more intimately connected with the laws themselves, and the manners of the people, than with the nature of the country. But does it follow that the same causes would of themselves produce the same results, if they were put into operation elsewhere; and if the country is no adequate substitute for laws and manners, can laws and manners in their turn prove a substitute for a country? It will readily be understood that the necessary elements of a reply to this question are wanting: other peoples are to be found in the New World beside the Anglo-Americans, and as these peoples are affected by the same physical circumstances as the latter, they may fairly be compared together. But there are no nations out of America which have adopted the same laws and manners, being destitute of the physical advantages peculiar to the Anglo-Americans. No standard of comparison therefore exists, and we can only hazard an opinion upon this subject.

It appears to me in the first place, that a careful distinction must be made between the institutions of the United States and democratic institutions in general. When I reflect upon the state of Europe, its mighty nations, its populous cities, its formidable armies, and the complex nature of its politics, I cannot suppose that even the Anglo-Americans, if they were transported to our hemisphere, with their ideas, their religion, and their manners, could exist without considerably altering their laws. But a democratic nation may be imagined, organized differently from the American people. It is not impossible to conceive a government really established upon the will of the majority; but in which the majority, repressing its natural propensity to equality, should consent, with a view to the order and the stability of the state, to invest a family or an individual with all the prerogatives of the executive. A democratic society might exist, in which the forces of the nation would be more centralized than they are in the United States; the people would exercise a less direct and less irresistible influence upon public affairs, and yet every citizen, invested with certain rights, would participate, within his sphere, in the conduct of the government. The observations I made among the Anglo-Americans induce me to believe that democratic institutions of this kind, prudently introduced into society, so as gradually to mix with the habits and to be infused with the opinions of the people, might subsist in other countries beside America. If the laws of the United States were the only imaginable democratic laws, or the most perfect which it is possible to conceive, I should admit that the success of those institutions affords no proof of the success of democratic institutions in general, in a country less favored by natural circumstances. But as the laws of America appear to me to be defective in several respects, and as I can readily imagine others of the same general nature, the peculiar advantages of that country do not prove that democratic institutions cannot succeed in a nation less favored by circumstances, if ruled by better laws.

If human nature were different in America from what it is elsewhere; or if the social condition of the Americans engendered habits and opinions among them different from those which originate in the same social condition in the Old World, the American democracies would afford no means of predicting what may occur in other democracies. If the Americans displayed the same propensities as all other democratic nations, and if their legislators had relied upon the nature of the country and the favor of circumstances to restrain those propensities within due limits, the prosperity of the United States would be exclusively attributable to physical causes, and it would afford no encouragement to a people inclined to imitate their example, without sharing their natural advantages. But neither of these suppositions is borne out by facts.

In America the same passions are to be met with as in Europe; some originating in human nature, others in the democratic condition of society. Thus in the United States I found that restlessness of heart which is natural to men, when all ranks are nearly equal and the chances of elevation are the same to all. I found the democratic feeling of envy expressed under a thousand different forms. I remarked that the people frequently displayed, in the conduct of affairs, a consummate mixture of ignorance and presumption; and I inferred that, in America, men are liable to the same failings and the same absurdities as among ourselves. But upon examining the state of society more attentively, I speedily discovered that the Americans had made great and successful efforts to counteract these imperfections of human nature, and to correct the natural defects of democracy. Their divers municipal laws appeared to me to be a means of restraining the ambition of the citizens within a narrow sphere, and of turning those same passions, which might have worked havoc in the state, to the good of the township or the parish. The American legislators have succeeded to a certain extent in opposing the notion of rights, to the feelings of envy; the permanence of the religious world, to the continual shifting of politics; the experience of the people, to its theoretical ignorance; and its practical knowledge of business, to the impatience of its desires.

The Americans, then, have not relied upon the nature of their country, to counterpoise those dangers which originate in their constitution and in their political laws. To evils which are common to all democratic peoples, they have applied remedies which none but themselves had ever thought of before; and although they were the first to make the experiment, they have succeeded in it.

The manners and laws of the Americans are not the only ones which may suit a democratic people; but the Americans have shown that it would be wrong to despair of regulating democracy by the aid of manners and of laws. If other nations should borrow this general and pregnant idea from the Americans, without however intending to imitate them in the peculiar application which they have made of it; if they should attempt to fit themselves for that social condition, which it seems to be the will of Providence to impose upon the generations of this age, and so to escape from the despotism of the anarchy which threatens them; what reason is there to suppose that their efforts would not be crowned with success? The organization and the establishment of democracy in Christendom, is the great political problem of the time. The Americans, unquestionably, have not resolved this problem, but they furnish useful data to those who undertake the task.

IMPORTANCE OF WHAT PRECEDES WITH RESPECT TO THE STATE OF EUROPE.

It may readily be discovered with what intention I undertook the foregoing inquiries. The question here discussed is interesting not only to the United States, but to the whole world; it concerns, not a nation, but all mankind. If those nations whose social condition is democratic could only remain free as long as they are inhabitants of the wilds, we could not but despair of the future destiny of the human race; for democracy is rapidly acquiring a more extended sway, and the wilds are gradually peopled with men. If it were true that laws and manners are insufficient to maintain democratic institutions, what refuge would remain open to the nations except the despotism of a single individual? I am aware that there are many worthy persons at the present time who are not alarmed at this latter alternative, and who are so tired of liberty as to be glad of repose, far from those storms by which it is attended. But these individuals are ill acquainted with the haven to which they are bound. They are so deluded by their recollections, as to judge the tendency of absolute power by what it was formerly, and not what it might become at the present time.

If absolute power were re-established among the democratic nations of Europe, I am persuaded that it would assume a new form, and appear under features unknown to our forefathers. There was a time in Europe, when the laws and the consent of the people had invested princes with almost unlimited authority; but they scarcely ever availed themselves of it. I do not speak of the prerogatives of the nobility, of the authority of supreme courts of justice, of corporations and their chartered rights, or of provincial privileges, which served to break the blows of the sovereign authority, and to maintain a spirit of resistance in the nation. Independently of these political institutions—which, however opposed they might be to personal liberty, served to keep alive the love of freedom in the mind of the public, and which may be esteemed to have been useful in this respect—the manners and opinions of the nation confined the royal authority within barriers which were not less powerful, although they were less conspicuous. Religion, the affections of the people, the benevolence of the prince, the sense of honor, family pride, provincial prejudices, custom, and public opinion, limited the power of kings, and restrained their authority within an invisible circle. The constitution of nations was despotic at that time, but their manners were free. Princes had the right, but they had neither the means nor the desire, of doing whatever they pleased.

But what now remains of those barriers which formerly arrested the aggressions of tyranny? Since religion has lost its empire over the souls of men, the most prominent boundary which divided good from evil is overthrown: the very elements of the moral world are indeterminate; the princes and the peoples of the earth are guided by chance, and none can define the natural limits of despotism and the bounds of license. Long revolutions have for ever destroyed the respect which surrounded the rulers of the state; and since they have been relieved from the burden of public esteem, princes may henceforward surrender themselves without fear to the seductions of arbitrary power.

When kings find that the hearts of their subjects are turned toward them, they are clement, because they are conscious of their strength; and they are chary of the affection of their people, because the affection of their people is the bulwark of the throne. A mutual interchange of good will then takes place between the prince and the people, which resembles the gracious intercourse of domestic society. The subjects may murmur at the sovereign's decree, but they are grieved to displease him; and the sovereign chastises his subjects with the light hand of parental affection.

But when once the spell of royalty is broken in the tumult of revolution; when successive monarchs have occupied the throne, and alternately displayed to the people the weakness of right, and the harshness of power, the sovereign is no longer regarded by any as the father of the state, and he is feared by all as its master. If he be weak, he is despised; if he be strong, he is detested. He is himself full of animosity and alarm; he finds that he is a stranger in his own country, and he treats his subjects like conquered enemies.

When the provinces and the towns formed so many different nations in the midst of their common country, each of them had a will of its own, which was opposed to the general spirit of subjection; but now that all the parts of the same empire, after having lost their immunities, their customs, their prejudices, their traditions, and their names, are subjected and accustomed to the same laws, it is not more difficult to oppress them collectively, than it was formerly to oppress them singly.

While the nobles enjoyed their power, and indeed long

after that power was lost. the honor of aristocracy conferred an extraordinary degree of force upon their personal opposition. They afforded instances of men who, notwithstanding their weakness, still entertained a high opinion of their personal value, and dared to cope single-handed with the efforts of the public authority. But at the present day, when all ranks are more and more confounded, when the individual disappears in the throng, and is easily lost in the midst of a common obscurity, when the honor of monarchy has almost lost its empire without being succeeded by public virtue, and when nothing can enable man to rise above himself, who shall say at what point the exigencies of power and servility of weakness will stop ?

As long as family feeling was kept alive, the antagonist of oppression was never alone ; he looked about him, and found his clients, his hereditary friends, and his kinsfolk. If this support was wanting, he was sustained by his ancestors and animated by his posterity. But when patrimonial estates are divided, and when a few years suffice to confound the distinctions of a race, where can family feeling be found ? What force can there be in the customs of a country which has changed, and is still perpetually changing its aspect ; in which every act of tyranny has a precedent, and every crime an example ; in which there is nothing so old that its antiquity can save it from destruction, and nothing so unparalleled that its novelty can prevent it from being done ? What resistance can be offered by manners of so pliant a make, that they have already often yielded ? What strength can even public opinion have retained, when no twenty persons are connected by a common tie ; when not a man, nor a family, nor chartered corporation, nor class, nor free institution, has the power of representing that opinion ; and when every citizen—being equally weak, equally poor, and equally dependant—has only his personal impotence to oppose to the organized force of the government ?

The annals of France furnish nothing analogous to the condition in which that country might then be thrown. But it may more aptly be assimilated to the times of old, and to those hideous eras of Roman oppression, when the manners of the people were corrupted, their traditions obliterated, their habits destroyed, their opinions shaken, and freedom, expelled from the laws, could find no refuge in the land ; when nothing protected the citizens, and the citizens no longer protected themselves ; when human nature was the sport of man, and princes wearied out the clemency of Heaven before they exhausted the patience of their subjects. Those who hope to revive the monarchy of Henry IV. or of Louis XIV., appear to me to be afflicted with mental blindness; and when I consider the present condition of several European nations—a condition to which all the others tend—I am led to believe that they will soon be left with no other alternative than democratic liberty, or the tyranny of the Cesars.

And, indeed, it is deserving of consideration, whether men are to be entirely emancipated, or entirely enslaved; whether their rights are to be made equal, or wholly taken away from them. If the rulers of society were reduced either gradually to raise the crowd to their own level, or to sink the citizens below that of humanity, would not the doubts of many be resolved, the consciences of many be healed, and the community be prepared to make great sacrifices with little difficulty? In that case, the gradual growth of democratic manners and institutions should be regarded, not as the best, but as the only means of preserving freedom; and without liking the government of democracy, it might be adopted as the most applicable and the fairest remedy for the present ills of society.

It is difficult to associate a people in the work of government; but it is still more difficult to supply it with experience, and to inspire it with the feelings which it requires in order to govern well. I grant that the caprices of democracy are perpetual; its instruments are rude, its laws imperfect. But if it were true that soon no just medium would exist between the empire of democracy and the dominion of a single arm, should we not rather incline toward the former, than submit voluntarily to the latter? And if complete equality be our fate, is it not better to be levelled by free institutions than by despotic power?

Those who, after having read this book, should imagine that my intention in writing it has been to propose the laws and manners of the Anglo-Americans for the imitation of all democratic peoples, would commit a very great mistake; they must have paid more attention to the form than to the substance of my ideas. My aim has been to show, by the example of America, that laws, and especially manners, may exist, which will allow a democratic people to remain free. But I am very far from thinking that we ought to follow the example of the American democracy, and copy the means which it has employed to attain its ends; for I am well aware of the influence which the nature of a country and its political precedents exercise upon a constitution; and I should regard it as a great misfortune for mankind, if liberty were to exist, all over the world, under the same forms.

But I am of opinion that if we do not succeed in gradually introducing democratic institutions into France, and if we despair of imparting to the citizens those ideas and sentiments which first prepare them for freedom, and afterward allow them to enjoy it, there will be no independence at all, either for the middling classes or the nobility, for the poor or for the rich, but an equal tyranny over all; and I foresee that if the peaceable empire of the majority be not founded among us in time, we shall sooner or later arrive at the unlimited authority of a single despot.

CHAPTER XVIII.

THE PRESENT AND PROBABLE FUTURE CONDITION OF THE THREE RACES WHICH INHABIT THE TERRITORY OF THE UNITED STATES.

The principal part of the task which I had imposed upon myself is now performed: I have shown, as far as I was able, the laws and manners of the American democracy. Here I might stop; but the reader would perhaps feel that I had not satisfied his expectations.

The absolute supremacy of democracy is not all that we meet with in America; the inhabitants of the New World may be considered from more than one point of view. In the course of this work, my subject has often led me to speak of the Indians and the negroes; but I have never been able to stop in order to show what places these two races occupy, in the midst of the democratic people whom I was engaged in describing. I have mentioned in what spirit, and according to what laws, the Anglo-American Union was formed; but I could only glance at the dangers which menace that confederation, while it was equally impossible for me to give a detailed account of its chances of duration, independently of its laws and manners. When speaking of the United republican States, I hazarded no conjectures upon the permanence of republican forms in the New World; and when making frequent allusion to the commercial activity which reigns in the Union, I was unable to inquire into the future condition of the Americans as a commercial people.

These topics are collaterally connected with my subject, without forming a part of it; they are American, without being democratic; and to portray democracy has been my principal aim. It was therefore necessary to postpone these questions, which I now take up as the proper termination of my work.

The territory now occupied or claimed by the American Union, spreads from the shores of the Atlantic to those of the Pacific ocean. On the east and west its limits are those of the continent itself. On the south it advances nearly to the tropic, and it extends upward to the icy regions of the north.*

The human beings who are scattered over this space do not form, as in Europe, so many branches of the same stock. Three races naturally distinct, and I might almost say hostile to each other, are discoverable among them at the first glance. Almost insurmountable barriers had been raised between them by education and by law, as well as by their origin and outward characteristics; but fortune has brought them together on the same soil, where, although they are mixed, they do not amalgamate, and each race fulfils its destiny apart.

Among these widely differing families of men, the first which attracts attention, the superior in intelligence, in power, and in enjoyment, is the white or European, the MAN pre-eminent; and in subordinate grades, the negro and the Indian. These two unhappy races have nothing in common; neither birth, nor features, nor language, nor habits. Their only resemblance lies in their misfortunes. Both of them occupy an inferior rank in the country they inhabit; both suffer from tyranny; and if their wrongs are not the same, they originate at any rate with the same authors.

If we reasoned from what passes in the world, we should almost say that the European is to the other races of mankind, what man is to the lower animals;—he makes them subservient to his use; and when he cannot subdue, he destroys them. Oppression has at one stroke deprived the descendants of the Africans of almost all the privileges of humanity. The negro of the United States has lost all remembrance of his country; the language which his forefathers spoke is never heard around him; he abjured their religion and forgot their customs when he ceased to belong to Africa, without acquiring any claim to European privileges. But he remains half-way between the two communities; sold by the

* See the map.

one, repulsed by the other; finding not a spot in the universe to call by the name of country, except the faint image of a home which the shelter of his master's roof affords.

The negro has no family; woman is merely the temporary companion of his pleasures, and his children are upon an equality with himself from the moment of their birth. Am I to call it a proof of God's mercy, or a visitation of his wrath, that man in certain states appears to be insensible to his extreme wretchedness, and almost affects with a depraved taste the cause of his misfortunes? The negro, who is plunged in this abyss of evils, scarcely feels his own calamitous situation. Violence made him a slave, and the habit of servitude gives him the thoughts and desires of a slave; he admires his tyrants more than he hates them, and finds his joy and his pride in the servile imitation of those who oppress him: his understanding is degraded to the level of his soul.

The negro enters upon slavery as soon as he is born; nay, he may have been purchased in the womb, and have begun his slavery before he began his existence. Equally devoid of wants and of enjoyment, and useless to himself, he learns, with his first notions of existence, that he is the property of another who has an interest in preserving his life, and that the care of it does not devolve upon himself; even the power of thought appears to him a useless gift of Providence, and he quietly enjoys the privileges of his debasement.

If he becomes free, independence is often felt by him to be a heavier burden than slavery; for having learned, in the course of his life, to submit to everything except reason, he is too much unacquainted with her dictates to obey them. A thousand new desires beset him, and he is destitute of the knowledge and energy necessary to resist them: these are masters which it is necessary to contend with, and he has learned only to submit and obey. In short, he sinks to such a depth of wretchedness, that while servitude brutalizes, liberty destroys him.

Oppression has been no less fatal to the Indian than to the negro race, but its effects are different. Before the arrival of the white men in the New World, the inhabitants of North America lived quietly in their woods, enduring the vicissitudes, and practising the virtues and vices common to savage nations. The Europeans, having dispersed the Indian tribes and driven them into the deserts, condemned them to a wandering life full of inexpressible sufferings.

Savage nations are only controlled by opinion and by custom. When the North American Indians had lost their sentiment of attachment to their country ; when their families were dispersed, their traditions obscured, and the chain of their recollections broken ; when all their habits were changed, and their wants increased beyond measure, European tyranny rendered them more disorderly and less civilized than they were before. The moral and physical condition of these tribes continually grew worse, and they became more barbarous as they became more wretched. Nevertheless the Europeans have not been able to metamorphose the character of the Indians ; and though they have had power to destroy them, they have never been able to make them submit to the rules of civilized society.

The lot of the negro is placed on the extreme limit of servitude, while that of the Indian lies on the utmost verge of liberty ; and slavery does not produce more fatal effects upon the first, than independence upon the second. The negro has lost all property in his own person, and he cannot dispose of his existence without committing a sort of fraud : but the savage is his own master as soon as he is able to act ; parental authority is scarcely known to him ; he has never bent his will to that of any of his kind, or learned the difference between voluntary obedience and a shameful subjection ; and the very name of law is unknown to him. To be free, with him, signifies to escape from all the shackles of society. As he delights in this barbarous independence, and would rather perish than sacrifice the least part of it, civilisation has little power over him.

The negro makes a thousand fruitless efforts to insinuate himself among men who repulse him ; he conforms to the taste of his oppressors, adopts their opinions, and hopes by imitating them to form a part of their community. Having been told from infancy that his race is naturally inferior to that of the whites, he assents to the proposition, and is ashamed of his own nature. In each of his features he discovers a trace of slavery, and, if it were in his power, he would willingly rid himself of everything that makes him what he is.

The Indian, on the contrary, has his imagination inflated with the pretended nobility of his origin, and lives and dies in the midst of these dreams of pride. Far from desiring to conform his habits to ours, he loves his savage life as the distinguishing mark of his race, and he repels every advance to civilisation, less perhaps from the hatred which he entertains for it, than from a dread of resembling the Europeans.*

* The native of North America retains his opinions and the most insignificant of his habits with a degree of tenacity which has no parallel

While he has nothing to oppose to our perfection in the arts but the resources of the desert, to our tactics nothing but undisciplined courage; while our well-digested plans are met by the spontaneous instincts of savage life, who can wonder if he fails in this unequal contest?

The negro who earnestly desires to mingle his race with that of the European, cannot effect it; while the Indian, who might succeed to a certain extent, disdains to make the attempt. The servility of the one dooms him to slavery, the pride of the other to death.

I remember that while I was travelling through the forests which still cover the state of Alabama, I arrived one day at the log house of a pioneer. I did not wish to penetrate into the dwelling of the American, but retired to rest myself for a while on the margin of a spring, which was not far off, in the woods. While I was in this place (which was in the neighborhood of the Creek territory), an Indian woman appeared, followed by a negress, and holding by the hand a little white girl of five or six years old, whom I took to be the daughter of the pioneer. A sort of barbarous luxury set off the costume of the Indian; rings of metal were hanging from her nostrils and ears; her hair, which was adorned with glass beads, fell loosely upon her shoulders; and I saw that she was not married, for she still wore the necklace of shells which the

in history. For more than two hundred years the wandering tribes of North America have had daily intercourse with the whites, and they have never derived from them either a custom or an idea. Yet the Europeans have exercised a powerful influence over the savages: they have made them more licentious, but not more European. In the summer of 1831, I happened to be beyond Lake Michigan, at a place called Green Bay, which serves as the extreme frontier between the United States and the Indians on the northwestern side. Here I became acquainted with an American officer, Major H., who, after talking to me at length on the inflexibility of the Indian character, related the following fact: "I formerly knew a young Indian," said he, "who had been educated at a college in New England, where he had greatly distinguished himself, and had acquired the external appearance of a member of civilized society. When the war broke out between ourselves and the English, in 1810, I saw this young man again; he was serving in our army at the head of the warriors of his tribe; for the Indians were admitted among the ranks of the Americans, upon condition that they would abstain from their horrible custom of scalping their victims. On the evening of the battle of * * *, C. came and sat himself down by the fire of our bivouac. I asked him what had been his fortune that day: he related his exploits; and growing warm and animated by the recollection of them, he concluded by suddenly opening the breast of his coat, saying, 'You must not betray me—see here!' And I actually beheld," said the major, "between his body and his shirt, the skin and hair of an English head still dripping with gore."

bride always deposites on the nuptial couch. The negress was clad in squalid European garments.

They all three came and seated themselves upon the banks of the fountain; and the young Indian, taking the child in her arms, lavished upon her such fond caresses as mothers give; while the negress endeavored by various little artifices to attract the attention of the young creole. The child displayed in her slightest gestures a consciousness of superiority which formed a strange contrast with her infantine weakness; as if she received the attentions of her companions with a sort of condescension.

The negress was seated on the ground before her mistress, watching her smallest desires, and apparently divided between strong affection for the child and servile fear; while the savage displayed, in the midst of her tenderness, an air of freedom and of pride which was almost ferocious. I had approached the group, and I contemplated them in silence; but my curiosity was probably displeasing to the Indian woman, for she suddenly rose, pushed the child roughly from her, and giving me an angry look, plunged into the thicket.

I had often chanced to see individuals met together in the same place, who belonged to the three races of men which people North America. I had perceived from many different results the preponderance of the whites. But in the picture which I have just been describing there was something peculiarly touching; a bond of affection here united the oppressors with the oppressed, and the effort of Nature to bring them together rendered still more striking the immense distance placed between them by prejudice and by law.

THE PRESENT AND PROBABLE FUTURE CONDITION OF THE INDIAN TRIBES WHICH INHABIT THE TERRITORY POSSESSED BY THE UNION.

Gradual disappearance of the native Tribes.—Manner in which it takes place.—Miseries accompanying the forced Migrations of the Indians.—The Savages of North America had only two ways of escaping Destruction; War or Civilisation.—They are no longer able to make War.—Reasons why they refused to become civilized when it was in their Power, and why they cannot become so now that they desire it.—Instance of the Creek and Cherokees.—Policy of the particular States toward these Indians.—Policy of the federal Government.

None of the Indian tribes which formerly inhabited the territory of New England—the Narragansets, the Mohicans, the

Pequots—have any existence but in the recollection of man. The Lenapes, who received William Penn a hundred and fifty years ago upon the banks of the Delaware, have disappeared; and I myself met with the last of the Iroquois, who were begging alms. The nations I have mentioned formerly covered the country to the seacoast; but a traveller at the present day must penetrate more than a hundred leagues into the interior of the continent to find an Indian. Not only have these wild tribes receded, but they are destroyed;* and as they give way or perish, an immense and increasing people fills their place. There is no instance on record of so prodigious a growth, or so rapid a destruction; the manner in which the latter change takes place is not difficult to describe.

When the Indians were the sole inhabitants of the wilds whence they have been expelled, their wants were few. Their arms were of their own manufacture, their only drink was the water of the brook, and their clothes consisted of the skin of animals, whose flesh furnished them with food.

The Europeans introduced among the savages of North America firearms, ardent spirits, and iron: they taught them to exchange for manufactured stuffs the rough garments which had previously satisfied their untutored simplicity. Having acquired new tastes, without the arts by which they could be gratified, the Indians were obliged to have recourse to the workmanship of the whites; but in return for their productions, the savage had nothing to offer except the rich furs which still abounded in his woods. Hence the chase became necessary, not merely to provide for his subsistence, but in order to procure the only objects of barter which he could furnish to Europe.† While the wants of the natives

* In the thirteen original states, there are only 6,273 Indians remaining. (See Legislative Documents, 20th congress, No. 117, p. 90.)

† Messrs. Clarke and Cass, in their report to congress, the 4th February, 1829, p. 23, expressed themselves thus: "The time when the Indians generally could supply themselves with food and clothing, without any of the articles of civilized life, has long since passed away. The more remote tribes, beyond the Mississippi, who live where immense herds of buffalo are yet to be found, and who follow those animals in their periodical migrations, could more easily than any others recur to the habits of their ancestors, and live without the white man or any of his manufactures. But the buffalo is constantly receding. The smaller animals—the bear, the deer, the beaver, the otter, the muskrat, &c., principally minister to the comfort and support of the Indians; and these cannot be taken without guns, ammunition, and traps.

were thus increasing, their resources continued to diminish. From the moment when a European settlement is formed in the neighborhood of the territory occupied by the Indians, the beasts of chase take the alarm.* Thousands of savages, wandering in the forest and destitute of any fixed dwelling, did not disturb them; but as soon as the continuous sounds of European labor are heard in the neighborhood, they begin to flee away, and retire to the west, where their instinct teaches them that they will find deserts of immeasurable extent. "The buffalo is constantly receding," say Messrs. Clarke and Cass in their Report of the year 1829; "a few years since they approached the base of the Alleghany; and a few years hence they may even be rare upon the immense plains which extend to the base of the Rocky mountains." I have been assured that this effect of the approach of the whites is often felt at two hundred leagues' distance from the frontier. Their influence is thus exerted over tribes whose name is unknown to them, and who suffer the evils of usurpation long before they are acquainted with the authors of their distress.†

Bold adventurers soon penetrate into the country the Indians have deserted, and when they have advanced about fifteen or twenty leagues from the extreme frontiers of the whites, they begin to build habitations for civilized beings

"Among the northwestern Indians particularly, the labor of supplying a family with food is excessive. Day after day is spent by the hunter without success, and during this interval his family must subsist upon bark or roots, or perish. Want and misery are around them and among them. Many die every winter from actual starvation."

The Indians will not live as Europeans live; and yet they can neither subsist without them, nor exactly after the fashion of their fathers. This is demonstrated by a fact which I likewise give upon official authority. Some Indians of a tribe on the banks of Lake Superior had killed a European; the American government interdicted all traffic with the tribe to which the guilty parties belonged, until they were delivered up to justice. This measure had the desired effect.

* "Five years ago," says Volney in his Tableaux des Etats Unis, p. 370, "in going from Vincennes to Kaskaskia, a territory which now forms part of the State of Illinois, but which at the time I mention was completely wild (1797), you could not cross a prairie without seeing herds of from four to five hundred buffaloes. There are now none remaining; they swam across the Mississippi to escape from the hunters, and more particularly from the bells of the American cows."

† The truth of what I here advance may be easily proved by consulting the tabular statement of Indian tribes inhabiting the United States, and their territories. (Legislative Documents, 20th congress, No. 117, pp. 90–105.) It is there shown that the tribes of America are rapidly decreasing, although the Europeans are at a considerable distance from them.

in the midst of the wilderness. This is done without difficulty, as the territory of a hunting nation is ill defined; it is the common property of the tribe, and belongs to no one in particular, so that individual interests are not concerned in the protection of any part of it.

A few European families, settled in different situations at a considerable distance from each other, soon drive away the wild animals which remain between their places of abode. The Indians, who had previously lived in a sort of abundance, then find it difficult to subsist, and still more difficult to procure the articles of barter which they stand in need of.

To drive away their game is to deprive them of the means of existence, as effectually as if the fields of our agriculturists were stricken with barrenness; and they are reduced, like famished wolves, to prowl through the forsaken woods in quest of prey. Their instinctive love of their country attaches them to the soil which gave them birth,* even after it has ceased to yield anything but misery and death. At length they are compelled to acquiesce, and to depart: they follow the traces of the elk, the buffalo, and the beaver,. and are guided by those wild animals in the choice of their future country. Properly speaking, therefore, it is not the Europeans who drive away the native inhabitants of America; it is famine which compels them to recede; a happy distinction, which had escaped the casuists of former times, and for which we are indebted to modern discovery.

It is impossible to conceive the extent of the sufferings which attend these forced emigrations. They are undertaken by a people already exhausted and reduced; and the countries to which the new-comers betake themselves are inhabited by other tribes which receive them with jealous hostility. Hunger is in the rear war awaits them, and misery besets them on all sides. In the hope of escaping from such a host of enemies, they separate, and each individual endeavors to procure the means of supporting his existence in solitude and secresy, living in the immensity of

* "The Indians," says Messrs. Clarke and Cass in their report to congress, p. 15, "are attached to their country by the same feelings which bind us to ours; and, besides, there are certain superstitious notions connected with the alienation of what the Great Spirit gave to their ancestors, which operate strongly upon the tribes who have made few or no cessions, but which are gradually weakened as our intercourse with them is extended. 'We will not sell the spot which contains the bones of our fathers,' is almost always the first answer to a proposition for a sale."

the desert like an outcast in civilized society. The social tie, which distress had long since weakened, is then dissolved; they have lost their country, and their people soon deserts them; their very families are obliterated; the names they bore in common are forgotten, their language perishes, and all the traces of their origin disappear. Their nation has ceased to exist, except in the recollection of the antiquaries of America and a few of the learned of Europe.

I should be sorry to have my reader suppose that I am coloring the picture too highly: I saw with my own eyes several of the cases of misery which I have been describing; and I was the witness of sufferings which I have not the power to portray.

At the end of the year 1831, while I was on the left bank of the Mississippi, at a place named by Europeans Memphis, there arrived a numerous band of Choctaws (or Chactas, as they are called by the French in Louisiana). These savages had left their country, and were endeavoring to gain the right bank of the Mississippi, where they hoped to find an asylum which had been promised them by the American government. It was then in the middle of winter, and the cold was unusually severe; the snow had frozen hard upon the ground, and the river was drifting huge masses of ice. The Indians had their families with them; and they brought in their train the wounded and the sick, with children newly born, and old men upon the verge of death. They possessed neither tents nor wagons, but only their arms and some provisions. I saw them embark to pass the mighty river, and never will that solemn spectacle fade from my remembrance. No cry, no sob was heard among the assembled crowd: all were silent. Their calamities were of ancient date, and they knew them to be irremediable. The Indians had all stepped into the bark which was to carry them across, but their dogs remained upon the bank. As soon as these animals perceived that their masters were finally leaving the shore, they set up a dismal howl, and plunging all together into the icy waters of the Mississippi, they swam after the boat.

The ejectment of the Indians very often takes place at the present day, in a regular, and, as it were, a legal manner. When the European population begins to approach the limit of the desert inhabited by a savage tribe, the government of the United States usually despatches envoys to them, who assemble the Indians in a large plain, and having first eaten and drunk with them, accost them in the following manner: "What have you to do in the land of your fathers? Before long you must dig up their bones in order to live. In what respect is the country you inhabit better than another? Are there no woods, marshes, or prairies, except where you dwell? And can you live nowhere but under your own sun? Beyond those mountains which you see at the horizon, beyond the lake which bounds your territory on the west, there lie vast countries where beasts of chase are found in great abundance; sell your land to us, and go to live happily in those solitudes." After holding this language, they spread before the eyes of the Indians fire-arms, woollen garments, kegs of brandy, glass necklaces, bracelets of tinsel, ear-rings, and looking-glasses.* If, when they have beheld all these riches, they still hesitate, it is insinuated that they have not the means of refusing their required consent, and that the government itself will not long have the power of protecting them in their rights. What are they to do? Half convinced and half compelled, they go to inhabit new deserts, where the importunate whites will not let them remain ten years in tranquillity. In this manner do the Americans obtain at a very low price whole provinces, which the richest sovereigns of Europe could not purchase.*

* See in the legislative documents of congress (Doc. 117), the narrative of what takes place on these occasions. This curious passage is from the abovementioned report, made to congress by Messrs. Clarke and Cass, in February, 1829. Mr. Cass is now secretary of war.

"The Indians," says the report, "reach the treaty-ground poor, and almost naked. Large quantities of goods are taken there by the traders, and are seen and examined by the Indians. The women and children become importunate to have their wants supplied, and their influence is soon exerted to induce a sale. Their improvidence is habitual and unconquerable. The gratification of his immediate wants and desires is the ruling passion of an Indian: the expectation of future advantages seldom produces much effect. The experience of the past is lost, and the prospects of the future disregarded. It would be utterly hopeless to demand a cession of land unless the means were at hand of gratifying their immediate wants; and when their condition and circumstances are fairly considered, it ought not to surprise us that they are so anxious to relieve themselves."

† On the 19th of May, 1830, Mr. Edward Everett affirmed before the house of representatives, that the Americans had already acquired by *treaty*, to the east and west of the Mississippi, 230,000,000 of acres. In 1808, the Osages gave up 48,000,000 acres for an annual payment of 1,000 dollars. In 1818, the Quapaws yielded up 29,000,000 acres for 4,000 dollars. They reserved for themselves a territory of 1,000,000 acres for a hunting-ground. A solemn oath was taken that it should be respected: but before long it was invaded like the rest.

Mr. Bell, in his "Report of the Committee on Indian Affairs," February 24th, 1830, has these words: "To pay an Indian tribe what their ancient hunting-grounds are worth to them, after the game is fled or destroyed, as a mode of appropriating wild lands claimed by In-

These are great evils, and it must be added that they appear to me to be irremediable. I believe that the Indian nations of North America are doomed to perish: and that whenever the Europeans shall be established on the shores of the Pacific ocean, that race of men will be no more.* The Indians had only the two alternatives of war or civilisation; in other words, they must either have destroyed the Europeans or become their equals.

At the first settlement of the colonies they might have found it possible, by uniting their forces, to deliver themselves from the small bodies of strangers who landed on their continent.† They several times attempted to do it, and were on the point of succeeding; but the disproportion of their resources, at the present day, when compared with those of the whites, is too great to allow such an enterprise to be thought of. Nevertheless, there do arise from time to time among the Indians men of penetration, who foresee the final destiny which awaits the native population, and who exert themselves to unite all the tribes in common hostility to the Europeans; but their efforts are unavailing. Those tribes which are in the neighborhood of the whites are too much weakened to offer an effectual resistance; while the others, giving way to that childish carelessness of the morrow which characterizes savage life, wait for the near approach of dan-

dians, has been found more convenient, and certainly it is more agreeable to the forms of justice, as well as more merciful, than to assert the possession of them by the sword. Thus the practice of buying Indian titles is but the substitute which humanity and expediency have imposed, in place of the sword, in arriving at the actual enjoyment of property claimed by the right of discovery, and sanctioned by the natural superiority allowed to the claims of civilized communities over those of savage tribes. Up to the present time, so invariable has been the operation of certain causes, first in diminishing the value of forest lands to the Indians, and secondly in disposing them to sell readily, that the plan of buying their right of occupancy has never threatened to retard, in any perceptible degree, the prosperity of any of the states.' (Legislative documents, 21st congress, No. 227, p. 6.)

* This seems, indeed, to be the opinion of almost all the American statesmen. "Judging of the future by the past," says Mr. Cass, "we cannot err in anticipating a progressive diminution of their numbers, and their eventual extinction, unless our border should become stationary, and they be removed beyond it, or unless some radical change should take place in the principles of our intercourse with them, which it is easier to hope for than to expect."

† Among other warlike enterprises, there was one of the Wampanoags, and other confederate tribes, under Metacom in 1675, against the colonists of New England; the English were also engaged in war in Virginia in 1622

ger before they prepare to meet it: some are unable, the others are unwilling to exert themselves.

It is easy to foresee that the Indians will never conform to civilisation; or that it will be too late, whenever they may be inclined to make the experiment.

Civilisation is the result of a long social process which takes place in the same spot, and is handed down from one generation to another, each one profiting by the experience of the last. Of all nations, those submit to civilisation with the most difficulty, which habitually live by the chase. Pastoral tribes, indeed, often change their place of abode; but they follow in regular order in their migrations, and often return again to their old stations, while the dwelling of the hunter varies with that of the animals he pursues.

Several attempts have been made to diffuse knowledge among the Indians, without controlling their wandering propensities; by the Jesuits in Canada, and by the puritans in New England;* but none of these endeavors were crowned by any lasting success. Civilisation began in the cabin, but it soon retired to expire in the woods; the great error of these legislators of the Indians was their not understanding, that in order to succeed in civilizing a people, it is first necessary to fix it; which cannot be done without inducing it to cultivate the soil: the Indians ought in the first place to have been accustomed to agriculture. But not only are they destitute of this indispensable preliminary to civilisation, they would even have great difficulty in acquiring it. Men who have once abandoned themselves to the restless and adventurous life of the hunter, feel an insurmountable disgust for the constant and regular labor which tillage requires. We see this proved in the bosom of our own society; but it is far more visible among peoples whose partiality for the chase is a part of their natural character.

Independently of this general difficulty, there is another, which applies peculiarly to the Indians; they consider labor not merely as an evil, but as a disgrace; so that their pride prevents them from becoming civilized, as much as their indolence.†

* See the "Histoire de la Nouvelle France," by Charlevoix, and the work entitled "Lettres Edifiantes."

† "In all the tribes," says Volney, in his "Tableau des Etats Unis," p. 423, "there still exists a generation of old warriors, who cannot forbear, when they see their countrymen using the hoe, from exclaiming against the degradation of ancient manners, and asserting that the savages owe their decline to these innovations: adding, that they have only to return to their primitive habits, in order to recover their power and their glory."

There is no Indian so wretched as not to retain, under his hut of bark, a lofty idea of his personal worth; he considers the cares of industry and labor as degrading occupations; he compares the husbandman to the ox which traces the furrow; and even in our most ingenious handicraft, he can see nothing but the labor of slaves. Not that he is devoid of admiration for the power and intellectual greatness of the whites; but although the result of our efforts surprises him, he contemns the means by which we obtain it; and while he acknowledges our ascendency, he still believes in his superiority. War and hunting are the only pursuits which appear to him worthy to be the occupations of a man.* The Indian, in the dreary solitude of his woods, cherishes the same ideas, the same opinions, as the noble of the middle ages in his castle, and he only requires to become a conqueror to complete the resemblance; thus, however strange it may seem, it is in the forests of the New World, and not among the Europeans who people its coasts, that the ancient prejudices of Europe are still in existence.

More than once, in the course of this work, I have endeavored to explain the prodigious influence which the social condition appears to exercise upon the laws and the manners of men; and I beg to add a few words on the same subject. When I perceive the resemblance which exists between the political institutions of our ancestors, the Germans, and of the wandering tribes of North America: between the customs described by Tacitus, and those of which I have sometimes been a witness, I cannot help thinking that the same cause has brought about the same results in both hemispheres; and that in the midst of the apparent diversity of human affairs, a certain number of primary facts may be discovered, from which all the others are derived. In what we usually call the German institutions, then, I am inclined only to perceive

* The following description occurs in an official document: "Until a young man has been engaged with an enemy, and has performed some acts of valor, he gains no consideration, but is regarded nearly as a woman. In their great war-dances all the warriors in succession strike the post, as it is called, and recount their exploits. On these occasions their auditory consists of the kinsmen, friends, and comrades of the narrator. The profound impression which his discourse produces on them is manifested by the silent attention it receives, and by the loud shouts which hail its termination. The young man who finds himself at such a meeting without anything to recount, is very unhappy; and instances have sometimes occurred of young warriors whose passions had been thus inflamed, quitting the war-dance suddenly, and going off alone to seek for trophies which they might exhibit, and adventures which they might be allowed to relate.

barbarian habits; and the opinions of savages, in what we style feudal principles.

However strongly the vices and prejudices of the North American Indians may be opposed to their becoming agricultural and civilized, necessity sometimes obliges them to it. Several of the southern nations, and among them the Cherokees and the Creeks,* were surrounded by Europeans, who had landed on the shores of the Atlantic, and who, either descending the Ohio or proceeding up the Mississippi, arrived simultaneously upon their borders. These tribes have not been driven from place to place, like their northern brethren; but they have been gradually enclosed within narrow limits, like the game within the thicket before the huntsmen plunge into the interior. The Indians, who were thus placed between civilisation and death, found themselves obliged to live by ignominious labor like the whites. They took to agriculture, and without entirely forsaking their old habits or manners, sacrificed only as much as was necessary to their existence.

The Cherokees went further; they created a written language; established a permanent form of government; and as everything proceeds rapidly in the New World, before they had all of them clothes, they set up a newspaper.†

The growth of European habits has been remarkably accelerated among these Indians by the mixed race which has sprung up.‡ Deriving intelligence from the father's side, without entirely losing the savage customs of the mother, the half-blood forms the natural link between civilisation and

* These nations are now swallowed up in the states of Georgia, Tennessee, Alabama, and Mississippi. There were formerly in the south four great nations (remnants of which still exist), the Choctaws, the Chickasaws, the Creeks, and the Cherokees. The remnants of these four nations amounted, in 1830, to about 75,000 individuals. It is computed that there are now remaining in the territory occupied or claimed by the Anglo-American Union about 300,000 Indians. (See proceedings of the Indian board in the city of New York.) The official documents supplied to congress make the number amount to 313,130. The reader who is curious to know the names and numerical strength of all the tribes which inhabit the Anglo-American territory, should consult the documents I refer to. (Legislative Documents, 28th congress, No. 117, pp. 90–105.)

† I brought back with me to France, one or two copies of this singular publication.

‡ See in the report of the committee on Indian affairs, 21st congress, No. 227, p. 23, the reasons for the multiplication of Indians of mixed blood among the Cherokees. The principal cause dates from the war of independence. Many Anglo-Americans of Georgia, having taken the side of England, were obliged to retreat among the Indians, where they married.

barbarism. Wherever this race has multiplied, the savage state has become modified, and a great change has taken place in the manners of the people.*

The success of the Cherokees proves that the Indians are capable of civilisation, but it does not prove that they will succeed in it. The difficulty which the Indians find in submitting to civilisation proceeds from the influence of a general cause, which it is almost impossible for them to escape. An attentive survey of history demonstrates that, in general, barbarous nations have raised themselves to civilisation by degrees, and by their own efforts. Whenever they derived knowledge from a foreign people, they stood toward it in the relation of conquerors, not of a conquered nation. When the conquered nation is enlightened, and the conquerors are half savage, as in the case of the invasion of Rome by the northern nations, or that of China by the Moguls, the power which victory bestows upon the barbarian is sufficient to keep up his importance among civilized men, and permit him to rank as their equal, until he becomes their rival: the one has might on his side, the other has intelligence; the former admires the knowledge and the arts of the conquered, the latter envies the power of the conquerors. The barbarians at length admit civilized man into their palaces, and he in turn opens his schools to the barbarians. But when the side on

* Unhappily the mixed race has been less numerous and less influential in North America than in any other country. The American continent was peopled by two great nations of Europe, the French and the English. The former were not slow in connecting themselves with the daughters of the natives; but there was an unfortunate affinity between the Indian character and their own: instead of giving the tastes and habits of civilized life to the savages, the French too often grew passionately fond of the state of wild freedom they found them in. They became the most dangerous of the inhabitants of the desert, and won the friendship of the Indian by exaggerating his vices and his virtues. M. de Senonville, the governor of Canada, wrote thus to Louis XIV., in 1685: "It has long been believed that in order to civilize the savages we ought to draw them nearer to us, but there is every reason to suppose we have been mistaken. Those which have been brought into contact with us have not become French, and the French who have lived among them are changed into savages, affecting to live and dress like them." (History of New France, by Charlevoix, vol. ii., p. 345). The Englishman, on the contrary, continuing obstinately attached to the customs and the most insignificant habits of his forefathers, has remained in the midst of the American solitudes just what he was in the bosom of European cities; he would not allow of any communication with savages whom he despised, and avoided with care the union of his race with theirs. Thus, while the French exercised no salutary influence over the Indians, the English have always remained alien from them.

which the physical force lies, also possesses an intellectual preponderance, the conquered party seldom becomes civilized; it retreats, or is destroyed. It may therefore be said, in a general way, that savages go forth in arms to seek knowledge, but that they do not receive it when it comes to them.

If the Indian tribes which now inhabit the heart of the continent could summon up energy enough to attempt to civilize themselves, they might possibly succeed. Superior already to the barbarous nations which surround them, they would gradually gain strength and experience; and when the Europeans should appear upon their borders, they would be in a state, if not to maintain their independence, at least to assert their right to the soil, and to incorporate themselves with the conquerors. But it is the misfortune of Indians to be brought into contact with a civilized people, which is also (it may be owned) the most avaricious nation on the globe, while they are still semi-barbarian: to find despots in their instructers, and to receive knowledge from the hand of oppression. Living in the freedom of the woods, the North American Indian was destitute, but he had no feeling of inferiority toward any one; as soon, however, as he desires to penetrate into the social scale of the whites, he takes the lowest rank in society, for he enters ignorant and poor within the pale of science and wealth. After having led a life of agitation, beset with evils and dangers, but at the same time filled with proud emotions,* he is obliged to submit to a wearisome,

* There is in the adventurous life of the hunter a certain irresistible charm which seizes the heart of man, and carries him away in spite of reason and experience. This is plainly shown by the memoirs of Tanner. Tanner is a European who was carried away at the age of six by the Indians, and has remained thirty years with them in the woods. Nothing can be conceived more appalling than the miseries which he describes. He tells us of tribes without a chief, families without a nation to call their own, men in a state of isolation, wrecks of powerful tribes wandering at random amid the ice and snow and desolate solitudes of Canada. Hunger and cold pursue them; every day their life is in jeopardy. Among these men manners have lost their empire, traditions are without power. They become more and more savage. Tanner shared in all these miseries; he was aware of his European origin; he was not kept away from the whites by force; on the contrary, he came every year to trade with them, entered their dwellings, and saw their enjoyments; he knew that whenever he chose to return to civilized life, he was perfectly able to do so—and he remained thirty years in the deserts. When he came to civilized society, he declared that the rude existence which he described had a secret charm for him which he was unable to define: he returned to it again and again: at length he abandoned it with poignant regret; and when he was at length fixed among the whites, several of his children refused to share his tranquil and easy situation. I saw Tanner myself

obscure, and degraded state, and to gain the bread which nourishes him by hard and ignoble labor; such are in his eyes the only results of which civilisation can boast: and even this much he is not sure to obtain.

When the Indians undertake to imitate their European neighbors, and to till the earth like the settlers, they are immediately exposed to a very formidable competition. The white man is skilled in the craft of agriculture; the Indian is a rough beginner in an art with which he is unacquainted. The former reaps abundant crops without difficulty, the latter meets with a thousand obstacles in raising the fruits of the earth.

The European is placed among a population whose wants he knows and partakes. The savage is isolated in the midst of a hostile people, with whose manners, language and laws, he is imperfectly acquainted, but without whose assistance he cannot live. He can only procure the materials of comfort by bartering his commodities against the goods of the European, for the assistance of his countrymen is wholly insufficient to supply his wants. When the Indian wishes to sell the produce of his labor, he cannot always meet with a purchaser, while the European readily finds a market; and the former can only produce at a considerable cost, that which the latter vends at a very low rate. Thus the Indian has no sooner escaped those evils to which barbarous nations are exposed, than he is subjected to the still greater miseries of civilized communities; and he finds it scarcely less difficult to live in the midst of our abundance, than in the depth of his own wilderness.

He has not yet lost the habits of his erratic life; the traditions of his fathers and his passion for the chase are still alive within him. The wild enjoyments which formerly animated him in the woods painfully excite his troubled imagination; and his former privations appear to be less keen, his former perils less appalling. He contrasts the independence which he possessed among his equals with the servile position which he occupies in civilized society. On the other hand, the solitudes which were so long his free home are still at hand; a few hours' march will bring him back to them once more. The whites offer him a sum, which seems to him to be considerable, for the ground which he has begun to clear. This money of the Europeans may possibly furnish him with the

at the lower end of Lake Superior; he seemed to be more like a savage than a civilized being. His book is written without either taste or order; but he gives, even unconsciously, a lively picture of the prejudices, the passions, vices, and, above all, of the destitution in which he lived.

means of a happy and peaceful subsistence in remote regions; and he quits the plough, resumes his native arms, and returns to the wilderness for ever.* The condition of the Creeks and Cherokees, to which I have already alluded, sufficiently corroborates the truth of this deplorable picture.

The Indians, in the little which they have done, have unquestionably displayed as much natural genius as the peoples of Europe in their most important designs; but nations as well as men require time to learn, whatever may be their intelligence and their zeal. While the savages were engaged in the work of civilisation, the Europeans continued to surround them on every side, and to confine them within narrower limits; the two races gradually met, and they are now in immediate juxtaposition to each other. The Indian is already superior to his barbarous parent, but he is still very far below his white neighbor. With their resources and acquired knowledge, the Europeans soon appropriated to them-

* The destructive influence of highly civilized nations upon others which are less so, has been exemplified by the Europeans themselves. About a century ago the French founded the town of Vincennes upon the Wabash, in the middle of the desert; and they lived there in great plenty, until the arrival of the American settlers, who first ruined the previous inhabitants by their competition, and afterward purchased their lands at a very low rate. At the time when M. de Volney, from whom I borrow these details, passed through Vincennes, the number of the French was reduced to a hundred individuals, most of whom were about to pass over to Louisiana or to Canada. These French settlers were worthy people, but idle and uninstructed: they had contracted many of the habits of the savages. The Americans, who were perhaps their inferiors in a moral point of view, were immeasurably superior to them in intelligence: they were industrious, well-informed, rich, and accustomed to govern their own community.

I myself saw in Canada, where the intellectual difference between the two races is less striking, that the English are the masters of commerce and manufacture in the Canadian country, that they spread on all sides, and confine the French within limits which scarcely suffice to contain them. In like manner, in Louisiana, almost all activity in commerce and manufacture centres in the hands of the Anglo-Americans.

But the case of Texas is still more striking: the state of Texas is a part of Mexico, and lies upon the frontier between that country and the United States. In the course of the last few years the Anglo-Americans have penetrated into this province, which is still thinly peopled; they purchase land, they produce the commodities of the country, and supplant the original population. It may easily be foreseen that if Mexico takes no steps to check this change, the province of Texas will very shortly cease to belong to that government.

If the different degrees, comparatively so light, which exist in European civilisation, produce results of such magnitude, the consequences which must ensue from the collision of the most perfect European civilisation with Indian savages may readily be conceived.

selves most of the advantages which the natives might have derived from the possession of the soil: they have settled in the country, they have purchased land at a very low rate or have occupied it by force, and the Indians have been ruined by a competition which they had not the means of resisting. They were isolated in their own country, and their race only constituted a colony of troublesome aliens in the midst of a numerous and domineering people.*

Washington said in one of his messages to congress, "We are more enlightened and powerful than the Indian nations, we are therefore bound in honor to treat them with kindness and even with generosity." But this virtuous and high-minded policy has not been followed. The rapacity of the settlers is usually backed by the tyranny of the government. Although the Cherokees and the Creeks are established upon the territory which they inhabited before the settlement of the Europeans, and although the Americans have frequently treated with them as with foreign nations, the surrounding states have not consented to acknowledge them as an independent people, and attempts have been made to subject these children of the woods to Anglo-American magistrates, laws, and customs.† Destitution had driven these unfortu-

* See in the legislative documents (21st congress, No. 89), instances of excesses of every kind committed by the whites upon the territory of the Indians, either in taking possession of a part of their lands, until compelled to retire by the troops of congress, or carrying off their cattle, burning their houses, cutting down their corn, and doing violence to their persons.

It appears, nevertheless, from all these documents, that the claims of the natives are constantly protected by the government from the abuse of force. The Union has a representative agent continually employed to reside among the Indians; and the report of the Cherokee agent, which is among the documents I have referred to, is almost always favorable to the Indians. "The intrusion of whites," he says, "upon the lands of the Cherokees would cause ruin to the poor, helpless, and inoffensive inhabitants." And he farther remarks upon the attempt of the state of Georgia to establish a division line for the purpose of limiting the boundaries of the Cherokees, that the line drawn having been made by the whites, and entirely upon *exparte* evidence of their several rights, was of no validity whatever.

† In 1829 the state of Alabama divided the Creek territory into counties, and subjected the Indian population to the power of European magistrates.

In 1830 the state of Mississippi assimilated the Choctaws and Chickasaws to the white population, and declared that any of them that should take the title of chief would be punished by a fine of 1,000 dollars and a year's imprisonment. When these laws were enforced upon the Choctaws who inhabited that district, the tribes assembled, their chief communicated to them the intentions of the whites, and

nate Indians to civilisation, and oppression now drives them back to their former condition; many of them abandon the soil which they had begun to clear, and return to their savage course of life.

If we consider the tyrannical measures which have been adopted by the legislatures of the southern states, the conduct of their governors, and the decrees of their courts of justice, we shall be convinced that the entire expulsion of the Indians is the final result to which the efforts of their policy are directed. The Americans of that part of the Union look with jealousy upon the aborigines,* they are aware that these tribes have not yet lost the traditions of savage life, and before civilisation has permanently fixed them to the soil, it is intended to force them to recede by reducing them to despair. The Creeks and Cherokees, oppressed by the several states, have appealed to the central government, which is by no means insensible to their misfortunes, and is sincerely desirous of saving the remnant of the natives, and of maintaining them in the free possession of that territory which the Union is pledged to respect.† But the several states oppose so formidable a resistance to the execution of this design, that the government is obliged to consent to the extirpation of a few barbarous tribes in order not to endanger the safety of the American Union.

But the federal government, which is not able to protect the Indians, would fain mitigate the hardships of their lot; and, with this intention, proposals have been made to transport them into more remote regions at the public cost.

Between the 33d and 37th degrees of north latitude, a vast tract of country lies, which has taken the name of Arkansas, from the principal river that waters its extent. It is bounded on the one side by the confines of Mexico, on the other by the Mississippi. Numberless streams cross it in every direction; the climate is mild, and the soil productive, but it is only in-

read to them some of the laws to which it was intended that they should submit; and they unanimously declared that it was better at once to retreat again into the wilds.

* The Georgians, who are so much annoyed by the proximity of the Indians, inhabit a territory which does not at present contain more than seven inhabitants to the square mile. In France there are one hundred and sixty-two inhabitants to the same extent of country.

† In 1818 congress appointed commissioners to visit the Arkansas territory accompanied by a deputation of Creeks, Choctaws, and Chickasaws. This expedition was commanded by Messrs. Kennerly, M'Coy, Wash Hood, and John Bell. See the different reports of the commissioners, and their journal, in the documents of congress, No. 87, house of representatives.

habited by a few wandering hordes of savages. The government of the Union wishes to transport the broken remnants of the indigenous population of the south, to the portion of this country which is nearest to Mexico, and at a great distance from the American settlements.

We were assured, toward the end of the year 1831, that 10,000 Indians had already gone to the shores of the Arkansas; and fresh detachments were constantly following them; but congress has been unable to excite a unanimous determination in those whom it is disposed to protect. Some, indeed, are willing to quit the seat of oppression, but the most enlightened members of the community refuse to abandon their recent dwellings and the springing crops; they are of opinion that the work of civilisation, once interrupted, will never be resumed; they fear that those domestic habits which have been so recently contracted, may be irrecoverably lost in the midst of a country which is still barbarous, and where nothing is prepared for the subsistence of an agricultural people; they know that their entrance into those wilds will be opposed by inimical hordes, and that they have lost the energy of barbarians, without acquiring the resources of civilisation to resist their attacks. Moreover the Indians readily discover that the settlement which is proposed to them is merely a temporary expedient. Who can assure them that they will at length be allowed to dwell in peace in their new retreat? The United States pledge themselves to the observance of the obligation; but the territory which they at present occupy was formerly secured to them by the most solemn oaths of Anglo-American faith.* The American government does not indeed rob them of their lands, but it allows perpetual incursions to be made on them. In a few years the same white population which now flocks around them, will track them to the solitudes of the Arkansas; they will then be exposed to the same evils without the same remedies; and as the limits

* The fifth article of the treaty made with the Creeks in August, 1790, is in the following words: "The United States solemnly guaranty to the Creek nation all their land within the limits of the Uni ed States."

The seventh article of the treaty concluded in 1791 with the Chero kees says: "The United States solemnly guaranty to the Cherokee nation all their lands not hereby ceded." The following article declared that if any citizen of the United States or other settler not of the Indian race, should establish himself upon the territory of the Cherokees, the United States would withdraw their protection from that individual, and give him up to be punished as the Cherokee nation should think fit.

of the earth will at last fail them, their only refuge is the grave.

The Union treats the Indians with less cupidity and rigor than the policy of the several states, but the two governments are alike destitute of good faith. The states extend what they are pleased to term the benefits of their laws to the Indians, with a belief that the tribes will recede rather than submit; and the central government, which promises a permanent refuge to these unhappy beings, is well aware of its inability to secure it to them.*

Thus the tyranny of the states obliges the savages to retire, the Union, by its promises and resources, facilitates their retreat; and these measures tend to precisely the same end.† "By the will of our Father in heaven, the governor of the whole world," said the Cherokees in their petition to congress,‡ "the red man of America has become small, and the white man great and renowned. When the ancestors of the people of these United States first came to the shores of America, they found the red man strong: though he was ignorant and savage, yet he received them kindly, and gave them dry land to rest their weary feet. They met in peace, and shook hands in token of friendship. Whatever the white man wanted and asked of the Indian, the latter willingly

* This does not prevent them from promising in the most solemn manner to do so. See the letter of the president addressed to the Creek Indians, 23d March, 1829. ("Proceedings of the Indian Board, in the City of New York," p. 5.) "Beyond the great river Mississippi, where a part of your nation has gone, your father has provided a country large enough for all of you, and he advises you to remove to it. There your white brothers will not trouble you; they will have no claim to the land, and you can live upon it, you and all your children, as long as the grass grows or the water runs, in peace and plenty. *It will be yours for ever.*"

The secretary of war, in a letter written to the Cherokees, April 18th, 1829 (see the same work, page 6), declares to them that they cannot expect to retain possession of the land, at the time occupied by them, but gives them the most positive assurance of uninterrupted peace if they would remove beyond the Mississippi: as if the power which could not grant them protection then, would be able to afford it them hereafter!

† To obtain a correct idea of the policy pursued by the several states and the Union with respect to the Indians, it is necessary to consult, 1st, "The laws of the colonial and state governments relating to the Indian inhabitants." (See the legislative documents, 21st congress, No. 319.) 2d, "The laws of the Union on the same subject, and especially that of March 20th, 1802." See Story's Laws of the United States.) 3d, "The report of Mr. Cass, secretary of war, relative to Indian affairs, November 29th, 1823.

‡ December 18th, 1829

gave. At that time the Indian was the lord, and the white man the suppliant. But now the scene has changed. The strength of the red man has become weakness. As his neighbors increased in numbers, his power became less and less, and now, of the many and powerful tribes who once covered the United States, only a few are to be seen—a few whom a sweeping pestilence had left. The northern tribes, who were once so numerous and powerful, are now nearly extinct. Thus it has happened to the red man of America. Shall we, who are remnants, share the same fate?

"The land on which we stand we have received as an in heritance from our fathers who possessed it from time imme morial, as a gift from our common Father in heaven. They bequeathed it to us as their children, and we have sacredly kept it, as containing their remains. This right of inheritance we have never ceded, nor ever forfeited. Permit us to ask what better right can the people have to a country than the right of inheritance and immemorial peaceable possession? We know it is said of late by the state of Georgia and by the executive of the United States, that we have forfeited this right; but we think it is said gratuitously. At what time have we made the forfeit? What great crime have we committed, whereby we must for ever be divested of our country and rights? Was it when we were hostile to the United States, and took part with the king of Great Britain, during the struggle for independence? If so, why was not this forfeiture declared in the first treaty which followed that war? Why was not such an article as the following inserted in the treaty: 'The United States give peace to the Cherokees, but for the part they took in the last war, declare them to be but tenants at will, to be removed when the convenience of the states, within whose chartered limits they live, shall require it?' That was the proper time to assume such a possession. But it was not thought of, nor would our forefathers have agreed to any treaty, whose tendency was to deprive them of their rights and their country."

Such is the language of the Indians: their assertions are true, their forebodings inevitable. From whichever side we consider the destinies of the aborigines of North America, their calamities appear to be irremediable: if they continue barbarous, they are forced to retire: if they attempt to civilize their manners, the contact of a more civilized community subjects them to oppression and destitution. They perish if they continue to wander from waste to waste, and if they attempt to settle, they still must perish; the assistance of Europeans is necessary to instruct them, but the approach of Europeans corrupts and repels them into savage life; they refuse to change their habits as long as their solitudes are their own, and it is too late to change them when they are constrained to submit.

The Spaniards pursued the Indians with blood-hounds, like wild beasts; they sacked the New World with no more temper or compassion than a city taken by storm: but destruction must cease, and phrensy be stayed; the remnant of the Indian population, which had escaped the massacre, mixed with its conquerors and adopted in the end their religion and their manners.* The conduct of the Americans of the United States toward the aborigines is characterized, on the other hand, by a singular attachment to the formalities of law. Provided that the Indians retain their barbarous condition, the Americans take no part in their affairs: they treat them as independent nations, and do not possess themselves of their hunting grounds without a treaty of purchase; and if an Indian nation happens to be so encroached upon as to be unable to subsist upon its territory, they afford it brotherly assistance in transporting it to a grave sufficiently remote from the land of its fathers.

The Spaniards were unable to exterminate the Indian race by those unparalleled atrocities which brand them with indelible shame, nor did they even succeed in wholly depriving it of its rights; but the Americans of the United States have accomplished this twofold purpose with singular felicity; tranquilly, legally, philanthropically, without shedding blood, and without violating a single great principle of morality in the eyes of the world.† It is impossible to destroy men with more respect for the laws of humanity.

* The honor of this result is, however, by no means due to the Spaniards. If the Indian tribes had not been tillers of the ground at the time of the arrival of the Europeans, they would unquestionably have been destroyed in South as well as in North America.

† See among other documents, the report made by Mr. Bell in the name of the committee on Indian affairs, Feb. 24th, 1830, in which it is most logically established and most learnedly proved, that "the fundamental principle, that the Indians had no right by virtue of their ancient possession either of will or sovereignty, has never been abandoned either expressly or by implication."

In perusing this report, which is evidently drawn up by an able hand, one is astonished at the facility with which the author gets rid of all arguments founded upon reason and natural right, which he designates as abstract and theoretical principles. The more I contemplate the difference between civilized and uncivilized man with regard to the principles of justice, the more I observe that the former contests the justice of those rights, which the latter simply violates.

SITUATION OF THE BLACK POPULATION IN THE UNITED STATES, AND DANGERS WITH WHICH ITS PRESENCE THREATENS THE WHITES.

Why it is more difficult to abolish Slavery, and to efface all Vestiges of it among the Moderns, than it was among the Ancients.—In the United States the prejudices of the Whites against the Blacks seem to increase in Proportion as Slavery is abolished.—Situation of the Negroes in the Northern and Southern States.—Why the Americans abolish Slavery.—Servitude, which debases the Slave, impoverishes the Master.—Contrast between the left and the right Bank of the Ohio.—To what attributable.—The black Race, as well as Slavery, recedes toward the South.—Explanation of this fact.—Difficulties attendant upon the Abolition of Slavery in the South.—Dangers to come.—General Anxiety.—Foundation of a black Colony in Africa.—Why the Americans of the South increase the Hardships of Slavery, while they are distressed at its Continuance.

The Indians will perish in the same isolated condition in which they have lived; but the destiny of the negroes is in some measure interwoven with that of the Europeans. These two races are attached to each other without intermingling; and they are alike unable entirely to separate or to combine. The most formidable of all the ills which threaten the future existence of the United States, arises from the presence of a black population upon its territory; and in contemplating the causes of the present embarrassments or of the future dangers of the United States, the observer is invariably led to consider this as a primary fact.

The permanent evils to which mankind is subjected are usually produced by the vehement or the increasing efforts of men; but there is one calamity which penetrated furtively into the world, and which was at first scarcely distinguishable amid the ordinary abuses of power: it originated with an individual whose name history has not preserved; it was wafted like some accursed germ upon a portion of the soil, but it afterward nurtured itself, grew without effort, and spreads naturally with the society to which it belongs. I need scarcely add that this calamity is slavery. Christianity suppressed slavery, but the Christians of the sixteenth century re-established it—as an exception, indeed, to their social system, and restricted to one of the races of mankind; but the wound thus inflicted upon humanity, though less extensive, was at the same time rendered far more difficult of cure.

It is important to make an accurate distinction between slavery itself, and its consequences. The immediate evils which are produced by slavery were very nearly the same in antiquity as they are among the moderns; but the consequences of these evils were different. The slave, among the ancients, belonged to the same race as his master, and he was often the superior of the two in education* and instruction. Freedom was the only distinction between them; and when freedom was conferred, they were easily confounded together. The ancients, then, had a very simple means of avoiding slavery and its evil consequences, which was that of enfranchisement; and they succeeded as soon as they adopted this measure generally. Not but, in ancient states, the vestiges of servitude subsisted for some time after servitude was abolihed. There is a natural prejudice which prompts men to despise whomsoever has been their inferior, long after he has become their equal; and the real inequality which is produced by fortune or by law, is always succeeded by an imaginary inequality which is implanted in the manners of the people. Nevertheless, this secondary consequence of slavery was limited to a certain term among the ancients; for the freedman bore so entire a resemblance to those born free, that it soon became impossible to distinguish him from among them.

The greatest difficulty in antiquity was that of altering the law; among the moderns it is of altering the manners; and, as far as we are concerned, the real obstacles begin where those of the ancients left off. This arises from the circumstance that, among the moderns, the abstract and transient fact of slavery is fatally united to the physical and permanent fact of color. The tradition of slavery dishonors the race, and the peculiarity of the race perpetuates the tradition of slavery. No African has ever voluntarily emigrated to the shores of the New World; whence it must be inferred, that all the blacks who are now to be found in that hemisphere are either slaves or freedmen. Thus the negro transmits the eternal mark of his ignominy to all his descendants; and although the law may abolish slavery, God alone can obliterate the traces of its existence.

The modern slave differs from his master not only in his condition, but in his origin. You may set the negro free, but you cannot make him otherwise than an alien to the European. Nor is this all; we scarcely acknowledge the common fea-

* It is well known that several of the most distinguished authors of antiquity, and among them Æsop and Terence, were or had been slaves. Slaves were not always taken from barbarous nations, and the chances of war reduced highly civilized men to servitude.

tures of mankind in this child of debasement whom slavery has brought among us. His physiognomy is to our eyes hideous, his understanding weak, his tastes low; and we are almost inclined to look upon him as a being intermediate between man and the brutes.* The moderns, then, after they have abolished slavery, have three prejudices to contend against, which are less easy to attack, and far less easy to conquer, than the mere fact of servitude: the prejudice of the master, the prejudice of the race, and the prejudice of color.

It is difficult for us, who have had the good fortune to be born among men like ourselves by nature, and equal to ourselves by law, to conceive the irreconcilable differences which separate the negro from the European in America. But we may derive some faint notion of them from analogy. France was formerly a country in which numerous distinctions of rank existed, that had been created by the legislation. Nothing can be more fictitious than a purely legal inferiority; nothing more contrary to the instinct of mankind than these permanent divisions which had been established between beings evidently similar. Nevertheless these divisions subsisted for ages; they still subsist in many places; and on all sides they have left imaginary vestiges, which time alone can efface. If it be so difficult to root out an inequality which solely originates in the law, how are those distinctions to be destroyed which seem to be founded upon the immutable laws of nature herself? When I remember the extreme difficulty with which aristocratic bodies, of whatever nature they may be, are commingled with the mass of the people; and the exceeding care which they take to preserve the ideal boundaries of their caste inviolate, I despair of seeing an aristocracy disappear which is founded upon visible and indelible signs. Those who hope that the Europeans will ever mix with the negroes, appear to me to delude themselves; and I am not led to any such conclusion by my own reason, or by the evidence of facts.

Hitherto, wherever the whites nave been the most powerful, they have maintained the blacks in a subordinate or a servile position; wnerever the negroes have been strongest, they have destroyed the whites; such has been the only

* To induce the whites to abandon the opinion they have conceived of the moral and intellectual inferiority of their former slaves, the negroes must change; but as long as this opinion subsists, to change is impossible.

course of events which has ever taken place between the two races.

I see that in a certain portion of the territory of the United States at the present day, the legal barrier which separated the two races is tending to fall away, but not that which exists in the manners of the country; slavery recedes, but the prejudice to which it has given birth remains stationary. Whosoever has inhabited the United States, must have perceived, that in those parts of the Union in which the negroes are no longer slaves, they have in nowise drawn nearer to the whites. On the contrary, the prejudice of the race appears to be stronger in the states which have abolished slavery, than in those where it still exists; and nowhere is it so intolerant as in those states where servitude has never been known.

It is true, that in the north of the Union, marriages may be legally contracted between negroes and whites, but public opinion would stigmatize a man who should connect himself with a negress as infamous, and it would be difficult to meet with a single instance of such a union. The electoral franchise has been conferred upon the negroes in almost all the states in which slavery has been abolished; but if they come forward to vote, their lives are in danger. If oppressed, they may bring an action at law, but they will find none but whites among their judges; and although they may legally serve as jurors, prejudice repulses them from that office. The same schools do not receive the child of the black and of the European. In the theatres, gold cannot procure a seat for the servile race beside their former masters; in the hospitals they lie apart; and although they are allowed to invoke the same Divinity as the whites, it must be at a different altar, and in their own churches, with their own clergy. The gates of heaven are not closed against these unhappy beings; but their inferiority is continued to the very confines of the other world. When the negro is defunct, his bones are cast aside, and the distinction of condition prevails even in the equality of death. The negro is free, but he can share neither the rights, nor the pleasure, nor the labor, nor the afflictions, nor the tomb of him whose equal he has been declared to be; and he cannot meet him upon fair terms in life or in death.

In the south, where slavery still exists, the negroes are less carefully kept apart; they sometimes share the labor and the recreations of the whites; the whites consent to intermix with them to a certain extent, and although the legislation treats them more harshly, the habits of the people are more tolerant and compassionate. In the south the master is not afraid to raise his slave to his own standing, because he knows that he can in a moment reduce him to the dust at pleasure. In the north, the white no longer distinctly perceives the barrier which separates him from the degraded race, and he shuns the negro with the more pertinacity, because he fears lest they should be some day confounded together.

Among the Americans of the south, nature sometimes reasserts her rights, and restores a transient equality between the blacks and the whites; but in the north, pride restrains the most imperious of human passions. The American of the northern states would perhaps allow the negress to share his licentious pleasures, if the laws of his country did not declare that she may aspire to be the legitimate partner of his bed; but he recoils with horror from her who might become his wife.

Thus it is, in the United States, that the prejudice which repels the negroes seems to increase in proportion as they are emancipated, and inequality is sanctioned by the manners while it is effaced from the laws of the country. But if the relative position of the two races which inhabit the United States, is such as I have described, it may be asked why the Americans have abolished slavery in the north of the Union, why they maintain it in the south, and why they aggravate its hardships there? The answer is easily given. It is not for the good of the negroes, but for that of the whites, that measures are taken to abolish slavery in the United States.

The first negroes were imported into Virginia about the year 1621.* In America, therefore, as well as in the rest of the globe, slavery originated in the south. Thence it spread from one settlement to another; but the number of slaves diminished toward the northern states, and the negro population was always very limited in New England.†

* See Beverley's History of Virginia. See also in Jefferson's Memoirs some curious details concerning the introduction of negroes into Virginia, and the first act which prohibited the importation of them in 1778.

† The number of slaves was less considerable in the north, but the advantages resulting from slavery were not more contested there than in the south. In 1740, the legislature of the state of New York declared that the direct importation of slaves ought to be encouraged as much as possible, and smuggling severely punished, in order not to discourage the fair trader. (Kent's Commentaries, vol. ii., p. 206.) Curious researches, by Belknap, upon slavery in New England, are to be found in the Historical Collections of Massachusetts, vol. iv., p. 193. It appears that negroes were introduced there in 1630, but that the

A century had scarcely elapsed since the foundation of the colonies, when the attention of the planters was struck by the extraordinary fact, that the provinces which were comparatively destitute of slaves, increased in population, in wealth, and in prosperity, more rapidly than those which contained the greatest number of negroes. In the former, however, the inhabitants were obliged to cultivate the soil themselves, or by hired laborers; in the latter, they were furnished with hands for which they paid no wages; yet, although labor and expense were on the one side, and ease with economy on the other, the former were in possession of the most advantageous system. This consequence seemed to be the more difficult to explain, since the settlers, who all belonged to the same European race, had the same habits, the same civilisation, the same laws, and their shades of difference were extremely slight.

Time, however, continued to advance; and the Anglo-Americans, spreading beyond the coasts of the Atlantic ocean, penetrated farther and farther into the solitudes of the west; they met with a new soil and an unwonted climate; the obstacles which opposed them were of the most various character; their races intermingled, the inhabitants of the south went up toward the north, those of the north descended to the south; but in the midst of all these causes, the same result recurred at every step; and in general, the colonies in which there were no slaves became more populous and more rich than those in which slavery flourished. The more progress was made, the more was it shown that slavery, which is so cruel to the slave, is prejudicial to the master.

But this truth was most satisfactorily demonstrated when civilisation reached the banks of the Ohio. The stream which the Indians had distinguished by the name of Ohio, or Beautiful river, waters one of the most magnificent valleys which have ever been made the abode of man. Undulating lands extend upon both shores of the Ohio, whose soil affords inexhaustible treasures to the laborer; on either bank the air is wholesome and the climate mild; and each of them forms the extreme frontier of a vast state: that which follows the numerous windings of the Ohio upon the left is called Kentucky; that upon the right bears the name of the river. These two states only differ in a single respect; Kentucky

legislation and manners of the people were opposed to slavery from the first; see also, in the same work, the manner in which public opinion, and afterward the laws, finally put an end to slavery.

has admitted slavery, but the state of Ohio has prohibited the existence of slaves within its borders.*

Thus the traveller who floats down the current of the Ohio, to the spot where that river falls into the Mississippi, may be said to sail between liberty and servitude; and a transient inspection of the surrounding objects will convince him which of the two is most favorable to mankind.

Upon the left bank of the stream the population is rare; from time to time one descries a troop of slaves loitering in the half-desert fields; the primeval forest recurs at every turn; society seems to be asleep, man to be idle, and nature alone offers a scene of activity and of life.

From the right bank, on the contrary, a confused hum is heard, which proclaims the presence of industry; the fields are covered with abundant harvests; the elegance of the dwellings announces the taste and activity of the laborer; and man appears to be in the enjoyment of that wealth and contentment which are the reward of labor.†

The state of Kentucky was founded in 1775, the state of Ohio only twelve years later; but twelve years are more in America than half a century in Europe, and, at the present day, the population of Ohio exceeds that of Kentucky by 250,000 souls.‡ These opposite consequences of slavery and freedom may readily be understood; and they suffice to explain many of the differences which we remark between the civilisation of antiquity and that of our own time.

Upon the left bank of the Ohio labor is confounded with the idea of slavery, upon the right bank it is identified with that of prosperity and improvement; on the one side it is degraded, on the other it is honored; on the former territory no white laborers can be found, for they would be afraid of assimilating themselves to the negroes; on the latter no one is idle, for the white population extends its activity and its intelligence to every kind of employment. Thus the men

* Not only is slavery prohibited in Ohio, but no free negroes are allowed to enter the territory of that state, or to hold property in it See the statutes of Ohio.

† The activity of Ohio is not confined to individuals, but the undertakings of the state are surprisingly great: a canal has been established between Lake Erie and the Ohio, by means of which the valley of the Mississippi communicates with the river of the north, and the European commodities with arrive at New York, may be forwarded by water to New Orleans across five hundred leagues of continent.

‡ The exact numbers given by the census of 1830 were: Kentucky, 688,844; Ohio, 937,679.

[In 1840 the census gave, Kentucky 779,828; Ohio 1,519,467.]

whose task it is to cultivate the rich soil of Kentucky are ignorant and lukewarm; while those who are active and enlightened either do nothing, or pass over into the state of Ohio, where they may work without dishonor.

It is true that in Kentucky the planters are not obliged to pay wages to the slaves whom they employ; but they derive small profits from their labor, while the wages paid to free workmen would be returned with interest in the value of their services. The free workman is paid, but he does his work quicker than the slave; and rapidity of execution is one of the great elements of economy. The white sells his services, but they are only purchased at the times at which they may be useful; the black can claim no remuneration for his toil, but the expense of his maintenance is perpetual; he must be supported in his old age as well as in the prime of manhood, in his profitless infancy as well as in the productive years of youth. Payment must equally be made in order to obtain the services of either class of men; the free workman receives his wages in money; the slave in education, in food, in care, and in clothing. The money which a master spends in the maintenance of his slaves, goes gradually and in detail, so that it is scarcely perceived; the salary of the free workman is paid in a round sum, which appears only to enrich the individual who receives it; but in the end the slave has cost more than the free servant, and his labor is less productive.*

The influence of slavery extends still farther; it affects the character of the master, and imparts a peculiar tendency to his ideas and his tastes. Upon both banks of the Ohio, the character of the inhabitants is enterprising and energetic; but this vigor is very differently exercised in the two states.

* Independently of these causes which, wherever free workmen abound, render their labor more productive and more economical than that of slaves, another cause may be pointed out which is peculiar to the United States: the sugar-cane has hitherto been cultivated with success only upon the banks of the Mississippi, near the mouth of that river in the gulf of Mexico. In Louisiana the cultivation of the sugar-cane is exceedingly lucrative; nowhere does a laborer earn so much by his work: and, as there is always a certain relation between the cost of production and the value of the produce, the price of slaves is very high in Louisiana. But Louisiana is one of the confederate states, and slaves may be carried thither from all parts of the Union; the price given for slaves in New Orleans consequently raises the value of slaves in all the other markets. The consequence of this is, that in the countries where the land is less productive, the cost of slave labor is still very considerable, which gives an additional advantage to the competition of free labor.

The white inhabitant of Ohio, who is obliged to subsist by his own exertions, regards temporal prosperity as the principal aim of his existence; and as the country which he occupies presents inexhaustible resources to his industry, and ever-varying lures to his activity, his acquisitive ardor surpasses the ordinary limits of human cupidity: he is tormented by the desire of wealth, and he boldly enters upon every path which fortune opens to him; he becomes a sailor, pioneer, an artisan, or a laborer, with the same indifference, and he supports, with equal constancy, the fatigues and the dangers incidental to these various professions; the resources of his intelligence are astonishing, and his avidity in the pursuit of gain amounts to a species of heroism.

But the Kentuckian scorns not only labor, but all the undertakings which labor promotes; as he lives in an idle independence, his tastes are those of an idle man; money loses a portion of its value in his eyes; he covets wealth much less than pleasure and excitement; and the energy which his neighbor devotes to gain, turns with him to a passionate love of field sports and military exercises; he delights in violent bodily exertion, he is familiar with the use of arms, and is accustomed from a very early age to expose his life in single combat. Thus slavery not only prevents the whites from becoming opulent, but even from desiring to become so.

As the same causes have been continually producing opposite effects for the last two centuries in the British colonies of North America, they have established a very striking difference between the commercial capacity of the inhabitants of the south and that of the north. At the present day, it is only the northern states which are in possession of shipping, manufactures, railroads, and canals. This difference is perceptible not only in comparing the north with the south, but in comparing the several southern states. Almost all the individuals who carry on commercial operations, or who endeavor to turn slave-labor to account in the most southern districts of the Union, have emigrated from the north. The natives of the northern states are constantly spreading over that portion of the American territory, where they have less to fear from competition; they discover resources there, which escaped the notice of the inhabitants; and, as they comply with a system which they do not approve, they succeed in turning it to better advantage than those who first founded, and who still maintain it.

Were I inclined to continue this parallel, I could easily prove that almost all the differences, which may be remarked between the characters of the Americans in the southern and in the northern states, have originated in slavery; but this would divert me from my subject, and my present intention is not to point out all the consequences of servitude, but those effects which it has produced upon the prosperity of the countries which have admitted it.

The influence of slavery upon the production of wealth must have been very imperfectly known in antiquity, as slavery then obtained throughout the civilized world, and the nations which were unacquainted with it were barbarous. And indeed Christianity only abolished slavery by advocating the claims of the slave; at the present time it may be attacked in the name of the master; and, upon this point, interest is reconciled with morality.

As these truths became apparent in the United States, slavery receded before the progress of experience. Servitude had begun in the south, and had thence spread toward the north; but it now retires again. Freedom, which started from the north, now descends uninterruptedly toward the south. Among the great states, Pennsylvania now constitutes the extreme limit of slavery to the north; but even within those limits the slave-system is shaken; Maryland, which is immediately below Pennsylvania, is preparing for its abolition; and Virginia, which comes next to Maryland, is already discussing its utility and its dangers.*

No great change takes place in human institutions, without involving among its causes the law of inheritance. When the law of primogeniture obtained in the south, each family was represented by a wealthy individual, who was neither compelled nor induced to labor; and he was surrounded, as by parasitic plants, by the other members of his family, who were then excluded by law from sharing the common inheritance, and who led the same kind of life as himself. The very same thing then occurred in all the families of the south that still happens in the wealthy families of some countries in Europe, namely, that the younger sons remain in the

* A peculiar reason contributes to detach the two last-mentioned states from the cause of slavery. The former wealth of this part of the Union was principally derived from the cultivation of tobacco. This cultivation is specially carried on by slaves; but within the last few years the market-price of tobacco has diminished, while the value of the slaves remains the same. Thus the ratio between the cost of production and the value of the produce is changed. The natives of Maryland and Virginia are therefore more disposed than they were thirty years ago, to give up slave labor in the cultivation of tobacco, or to give up slavery and tobacco at the same time.

same state of idleness as their elder brother, without being as rich as he is. This identical result seems to be produced in Europe and in America by wholly analogous causes. In the south of the United States, the whole race of whites formed an aristocratic body, which was headed by a certain number of privileged individuals, whose wealth was permanent, and whose leisure was hereditary. These leaders of the American nobility kept alive the traditional prejudices of the white race in the body of which they were the representatives, and maintained the honor of inactive life. This aristocracy contained many who were poor, but none who would work; its members preferred want to labor; consequently no competition was set on foot against negro laborers and slaves, and whatever opinion might be entertained as to the utility of their efforts, it was indispensable to employ them, since there was no one else to work.

No sooner was the law of primogeniture abolished than fortunes began to diminish, and all the families of the country were simultaneously reduced to a state in which labor became necessary to procure the means of subsistence: several of them have since entirely disappeared; and all of them learned to look forward to the time at which it would be necessary for every one to provide for his own wants. Wealthy individuals are still to be met with, but they no longer constitute a compact and hereditary body, nor have they been able to adopt a line of conduct in which they could persevere, and which they could infuse into all ranks of society. The prejudice which stigmatized labor was in the first place abandoned by common consent; the number of needy men was increased, and the needy were allowed to gain a laborious subsistence without blushing for their exertions. Thus one of the most immediate consequences of the partible quality of estates has been to create a class of free laborers. As soon as a competition was set on foot between the free laborer and the slave, the inferiority of the latter became manifest, and slavery was attacked in its fundamental principles, which is, the interest of the master.

As slavery recedes, the black population follows its retrograde course, and returns with it to those tropical regions from which it originally came. However singular this fact may at first appear to be, it may readily be explained. Although the Americans abolish the principle of slavery, they do not set their slaves free. To illustrate this remark I will quote the example of the state of New York. In 1788, the state of New York prohibited the sale of slaves within its limits; which was an indirect method of prohibiting the importation of blacks. Thenceforward the number of negroes could only increase according to the ratio of the natural increase of population. But eight years later a more decisive measure was taken, and it was enacted that all children born of slave parents after the 4th of July, 1799, should be free. No increase could then take place, and although slaves still existed, slavery might be said to be abolished.

From the time at which a northern state prohibited the importation of slaves, no slaves were brought from the south to be sold in its markets. On the other hand, as the sale of slaves was forbidden in that state, an owner was no longer able to get rid of his slaves (who thus became a burdensome possession) otherwise than by transporting him to the south. But when a northern state declared that the son of the slave should be born free, the slave lost a large portion of his market value, since his posterity was no longer included in the bargain, and the owner had then a strong interest in transporting him to the south. Thus the same law prevents the slaves of the south from coming to the northern states, and drives those of the north to the south.

The want of free hands is felt in a state in proportion as the number of slaves decreases. But in proportion as labor is performed by free hands, slave-labor becomes less productive; and the slave is then a useless or an onerous possession, whom it is important to export to those southern states where the same competition is not to be feared. Thus the abolition of slavery does not set the slave free, but it merely transfers him from one master to another, and from the north to the south.

The emancipated negroes, and those born after the abolition of slavery, do not, indeed, migrate from the north to the south; but their situation with regard to the Europeans is not unlike that of the aborigines of America; they remain half civilized, and deprived of their rights in the midst of a population which is far superior to them in wealth and in knowledge; where they are exposed to the tyranny of the laws,* and the intolerance of the people. On some accounts they are still more to be pitied than the Indians, since they are haunted by the reminiscence of slavery, and they cannot

* The states in which slavery is abolished usually do what they can to render their territory disagreeable to the negroes as a place of residence; and as a kind of emulation exists between the different states in this respect, the unhappy blacks can only choose the least of the evils which beset them.

claim possession of a single portion of the soil: many of them perish miserably,* and the rest congregate in the great towns, where they perform the meanest offices, and lead a wretched and precarious existence.

But even if the number of negroes continued to increase as rapidly as when they were still in a state of slavery, as the number of whites augments with twofold rapidity since the abolition of slavery, the blacks would soon be, as it were, lost in the midst of a strange population.

A district which is cultivated by slaves is in general more scantily peopled than a district cultivated by free labor: moreover, America is still a new country, and a state is therefore not half peopled at the time when it abolished slavery. No sooner is an end put to slavery, than the want of free labor is felt, and a crowd of enterprising adventurers immediately arrive from all parts of the country, who hasten to profit by the fresh resources which are then opened to industry. The soil is soon divided among them, and a family of white settlers takes possession of each tract of country. Besides which, European emigration is exclusively directed to the free states; for what would be the fate of a poor emigrant who crosses the Atlantic in search of ease and happiness, if he were to land in a country where labor is stigmatized as degrading?

Thus the white population grows by its natural increase, and at the same time by the immense influx of emigrants; while the black population receives no emigrants, and is upon its decline. The proportion which existed between the two races is soon inverted. The negroes constitute a scanty remnant, a poor tribe of vagrants, which is lost in the midst of an immense people in full possession of the land; and the presence of the blacks is only marked by the injustice and the hardships of which they are the unhappy victims.

In several of the western states the negro race never made its appearance; and in all the northern states it is rapidly declining. Thus the great question of its future condition is confined within a narrow circle, where it becomes less formidable, though not more easy of solution.

* There is a very great difference between the mortality of the blacks and of the whites in the states in which slavery is abolished; from 1820 to 1831 only one out of forty-two individuals of the white population died in Philadelphia; but one negro out of twenty-one individuals of the black population died in the same space of time. The mortality is by no means so great among the negroes who are still slaves. (See Emmerson's Medical Statistics, p. 28.)

The more we descend toward the south, the more difficult does it become to abolish slavery with advantage: and this arises from several physical causes, which it is important to point out.

The first of these causes is the climate: it is well known that in proportion as Europeans approach the tropics, they suffer more from labor. Many of the Americans even assert, that within a certain latitude the exertions which a negro can make without danger are fatal to them;* but I do not think that this opinion, which is so favorable to the indolence of the inhabitants of southern regions, is confirmed by experience. The southern parts of the Union are not hotter than the south of Italy and of Spain;† and it may be asked why the European cannot work as well there as in the two latter countries. If slavery has been abolished in Italy and in Spain without causing the destruction of the masters, why should not the same thing take place in the Union? I cannot believe that Nature has prohibited the Europeans in Georgia and the Floridas, under pain of death, from raising the means of subsistence from the soil; but their labor would unquestionably be more irksome and less productive‡ to them than the inhabitants of New England. As the free workman thus loses a portion of his superiority over the slave in the southern states, there are fewer inducements to abolish slavery.

All the plants of Europe grow in the northern parts of the Union; the south has special productions of its own. It has been observed that slave labor is a very expensive method of cultivating corn. The farmer of corn-land in a country where slavery is unknown, habitually retains a small number of laborers in his service, and at seed-time and harvest he hires several additional hands, who only live at his cost for a short period. But the agriculturist in a slave state is obliged to keep a large number of slaves the whole year round, in

* This is true of the spots in which rice is cultivated; rice-grounds, which are unwholesome in all countries, are particularly dangerous in those regions which are exposed to the beams of a tropical sun. Europeans would not find it easy to cultivate the soil in that part of the New World if it must necessarily be made to produce rice; but may they not subsist without rice-grounds?

† These states are nearer to the equator than Italy and Spain, but the temperature of the continent of America is very much lower than that of Europe.

‡ The Spanish government formerly caused a certain number of peasants from the Azores to be transported into a district of Louisiana called Attakapas, by way of experiment. These settlers still cultivate the soil without the assistance of slaves, but their industry is so languid as scarcely to supply their most necessary wants

order to sow his fields and to gather in his crops, although their services are only required for a few weeks; but slaves are unable to wait till they are hired, and to subsist by their own labor in the meantime like free laborers; in order to have their services, they must be bought. Slavery, independently of its general disadvantages, is therefore still more inapplicable to countries in which corn is cultivated than to those which produce crops of a different kind.

The cultivation of tobacco, of cotton, and especially of the sugar-cane, demands, on the other hand, unremitting attention: and women and children are employed in it, whose services are of but little use in the cultivation of wheat. Thus slavery is naturally more fitted to the countries from which these productions are derived.

Tobacco, cotton, and the sugar-cane, are exclusively grown in the south, and they form one of the principal sources of the wealth of those states. If slavery were abolished, the inhabitants of the south would be constrained to adopt one of two alternatives: they must either change their system of cultivation, and then they would come into competition with the more active and more experienced inhabitants of the north; or, if they continued to cultivate the same produce without slave labor, they would have to support the competition of the other states of the south, which might still retain their slaves. Thus, peculiar reasons for maintaining slavery exist in the south which do not operate in the north.

But there is yet another motive which is more cogent than all the others; the south might indeed, rigorously speaking, abolish slavery, but how should it rid its territory of the black population? Slaves and slavery are driven from the north by the same law, but this twofold result cannot be hoped for in the south.

The arguments which I have adduced to show that slavery is more natural and more advantageous in the south than in the north, sufficiently prove that the number of slaves must be far greater in the former districts. It was to the southern settlements that the first Africans were brought, and it is there that the greatest number of them have always been imported. As we advance toward the south, the prejudice which sanctions idleness increases in power. In the states nearest to the tropics there is not a single white laborer; the negroes are consequently much more numerous in the south than in the north. And, as I have already observed, this disproportion increases daily, since the negroes are transferred to one part of the Union as soon as slavery is abolished in the other.

Thus the black population augments in the south, not only by its natural fecundity, but by the compulsory emigration of the negroes from the north; and the African race has causes of increase in the south very analogous to those which so powerfully accelerate the growth of the European race in the north.

In the state of Maine there is one negro in three hundred inhabitants; in Massachusetts, one in one hundred; in New York, two in one hundred; in Pennsylvania, three in the same number; in Maryland, thirty-four; in Virginia, forty-two; and lastly, in South Carolina, fifty-five per cent.* Such was the proportion of the black population to the whites in the year 1830. But this proportion is perpetually changing, as it constantly decreases in the north and augments in the south.

It is evident that the most southern states of the Union cannot abolish slavery without incurring very great dangers, which the north had no reason to apprehend when it emancipated its black population. We have already shown the system by which the northern states secure the transition from slavery to freedom, by keeping the present generation in chains, and setting their descendants free; by this means the negroes are gradually introduced into society; and while the men who might abuse their freedom are kept in a state of servitude, those who are emancipated may learn the art of being free before they become their own masters. But it would be difficult to apply this method in the south. To declare that all the negroes born after a certain period shall be free, is to introduce the principle and the notion of liberty into the heart of slavery; the blacks, whom the law thus maintains in a state of slavery from which their children are delivered, are astonished at so unequal a fate, and their aston-

* We find it asserted in an American work, entitled, "Letters on the Colonization Society," by Mr. Carey, 1833, that "for the last forty years the black race has increased more rapidly than the white race in the state of South Carolina; and that if we take the average population of the five states of the south into which slaves were first introduced, viz., Maryland, Virginia, South Carolina, North Carolina, and Georgia, we shall find that from 1790 to 1830, the whites have augmented in the proportion of 80 to 100, and the blacks in that of 112 to 100."

In the United States, 1830, the population of the two races stood as follows:—

States where slavery is abolished, 6,565,434 whites; 120,520 blacks

Slave states, 3,960,814 whites; 2,208,112 blacks.

[By the census of 1840, the population of the two races was as follows: States where slavery is abolished, 9,556,065 whites; 171,854 blacks. Slave states, 4,633,153 whites; 2,581,688 blacks]

ishment is only the prelude to their impatience and irritation. Thenceforward slavery loses in their eyes that kind of moral power which it derived from time and habit; it is reduced to a mere palpable abuse of force. The northern states had nothing to fear from the contrast, because in them the blacks were few in number, and the white population was very considerable. But if this faint dawn of freedom were to show two millions of men their true position, the oppressors would have reason to tremble. After having enfranchised the children of their slaves, the Europeans of the southern states would very shortly be obliged to extend the same benefit to the whole black population.

In the north, as I have already remarked, a two-fold migration ensues upon the abolition of slavery, or even precedes that event when circumstances have rendered it probable; the slaves quit the country to be transported southward; and the whites of the northern states as well as the emigrants from Europe hasten to fill up their place. But these two causes cannot operate in the same manner in the southern states. On the one hand, the mass of slaves is too great for any expectation of their ever being removed from the country to be entertained; and on the other hand, the Europeans and the Anglo-Americans of the north are afraid to come to inhabit a country, in which labor has not yet been reinstated in its rightful honors. Besides, they very justly look upon the states in which the proportion of the negroes equals or exceeds that of the whites, as exposed to very great dangers; and they refrain from turning their activity in that direction.

Thus the inhabitants of the south would not be able, like their northern countrymen, to initiate the slaves gradually into a state of freedom, by abolishing slavery; they have no means of perceptibly diminishing the black population, and they would remain unsupported to repress its excesses. So that in the course of a few years, a great people of free negroes would exist in the heart of a white nation of equal size.

The same abuses of power which still maintain slavery, would then become the source of the most alarming perils, which the white population of the south might have to apprehend. At the present time the descendants of the Europeans are the sole owners of the land; the absolute masters of all labor; and the only persons who are possessed of wealth, knowledge, and arms. The black is destitute of all these advantages, but he subsists without them because he is a slave. If he were free, and obliged to provide for his own subsistence, would it be possible for him to remain without these things and to support life? Or would not the very instruments of the present superiority of the white, while slavery exists, expose him to a thousand dangers if it were abolished?

As long as the negro remains a slave, he may be kept in a condition not very far removed from that of the brutes; but, with his liberty, he cannot but acquire a degree of instruction which will enable him to appreciate his misfortunes, and to discern a remedy for them. Moreover, there exists a singular principle of relative justice which is very firmly implanted in the human heart. Men are much more forcibly struck by those inequalities which exist within the circles of the same class, than with those which may be remarked between different classes. It is more easy for them to admit slavery, than to allow several millions of citizens to exist under a load of eternal infamy and hereditary wretchedness. In the north, the population of freed negroes feels these hardships and resents these indignities; but its members and its powers are small, while in the south it would be numerous and strong.

As soon as it is admitted that the whites and the emancipated blacks are placed upon the same territory in the situation of two alien communities, it will readily be understood that there are but two alternatives for the future; the negroes and the whites must either wholly part or wholly mingle. I have already expressed the conviction which I entertain as to the latter event.* I do not imagine that the white and the black races will ever live in any country upon an equal footing. But I believe the difficulty to be still greater in the United States than elsewhere. An isolated individual may surmount the prejudices of religion, of his country, or of his race, and if this individual is a king he may effect surprising changes in society; but a whole people cannot rise, as it were, above itself. A despot who should subject the Americans and their former slaves to the same yoke, might perhaps succeed in commingling their races; but as long as the American democracy remains at the head of affairs, no one will undertake so difficult a task; and it may be foreseen that the freer

* This opinion is sanctioned by authorities infinitely weightier than anything that I can say; thus, for instance, it is stated in the Memoirs of Jefferson (as collected by M. Conseil), "Nothing is more clearly written in the book of destiny than the emancipation of the blacks; and it is equally certain that the two races will never live in a state of equal freedom under the same government, so insurmountable are the barriers which nature, habit, and opinions, have established between them"

the white population of the United States becomes, the more isolated will it remain.*

I have previously observed that the mixed race is the true bond of union between the Europeans and the Indians; just so the mulattoes are the true means of transition between the white and the negro; so that wherever mulattoes abound, the intermixture of the two races is not impossible. In some parts of America the European and the negro races are so crossed by one another, that it is rare to meet with a man who is entirely black or entirely white: when they are arrived at this point, the two races may really be said to be combined; or rather to have been absorbed in a third race, which is connected with both, without being identical with either.

Of all the Europeans the English are those who have mixed least with the negroes. More mulattoes are to be seen in the south of the Union than in the north, but still they are infinitely more scarce than in any other European colony: Mulattoes are by no means numerous in the United States; they have no force peculiar to themselves, and when quarrels originating in differences of color take place, they generally side with the whites, just as the lacqueys of the great in Europe assume the contemptuous airs of nobility to the lower orders.

The pride of origin, which is natural to the English, is singularly augmented by the personal pride which democratic liberty fosters among the Americans: the white citizen of the United States is proud of his race, and proud of himself. But if the whites and the negroes do not intermingle in the north of the Union, how should they mix in the south? Can it be supposed for an instant, that an American of the southern states, placed, as he must for ever be, between the white man with all his physical and moral superiority, and the negro, will ever think of preferring the latter? The Americans of the southern states have two powerful passions, which will always keep them aloof; the first is the fear of being assimilated to the negroes, their former slaves; and the second, the dread of sinking below the whites, their neighbors.

If I were called upon to predict what will probably occur at some future time, I should say, that the abolition of slavery in the south, will, in the common course of things, increase the repugnance of the white population for the men of color.

* If the British West India planters had governed themselves, they would assuredly not have passed the slave emancipation bill which the mother country has recently imposed upon them.

I found this opinion upon the analogous observation which I already had occasion to make in the north. I there remarked, that the white inhabitants of the north avoid the negroes with increasing care, in proportion as the legal barriers of separation are removed by the legislature; and why should not the same result take place in the south? In the north, the whites are deterred from intermingling with the blacks by the fear of an imaginary danger; in the south, where the danger would be real, I cannot imagine that the fear would be less general.

If, on the one hand, it be admitted (and the fact is unquestionable), that the colored population perpetually accumulates in the extreme south, and that it increases more rapidly than that of the whites; and if, on the other hand, it be allowed that it is impossible to foresee a time at which the whites and the blacks will be so intermingled as to derive the same benefits from society; must it not be inferred, that the blacks and the whites will, sooner or later, come to open strife in the southern states of the Union? But if it be asked what the issue of the struggle is likely to be, it will readily be understood, that we are here left to form a very vague surmise of the truth. The human mind may succeed in tracing a wide circle, as it were, which includes the course of future events; but within that circle a thousand various chances and circumstances may direct it in as many different ways; and in every picture of the future there is a dim spot, which the eye of the understanding cannot penetrate. It appears, however, to be extremely probable, that in the West India islands the white race is destined to be subdued, and the black population to share the same fate upon the continent.

In the West India islands the white planters are surrounded by an immense black population; on the continent, the blacks are placed between the ocean and an innumerable people, which already extends over them in a dense mass from the icy confines of Canada to the frontiers of Virginia, and from the banks of the Missouri to the shores of the Atlantic. If the white citizens of North America remain united, it cannot be supposed that the negroes will escape the destruction with which they are menaced; they must be subdued by want or by the sword. But the black population which is accumulating along the coast of the gulf of Mexico, has a chance of success, if the American Union is dissolved when the struggle between the two races begins. If the federal tie were broken, the citizens of the south would be wrong to rely upon any lasting succor from their northern countrymen. The latter are well aware that the danger can never reach them; and unless they are constrained to march to the assistance of the south by a positive obligation, it may be foreseen that the sympathy of color will be insufficient to stimulate their exertions.

Yet, at whatever period the strife may break out, the whites of the south, even if they are abandoned to their own resources, will enter the lists with an immense superiority of knowledge and of the means of warfare: but the blacks will have numerical strength and the energy of despair upon their side; and these are powerful resources to men who have taken up arms. The fate of the white population of the southern states will, perhaps, be similar to that of the Moors in Spain. After having occupied the land for centuries, it will perhaps be forced to retire to the country whence its ancestors came, and to abandon to the negroes the possession of a territory, which Providence seems to have more peculiarly destined for them, since they can subsist and labor in it more easily than the whites.

The danger of a conflict between the white and the black inhabitants of the southern states of the Union—a danger which, however remote it may be, is inevitable—perpetually haunts the imagination of the Americans. The inhabitants of the north make it a common topic of conversation, although they have no direct injury to fear from the struggle; but they vainly endeavor to devise some means of obviating the misfortunes which they foresee. In the southern states the subject is not discussed: the planter does not allude to the future in conversing with strangers; the citizen does not communicate his apprehensions to his friends: he seeks to conceal them from himself: but there is something more alarming in the tacit forebodings of the south, than in the clamorous fears of the northern states.

This all-pervading disquietude has given birth to an undertaking which is but little known, but which may have the effect of changing the fate of a portion of the human race. From apprehension of the dangers which I have just been describing, a certain number of American citizens have formed a society for the purpose of exporting to the coast of Guinea, at their own expense, such free negroes as may be willing to escape from the oppression to which they are subject.*

* This society assumed the name "The Society for the Colonization of the Blacks." See its annual reports; and more particularly the fifteenth. See also the pamphlet, to which allusion has already been made, entitled "Letters on the Colonization Society, and on its probable results," by Mr. Carey, Philadelphia, April, 1833.

In 1820, the society to which I allude formed a settlement in Africa, upon the 7th degree of north latitude, which bears the name of Liberia. The most recent intelligence informs us that two thousand five hundred negroes are collected there; they have introduced the democratic institutions of America into the country of their forefathers; and Liberia has a representative system of government, negro-jurymen, negro-magistrates, and negro-priests; churches have been built, newspapers established, and, by a singular change in the vicissitudes of the world, white men are prohibited from sojourning within the settlement.*

This is indeed a strange caprice of fortune. Two hundred years have now elapsed since the inhabitants of Europe undertook to tear the negro from his family and his home, in order to transport him to the shores of North America; at the present day, the European settlers are engaged in sending back the descendants of those very negroes to the continent from which they were originally taken; and the barbarous Africans have been brought into contact with civilisation in the midst of bondage, and have become acquainted with free political institutions in slavery. Up to the present time Africa has been closed against the arts and sciences of the whites; but the inventions of Europe will perhaps penetrate into those regions, now that they are introduced by Africans themselves. The settlement of Liberia is founded upon a lofty and a most fruitful idea; but whatever may be its results with regard to the continent of Africa, it can afford no remedy to the New World.

In twelve years the Colonization society has transported two thousand five hundred negroes to Africa; in the same space of time about seven hundred thousand blacks were born in the United States. If the colony of Liberia were so situated as to be able to receive thousands of new inhabitants every year, and if the negroes were in a state to be sent thither with advantage; if the Union were to supply the society with annual subsidies,† and to transport the negroes to

* This last regulation was laid down by the founders of the settlement; they apprehended that a state of things might arise in Africa, similar to that which exists on the frontiers of the United States, and that if the negroes, like the Indians, were brought into collision with a people more enlightened than themselves, they would be destroyed before they could be civilized.

† Nor would these be the only difficulties attendant upon the undertaking; if the Union undertook to buy up the negroes now in America, in order to transport them to Africa, the price of slaves, increasing with their scarcity, would soon become enormous; and the states

Africa in vessels of the state, it would be still unable to counterpoise the natural increase of population among the blacks; and as it would not remove as many men in a year as are born upon its territory within the same space of time, it would fail in suspending the growth of the evil which is daily increasing in the states.* The negro race will never leave those shores of the American continent, to which it was brought by the passions and the vices of Europeans; and it will not disappear from the New World as long as it continues to exist. The inhabitants of the United States may retard the calamities which they apprehend, but they cannot now destroy their efficient cause.

I am obliged to confess that I do not regard the abolition of slavery as a means of warding off the struggle of the two races in the United States. The negroes may long remain slaves without complaining; but if they are once raised to the level of freemen, they will soon revolt at being deprived of all their civil rights; and as they cannot become the equals of the whites, they will speedily declare themselves as enemies. In the north everything contributed to facilitate the emancipation of the slaves; and slavery was abolished, without placing the free negroes in a position which could become formidable, since their number was too small for them ever to claim the exercise of their rights. But such is not the case in the south. The question of slavery was a question of commerce and manufacture for the slave-owners in the north; for those of the south, it is a question of life and death. God forbid that I should seek to justify the principle of negro slavery, as has been done by some American writers! But I only observe that all the countries which formerly adopted that execrable principle are not equally able to abandon it at the present time.

When I contemplate the condition of the south, I can only discover two alternatives which may be adopted by the white inhabitants of those states: viz., either to emancipate the

of the north would never consent to expend such great sums, for a purpose which would procure such small advantages to themselves. If the Union took possession of the slaves in the southern states by force, or at a rate determined by law, an insurmountable resistance would arise in that part of the country. Both alternatives are equally impossible.

* In 1830 there were in the United States 2,010,327 slaves and 319,439 blacks, in all 2,329,766 negroes, which formed about one-fifth of the total population of the United States at that time.

[In 1840 there were in the United States 2,486,348 slaves, and 386,232 free blacks; in all, 2,872,580 negroes, which formed about one-sixth of the total population.]

negroes, and to intermingle with them ; or, remaining isolated from them, to keep them in a state of slavery as long as possible. All intermediate measures seem to me likely to terminate, and that shortly, in the most horrible of civil wars, and perhaps in the extirpation of one or other of the two races. Such is the view which the Americans of the south take of the question, and they act consistently with it. As they are determined not to mingle with the negroes, they refuse to emancipate them.

Not that the inhabitants of the south regard slavery as necessary to the wealth of the planter ; for on this point many of them agree with their northern countrymen in freely admitting that slavery is prejudicial to their interests ; but they are convinced that, however prejudicial it may be, they hold their lives upon no other tenure. The instruction which is now diffused in the south has convinced the inhabitants that slavery is injurious to the slave-owner, but it has also shown them, more clearly than before, that no means exist of getting rid of its bad consequences. Hence arises a singular contrast ; the more the utility of slavery is contested, the more firmly is it established in the laws ; and while the principle of servitude is gradually abolished in the north, that self-same principle gives rise to more and more rigorous consequences in the south.

The legislation of the southern states, with regard to slaves, presents at the present day such unparalleled atrocities, as suffice to show how radically the laws of humanity have been perverted, and to betray the desperate position of the community in which that legislation has been promulgated. The Americans of this portion of the Union have not, indeed, augmented the hardships of slavery ; they have, on the contrary, bettered the physical condition of the slaves. The only means by which the ancients maintained slavery were fetters and death ; the Americans of the south of the Union have discovered more intellectual securities for the duration of their power. They have employed their despotism and their violence against the human mind. In antiquity, precautions were taken to prevent the slave from breaking his chains ; at the present day measures are adopted to deprive him even of the desire of freedom. The ancients kept the bodies of their slaves in bondage, but they placed no restraint upon the mind and no check upon education ; and they acted consistently with their established principle, since a natural termination of slavery then existed, and one day or other the slave might be set free, and become the equal of his master. But the Americans of the south, who do not admit that the negroes can ever be commingled with themselves, have forbidden them to be taught to read or to write, under severe penalties; and as they will not raise them to their own level, they sink them as nearly as possible to that of the brutes.

The hope of liberty had always been allowed to the slave to cheer the hardships of his condition. But the Americans of the south are well aware that emancipation cannot but be dangerous, when the freed man can never be assimilated to his former master. To give a man his freedom, and to leave him in wretchedness and ignominy, is nothing less than to prepare a future chief for a revolt of the slaves. Moreover, it has long been remarked, that the presence of a free negro vaguely agitates the minds of his less fortunate brethren, and conveys to them a dim notion of their rights. The Americans of the south have consequently taken measures to prevent slave-owners from emancipating their slaves in most cases; not indeed by a positive prohibition, but by subjecting that step to various forms which it is difficult to comply with.

I happened to meet with an old man, in the south of the Union, who had lived in illicit intercourse with one of his negresses, and had had several children by her, who were born the slaves of their father. He had indeed frequently thought of bequeathing to them at least their liberty; but years had elapsed without his being able to surmount the legal obstacles to their emancipation, and in the meanwhile his old age was come, and he was about to die. He pictured to himself his sons dragged from market to market, and passing from the authority of a parent to the rod of the stranger, until these horrid anticipations worked his expiring imagination into phrensy. When I saw him he was a prey to all the anguish of despair, and he made me feel how awful is the retribution of Nature upon those who have broken her laws.

These evils are unquestionably great; but they are the necessary and foreseen consequences of the very principle of modern slavery. When the Europeans chose their slaves from a race differing from their own, which many of them considered as inferior to the other races of mankind, and which they all repelled with horror from any notion of intimate connexion, they must have believed that slavery would last for ever; since there is no intermediate state which can be durable, between the excessive inequality produced by servitude, and the complete equality which originates in independence. The Europeans did imperfectly feel this truth, but without acknowledging it even to themselves. Whenever they have had to do with negroes, their conduct has either been dictated by their interest and their pride, or by their compassion. They first violated every right of humanity by their treatment of the negro; and they afterward informed him that those rights were precious and inviolable. They affected to open their ranks to the slave, but the negroes who attempted to penetrate into the community were driven back with scorn; and they have incautiously and involuntarily been led to admit of freedom instead of slavery, without having the courage to be wholly iniquitous, or wholly just. (*a*)

If it be impossible to anticipate a period at which the Americans of the south will mingle their blood with that of the negroes, can they allow their slaves to become free without compromising their own security? And if they are obliged to keep that race in bondage, in order to save their own families, may they not be excused for availing themselves of the means best adapted to that end? The events which are taking place in the southern states of the Union, appear to be at once the most horrible and the most natural results of slavery. When I see the order of nature overthrown, and when I hear the cry of humanity in its vain struggle against the laws, my indignation does not light upon the men of our own time who were the instruments of these outrages; but I reserve my execration for those who, after a thousand years of freedom, brought back slavery into the world once more.

Whatever may be the efforts of the Americans of the south to maintain slavery, they will not always succeed. Slavery, which is now confined to a single tract of the civilized earth, which is attacked by Christianity as unjust, and by political economy as prejudicial, and which is now contrasted with democratic liberties and the information of our age, cannot survive. By the choice of the master or the will of the slave, it will cease; and in either case great calamities may be expected to ensue. If liberty be refused to the negroes of the south, they will in the end seize it for themselves by force; if it be given, they will abuse it ere long.

(*a*) In the original, "Voulant la servitude, il se sont laissé entrainer, malgré eux ou à leur insu, vers la liberté."

"Desiring servitude, they have suffered themselves, involuntarily or ignorantly, to be drawn toward liberty."—*Reviser*

WHAT ARE THE CHANCES IN FAVOR OF THE DURATION OF THE AMERICAN UNION, AND WHAT DANGERS THREATEN IT.

Reasons why the preponderating Force lies in the States rather than in the Union —The Union will only last as long as all the States choose to belong to it.—Causes which tend to keep them united.—Utility of the Union to resist foreign Enemies, and to prevent the Existence of Foreigners in America.—No natural Barriers between the several States.—No conflicting Interests to divide them.—Reciprocal Interests of the Northern, Southern, and Western States.—Intellectual ties of Union —Uniformity of Opinions.—Dangers of the Union resulting from the different Characters and the Passions of its Citizens.—Character of the Citizens in the South and in the North.—The rapid growth of the Union one of its greatest Dangers.—Progress of the Population to the Northwest.—Power gravitates in the same Direction.—Passions originating from sudden turns of Fortune.—Whether the existing Government of the Union tends to gain strength, or to lose it.—Various signs of its Decrease.—Internal Inprovement.—Waste Lands.—Indians.—The Bank.—The Tariff.—General Jackson.

The maintenance of the existing institutions of the several states depends in some measure upon the maintenance of the Union itself. It is therefore important in the first instance to inquire into the probable fate of the Union. One point may indeed be assumed at once; if the present confederation were dissolved, it appears to me to be incontestable that the states of which it is now composed would not return to their original isolated condition; but that several Unions would then be formed in the place of one. It is not my intention to inquire into the principles upon which these new Unions would probably be established, but merely to show what the causes are which may effect the dismemberment of the existing confederation.

With this object I shall be obliged to retrace some of the steps which I have already taken, and to revert to topics which I have before discussed. I am aware that the reader may accuse me of repetition, but the importance of the matter which still remains to be treated is my excuse; I had rather say too much, than say too little to be thoroughly understood, and I prefer injuring the author to slighting the subject.

The legislators who formed the constitution of 1789 endeavored to confer a distinct and preponderating authority upon the federal power. But they were confined by the conditions of the task which they had undertaken to perform. They were not appointed to constitute the government of a single people, but to regulate the association of several states; and, whatever their inclinations might be, they could not but divide the exercise of sovereignty in the end.

In order to understand the consequences of this division, it is necessary to make a short distinction between the affairs of government. There are some objects which are national by their very nature, that is to say, which affect the nation as a body, and can only be intrusted to the man or the assembly of men who most completely represent the entire nation. Among these may be reckoned war and diplomacy. There are other objects which are provincial by their very nature, that is to say, which only affect certain localities, and which can only be properly treated in that locality. Such, for instance, is the budget of municipality. Lastly, there are certain objects of a mixed nature, which are national inasmuch as they affect all the citizens who compose the nation, and which are provincial inasmuch as it is not necessary that the nation itself should provide for them all. Such are the rights which regulate the civil and political condition of the citizens. No society can exist without civil and political rights. These rights therefore interest all the citizens alike; but it is not always necessary to the existence and the prosperity of the nation that these rights should be uniform, nor consequently, that they should be regulated by the central authority.

There are, then, two distinct categories of objects which are submitted to the direction of the sovereign power; and these categories occur in all well-constituted communities, whatever the basis of the political constitution may otherwise be. Between these two extremes, the objects which I have termed mixed may be considered to lie. As these objects are neither exclusively national nor entirely provincial, they may be attained by a national or a provincial government, according to the agreement of the contracting parties, without in any way impairing the contract of association.

The sovereign power is usually formed by the union of separate individuals, who compose a people; and individual powers or collective forces, each representing a very small portion of the sovereign authority, are the sole elements which are subjected to the general government of their choice. In this case the general government is more naturally called upon to regulate, not only those affairs which are of essential national importance, but those which are of a more local interest; and the local governments are reduced to that small share of sovereign authority which is indispensable to their prosperity.

But sometimes the sovereign authority is composed of preorganized political bodies, by virtue of circumstances anterior to their union; and in this case the provincial governments assume the control, not only of those affairs which more peculiarly belong to their province, but of all, or of a part of the mixed affairs to which allusion has been made. For the confederate nations which were independent sovereign states before their Union, and which still represent a very considerable share of the sovereign power, have only consented to cede to the general government the exercise of those rights which are indispensable to the Union.

When the national government, independently of the prerogative inherent in its nature, is invested with the right of regulating the affairs which relate partly to the general and partly to the local interest, it possesses a preponderating influence. Not only are its own rights extensive, but all the rights which it does not possess exist by its sufferance, and it may be apprehended that the provincial governments may be deprived of their natural and necessary prerogatives by its influence.

When, on the other hand, the provincial governments are invested with the power of regulating those same affairs of mixed interest, an opposite tendency prevails in society. The preponderating force resides in the province, not in the nation; and it may be apprehended that the national government may in the end be stripped of the privileges which are necessary to its existence.

Independent nations have therefore a natural tendency to centralization, and confederations to dismemberment.

It now only remains for us to apply these general principles to the American Union. The several states were necessarily possessed of the right of regulating all exclusively provincial affairs. Moreover these same states retained the right of determining the civil and political competency of the citizens, of regulating the reciprocal relations of the members of the community, and of dispensing justice; rights which are of a general nature, but which do not necessarily appertain to the national government. We have shown that the government of the Union is invested with the power of acting in the name of the whole nation, in those cases in which the nation has to appear as a single and undivided power; as, for instance, in foreign relations, and in offering a common resistance to a common enemy; in short, in conducting those affairs which I have styled exclusively national.

In this division of the rights of sovereignty, the share of the Union seems at first sight to be more considerable than that of the states; but a more attentive investigation shows it to be less so. The undertakings of the government of the Union are more vast, but their influence is more rarely felt. Those of the provincial government are comparatively small, but they are incessant, and they serve to keep alive the authority which they represent. The government of the Union watches the general interests of the country; but the general interests of a people have a very questionable influence upon individual happiness; while provincial interests produce a most immediate effect upon the welfare of the inhabitants. The Union secures the independence and the greatness of the nation, which do not immediately affect private citizens; but the several states maintain the liberty, regulate the rights, protect the fortune, and secure the life and the whole future prosperity of every citizen.

The federal government is very far removed from its subjects, while the provincial governments are within the reach of them all, and are ready to attend to the smallest appeal. The central government has upon its side the passions of a few superior men who aspire to conduct it; but upon the side of the provincial governments are the interests of all those second-rate individuals who can only hope to obtain power within their own state, and who nevertheless exercise the largest share of authority over the people because they are placed nearest to its level.

The Americans have therefore much more to hope and to fear from the states than from the Union; and, in conformity with the natural tendency of the human mind, they are more likely to attach themselves to the former than to the latter. In this respect their habits and feelings harmonize with their interests.

When a compact nation divides its sovereignty, and adopts a confederate form of government, the traditions, the customs, and the manners of the people are for a long time at variance with their legislation; and the former tend to give a degree of influence to the central government which the latter forbids. When a number of confederate states unite to form a single nation, the same causes operate in an opposite direction. I have no doubt that if France were to become a confederate republic like that of the United States, the government would at first display more energy than that of the Union; and if the Union were to alter its constitution to a monarchy like that of France, I think that the American government would be a long time in acquiring the force which now rules the latter nation. When the national existence of the Anglo-Americans began, their provincial existence was already of long standing; necessary relations were established between the townships and the individual citizens of the same states; and they were accustomed to consider some objects as common to them all, and to conduct other affairs as exclusively relating to their own special interests.

The Union is a vast body, which presents no definite object to patriotic feeling. The forms and limits of the state are distinct and circumscribed; since it represents a certain number of objects which are familiar to the citizens and beloved by all. It is identified with the very soil, with the right of property and the domestic affections, with the recollections of the past, the labors of the present, and the hopes of the future. Patriotism, then, which is frequently a mere extension of individual egotism, is still directed to the state, and is not excited by the Union. Thus the tendency of the interests, the habits, and the feelings of the people, is to centre political activity in the states, in preference to the Union.

It is easy to estimate the different forces of the two governments, by remarking the manner in which they fulfil their respective functions. Whenever the government of a state has occasion to address an individual, or an assembly of individuals, its language is clear and imperative; and such is also the tone of the federal government in its intercourse with individuals; but no sooner has it anything to do with a state, than it begins to parley, to explain its motives, and to justify its conduct, to argue, to advise, and in short, anything but to command. If doubts are raised as to the limits of the constitutional powers of each government, the provincial government prefers its claims with boldness, and takes prompt and energetic steps to support it. In the meanwhile the government of the Union reasons, it appeals to the interests, to the good sense, to the glory of the nation; it temporizes, it negotiates, and does not consent to act until it is reduced to the last extremity. At first sight it might readily be imagined that it is the provincial government which is armed with the authority of the nation, and that congress represents a single state.

The federal government is, therefore, notwithstanding the precautions of those who founded it, naturally so weak, that it more peculiarly requires the free consent of the governed to enable it to subsist. It is easy to perceive that its object is to enable the states to realize with facility their determination of remaining united; and, as long as this preliminary consideration exists, its authority is great, temperate, and effective. The constitution fits the government to control individuals, and easily to surmount such obstacles as they may be inclined to offer, but it was by no means established with a view to the possible separation of one or more of the states from the Union.

If the sovereignty of the Union were to engage in a struggle with that of the states at the present day, its defeat may be confidently predicted; and it is not probable that such a struggle would be seriously undertaken. As often as steady resistance is offered to the federal government, it will be found to yield. Experience has hitherto shown that whenever a state has demanded anything with perseverance and resolution, it has invariably succeeded; and that if a separate government has distinctly refused to act, it was left to do as it thought fit.*

But even if the government of the Union had any strength inherent in itself, the physical situation of the country would render the exercise of that strength very difficult.† The United States cover an immense territory; they are separated from each other by great distances; and the population is disseminated over the surface of a country which is still half a wilderness. If the Union were to undertake to enforce the allegiance of the confederate states by military means, it would be in a position very analogous to that of England at the time of the war of independence.

However strong a government may be, it cannot easily escape from the consequences of a principle which it has once admitted as the foundation of its constitution. The Union was formed by the voluntary agreement of the states; and, in uniting together, they have not forfeited their nationality, nor have they been reduced to the condition of one and the same people. If one of the states chose to withdraw its name from the compact, it would be difficult to disprove its right of doing so; and the federal government would have no means of maintaining its claims directly, either by force or by right. In order to enable the federal government easily to conquer the resistance which may be offered to it by any one of its subjects, it would be necessary that one or more of

* See the conduct of the northern states in the war of 1812. "During that war," said Jefferson, in a letter to General Lafayette, "four of the eastern states were only attached to the Union, like so many inanimate bodies to living men."

† The profound peace of the Union affords no pretext for a standing army; and without a standing army a government is not prepared to profit by a favorable opportunity to conquer resistance, and take the sovereign power by surprise.

them should be especially interested in the existence of the Union, as has frequently been the case in the history of confederations.

If it be supposed that among the states which are united by the federal tie, there are some which exclusively enjoy the principal advantages of union, or whose prosperity depends on the duration of that union, it is unquestionable that they will always be ready to support the central government in enforcing the obedience of the others. But the government would then be exerting a force not derived from itself, but from a principle contrary to its nature. States form confederations in order to derive equal advantages from their union; and in the case just alluded to, the federal government would derive its power from the unequal distribution of those benefits among the states.

If one of the confederated states have acquired a preponderance sufficiently great to enable it to take exclusive possession of the central authority, it will consider the other states as subject provinces, and will cause its own supremacy to be respected under the borrowed name of the sovereignty of the Union. Great things may then be done in the name of the federal government, but in reality that government will have ceased to exist.* In both these cases, the power which acts in the name of the confederation becomes stronger, the more it abandons the natural state and the acknowledged principles of confederations.

In America the existing Union is advantageous to all the states, but it is not indispensable to any one of them. Several of them might break the federal tie without compromising the welfare of the others, although their own prosperity would be lessened. As the existence and the happiness of none of the states are wholly dependent on the present constitution, they would none of them be disposed to make great personal sacrifices to maintain it. On the other hand, there is no state which seems, hitherto, to have its ambition much interested in the maintenance of the existing Union. They certainly do not all exercise the same influence in the federal councils, but no one of them can hope to domineer over the rest, or to treat them as its inferiors or as its subjects.

It appears to me unquestionable, that if any portion of the Union seriously desired to separate itself from the other states,

* Thus the province of Holland in the republic of the Low Countries, and the emperor in the Germanic Confederation, have sometimes put themselves in the place of the Union, and have employed the federal authority to their own advantage.

they would not be able, nor indeed would they attempt, to prevent it; and that the present Union will only last as long as the states which compose it choose to continue members of the confederation. If this point be admitted, the question becomes less difficult; and our object is not to inquire whether the states of the existing Union are capable of separating, but whether they will choose to remain united.

[The remarks respecting the inability of the federal government to retain within the Union any state that may choose "to withdraw its name from the contract," ought not to pass through an American edition of this work, without the expression of a dissent by the editor from the opinion of the author. The laws of the United States must remain in force in a revolted state, until repealed by congress; the customs and postages must be collected; the courts of the United States must sit, and must decide the causes submitted to them; as has been very happily explained by the author, the courts act upon individuals. If their judgments are resisted, the executive arm must interpose, and if the state authorities aid in the resistance, the military power of the whole Union must be invoked to overcome it. So long as the laws affecting the citizens of such a state remain, and so long as there remain any officers of a general government to enforce them, these results must follow not only theoretically but actually. The author probably formed the opinions which are the subject of these remarks, at the commencement of the controversy with South Carolina respecting the tariff And when they were written and published, he had not learned the result of that controversy, in which the supremacy of the Union and its laws was triumphant. There was doubtless great reluctance in adopting the necessary measures to collect the customs, and to bring every legal question that could possibly arise out of the controversy, before the judiciary of the United States, but they were finally adopted, and were not the less successful for being the result of deliberation and of necessity. Out of that controversy have arisen some advantages of a permanent character, produced by the legislation which it required. There were defects in the laws regulating the manner of bringing from the state courts into those of the United States, a cause involving the constitutionality of acts of congress or of the states, through which the federal authority might be evaded. Those defects were remedied by the legislation referred to; and it is now more emphatically and universally true, than when the author wrote, that the acts of the general government operate through the judiciary, upon individual citizens, and not upon the states.—*American Editor.*]

Among the various reasons which tend to render the existing Union useful to the Americans, two principal causes are peculiarly evident to the observer. Although the Americans are, as it were, alone upon their continent, their commerce makes them the neighbors of all the nations with which they trade. Notwithstanding their apparent isolation, the Americans require a certain degree of strength, which they cannot retain otherwise than by remaining united to each other. If the states were to split, they would not only diminish the strength which they are now able to display toward foreign nations, but they would soon create foreign powers upon their own territory. A system of inland custom-houses would then be established; the valleys would be divided by imaginary boundary lines; the courses of the rivers would be confined by territorial distinctions; and a multitude of hindrances would prevent the Americans from exploring the whole of that vast continent which Providence has allotted to them for a dominion. At present they have no invasion to fear, and consequently no standing armies to maintain, no taxes to levy. If the Union were dissolved, all these burdensome measures might ere long be required. The Americans are then very powerfully interested in the maintenance of their Union. On the other hand, it is almost impossible to discover any sort of material interest which might at present tempt a portion of the Union to separate from the other states.

When we cast our eyes upon the map of the United States, we perceive the chain of the Allegany mountains, running from the northeast to the southwest, and crossing nearly one thousand miles of country; and we are led to imagine that the design of Providence was to raise, between the valley of the Mississippi and the coasts of the Atlantic ocean, one of those natural barriers which break the mutual intercourse of men, and form the necessary limits of different states. But the average height of the Alleganies does not exceed 2,500 feet; their greatest elevation is not above 4,000 feet; their rounded summits, and the spacious valleys which they conceal within their passes, are of easy access from several sides. Beside which, the principal rivers that fall into the Atlantic ocean, the Hudson, the Susquehannah, and the Potomac, take their rise beyond the Alleganies, in an open district, which borders upon the valley of the Mississippi. These streams quit this tract of country,* make their way through the barrier which would seem to turn them westward, and as they wind through the mountains, they open an easy and natural passage to man.

No natural barrier exists in the regions which are now inhabited by the Anglo-Americans; the Alleganies are so far from serving as a boundary to separate nations, that they do not even serve as a frontier to the states. New York, Pennsylvania, and Virginia, comprise them within their bor-

* See Darby's View of the United States, pp 64. 79.

ders, and extend as much to the west as to the east of the line.

The territory now occupied by the twenty-four states of the Union, and the three great districts which have not yet acquired the rank of states, although they already contain inhabitants, covers a surface of 1,002,600 square miles,* which is about equal to five times the extent of France. Within these limits the qualities of the soil, the temperature, and the produce of the country, are extremely various. The vast extent of territory occupied by the Anglo-American republics has given rise to doubts as to the maintenance of the Union. Here a distinction must be made; contrary interests sometimes arise in the different provinces of a vast empire, which often terminate in open dissensions; and the extent of the country is then most prejudicial to the power of the state. But if the inhabitants of these vast regions are not divided by contrary interests, the extent of the territory may be favorable to their prosperity; for the unity of the government promotes the interchange of the different productions of the soil, and increases their value by facilitating their consumption.

It is indeed easy to discover different interests in the different parts of the Union, but I am unacquainted with any which are hostile to each other. The southern states are almost exclusively agricultural : the northern states are more peculiarly commercial and manufacturing: the states of the west are at the same time agricultural and manufacturing. In the south the crops consist of tobacco, of rice, of cotton, and of sugar; in the north and the west, of wheat and maize: these are different sources of wealth; but union is the means by which these sources are opened to all, and rendered equally advantageous to the several districts.

The north, which ships the produce of the Anglo-Americans to all parts of the world, and brings back the produce of the globe to the Union, is evidently interested in maintaining the confederation in its present condition, in order that the num-

* See Darby's View of the United States, p. 435. [In Carey & Lea's Geography of America, the United States are said to form an area of 2,076,400 square miles.—*Translator's Note.*]

[The discrepance between Darby's estimate of the area of the United States given by the author, and that stated by the translator, is not easily accounted for. In Bradford's comprehensive Atlas, a work generally of great accuracy, it is said that "as claimed by this country, the territory of the United States extends from 25° to 54° north latitude, and from 67° 49′ to 125° west longitude, over an area of about 2,200,000 square miles."—*American Editor.*]

ber of American producers and consumers may remain as large as possible. The north is the most natural agent of communication between the south and the west of the Union on the one hand, and the rest of the world upon the other; the north is therefore interested in the union and prosperity of the south and the west, in order that they may continue to furnish raw materials for its manufactures, and cargoes for its shipping.

The south and the west, on their side, are still more directly interested in the preservation of the Union, and the prosperity of the north. The produce of the south is for the most part exported beyond seas; the south and the west consequently stand in need of the commercial resources of the north. They are likewise interested in the maintenance of a powerful fleet by the Union, to protect them efficaciously. The south and the west have no vessels, but they cannot refuse a willing subsidy to defray the expenses of the navy; for if the fleets of Europe were to blockade the ports of the south and the delta of the Mississippi, what would become of the rice of the Carolinas, the tobacco of Virginia, and the sugar and cotton which grow in the valley of the Mississippi? Every portion of the federal budget does therefore contribute to the maintenance of material interests which are common to all the confederate states.

Independently of this commercial utility, the south and the west of the Union derive great political advantages from their connexion with the north. The south contains an enormous slave population; a population which is already alarming, and still more formidable for the future. The states of the west lie in the remoter part of a single valley; and all the rivers which intersect their territory rise in the Rocky mountains or in the Alleganies, and fall into the Mississippi, which bears them onward to the gulf of Mexico. The western states are consequently entirely cut off, by their position, from the traditions of Europe and the civilisation of the Old World. The inhabitants of the south, then, are induced to support the Union in order to avail themselves of its protection against the blacks; and the inhabitants of the west, in order not to be excluded from a free communication with the rest of the globe, and shut up in the wilds of central America. The north cannot but desire the maintenance of the Union, in order to remain, as it now is, the connecting link between that vast body and the other parts of the world.

The temporal interests of all the several parts of the Union are, then, intimately connected; and the same assertion holds true respecting those opinions and sentiments which may be termed the immaterial interests of men.

The inhabitants of the United States talk a great deal of their attachment to their country; but I confess that I do not rely upon that calculating patriotism which is founded upon interest, and which a change in the interest at stake may obliterate. Nor do I attach much importance to the language of the Americans, when they manifest in their daily conversation, the intention of maintaining the federal system adopted by their forefathers. A government retains its sway over a great number of citizens, far less by the voluntary and rational consent of the multitude, than by that instinctive and, to a certain extent, involuntary agreement, which results from similarity of feelings and resemblances of opinion. I will never admit that men constitute a social body, simply because they obey the same head and the same laws. Society can only exist when a great number of men consider a great number of things in the same point of view; when they hold the same opinions upon many subjects, and when the same occurrences suggest the same thoughts and impressions to their minds.

The observer who examines the present condition of the United States upon this principle, will readily discover, that although the citizens are divided into twenty-four distinct sovereignties, they nevertheless constitute a single people; and he may perhaps be led to think that the state of the Anglo-American Union is more truly a state of society, than that of certain nations of Europe which live under the same legislation and the same prince.

Although the Anglo-Americans have several religious sects, they all regard religion in the same manner. They are not always agreed upon the measures which are most conducive to good government, and they vary upon some of the forms of government which it is expedient to adopt; but they are unanimous upon the general principles which ought to rule human society. From Maine to the Floridas, and from Missouri to the Atlantic ocean, the people is held to be the legitimate source of all power. The same notions are entertained respecting liberty and equality, the liberty of the press, the right of association, the jury, and the responsibility of the agents of government.

If we turn from their political and religious opinions to the moral and philosophical principles which regulate the daily actions of life, and govern their conduct, we shall still find the same uniformity. The Anglo-Americans* acknowledge the absolute moral authority of the reason of the community, as they acknowledge the political authority of the mass of citizens; and they hold that public opinion is the surest arbiter of what is lawful or forbidden, true or false. The majority of them believe that a man will be led to do what is just and good by following his own interests, rightly understood. They hold that every man is born in possession of the right of self-government, and that no one has the right of constraining his fellow-creatures to be happy. They have all a lively faith in the perfectibility of man; they are of opinion that the effects of the diffusion of knowledge must necessarily be advantageous, and the consequences of ignorance fatal; they all consider society as a body in a state of improvement, humanity as a changing scene, in which nothing is, or ought to be, permanent; and they admit that what appears to them to be good to-day may be superseded by something better to-morrow. I do not give all these opinions as true, but I quote them as characteristic of the Americans.

The Anglo-Americans are not only united together by those common opinions, but they are separated from all other nations by a common feeling of pride. For the last fifty years, no pains have been spared to convince the inhabitants of the United States that they constitute the only religious, enlightened, and free people. They perceive that, for the present, their own democratic institutions succeed, while those of other countries fail; hence they conceive an overweening opinion of their superiority, and they are not very remote from believing themselves to belong to a distinct race of mankind.

The dangers which threaten the American Union do not originate in the diversity of interests or opinions; but in the various characters and passions of the Americans. The men who inhabit the vast territory of the United States are almost all the issue of a common stock; but the effects of the climate, and more especially of slavery, have gradually introduced very striking differences between the British settler of the southern states, and the British settler of the north. In Europe it is generally believed that slavery has rendered the interests of one part of the Union contrary to those of another part; but I by no means remarked this to be the case; slave-

* It is scarcely necessary for me to observe that by the expression *Anglo-Americans*, I only mean to designate the great majority of the nation; for a certain number of isolated individuals are of course to be met with holding very different opinions

ry has not created interests in the south contrary to those of the north, but it has modified the character and changed the habits of the natives of the south.

I have already explained the influence which slavery has exerted upon the commercial ability of the Americans in the south; and this same influence equally extends to their manners. The slave is a servant who never remonstrates, and who submits to everything without complaint. He may sometimes assassinate, but he never withstands, his master. In the south there are no families so poor as not to have slaves. The citizen of the southern states of the Union is invested with a sort of domestic dictatorship from his earliest years; the first notion he acquires in life is, that he is born to command, and the first habit he contracts is that of being obeyed without resistance. His education tends, then, to give him the character of a supercilious and a hasty man; irascible, violent, and ardent in his desires, impatient of obstacles, but easily discouraged if he cannot succeed upon his first attempt.

The American of the northern states is surrounded by no slaves in his childhood; he is even unattended by free servants; and is usually obliged to provide for his own wants. No sooner does he enter the world than the idea of necessity assails him on every side; he soon learns to know exactly the natural limits of his authority; he never expects to subdue those who withstand him, by force; and he knows that the surest means of obtaining the support of his fellow-creatures, is to win their favor. He therefore becomes patient, reflecting, tolerant, slow to act, and persevering in his designs.

In the southern states the more immediate wants of life are always supplied; the inhabitants of those parts are not busied in the material cares of life, which are always provided for by others; and their imagination is diverted to more captivating and less definite objects The American of the south is fond of grandeur, luxury, and renown, of gaiety, of pleasure, and above all, of idleness; nothing obliges him to exert himself in order to subsist; and as he has no necessary occupations, he gives way to indolence, and does not even attempt what would be useful.

But the equality of fortunes, and the absence of slavery in the north, plunge the inhabitants in those same cares of daily life which are disdained by the white population of the south. They are taught from infancy to combat want, and to place comfort above all the pleasures of the intellect or the heart.

The imagination is extinguished by the trivial details of life; and the ideas become less numerous and less general, but far more practical and more precise. As prosperity is the sole aim of exertion, it is excellently well attained; nature and mankind are turned to the best pecuniary advantage; and society is dexterously made to contribute to the welfare of each of its members, while individual egotism is the source of general happiness.

The citizen of the north has not only experience, but knowledge: nevertheless, he sets but little value upon the pleasures of knowledge; he esteems it as the means of obtaining a certain end, and he is only anxious to seize its more lucrative applications. The citizen of the south is more given to act upon impulse; he is more clever, more frank, more generous, more intellectual, and more brilliant. The former, with a greater degree of activity, of common sense, of information, and of general aptitude, has the characteristic good and evil qualities of the middle classes. The latter has the tastes, the prejudices, the weaknesses, and the magnanimity of all aristocracies.

If two men are united in society, who have the same interests, and to a certain extent the same opinions, but different characters, different acquirements, and a different style of civilisation, it is probable that these men will not agree. The same remark is applicable to a society of nations.

Slavery then does not attack the American Union directly in its interests, but indirectly in its manners.

The states which gave their assent to the federal contract in 1790 were thirteen in number; the Union now consists of twenty-four members. The population which amounted to nearly four millions in 1790, had more than tripled in the space of forty years; and in 1830 it amounted to nearly thirteen millions.* Changes of such magnitude cannot take place without some danger.

A society of nations, as well as a society of individuals, derive its principal chances of duration from the wisdom of its members, their individual weakness, and their limited number. The Americans who quit the coasts of the Atlantic ocean to plunge into the western wilderness, are adventurers impatient of restraint, greedy of wealth, and frequently men expelled from the states in which they were born. When they arrive in the deserts, they are unknown to each

* Census of 1790........ 3,929,328.
do 1830........12,856,165.
[do. 1840........17,068,666.]

other; and they have neither traditions, family feeling, nor the force of example to check their excesses. The empire of the laws is feeble among them; that of morality is still more powerless. The settlers who are constantly peopling the valley of the Mississippi are, then, in every respect inferior to the Americans who inhabit the older parts of the Union. Nevertheless, they already exercise a great influence in its councils; and they arrive at the government of the commonwealth before they have learned to govern themselves.*

The greater the individual weakness of each of the contracting parties, the greater are the chances of the duration of the contract; for their safety is then dependant upon their union. When, in 1790, the most populous of the American republics did not contain 500,000 inhabitants,† each of them felt its own insignificance as an independent people, and this feeling rendered compliance with the federal authority more easy. But when one of the confederate states reckons, like the State of New York, two millions of inhabitants, and covers an extent of territory equal in surface to a quarter of France,‡ it feels its own strength; and although it may continue to support the Union as advantageous to its prosperity, it no longer regards that body as necessary to its existence; and, as it continues to belong to the federal compact, it soon aims at preponderance in the federal assemblies. The probable unanimity of the states is diminished as their number increases. At present the interests of the different parts of the Union are not at variance; but who is able to foresee the multifarious changes of the future, in a country in which towns are founded from day to day, and states almost from year to year?

Since the first settlement of the British colonies, the number of inhabitants has about doubled every twenty-two years. I perceive no causes which are likely to check this progressive increase of the Anglo-American population for the next hundred years; and before that space of time has elapsed, I believe that the territories and dependencies of the United States will be covered by more than a hundred millions of inhabitants, and divided into forty states.§ I admit that these

* This indeed is only a temporary danger. I have no doubt that in time society will assume as much stability and regularity in the west, as it has already done upon the coast of the Atlantic ocean.

† Pennsylvania contained 431,373 inhabitants in 1790.

‡ The area of the state of New York is about 46,000 square miles. See Carey & Lea's American Geography, p. 142.

§ If the population continues to double every twenty-two years, as it has done for the last two hundred years, the number of inhabitants in

hundred millions of men have no hostile interests; I suppose, on the contrary, that they are all equally interested in the maintenance of the Union; but I am still of opinion, that where there are a hundred millions of men, and forty distinct nations unequally strong, the continuance of the federal government can only be a fortunate accident.

Whatever faith I may have in the perfectibility of man, until human nature is altered, and men wholly transformed, I shall refuse to believe in the duration of a government which is called upon to hold together forty different peoples, disseminated over a territory equal to one-half of Europe in extent; to avoid all rivalry, ambition, and struggles, between them; and to direct their independent activity to the accomplishment of the same designs.

But the greatest peril to which the Union is exposed by its increase, arises from the continual changes which take place in the position of its internal strength. The distance from Lake Superior to the gulf of Mexico extends from the 47th to the 30th degree of latitude, a distance of more than twelve hundred miles, as the bird flies. The frontier of the United States winds along the whole of this immense line; sometimes falling within its limits, but more frequently extending far beyond it, into the waste. It has been calculated that the whites advance a mean distance of seventeen miles along the whole of this vast boundary.* Obstacles, such as an unproductive district, a lake, or an Indian nation unexpectedly encountered, are sometimes met with. The advancing column then halts for a while; its two extremities fall back upon themselves, and as soon as they are reunited they proceed onward. This gradual and continuous progress of the European race toward the Rocky mountains, has the solemnity of a providential event; it is like a deluge of men rising unabatedly, and daily driven onward by the hand of God.

the United States in 1852, will be twenty millions: in 1874, forty-eight millions; and in 1896, ninety-six millions. This may still be the case even if the lands on the western slope of the Rocky mountains should be found to be unfit for cultivation. The territory which is already occupied can easily contain this number of inhabitants. One hundred millions of men disseminated over the surface of the twenty-four states, and the three dependencies, which constitute the Union, would give only 762 inhabitants to the square league: this would be far below the mean population of France, which is 1,063 to the square league; or of England, which is 1,457; and it would even be below the population of Switzerland, for that country, notwithstanding its lakes and mountains, contains 783 inhabitants to the square league (See Maltebrun, vol. vi., p. 92.)

* See Legislative Documents, 20th congress, No. 117, p. 105.

Within this first line of conquering settlers, towns are built, and vast states founded. In 1790 there were only a few thousand pioneers sprinkled along the valleys of the Mississippi; and at the present day these valleys contain as many inhabitants as were to be found in the whole Union in 1790. Their population amounts to nearly four millions.* The city of Washington was founded in 1800, in the very centre of the Union; but such are the changes which have taken place, that it now stands at one of the extremities; and the delegates of the most remote western states are already obliged to perform a journey as long as that from Vienna to Paris.†

All the states are borne onward at the same time in the path of fortune, but of course they do not all increase and prosper in the same proportion. In the north of the Union detached branches of the Allegany chain, extending as far as the Atlantic ocean, form spacious roads and ports, which are constantly accessible to vessels of the greatest burden. But from the Potomac to the mouth of the Mississippi, the coast is sandy and flat. In this part of the Union the mouths of almost all the rivers are obstructed; and the few harbors which exist among these lagunes, afford much shallower water to vessels, and much fewer commercial advantages than those of the north.

This first natural cause of inferiority is united to another cause proceeding from the laws. We have already seen that slavery, which is abolished in the north, still exists in the south; and I have pointed out its fatal consequences upon the prosperity of the planter himself.

The north is therefore superior to the south both in commerce‡ and manufacture; the natural consequence of which

* 3,672,317; census 1830.

† The distance of Jefferson, the capital of the state of Missouri, to Washington, is 1,018 miles. (American Almanac, 1831, p. 40.)

‡ The following statements will suffice to show the difference which exists between the commerce of the south and that of the north:—

In 1829, the tonnage of all the merchant-vessels belonging to Virginia, the two Carolinas, and Georgia (the four great southern states), amounted to only 5,243 tons. In the same year the tonnage of the vessels of the state of Massachusetts alone amounted to 17,322 tons. (See Legislative Documents, 21st congress, 2d session, No. 140, p. 244.) Thus the state of Massachusetts has three times as much shipping as the four abovementioned states. Nevertheless the area of the state of Massachusetts is only 7,335 square miles, and its population amounts to 610,014 inhabitants; while the area of the four other states I have quoted is 210,000 square miles, and their population 3,047,767. Thus the area of the state of Massachusetts forms only one thirtieth part of

is the more rapid increase of population and of wealth within its borders. The states situate upon the shores of the Atlantic ocean are already half-peopled. Most of the land is held by an owner; and these districts cannot therefore receive so many emigrants as the western states, where a boundless field is still open to their exertions. The valley of the Mississippi is far more fertile than the coast of the Atlantic ocean. This reason, added to all the others, contributes to drive the Europeans westward—a fact which may be rigorously demonstrated by figures. It is found that the sum total of the population of all the United States has about tripled in the course of forty years. But in the recent states adjacent to the Mississippi, the population has increased thirty-one fold within the same space of time.*

The relative position of the central federal power is continually displaced. Forty years ago the majority of the citizens of the Union was established upon the coast of the Atlantic, in the environs of the spot upon which Washington now stands; but the great body of the people is now advancing inland and to the north, so that in twenty years the majority will unquestionably be on the western side of the Alleganies. If the Union goes on to subsist, the basin of the Mississippi is evidently marked out, by its fertility and its extent, as the future centre of the federal government. In thirty or forty years, that tract of country will have assumed the rank which naturally belongs to it. It is easy to calculate that its population, compared to that of the coast of the Atlantic, will be, in round numbers, as 40 to 11. In a few years the states which founded the Union will lose the direction of its policy, and the population of the valleys of the Mississippi will preponderate in the federal assemblies.

This constant gravitation of the federal power and influence toward the northwest, is shown every ten years, when a general census of the population is made, and the number of

the area of the four states; and its population is five times smaller than theirs. (See Darby's View of the United States.) Slavery is prejudicial to the commercial prosperity of the south in several different ways; by diminishing the spirit of enterprise among the whites, and by preventing them from meeting with as numerous a class of sailors as they require. Sailors are generally taken from the lowest ranks of the population. But in the southern states these lowest ranks are composed of slaves, and it is very difficult to employ them at sea. They are unable to serve as well as a white crew, and apprehensions would always be entertained of their mutinying in the middle of the ocean, or of their escaping in the foreign countries at which they might touch

* Darby's view of the United States, p. 444

delegates which each state sends to congress is settled afresh.* In 1790 Virginia had nineteen representatives in congress. This number continued to increase until the year 1813, when it reached to twenty-three: from that time it began to decrease, and in 1833, Virginia elected only twenty-one representatives.† During the same period the state of New York advanced in the contrary direction; in 1790, it had ten representatives in congress; in 1813, twenty-seven; in 1823, thirty-four; and in 1833, forty. The state of Ohio had only one representative in 1803, and in 1833, it had already nineteen.

It is difficult to imagine a durable union of a people which is rich and strong, with one which is poor and weak, and if it were proved that the strength and wealth of the one are not the causes of the weakness and poverty of the other. But union is still more difficult to maintain at a time at which one party is losing strength, and the other is gaining it. This rapid and disproportionate increase of certain states threatens

* It may be seen that in the course of the last ten years (1820–'30) the population of one district, as for instance, the state of Delaware, has increased in the proportion of 5 per cent.; while that of another, as the territory of Michigan, has increased 250 per cent. Thus the population of Virginia has augmented 13 per cent., and that of the border state of Ohio 61 per cent., in the same space of time. The general table of these changes, which is given in the National Calendar, displays a striking picture of the unequal fortunes of the different states.

† It has just been said that in the course of the last term the population of Virginia has increased 13 per cent.; and it is necessary to explain how the number of representatives of a state may decrease, when the population of that state, far from diminishing, is actually upon the increase. I take the state of Virginia, to which I have already alluded, as my term of comparison. The number of representatives of Virginia in 1823 was proportionate to the total number of the representatives of the Union, and to the relation which its population bore to that of the whole Union; in 1833, the number of representatives of Virginia was likewise proportionate to the total number of the representatives of the Union, and to the relation which its population, augmented in the course of ten years, bore to the augmented population of the Union in the same space of time. The new number of Virginian representatives will then be to the old number, on the one hand, as the new number of all the representatives is to the old number; and, on the other hand, as the augmentation of the population of Virginia is to that of the whole population of the country. Thus, if the increase of the population of the lesser country be to that of the greater in an exact inverse ratio of the proportion between the new and the old numbers of all the representatives, the number of representatives of Virginia will remain stationary; and if the increase of the Virginian population be to that of the whole Union in a feebler ratio than the new number of representatives of the Union to the old number, the number of the representatives of Virginia must decrease

the independence of the others. New York might, perhaps, succeed with its two millions of inhabitants and its forty representatives, in dictating to the other states in congress. But even if the more powerful states make no attempt to bear down the lesser ones, the danger still exists; for there is almost as much in the possibility of the act as in the act itself. The weak generally mistrusts the justice and the reason of the strong. The states which increase less rapidily than the others, look upon those which are more favored by fortune, with envy and suspicion. Hence arise the deep-seated uneasiness and ill-defined agitation which are observable in the south, and which form so striking a contrast to the confidence and prosperity which are common to other parts of the Union. I am inclined to think that the hostile measures taken by the southern provinces upon a recent occasion, are attributable to no other cause. The inhabitants of the southern states are, of all the Americans, those who are most interested in the maintenance of the Union; they would assuredly suffer most from being left to themselves; and yet they are the only citizens who threaten to break the tie of confederation. But it is easy to perceive that the south, which has given four presidents, Washington, Jefferson, Madison, and Monroe, to the Union; which perceives that it is losing its federal influence, and that the number of its representatives in congress is diminishing from year to year, while those of the northern and western states are increasing; the south, which is peopled with ardent and irascible beings, is becoming more and more irritated and alarmed. The citizens reflect upon their present position and remember their past influence, with the melancholy uneasiness of men who suspect oppression: if they discover a law of the Union which is not unequivocally favorable to their interests, they protest against it as an abuse of force; and if their ardent remonstrances are not listened to, they threaten to quit an association which loads them with burdens while it deprives them of their due profits. "The tariff," said the inhabitants of Carolina in 1832, "enriches the north, and ruins the south; for if this were not the case, to what can we attribute the continually increasing power and wealth of the north, with its inclement skies and arid soil; while the south, which may be styled the garden of America, is rapidly declining."*

If the changes which I have described were gradual, so that

* See the report of its committees to the convention, which proclaimed the nullification of the tariff in South Carolina

each generation at least might have time to disappear with the order of things under which it had lived, the danger would be less; but the progress of society in America is precipitate, and almost revolutionary. The same citizen may have lived to see his state take the lead in the Union, and afterward become powerless in the federal assemblies; and an Anglo-American republic has been known to grow as rapidly as a man, passing from birth and infancy to maturity in the course of thirty years. It must not be imagined, however, that the states which lose their preponderance, also lose their population or or their riches; no stop is put to their prosperity, and they even go on to increase more rapidly than any kingdom in Europe.* But they believe themselves to be impoverished because their wealth does not augment as rapidly as that of their neighbors; and they think that their power is lost, because they suddenly come into collision with a power greater than their own.† Thus they are more hurt in their feelings and their passions, than in their interests. But this is amply sufficient to endanger the maintenance of the Union. If kings and peoples had only had their true interests in view, ever since the beginning of the world, the name of war would scarcely be known among mankind.

Thus the prosperity of the United States is the source of the most serious dangers that threaten them, since it tends to create in some of the confederate states that over-excitement which accompanies a rapid increase of fortune; and to awaken in others those feelings of envy, mistrust, and regret, which usually attend upon the loss of it. The Americans contemplate this extraordinary and hasty progress with exultation; but they would be wiser to consider it with sorrow and alarm. The Americans of the United States must inevitably become one of the greatest nations in the world;

* The population of a country assuredly constitutes the first element of its wealth. In the ten years (1820–'30) during which Virginia lost two of its representatives in congress, its population increased in the proportion of 13–7 per cent.; that of Carolina in the proportion of 15 per cent.; and that of Georgia 51–5 per cent. (See the American Almanac, 1832, p. 162.) But the population of Russia, which increases more rapidly than that of any other European country, only augments in ten years at the rate of 9–5 per cent.; of France at the rate of 7 per cent.; and of Europe in general at the rate of 4–7 per cent. (See Maltebrun, vol. vi., p. 95.)

† It must be admitted, however, that the depreciation which has taken place in the value of tobacco, during the last fifty years, has notably diminished the opulence of the southern planters; but this circumstance is as independent of the will of their northern brethren, as it is of their own

their offset will cover almost the whole of North America; the continent which they inhabit is their dominion, and it cannot escape them. What urges them to take possession of it so soon? Riches, power, and renown, cannot fail to be theirs at some future time; but they rush upon their fortune as if but a moment remained for them to make it their own.

I think I have demonstrated, that the existence of the present confederation depends entirely on the continued assent of all the confederates; and, starting from this principle, I have inquired into the causes which may induce any of the states to separate from the others. The Union may, however, perish in two different ways: one of the confederate states may choose to retire from the compact, and so forcibly sever the federal tie; and it is to this supposition that most of the remarks which I have made apply: or the authority of the federal government may be progressively intrenched on by the simultaneous tendency of the united republics to resume their independence. The central power, successively stripped of all its prerogatives, and reduced to impotence by tacit consent, would become incompetent to fulfil its purpose; and the second Union would perish, like the first, by a sort of senile inaptitude. The gradual weakening of the federal tie, which may finally lead to the dissolution of the Union, is a distinct circumstance, that may produce a variety of minor consequences before it operates so violent a change. The confederation might still subsist, although its government were reduced to such a degree of inanition as to paralyze the nation, to cause internal anarchy, and to check the general prosperity of the country.

After having investigated the causes which may induce the Anglo-Americans to disunite, it is important to inquire whether, if the Union continues to subsist, their government will extend or contract its sphere of action, and whether it will become more energetic or more weak.

The Americans are evidently disposed to look upon their future condition with alarm. They perceive that in most of the nations of the world, the exercise of the rights of sovereignty tends to fall under the control of a few individuals, and they are dismayed by the idea that such will also be the case in their own country. Even the statesmen feel, or affect to feel, these fears; for, in America, centralization is by no means popular, and there is no surer means of courting the majority, than by inveighing against the encroachments of the central power. The Americans do not perceive that the countries in which this alarming tendency to centralization exists, are inhabited by a single people; while the fact of the Union being composed of different confederate communities, is sufficient to baffle all the inferences which might be drawn from analogous circumstances. I confess that I am inclined to consider the fears of a great number of Americans as purely imaginary; and far from participating in their dread of the consolidation of power in the hands of the Union, I think that the federal government is visibly losing strength.

To prove this assertion I shall not have recourse to any remote occurrences, but to circumstances which I have myself observed, and which belong to our own time.

An attentive examination of what is going on in the United States, will easily convince us that two opposite tendencies exist in that country, like two distinct currents flowing in contrary directions in the same channel. The Union has now existed for forty-five years, and in the course of that time a vast number of provincial prejudices, which were at first hostile to its power, have died away. The patriotic feeling which attached each of the Americans to his own native state is become less exclusive; and the different parts of the Union have become more intimately connected the better they have become acquainted with each other. The post,* that great instrument of intellectual intercourse, now reaches into the backwoods; and steamboats have established daily means of communication between the different points of the coast. An inland navigation of unexampled rapidity conveys commodities up and down the rivers of the country.† And to these facilities of nature and art may be added those restless cravings, that busymindedness, and love of pelf, which are constantly urging the American into active life, and bringing him into contact with his fellow-citizens. He crosses the country in every direction; he visits all the various populations of the land; and there is not a province in France, in which the natives are so well known to each other as the thirteen millions of men who cover the territory of the United States.

* In 1832, the district of Michigan, which only contains 31,639 inhabitants, and is still an almost unexplored wilderness, possessed 940 miles of mail-roads. The territory of Arkansas, which is still more uncultivated, was already intersected by 1,938 miles of mail-roads (See report of the general post-office, 30th November, 1833.) The postage of newspapers alone in the whole Union amounted to $254,796.

† In the course of ten years, from 1821 to 1831, 271 steamboats have been launched upon the rivers which water the valley of the Mississippi alone. In 1829, 259 steamboats existed in the United States (See Legislative Documents, No. 140, p. 274.)

But while the Americans intermingle, they grow in resemblance of each other; the differences resulting from their climate, their origin, and their institutions diminish; and they all draw nearer and nearer to the common type. Every year, thousands of men leave the north to settle in different parts of the Union: they bring with them their faith, their opinions, and their manners; and as they are more enlightened than the men among whom they are about to dwell, they soon rise to the head of affairs, and they adapt society to their own advantage. This continual emigration of the north to the south is peculiarly favorable to the fusion of all the different provincial characters into one national character. The civilisation of the north appears to be the common standard, to which the whole nation will one day be assimilated.

The commercial ties which unite the confederate states are strengthened by the increasing manufactures of the Americans; and the union which began to exist in their opinions, gradually forms a part of their habits: the course of time has swept away the bugbear thoughts which haunted the imaginations of the citizens in 1789. The federal power is not become oppressive; it has not destroyed the independence of the states; it has not subjected the confederates to monarchical institutions; and the Union has not rendered the lesser states dependant upon the larger ones; but the confederation has continued to increase in population, in wealth, and in power. I am therefore convinced that the natural obstacles to the continuance of the American Union are not so powerful at the present time as they were in 1789; and that the enemies of the Union are not so numerous.

Nevertheless, a careful examination of the history of the United States for the last forty-five years, will readily convince us that the federal power is declining; nor is it difficult to explain the causes of this phenomenon. When the constitution of 1789 was promulgated, the nation was a prey to anarchy; the Union, which succeeded this confusion, excited much dread and much animosity; but it was warmly supported because it satisfied an imperious want. Thus, although it was more attacked than it is now, the federal power soon reached the maximum of its authority, as is usually the case with a government which triumphs after having braced its strength by the struggle. At that time the interpretation of the constitution seemed to extend rather than to repress, the federal sovereignty; and the Union offered, in several respects, the appearance of a single and undivided people, directed in its foreign and internal policy by a single government. But to attain this point the people had risen, to a certain extent, above itself.

The constitution had not destroyed the distinct sovereignty of the states; and all communities, of whatever nature they may be, are impelled by a secret propensity to assert their independence. This propensity is still more decided in a country like America, in which every village forms a sort of republic accustomed to conduct its own affairs. It therefore cost the states an effort to submit to the federal supremacy; and all efforts, however successful they may be, necessarily subside with the causes in which they originated.

As the federal government consolidated its authority, America resumed its rank among the nations, peace returned to its frontiers, and public credit was restored; confusion was succeeded by a fixed state of things which was favorable to the full and free exercise of industrious enterprise. It was this very prosperity which made the Americans forget the cause to which it was attributable; and when once the danger was passed, the energy and the patriotism which had enabled them to brave it, disappeared from among them. No sooner were they delivered from the cares which oppressed them, than they easily returned to their ordinary habits, and gave themselves up without resistance to their natural inclinations. When a powerful government no longer appeared to be necessary, they once more began to think it irksome. The Union encouraged a general prosperity, and the states were not inclined to abandon the Union; but they desired to render the action of the power which represented that body as light as possible. The general principle of union was adopted, but in every minor detail there was an actual tendency to independence. The principle of confederation was every day more easily admitted and more rarely applied; so that the federal government brought about its own decline, while it was creating order and peace.

As soon as this tendency of public opinion began to be manifested externally, the leaders of parties, who live by the passions of the people, began to work it to their own advantage. The position of the federal government then became exceedingly critical. Its enemies were in possession of the popular favor; and they obtained the right of conducting its policy by pledging themselves to lessen its influence. From that time forward, the government of the Union has invariably been obliged to recede, as often as it has attempted to enter the lists with the government of the states. And whenever an interpretation of the terms of the federal constitution has been called for, that interpretation has most frequently been opposed to the Union, and favorable to the states.

The constitution invested the federal government with the right of providing for the interests of the nation; and it has been held that no other authority was so fit to superintend the "internal improvements" which affected the prosperity of the whole Union; such, for instance, as the cutting of canals. But the states were alarmed at a power, distinct from their own, which could thus dispose of a portion of their territory, and they were afraid that the central government would, by this means, acquire a formidable extent of patronage within their own confines, and exercise a degree of influence which they intended to reserve exclusively to their own agents. The democratic party, which has constantly been opposed to the increase of the federal authority, then accused the congress of usurpation, and the chief magistrate of ambition. The central government was intimidated by the opposition; and it soon acknowledged its error, promising exactly to confine its influence, for the future, within the circle which was prescribed to it.

The constitution confers upon the Union the right of treating with foreign nations. The Indian tribes, which border upon the frontiers of the United States, have usually been regarded in this light. As long as these savages consented to retire before the civilized settlers, the federal right was not contested; but as soon as an Indian tribe attempted to fix its dwelling upon a given spot, the adjacent states claimed possession of the lands and the rights of sovereignty over the natives. The central government soon recognized both these claims; and after it had concluded treaties with the Indians as independent nations, it gave them up as subjects to the legislative tyranny of the states.*

Some of the states which had been founded upon the coast of the Atlantic, extended indefinitely to the west, into wild regions, where no European had ever penetrated. The states whose confines were irrevocably fixed, looked with a jealous eye upon the unbounded regions which the future would enable their neighbors to explore. The latter then agreed, with a view to conciliate the others, and to facilitate the act of union, to lay down their own boundaries, and to abandon all the territory which lay beyond those limits to the

* See in the legislative documents already quoted in speaking of the Indians, the letter of the President of the United States to the Cherokees, his correspondence on this subject with his agents, and his messages to congress.

confederation at large.* Thenceforward the federal government became the owner of all the uncultivated lands which lie beyond the borders of the thirteen states first confederated. It was invested with the right of parcelling and selling them, and the sums derived from this source were exclusively reserved to the public treasury of the Union, in order to furnish supplies for purchasing tracts of country from the Indians, for opening roads to the remote settlements, and for accelerating the increase of civilisation as much as possible. New states have, however, been formed in the course of time, in the midst of those wilds which were formerly ceded by the inhabitants of the shores of the Atlantic. Congress has gone on to sell, for the profit of the nation at large, the uncultivated lands which those new states contained. But the latter at length asserted that, as they were now fully constituted, they ought to enjoy the exclusive right of converting the produce of these sales to their own use. As their remonstrances became more and more threatening, congress thought fit to deprive the Union of a portion of the privileges which it had hitherto enjoyed; and at the end of 1832 it passed a law by which the greatest part of the revenue derived from the sale of lands was made over to the new western republics, although the lands themselves were not ceded to them.†

[The remark of the author, that "whenever an interpretation of the terms of the federal constitution has been called for, that interpretation has most frequently been opposed to the Union, and favorable to the states" requires considerable qualification. The instances which the author cites, are those of *legislative* interpretations, not those made by the judiciary. It may be questioned whether any of those cited by him are fair instances of *interpretation*. Although the then president and many of his friends doubted or denied the power of congress over many of the subjects mentioned by the author, yet the omission to exercise the power thus questioned, did not proceed wholly from doubts of the constitutional authority. It must be remembered that all these questions affected local interests of the states or districts represented in congress, and the author has elsewhere shown the tendency of the local feeling to overcome all regard for the abstract interest of the Union. Hence many members have voted on these questions without reference to the constitutional question, and indeed without entertaining any doubt of their power. These instances may afford proof that the federal power is declining, as the author contends, but they do not

* The first act of cession was made by the state of New York in 1780; Virginia, Massachusetts, Connecticut, South and North Carolina, followed this example at different times, and lastly, the act of cession of Georgia was made as recently as 1802.

† It is true that the president refused his assent to this law; but he completely adopted it in principle. See message of 8th December, 1833.

prove any actual interpretation of the constitution. And so numerous and various are the circumstances to influence the decision of a legislative body like the congress of the United States, that the people do not regard them as sound and authoritative expositions of the true sense of the constitution, except perhaps in those very few cases, where there has been a constant and uninterrupted practice from the organization of the government. The judiciary is looked to as the only authentic expounder of the constitution, and until a law of congress has passed that ordeal, its constitutionality is open to question: of which our history furnishes many examples. . . . . There are errors in some of the instances given by our author, which would materially mislead, if not corrected That in relation to the Indians proceeds upon the assumption that the United States claimed some rights over Indians or the territory occupied by them, inconsistent with the claims of the states. But this is a mistake. As to their lands, the United States never pretended to any right in them, except such as was granted by the cessions of the states. The principle universally acknowledged in the courts of the United States and of the several states, is, that by the treaty with Great Britain in which the independence of the colonies was acknowledged, the states became severally and individually independent, and as such succeeded to the rights of the crown of England to and over the lands within the boundaries of the respective states. The right of the crown in these lands was the absolute ownership, subject only to the rights of occupancy by the Indians so long as they remained a tribe. This right devolved to each state by the treaty which established their independence, and the United States have never questioned it. See 6th Cranch, 87; 8th Wheaton, 502, 884; 17th Johnson's Reports, 231. On the other hand, the right of holding treaties with the Indians has universally been conceded to the United States. The right of a state to the lands occupied by the Indians, within the boundaries of such state, does not in the least conflict with the right of holding treaties on national subjects by the United States with those Indians. With respect to Indians residing in any territory *without* the boundaries of any state, or on lands ceded to the United States, the case is different; the United States are in such cases the proprietors of the soil, subject to the Indian right of occupancy, and when that right is extinguished the proprietorship becomes absolute. It will be seen, then, that in relation to the Indians and their lands, no question could arise respecting the interpretation of the constitution. The observation that "as soon as an Indian tribe attempted to fix its dwelling upon a given spot, the adjacent states claimed possession of the lands, and the rights of sovereignty over the natives"—is a strange compound of error and of truth. As above remarked, the Indian right of occupancy has ever been recognized by the states, with the exception of the case referred to by the author, in which Georgia claimed the right to possess certain lands occupied by the Cherokees. This was anomalous, and grew out of treaties and cessions, the details of which are too numerous and complicated for the limits of a note. But in no other cases have the states ever claimed the possession of lands occupied by Indians, without having previously extinguished their right by purchase.

As to the rights of sovereignty over the natives, the principle admitted in the United States is that all persons within the territorial limits of a state are and of necessity must be, subject to the jurisdiction of its laws. While the Indian tribes were numerous, distinct, and separate from the whites, and possessed a government of their own, the state authorities, from considerations of policy, abstained from the exercise of criminal jurisdiction for offences committed by the Indians among themselves, although for offences against the whites they were subjected to the operation of the state laws. But as these tribes diminished in numbers, as those who remained among them became enervated by bad habits, and ceased to exercise any effectual government, humanity demanded that the power of the states should be interposed to protect the miserable remnants from the violence and outrage of each other. The first recorded instance of interposition in such a case was in 1821, when an Indian of the Seneca tribe in the state of New York was tried and convicted of murder on a squaw of the tribe. The courts declared their competency to take cognizance of such offences, and the legislature confirmed the declaration by a law.——Another instance of what the author calls interpretation of the constitution against the general government, is given by him in the proposed act of 1832, which passed both houses of congress, but was vetoed by the president, by which, as he says, "the greatest part of the revenue derived from the sale of lands, was made over to the new western republics." But this act was not founded on any doubt of the title of the United States to the lands in question, or of its constitutional power over them, and cannot be cited as any evidence of the interpretation of the constitution. An error of fact in this statement ought to be corrected. The bill to which the author refers, is doubtless that usually called Mr. Clay's land bill. Instead of making over the greatest part of the revenue to the new states, it appropriated twelve and a half per cent. to them, in addition to five per cent. which had been originally granted for the purpose of making roads. See Niles's Register, vol. 42, p. 355.—*American Editor.*]

The slightest observation in the United States enables one to appreciate the advantages which the country derives from the bank. These advantages are of several kinds, but one of them is peculiarly striking to the stranger. The bank-notes of the United States are taken upon the borders of the desert for the same value as at Philadelphia, where the bank conducts its operations.*

The bank of the United States is nevertheless an object of great animosity. Its directors have proclaimed their hostility to the president; and they are accused, not without some show of probability, of having abused their influence to thwart his election. The president therefore attacks the establishment which they represent, with all the warmth of personal enmity; and he is encouraged in the pursuit of his revenge by the conviction that he is supported by the secret propensities of the majority. The bank may be regarded as the great monetary tie of the Union, just as congress is the

* The present bank of the United States was established in 1816, with a capital of 35,000,000 dollars; its charter expires in 1836. Last year congress passed a law to renew it, but the president put his veto upon the bill. The struggle is still going on with great violence on either side, and the speedy fall of the bank may easily be foreseen.

great legislative tie; and the same passions which tend to render the states independent of the central power, contribute to the overthrow of the bank.

The bank of the United States always holds a great number of the notes issued by the provincial banks, which it can at any time oblige them to convert into cash. It has itself nothing to fear from a similar demand, as the extent of its resources enables it to meet all claims. But the existence of the provincial banks is thus threatened, and their operations are restricted, since they are only able to issue a quantity of notes duly proportioned to their capital. They submit with impatience to this salutary control. The newspapers which they have bought over, and the president, whose interest renders him their instrument, attack the bank with the greatest vehemence. They rouse the local passions, and the blind democratic instinct of the country to aid their cause; and they assert that the bank-directors form a permanent aristocratic body, whose influence must ultimately be felt in the government, and must affect those principles of equality upon which society rests in America.

The contest between the bank and its opponents is only an incident in the great struggle which is going on in America between the provinces and the central power; between the spirit of democratic independence, and the spirit of gradation and subordination. I do not mean that the enemies of the bank are identically the same individuals, who, on other points, attack the federal government; but I assert that the attacks directed against the bank of the United States originate in the propensities which militate against the federal government; and that the very numerous opponents of the former afford a deplorable symptom of the decreasing support of the latter.

The Union has never displayed so much weakness as in the celebrated question of the tariff.* The wars of the French revolution and of 1812 had created manufacturing establishments in the north of the Union, by cutting off all free communication between America and Europe. When peace was concluded, and the channel of intercourse reopened by which the produce of Europe was transmitted to the New World, the Americans thought fit to establish a system of import duties, for the twofold purpose of protecting their incipient manufactures, and of paying off the amount of the debt contracted

* See principally for the details of this affair, the legislative documents, 22d congress, 2d session, No 30.

during the war. The southern states, which have no manufactures to encourage, and which are exclusively agricultural, soon complained of this measure. Such were the simple facts, and I do not pretend to examine in this place whether their complaints were well founded or unjust.

As early as the year 1820, South Carolina declared, in a petition to Congress, that the tariff was "unconstitutional, oppressive, and unjust." And the states of Georgia, Virginia, North Carolina, Alabama, and Mississippi, subsequently remonstrated against it with more or less vigor. But Congress, far from lending an ear to these complaints, raised the scale of tariff duties in the years 1824 and 1828, and recognized anew the principle on which it was founded. A doctrine was then proclaimed, or rather revived, in the south, which took the name of nullification.

I have shown in the proper place that the object of the federal constitution was not to form a league, but to create a national government. The Americans of the United States form a sole and undivided people, in all the cases which are specified by that constitution; and upon these points the will of the nation is expressed, as it is in all constitutional nations, by the voice of the majority. When the majority has pronounced its decision, it is the duty of the minority to submit. Such is the sound legal doctrine, and the only one which agrees with the text of the constitution, and the known intention of those who framed it.

The partisans of nullification in the south maintain, on the contrary, that the intention of the Americans in uniting was not to reduce themselves to the condition of one and the same people; that they meant to constitute a league of independent states; and that each state, consequently, retains its entire sovereignty, if not *de facto*, at least *de jure;* and has the right of putting its own construction upon the laws of congress, and of suspending their execution within the limits of its own territory, if they are held to be unconstitutional or unjust.

The entire doctrine of nullification is comprised in a sentence uttered by Vice-President Calhoun, the head of that party in the south, before the senate of the United States, in the year 1833: "The constitution is a compact to which the states were parties in their sovereign capacity; now, whenever a contract is entered into by parties which acknowledge no tribunal above their authority to decide in the last resort, each of them has a right to judge for himself in relation to the nature, extent, and obligations of the instrument." It is evident that a similar doctrine destroys the very basis of the federal constitution, and brings back all the evils of the old confederation, from which the Americans were supposed to have had a safe deliverance.

When South Carolina perceived that Congress turned a deat ear to its remonstrances, it threatened to apply the doctrine of nullification to the federal tariff bill. Congress persisted in its former system; and at length the storm broke out. In the course of 1832 the citizens of South Carolina* named a national [state] convention, to consult upon the extraordinary measures which they were called upon to take; and on the 24th November of the same year, this convention promulgated a law, under the form of a decree, which annulled the federal law of the tariff, forbade the levy of the imposts which that law commands, and refused to recognize the appeal which might be made to the federal courts of law.† This decree was only to be put into execution in the ensuing month of February, and it was intimated, that if Congress modified the tariff before that period, South Carolina might be induced to proceed no farther with her menaces; and a vague desire was afterward expressed of submitting the question to an extraordinary assembly of all the confederate states.

In the meantime South Carolina armed her militia, and prepared for war. But congress, which had slighted its suppliant subjects, listened to their complaints as soon as they were found to have taken up arms.‡ A law was passed, by which

* That is to say, the majority of the people; for the opposite party, called the Union party, always formed a very strong and active minority. Carolina may contain about 47,000 electors; 30,000 were in favor of nullification, and 17,000 opposed to it.

† This decree was preceded by a report of the committee by which it was framed, containing the explanation of the motives and object of the law. The following passage occurs in it, p. 34: "When the rights reserved by the constitution to the different states are deliberately violated, it is the duty and the right of those states to interfere, in order to check the progress of the evil, to resist usurpation, and to maintain, within their respective limits, those powers and privileges which belong to them as *independent sovereign states.* If they were destitute of this right, they would not be sovereign. South Carolina declares that she acknowledges no tribunal upon earth above her authority. She has indeed entered into a solemn compact of union with the other states: but she demands, and will exercise, the right of putting her own construction upon it; and when this compact is violated by her sister states, and by the government which they have created, she is determined to avail herself of the unquestionable right of judging what is the extent of the infraction, and what are the measures best fitted to obtain justice."

‡ Congress was finally decided to take this step by the conduct of the powerful state of Virginia, whose legislature offered to serve as a

the tariff duties were to be progressively reduced for ten years, until they were brought so low as not to exceed the amount of supplies necessary to the government.* Thus congress completely abandoned the principle of the tariff; and substituted a mere fiscal impost for a system of protective duties.† The government of the Union, in order to conceal its defeat, had recourse to an expedient which is very much in vogue with feeble governments. It yielded the point *de facto*, but it remained inflexible upon the principles in question; and while congress was altering the tariff law, it passed another bill, by which the president was invested with extraordinary powers, enabling him to overcome by force a resistance which was then no longer to be apprehended.

But South Carolina did not consent to leave the Union in the enjoyment of these scanty trophies of success: the same national [state] convention which annulled the tariff bill, met again, and accepted the proffered concession: but at the same time it declared its unabated perseverance in the doctrine of nullification; and to prove what it said, it annulled the law investing the president with extraordinary powers, although it was very certain that the clauses of that law would never be carried into effect.

Almost all the controversies of which I have been speaking have taken place under the presidency of General Jackson; and it cannot be denied that in the question of the tariff he has supported the claims of the Union with vigor and with skill. I am however of opinion that the conduct of the individual who now represents the federal government, may be reckoned as one of the dangers which threaten its continuance.

Some persons in Europe have formed an opinion of the possible influence of General Jackson upon the affairs of his country, which appears highly extravagant to those who have seen more of the subject. We have been told that General Jackson has won sundry battles, that he is an energetic man, prone by nature and by habit to the use of force, covetous of power, and a despot by taste. All this may perhaps be true; but the inferences which have been drawn from these truths are exceedingly erroneous. It has been imagined that General Jackson is bent on establishing a dictatorship in America, on

mediator between the Union and South Carolina. Hitherto the latter state had appeared to be entirely abandoned even by the states which had joined her in her remonstrances.

* This law was passed on the 2d March, 1833.

† This bill was brought in by Mr. Clay, and it passed in four day through both houses of Congress, by an immense majority.

introducing a military spirit, and on giving a degree of influence to the central authority which cannot but be dangerous to provincial liberties. But in America, the time for similar undertakings, and the age for men of this kind, is not yet come; if General Jackson had entertained a hope of exercising his authority in this manner, he would infallibly have forfeited his political station, and compromised his life; accordingly he has not been so imprudent as to make any such attempt.

Far from wishing to extend the federal power, the president belongs to the party which is desirous of limiting that power to the bare and precise letter of the constitution, and which never puts a construction upon that act, favorable to the government of the Union; far from standing forth as the champion of centralization, General Jackson is the agent of all the jealousies of the states; and he was placed in the lofty station he occupies, by the passions of the people which are most opposed to the central government. It is by perpetually flattering these passions, that he maintains his station and his popularity. General Jackson is the slave of the majority: he yields to its wishes, its propensities, and its demands; say rather, that he anticipates and forestalls them.

Whenever the governments of the states come into collision with that of the Union, the president is generally the first to question his own rights: he almost always outstrips the legislature; and when the extent of the federal power is controverted, he takes part, as it were, against himself; he conceals his official interests, and extinguishes his own natural inclinations. Not indeed that he is naturally weak or hostile to the Union; for when the majority decided against the claims of the partisans of nullification, he put himself at its head, asserted the doctrines which the nation held, distinctly and energetically, and was the first to recommend forcible measures; but General Jackson appears to me, if I may use the American expressions, to be a federalist by taste, and a republican by calculation.

General Jackson stoops to gain the favor of the majority: but when he feels that his popularity is secure, he overthrows all obstacles in the pursuit of the objects which the community approves, or of those which it does not look upon with a jealous eye. He is supported by a power with which his predecessors were unacquainted; and he tramples on his personal enemies wherever they cross his path, with a facility which no former president ever enjoyed; he takes upon himself the responsibility of measures which no one, before him, would have ventured to attempt; he even treats the national representatives with disdain approaching to insult; he puts his veto upon the laws of congress, and frequently neglects to reply to that powerful body. He is a favorite who sometimes treats his master roughly. The power of General Jackson perpetually increases; but that of the President declines: in his hands the federal government is strong, but it will pass enfeebled into the hands of his successor.

I am strangely mistaken if the federal government of the United States be not constantly losing strength, retiring gradually from public affairs, and narrowing its circle of action more and more. It is naturally feeble, but it now abandons even its pretensions to strength. On the other hand, I thought that I remarked a more lively sense of independence, and a more decided attachment to provincial government, in the states. The Union is to subsist, but to subsist as a shadow; it is to be strong in certain cases, and weak in all others; in time of warfare, it is to be able to concentrate all the forces of the nation and all the resources of the country in its hands; and in time of peace its existence is to be scarcely perceptible: as if this alternate debility and vigor were natural or possible.

I do not foresee anything for the present which may be able to check this general impulse of public opinion: the causes in which it originated do not cease to operate with the same effect. The change will therefore go on, and it may be predicted that, unless some extraordinary event occurs, the government of the Union will grow weaker and weaker every day.

I think, however, that the period is still remote, at which the federal power will be entirely extinguished by its inability to protect itself and to maintain peace in the country. The Union is sanctioned by the manners and desires of the people; its results are palpable, its benefits visible. When it is perceived that the weakness of the federal government compromises the existence of the Union, I do not doubt that a reaction will take place with a view to increase its strength.

The government of the United States is, of all the federal governments which have hitherto been established, the one which is most naturally destined to act. As long as it is only indirectly assailed by the interpretation of its laws, and as long as its substance is not seriously altered, a change of opinion, an internal crisis, or a war, may restore all the vigor which it requires. The point which I have been most anxious to put in a clear light is simply this; many people, especially in France, imagine that a change of opinion is going on in the

United States, which is favorable to a centralization of power in the hands of the president and the congress. I hold that a contrary tendency may be distinctly observed. So far is the federal government from acquiring strength, and from threatening the sovereignty of the states, as it grows older, that I maintain it to be growing weaker and weaker, and that the sovereignty of the Union alone is in danger. Such are the facts which the present time discloses. The future conceals the final result of this tendency, and the events which may check, retard, or accelerate, the changes I have described; but I do not affect to be able to remove the veil which hides them from our sight.

OF THE REPUBLICAN INSTITUTIONS OF THE UNITED STATES, AND WHAT THEIR CHANCES OF DURATION ARE.

The Union is Accidental.—The Republican Institutions have more prospect of Permanence.—A Republic for the Present the Natural State of the Anglo-Americans.—Reason of this.—In order to destroy it, all Laws must be changed at the same time, and a great alteration take place in Manners —Difficulties experienced by the Americans in creating an Aristocracy.

THE dismemberment of the Union, by the introduction of war into the heart of those states which are now confederate, with standing armies, a dictatorship, and a heavy taxation, might eventually compromise the fate of the republican institutions. But we ought not to confound the future prospects of the republic with those of the Union. The Union is an accident, which will last only so long as circumstances are favorable to its existence; but a republican form of government seems to me to be the natural state of the Americans; which nothing but the continued action of hostile causes, always acting in the same direction, could change into a monarchy. The Union exists principally in the law which formed it; one revolution, one change in public opinion, might destroy it for ever; but the republic has a much deeper foundation to rest upon.

What is understood by republican government in the United States, is the slow and quiet action of society upon itself. It is a regular state of things really founded upon the enlightened will of the people. It is a conciliatory government under which resolutions are allowed time to ripen, and in which they are deliberately discussed, and executed with mature judgment. The republicans in the United States set a high value upon morality, respect religious belief, and acknowledge the existence of rights. They profess to think that a people ought to be moral, religious, and temperate, in proportion as it is free. What is called the republic in the United States, is the tranquil rule of the majority, which, after having had time to examine itself, and to give proof of its existence, is the common source of all the powers of the state. But the power of the majority is not of itself unlimited. In the moral world humanity, justice, and reason, enjoy an undisputed supremacy; in the political world vested rights are treated with no less deference. The majority recognizes these two barriers; and if it now and then overstep them, it is because, like individuals, it has passions, and like them, it is prone to do what is wrong, while it discerns what is right.

But the demagogues of Europe have made strange discoveries. A republic is not, according to them, the rule of the majority, as has hitherto been taught, but the rule of those who are strenuous partisans of the majority. It is not the people who preponderates in this kind of government, but those who best know what is for the good of the people. A happy distinction, which allows men to act in the name of nations without consulting them, and to claim their gratitude while their rights are spurned. A republican government, moreover, is the only one which claims the right of doing whatever it chooses, and despising what men have hitherto respected, from the highest moral obligations to the vulgar rules of common sense. It had been supposed, until our time, that despotism was odious, under whatever form it appeared. But it is a discovery of modern days that there are such things as legitimate tyranny and holy injustice, provided they are exercised in the name of the people.

The ideas which the Americans have adopted respecting the republican form of government, render it easy for them to live under it, and ensure its duration. If, in their country, this form be often practically bad, at least it is theoretically good; and, in the end, the people always acts in conformity with it.

It was impossible, at the foundation of the states, and it would still be difficult, to establish a central administration in America. The inhabitants are dispersed over too great a space, and separated by too many natural obstacles, for one man to undertake to direct the details of their existence. America is therefore pre-eminently the country of provincial and municipal government. To this cause, which was plainly felt by all the Europeans of the New World, the Anglo-Americans added several others peculiar to themselves.

At the time of the settlement of the North American colonies, municipal liberty had already penetrated into the laws as well as the manners of the English, and the emigrants adopted it, not only as a necessary thing, but as a benefit which they knew how to appreciate. We have already seen the manner in which the colonies were founded: every province, and almost every district, was peopled separately by men who were strangers to each other, or who associated with very different purposes. The English settlers in the United States, therefore, early perceived that they were divided into a great number of small and distinct communities which belonged to no common centre; and that it was needful for each of these little communities to take care of its own affairs, since there did not appear to be any central authority which was naturally bound and easily enabled to provide for them. Thus, the nature of the country, the manner in which the British colonies were founded, the habits of the first emigrants, in short everything, united to promote, in an extraordinary degree, municipal and provincial liberties.

In the United States, therefore, the mass of the institutions of the country is essentially republican; and in order permanently to destroy the laws which form the basis of the republic, it would be necessary to abolish all the laws at once. At the present day, it would be even more difficult for a party to succeed in founding a monarchy in the United States, than for a set of men to proclaim that France should henceforward be a republic. Royalty would not find a system of legislation prepared for it beforehand; and a monarchy would then exist, really surrounded by republican institutions. The monarchical principle would likewise have great difficulty in penetrating into the manners of the Americans.

In the United States, the sovereignty of the people is not an isolated doctrine bearing no relation to the prevailing manners and ideas of the people: it may, on the contrary, be regarded as the last link of a chain of opinions which binds the whole Anglo-American world. That Providence has given to every human being the degree of reason necessary to direct himself in the affairs which interest him exclusively; such is the grand maxim upon which civil and political society rests in the United States. The father of a family applies it to his children; the master to his servants; the township to its officers; the province to its townships; the state to the provinces; the Union to the states; and when extended to the nation, it becomes the doctrine of the sovereignty of the people.

Thus, in the United States, the fundamental principle of the republic is the same which governs the greater part of human actions ; republican notions insinuate themselves into all the ideas, opinions, and habits of the Americans, while they are formally recognized by the legislation : and before this legislation can be altered, the whole community must undergo very serious changes. In the United States, even the religion of most of the citizens is republican, since it submits the truths of the other world to private judgment: as in politics the care of its temporal interests is abandoned to the good sense of the people. Thus every man is allowed freely to take that road which he thinks will lead him to heaven ; just as the law permits every citizen to have the right of choosing his government.

It is evident that nothing but a long series of events, all having the same tendency, can substitute for this combination of laws, opinions, and manners, a mass of opposite opinions, manners and laws.

If republican principles are to perish in America, they can only yield after a laborious social process, often interrupted, and as often resumed ; they will have many apparent revivals, and will not become totally extinct until an entirely new people shall have succeeded to that which now exists. Now, it must be admitted that there is no symptom or presage of the approach of such a revolution. There is nothing more striking to a person newly arrived in the United States, than the kind of tumultuous agitation in which he finds political society. The laws are incessantly changing, and at first sight it seems impossible that a people so variable in its desires should avoid adopting, within a short space of time, a completely new form of government. Such apprehensions are, however, premature ; the instability which affects political institutions is of two kinds, which ought not to be confounded : the first, which modifies secondary laws, is not incompatible with a very settled state of society ; the other shakes the very foundations of the constitution, and attacks the fundamental principles of legislation ; this species of instability is always followed by troubles and revolutions, and the nation which suffers under it, is in a state of violent transition.

Experience shows that these two kinds of legislative instability have no necessary connexion ; for they have been found united or separate, according to times and circumstances. The first is common in the United States, but not the second: the Americans often change their laws, but the foundation of the constitution is respected.

In our days the republican principle rules in America, as the monarchical principle did in France under Louis XIV. The French of that period were not only friends of the monarchy, but they thought it impossible to put anything in its place; they received it as we receive the rays of the sun and the return of the seasons. Among them the royal power had neither advocates nor opponents. In like manner does the republican government exist in America, without contention or opposition; without proofs and arguments, by a tacit agreement, a sort of *consensus universalis*. It is, however, my opinion, that, by changing their administrative forms as often as they do, the inhabitants of the United States compromise the future stability of their government.

It may be apprehended that men, perpetually thwarted in their designs by the mutability of legislation, will learn to look upon republican institutions as an inconvenient form of society; the evil resulting from the instability of the secondary enactments, might then raise a doubt as to the nature of the fundamental principles of the constitution, and indirectly bring about a revolution; but this epoch is still very remote.

[It has been objected by an American review, that our author is mistaken in charging our laws with instability, and in answer to the charge, the permanence of our fundamental political institutions has been contrasted with the revolutions in France. But the objection proceeds upon a mistake of the author's meaning, which at this page is very clearly expressed. He refers to the instability which modifies *secondary laws*, and not to that which shakes the foundations of the constitution. The distinction is equally sound and philosophic, and those in the least acquainted with the history of our legislation, must bear witness to the truth of the author's remarks. The frequent revisions of the statutes of the states rendered necessary by the multitude, variety, and often the contradiction of the enactments, furnish abundant evidence of this instability.—*American Editor.*]

It may, however, be foreseen, even now, that when the Americans lose their republican institutions, they will speedily arrive at a despotic government, without a long interval of limited monarchy. Montesquieu remarked, that nothing is more absolute than the authority of a prince who immediately succeeds a republic, since the powers which had fearlessly been intrusted to an elected magistrate are then transferred to an hereditary sovereign. This is true in general, but it is more peculiarly applicable to a democratic republic. In the United States, the magistrates are not elected by a particular class of citizens, but by the majority of the nation; they are the immediate representatives of the passions of the multitude; and as they are wholly dependent upon its pleasure, they excite neither hatred nor fear: hence, as I have already shown, very little care has been taken to limit their influence, and they are left in possession of a vast deal of arbitrary power. This state of things has engendered habits which would outlive itself; the American magistrate would retain his power, but he would cease to be responsible for the exercise of it; and it is impossible to say what bounds could then be set to tyranny.

Some of our European politicians expect to see an aristocracy arise in America, and they already predict the exact period at which it will be able to assume the reins of government. I have previously observed, and I repeat my assertion, that the present tendency of American society appears to me to become more and more democratic. Nevertheless, I do not assert that the Americans will not, at some future time, restrict the circle of political rights in their country, or confiscate those rights to the advantage of a single individual; but I cannot imagine that they will ever bestow the exclusive exercise of them upon a privileged class of citizens, or, in other words, that they will ever found an aristocracy.

An aristocratic body is composed of a certain number of citizens, who, without being very far removed from the mass of the people, are, nevertheless, permanently stationed above it: a body which it is easy to touch, and difficult to strike; with which the people are in daily contact, but with which they can never combine. Nothing can be imagined more contrary to nature and to the secret propensities of the human heart, than a subjection of this kind; and men, who are left to follow their own bent, will always prefer the arbitrary power of a king to the regular administration of an aristocracy. Aristocratic institutions cannot subsist without laying down the inequality of men as a fundamental principle, as a part and parcel of the legislation, affecting the condition of the human family as much as it affects that of society; but these things are so repugnant to natural equity that they can only be extorted from men by constraint.

I do not think a single people can be quoted, since human society began to exist, which has, by its own free will and by its own exertions, created an aristocracy within its own bosom. All the aristocracies of the middle ages were founded by military conquest: the conqueror was the noble, the vanquished became the serf. Inequality was then imposed by force; and after it had been introduced into the manners of the country, it maintained its own authority, and was sanctioned by the legislation. Communities have existed which were aristocratic from their earliest origin, owing to circumstances anterior to that event, and which became more democratic in each succeeding age. Such was the destiny of the Romans, and of the Barbarians after them. But a people, having taken its rise in civilisation and democracy, which should gradually establish an inequality of conditions until it arrived at inviolable privileges and exclusive castes, would be a novelty in the world; and nothing intimates that America is likely to furnish so singular an example.

REFLECTIONS ON THE CAUSES OF THE COMMERCIAL PROSPERITY OF THE UNITED STATES.

The Americans destined by Nature to be a great maritime People.—Extent of their Coasts.—Depth of their Ports.—Size of their Rivers.—The commercial Superiority of the Anglo-Saxons less attributable, however, to physical Circumstances than to moral and intellectual Causes.—Reason of this Opinion.—Future Destiny of the Anglo-Americans as a commercial Nation.—The Dissolution of the Union would not check the maritime Vigor of the States.—Reason of this—Anglo-Americans will naturally supply the Wants of the inhabitants of South America.—They will become, like the English, the Factors of a great portion of the World.

THE coast of the United States, from the bay of Fundy to the Sabine river in the gulf of Mexico, is more than two thousand miles in extent. These shores form an unbroken line, and they are all subject to the same government. No nation in the world possesses vaster, deeper, or more secure ports for shipping than the Americans.

The inhabitants of the United States constitute a great civilized people, which fortune has placed in the midst of an uncultivated country, at a distance of three thousand miles from the central point of civilisation. America consequently stands in daily need of European trade. The Americans will, no doubt, ultimately succeed in producing or manufacturing at home most of the articles which they require; but the two continents can never be independent of each other, so numerous are the natural ties which exist between their wants, their ideas, their habits, and their manners.

The Union produces peculiar commodities which are now become necessary to us, but which cannot be cultivated, or can only be raised at an enormous expense, upon the soil of Europe. The Americans only consume a small portion of this produce, and they are willing to sell us the rest. Europe is therefore the market of America, as America is the market of Europe; and maritime commerce is no less necessary to enable the inhabitants of the United States to transport their raw materials to the ports of Europe, than it is to enable us to supply them with our manufactured produce. The United States were therefore necessarily reduced to the alternative of increasing the business of other maritime nations to a great extent, if they had themselves declined to enter into commerce, as the Spaniards of Mexico have hitherto done; or, in the second place, of becoming one of the first trading powers of the globe.

The Anglo-Americans have always displayed a very decided taste for the sea. The declaration of independence broke the commercial restrictions which united them to England, and gave a fresh and powerful stimulus to their maritime genius. Ever since that time, the shipping of the Union has increased in almost the same rapid proportion as the number of its inhabitants. The Americans themselves now transport to their own shores nine-tenths of the European produce which they consume.* And they also bring three-quarters of the exports of the New World to the European consumer.† The ships of the United States fill the docks of Havre and of Liverpool; while the number of English and French vessels which are to be seen at New York is comparatively small.‡

Thus, not only does the American merchant face competi-

* The total value of goods imported during the year which ended on the 30th September, 1332, was 101,129,266 dollars. The value of the cargoes of foreign vessels did not amount to 10,731,039 dollars, or about one-tenth of the entire sum.

† The value of goods exported during the same year amounted to 87,176,943 dollars; the value of goods exported by foreign vessels amounted to 21,036,183 dollars, or about one quarter of the whole sum. (Williams's Register, 1833, p. 398.)

‡ The tonnage of the vessels which entered all the ports of the Union in the years 1829, 1830, and 1831, amounted to 3,307,719 tons, of which 544,571 tons were foreign vessels; they stood therefore to the American vessels in a ratio of about 16 to 100. (National Calendar, 1833, p. 304.) The tonnage of the English vessels which entered the ports of London, Liverpool and Hull, in the years 1820, 1826, and 1831, amounted to 443,800 tons. The foreign vessels which entered the same ports during the same years, amounted to 159,431 tons. The ratio between them was therefore about 36 to 100. (Companion to the Almanac, 1834, p. 169.) In the year 1832 the ratio between the foreign and British ships which entered the ports of Great Britain was 29 to 100.

tion in his own country, but he even supports that of foreign nations in their own ports with success. This is readily explained by the fact that the vessels of the United States can cross the seas at a cheaper rate than any other vessels in the world. As long as the mercantile shipping of the United States preserves this superiority, it will not only retain what it has acquired, but it will constantly increase in prosperity.

It is difficult to say for what reason the Americans can trade at a lower rate than other nations; and one is at first led to attribute this circumstance to the physical or natural advantages which are within their reach; but this supposition is erroneous. The American vessels cost almost as much to build as our own;* they are not better built, and they generally last for a shorter time. The pay of the American sailor is more considerable than the pay on board European ships; which is proved by the great number of Europeans who are to be met with in the merchant-vessels of the United States. But I am of opinion that the true cause of their superiority must not be sought for in physical advantages, but that it is wholly attributable to their moral and intellectual qualities.

The following comparison will illustrate my meaning. During the campaigns of the revolution the French introduced a new system of tactics into the art of war, which perplexed the oldest generals, and very nearly destroyed the most ancient monarchies in Europe. They undertook (what had never been before attempted) to make shift without a number of things which had always been held to be indispensable in warfare; they required novel exertions on the part of their troops, which no civilized nations had ever thought of; they achieved great actions in an incredibly short space of time: and they risked human life without hesitation, to obtain the object in view. The French had less money and fewer men than their enemies; their resources were infinitely inferior; nevertheless they were constantly victorious, until their adversaries chose to imitate their example.

The Americans have introduced a similar system into their commercial speculations; and they do for cheapness what the French did for conquest. The European sailor navigates with prudence; he only sets sail when the weather is favorable; if an unforeseen accident befalls him, he puts into port; at night he furls a portion of his canvass; and when the whitening billows intimate the vicinity of land, he checks

* Materials are, generally speaking, less expensive in America than in Europe, but the price of labor is much higher.

his way, and takes an observation of the sun. But the American neglects these precautions and braves these dangers. He weighs anchor in the midst of tempestuous gales; by night and by day he spreads his sheets to the wind; he repairs as he goes along such damage as his vessel may have sustained from the storm; and when he at last approaches the term of his voyage, he darts onward to the shore as if he already descried a port. The Americans are often shipwrecked, but no trader crosses the seas so rapidly. And as they perform the same distance in a shorter time, they can perform it at a cheaper rate.

The European touches several times at different ports in the course of a long voyage; he loses a good deal of precious time in making the harbor, or in waiting for a favorable wind to leave it; and he pays daily dues to be allowed to remain there. The American starts from Boston to go to purchase tea in China: he arrives at Canton, stays there a few days and then returns. In less than two years he has sailed as far as the entire circumference of the globe, and he has seen land but once. It is true that during a voyage of eight or ten months he has drunk brackish water, and lived upon salt meat; that he has been in a continual contest with the sea, with disease, and with the tedium of monotony; but, upon his return, he can sell a pound of his tea for a halfpenny less than the English merchant, and his purpose is accomplished.

I cannot better explain my meaning than by saying that the Americans affect a sort of heroism in their manner of trading. But the European merchant will always find it very difficult to imitate his American competitor, who, in adopting the system which I have just described, follows not only a calculation of his gain, but an impulse of his nature.

The inhabitants of the United States are subject to all the wants and all the desires which result from an advanced stage of civilisation; but as they are not surrounded by a community admirably adapted, like that of Europe, to satisfy their wants, they are often obliged to procure for themselves the various articles which education and habit have rendered necessaries. In America it sometimes happens that the same individual tills his field, builds his dwelling, contrives his tools, makes his shoes, and weaves the coarse stuff of which his dress is composed. This circumstance is prejudicial to the excellence of the work: but it powerfully contributes to awaken the intelligence of the workman. Nothing tends to materialise man, and to deprive his work of the faintest trace of mind, more than extreme division of labor. In a country like America, where men devoted to special occupations are rare, a long apprenticeship cannot be required from any one who embraces a profession. The Americans therefore change their means of gaining a livelihood very readily; and they suit their occupations to the exigencies of the moment, in the manner most profitable to themselves. Men are to be met with who have successively been barristers, farmers, merchants, ministers of the gospel, and physicians. If the American be less perfect in each craft than the European, at least there is scarcely any trade with which he is utterly unacquainted. His capacity is more general, and the circle of his intelligence is enlarged.

The inhabitants of the United States are never fettered by the axioms of their profession; they escape from all the prejudices of their present station; they are not more attached to one line of operation than to another; they are not more prone to employ an old method than a new one; they have no rooted habits, and they easily shake off the influence which the habits of other nations might exercise upon their minds, from a conviction that their country is unlike any other, and that its situation is without a precedent in the world. America is a land of wonders, in which everything is in constant motion, and every movement seems an improvement. The idea of novelty is there indissolubly connected with the idea of melioration. No natural boundary seems to be set to the efforts of man; and what is not yet done is only what he has not yet attempted to do.

This perpetual change which goes on in the United States, these frequent vicissitudes of fortune, accompanied by such unforeseen fluctuations in private and in public wealth, serve to keep the minds of the citizens in a perpetual state of feverish agitation, which admirably invigorates their exertions, and keeps them in a state of excitement above the ordinary level of mankind. The whole life of an American is passed like a game of chance, a revolutionary crisis or a battle. As the same causes are continually in operation throughout the country, they ultimately impart an irresistible impulse to the national character. The American, taken as a chance specimen of his countrymen, must then be a man of singular warmth in his desires, enterprising, fond of adventure, and above all of innovation. The same bent is manifest in all that he does; he introduces it into his political laws, his religious doctrines, his theories of social economy, and his domestic occupations; he bears it with him in the depth of the backwoods, as well as in the business of the city. It is the same passion, applied to maritime commerce, which makes him the cheapest and the quickest trader in the world.

As long as the sailors of the United States retain these inspiriting advantages, and the practical superiority which they derive from them, they will not only continue to supply the wants of the producers and consumers of their own country, but they will tend more and more to become, like the English, the factors of all other peoples.* This prediction has already begun to be realized; we perceive that the American traders are introducing themselves as intermediate agents in the commerce of several European nations;† and America will offer a still wider field to their enterprise.

The great colonies which were founded in South America by the Spaniards and the Portuguese have since become empires. Civil war and oppression now lay waste those extensive regions. Population does not increase, and the thinly-scattered inhabitants are too much absorbed in the cares of self-defence even to attempt any melioration of their condition. Such, however, will not always be the case. Europe has succeeded by her own efforts in piercing the gloom of the middle ages; South America has the same Christian laws and Christian manners as we have; she contains all the germs of civilisation which have grown amid the nations of Europe or their offsets, added to the advantages to be derived from our example; why then should she always remain uncivilized? It is clear that the question is simply one of time; at some future period, which may be more or less remote, the inhabitants of South America will constitute flourishing and enlightened nations.

But when the Spaniards and Portuguese of South America begin to feel the wants common to all civilized nations, they will still be unable to satisfy those wants for themselves; as the youngest children of civilisation, they must perforce admit the superiority of their elder brethren. They will be agriculturists long before they succeed in manufactures or commerce, and they will require the mediation of strangers

* It must not be supposed that English vessels are exclusively employed in transporting foreign produce into England, or British produce to foreign countries: at the present day the merchant shipping of England may be regarded in the light of a vast system of public conveyances ready to serve all the producers of the world, and to open communications between all peoples. The maritime genius of the Americans prompts them to enter into competition with the English.

† Part of the commerce of the Mediterranean is already carried on by American vessels.

to exchange their produce beyond seas for those articles for which a demand will begin to be felt.

It is unquestionable that the Americans of the north will one day supply the wants of the Americans of the south. Nature has placed them in contiguity; and has furnished the former with every means of knowing and appreciating those demands, of establishing a permanent connexion with those states, and of gradually filling their markets. The merchant of the United States could only forfeit these natural advantages if he were very inferior to the merchant of Europe; to whom he is, on the contrary, superior in several respects. The Americans of the United States already exercise a very considerable moral influence upon all the people of the New World. They are the source of intelligence, and all the nations which inhabit the same continent are already accustomed to consider them as the most enlightened, the most powerful, and the most wealthy members of the great American family. All eyes are therefore turned toward the Union; and the states of which that body is composed are the models which the other communities try to imitate to the best of their power: it is from the United States that they borrow their political principles and their laws.

The Americans of the United States stand in precisely the same position with regard to the peoples of South America as their fathers, the English, occupy with regard to the Italians, the Spaniards, the Portuguese, and all those nations of Europe, which receive their articles of daily consumption from England, because they are less advanced in civilisation and trade. England is at this time the natural emporium of almost all the nations which are within its reach; the American Union will perform the same part in the other hemisphere; and every community which is founded, or which prospers in the New World, is founded and prospers to the advantage of the Anglo-Americans.

If the Union were to be dissolved, the commerce of the states which now compose it, would undoubtedly be checked for a time; but this consequence would be less perceptible than is generally supposed. It is evident that whatever may happen, the commercial states will remain united. They are all contiguous to each other; they have identically the same opinions, interests, and manners, and they are alone competent to form a very great maritime power. Even if the south of the Union were to become independent of the north, it would still require the service of those states. I have already observed that the south is not a commercial country, and nothing intimates that it is likely to become so. The Americans of the south of the United States will therefore be obliged, for a long time to come, to have recourse to strangers to export their produce, and to supply them with the commodities which are requisite to satisfy their wants. But the northern states are undoubtedly able to act as their intermediate agents cheaper than any other merchants. They will therefore retain that employment, for cheapness is the sovereign law of commerce. National claims and national pre judices cannot resist the influence of cheapness. Nothing can be more virulent than the hatred which exists between the Americans of the United States and the English. But, notwithstanding these inimical feelings, the Americans derive the greater part of their manufactured commodities from England, because England supplies them at a cheaper rate than any other nation. Thus the increasing prosperity of America turns, notwithstanding the grudges of the Americans, to the advantage of British manufactures.

Reason shows and experience proves that no commercial prosperity can be durable if it cannot be united, in case of need, to naval force. This truth is as well understood in the United States as it can be anywhere else: the Americans are already able to make their flag respected: in a few years they will be able to make it feared. I am convinced that the dismemberment of the Union would not have the effect of diminishing the naval power of the Americans, but that it would powerfully contribute to increase it. At the present time the commercial states are connected with others which have not the same interests, and which frequently yield an unwilling consent to the increase of a maritime power by which they are only indirectly benefited. If, on the contrary, the commercial states of the Union formed one independent nation, commerce would become the foremost of their national interests; they would consequently be willing to make very great sacrifices to protect their shipping, and nothing would prevent them from pursuing their designs upon this point.

Nations, as well as men, almost always betray the most prominent features of their future destiny in their earliest years. When I contemplate the ardor with which the Anglo-Americans prosecute commercial enterprise, the advantages which befriend them, and the success of their undertakings, I cannot refrain from believing that they will one day become the first maritime power of the globe. They are born to rule the seas, as the Romans were to conquer the world.

CONCLUSION.

I HAVE now nearly reached the close of my inquiry . hitherto, in speaking of the future destiny of the United States, I have endeavored to divide my subject into distinct portions, in order to study each of them with more attention. My present object is to embrace the whole from one single point; the remarks I shall make will be less detailed, but they will be more sure. I shall perceive each object less distinctly, but I shall descry the principal facts with more certainty. A traveller, who has just left the walls of an immense city, climbs the neighboring hill; as he goes farther off, he loses sight of the men whom he has so recently quitted; their dwellings are confused in a dense mass; he can no longer distinguish the public squares, and he can scarcely trace out the great thoroughfares; but his eye has less difficulty in following the boundaries of the city, and for the first time he sees the shape of the vast whole. Such is the future destiny of the British race in North America to my eye; the details of the stupendous picture are overhung with shade, but I conceive a clear idea of the entire subject.

The territory now occupied or possessed by the United States of America, forms about one-twentieth part of the habitable earth. But extensive as these confines are, it must not be supposed that the Anglo-American race will always remain within them; indeed, it has already far overstepped them.

There was once a time at which we also might have created a great French nation in the American wilds, to counterbalance the influence of the English upon the destinies of the New World. France formerly possessed a territory in North America, scarcely less extensive than the whole of Europe. The three greatest rivers of that continent then flowed within her dominions. The Indian tribes which dwelt between the mouth of the St. Lawrence and the delta of the Mississippi were unaccustomed to any tongue but ours; and all the European settlements scattered over that immense region recalled the traditions of our country. Louisburg, Montmorency, Duquesne, Saint-Louis, Vincennes, New Orleans (for such were the names they bore), are words dear to France and familiar to our ears.

But a concourse of circumstances, which it would be tedious to enumerate,* have deprived us of this magnificent inheritance. Wherever the French settlers were numerically weak and partially established, they have disappeared; those who remain are collected on a small extent of country, and are now subject to other laws. The 400,000 French inhabitants of Lower Canada constitute, at the present time, the remnant of an old nation lost in the midst of a new people. A foreign population is increasing around them unceasingly, and on all sides, which already penetrates among the ancient masters of the country, predominates in their cities, and corrupts their language. This population is identical with that of the United States; it is therefore with truth that I asserted that the British race is not confined within the frontiers of the Union, since it already extends to the northeast.

To the northwest nothing is to be met with but a few insignificant Russian settlements; but to the southwest, Mexico presents a barrier to the Anglo-Americans. Thus, the Spaniards and the Anglo-Americans are, properly speaking, the only two races which divide the possession of the New World. The limits of separation between them have been settled by a treaty; but although the conditions of that treaty are exceedingly favorable to the Anglo-Americans, I do not doubt that they will shortly infringe this arrangement. Vast provinces, extending beyond the frontiers of the Union toward Mexico, are still destitute of inhabitants. The natives of the United States will forestall the rightful occupants of these solitary regions. They will take possession of the soil, and establish social institutions, so that when the legal owner arrives at length, he will find the wilderness under cultivation, and strangers quietly settled in the midst of his inheritance.

The lands of the New World belong to the first occupant, and they are the natural reward of the swiftest pioneer. Even the countries which are already peopled will have some difficulty in securing themselves from this invasion. I have already alluded to what is taking place in the province of Texas. The inhabitants of the United States are perpetually migrating to Texas, where they purchase land; and although they conform to the laws of the country, they are gradually founding the empire of their own language and their own

* The foremost of these circumstances is, that nations which are accustomed to free institutions and municipal government are better able than any others to found prosperous colonies. The habit of thinking and governing for oneself is indispensable in a new country, where success necessarily depends, in a great measure, upon the individual exertions of the settlers.

manners. The province of Texas is still part of the Mex. can dominions, but it will soon contain no Mexicans: th same thing has occurred whenever the Anglo-American have come into contact with populations of a different origi

[The prophetic accuracy of the author, in relation to the prese actual condition of Texas, exhibits the sound and clear perception wit which he surveyed our institutions and character.—*American Editor.*

It cannot be denied that the British race has acquired a amazing preponderance over all the other European races i the New World; and that it is very superior to them in civilisation, in industry, and in power. As long as it is only sur rounded by desert or thinly-peopled countries, as long as i encounters no dense populations upon its route, through which it cannot work its way, it will assuredly continue to spread. The lines marked out by treaties will not stop it; but it will everywhere transgress these imaginary barriers.

The geographical position of the British race in the New World is peculiarly favorable to its rapid increase. Above its northern frontiers the icy regions of the pole extend; and a few degrees below its southern confines lies the burning climate of the equator. The Anglo-Americans are therefore placed in the most temperate and habitable zone of the continent.

It is generally supposed that the prodigious increase of population in the United States is posterior to their declaration of independence. But this is an error: the population increased as rapidly under the colonial system as it does at the present day; that is to say, it doubled in about twenty-two years. But this proportion, which is now applied to millions, was then applied to thousands, of inhabitants; and the same fact which was scarcely noticeable a century ago, is now evident to every observer.

The British subjects in Canada, who are dependent on a king, augment and spread almost as rapidly as the British settlers of the United States, who live under a republican government. During the war of independence, which lasted eight years, the population continued to increase without intermission in the same ratio. Although powerful Indian nations allied with the English existed, at that time, upon the western frontiers, the emigration westward was never checked. While the enemy laid waste the shores of the Atlantic, Kentucky, the western parts of Pennsylvania, and the states of Vermont and of Maine were filling with inhabitants. Nor did the unsettled state of the constitution, which succeeded the war, prevent the increase of the population, or stop its progress across the wilds. Thus, the difference of laws, the various conditions of peace and war, of order and of anarchy, have exercised no perceptible influence upon the gradual development of the Anglo-Americans. This may be readily understood: for the fact is, that no causes are sufficiently general to exercise a simultaneous influence over the whole of so extensive a territory. One portion of the country always offers a sure retreat from the calamities which afflict another part; and however great may be the evil, the remedy which is at hand is greater still.

It must not, then, be imagined that the impulse of the British race in the New World can be arrested. The dismemberment of the Union, and the hostilities which might ensue, the abolition of republican institutions, and the tyrannical government which might succeed it, may retard this impulse, but they cannot prevent it from ultimately fulfilling the destinies to which that race is reserved. No power upon earth can close upon the emigrants that fertile wilderness which offers resources to all industry and a refuge from all want. Future events, of whatever nature they may be, will not deprive the Americans of their climate or of their inland seas, of their great rivers or of their exuberant soil. Nor will bad laws, revolutions, and anarchy, be able to obliterate that love of prosperity and that spirit of enterprise which seem to be the distinctive characteristics of their race, or to extinguish that knowledge which guides them on their way.

Thus, in the midst of the uncertain future, one event at least is sure. At a period which may be said to be near (for we are speaking of the life of a nation), the Anglo-Americans will alone cover the immense space contained between the polar regions and the tropics, extending from the coasts of the Atlantic to the shores of the Pacific ocean. The territory which will probably be occupied by the Anglo-Americans at some future time, may be computed to equal three-quarters of Europe in extent.* The climate of the Union is upon the whole preferable to that of Europe, and its natural advantages are not less great; it is therefore evident that its population will at some future time be proportionate to our own. Europe, divided as it is between so many different nations, and torn as it has been by incessant wars and the barbarous

* The United States already extend over a territory equal to one half of Europe. The area of Europe is 500,000 square leagues, and its population 205,000,000 of inhabitants. (Maltebrun, liv. 114, vol., vi., p. 4.)

manners of the Middle Ages, has notwithstanding attained a population of 410 inhabitants to the square league.* What cause can prevent the United States from having as numerous a population in time?

Many ages must elapse before the divers offsets of the British race in America cease to present the same homogeneous characteristics; and the time cannot be foreseen at which a permanent inequality of conditions will be established in the New World. Whatever differences may arise, from peace or from war, from freedom or oppression, from prosperity or want, between the destinies of the different descendants of the great Anglo-American family, they will at least preserve an analogous social condition, and they will hold in common the customs and the opinions to which that social condition has given birth.

In the Middle Ages, the tie of religion was sufficiently powerful to imbue all the different populations of Europe with the same civilisation. The British of the New World have a thousand other reciprocal ties; and they live at a time when the tendency to equality is general among mankind. The Middle Ages were a period when everything was broken up; when each people, each province, each city, and each family, had a strong tendency to maintain its distinct individuality. At the present time an opposite tendency seems to prevail, and the nations seem to be advancing to unity. Our means of intellectual intercourse unite the most remote parts of the earth; and it is impossible for men to remain strangers to each other, or to be ignorant of the events which are taking place in any corner of the globe. The consequence is, that there is less difference, at the present day, between the Europeans and their descendants in the New World, than there was between certain towns in the thirteenth century, which were only separated by a river. If this tendency to assimilation brings foreign nations closer to each other, it must *à fortiori* prevent the descendants of the same people from becoming aliens to each other.

The time will therefore come when one hundred and fifty millions of men will be living in North America,† equal in condition, the progeny of one race, owing their origin to the same cause, and preserving the same civilisation, the same language, the same religion, the same habits, the same manners, and imbued with the same opinions, propagated under

* See Maltebrun, liv. 116, vol. vi., p. 92.

† This would be a population proportionate to that of Europe, taken at a mean rate of 410 inhabitants to the square league.

the same forms. The rest is uncertain, but this is certain; and it is a fact new to the world—a fact fraught with such portentous consequences as to baffle the efforts even of the imagination.

There are, at the present time, two great nations in the world, which seem to tend toward the same end, although they started from different points; I allude to the Russians and the Americans. Both of them have grown up unnoticed; and while the attention of mankind was directed elsewhere, they have suddenly assumed a most prominent place among the nations; and the world learned their existence and their greatness at almost the same time.

All other nations seem to have nearly reached their natural limits, and only to be charged with the maintenance of their power; but these are still in the act of growth;* all the others are stopped, or continue to advance with extreme difficulty; these are proceeding with ease and with celerity along a path to which the human eye can assign no term. The American struggles against the natural obstacles which oppose him; the adversaries of the Russian are men; the former combats the wilderness and savage life; the latter, civilisation with all its weapons and its arts; the conquests of the one are therefore gained by the ploughshare; those of the other, by the sword. The Anglo-American relies upon personal interest to accomplish his ends, and gives free scope to the unguided exertions and common sense of the citizens; the Russian centres all the authority of society in a single arm: the principal instrument of the former is freedom; of the latter, servitude. Their starting-point is different, and their courses are not the same; yet each of them seems to be marked out by the will of Heaven to sway the destinies of half the globe.

* Russia is the country in the Old World in which population increases most rapidly in proportion.

APPENDIX

APPENDIX A.—Page 17.

For information concerning all the countries of the West which have not been visited by Europeans, consult the account of two expeditions undertaken at the expense of congress by Major Long. This traveller particularly mentions, on the subject of the great American desert, that a line may be drawn nearly parallel to the 20th degree of longitude* (meridian of Washington), beginning from the Red river and ending at the river Platte. From this imaginary line to the Rocky mountains, which bound the valley of the Mississippi on the west, lie immense plains, which are almost entirely covered with sand, incapable of cultivation, or scattered over with masses of granite. In summer, these plains are quite destitute of water, and nothing is to be seen on them but herds of buffaloes and wild horses. Some hordes of Indians are also found there, but in no great number.

Major Long was told, that in travelling northward from the river Platte, you find the same desert constantly on the left; but he was unable to ascertain the truth of this report. (Long's Expedition, vol. ii., p. 361.)

However worthy of confidence may be the narrative of Major Long, it must be remembered that he only passed through the country of which he speaks, without deviating widely from the line which he had traced out for his journey.

APPENDIX B.—Page 18.

South America, in the regions between the tropics, produces an incredible profusion of climbing-plants, of which the Flora of the Antilles alone presents us with forty different species.

Among the most graceful of these shrubs is the passion-flower, which, according to Descourtiz, grows with such luxuriance in the Antilles, as to climb trees by means of the tendrils with which it is provided, and form moving bowers of rich and elegant festoons, decorated with blue and purple flowers, and fragrant with perfume. (Vol. i., p. 265).

The *mimosa scandens* (acacia à grandes gousses) is a creeper of enormous and rapid growth, which climbs from tree to tree, and sometimes covers more than half a league. (Vol. iii., p. 227.)

* The 20th degree of longitude according to the meridian of Washington, agrees very nearly with the 97th degree on the meridian of Greenwich.

APPENDIX C.—Page 2C

The languages which are spoken by the Indians of America, from the Pole to Cape Horn, are said to be all formed upon the same model, and subject to the same grammatical rules; whence it may fairly be concluded that all the Indian nations sprang from the same stock.

Each tribe of the American continent speaks a different dialect; but the number of languages, properly so called, is very small, a fact which tends to prove that the nations of the New World had not a very remote origin.

Moreover, the languages of America have a great degree of regularity; from which it seems probable that the tribes which employ them had not undergone any great revolutions, or been incorporated, voluntarily, or by constraint, with foreign nations. For it is generally the union of several languages into one which produces grammatical irregularities.

It is not long since the American languages, especially those of the north, first attracted the serious attention of philologists, when the discovery was made that this idiom of a barbarous people was the product of a complicated system of ideas and very learned combinations. These languages were found to be very rich, and great pains had been taken at their formation to render them agreeable to the ear.

The grammatical system of the Americans differs from all others in several points, but especially in the following:—

Some nations in Europe, among others the Germans, have the power of combining at pleasure different expressions, and thus giving a complex sense to certain words. The Indians have given a most surprising extension to this power, so as to arrive at the means of connecting a great number of ideas with a single term. This will be easily understood with the help of an example quoted by Mr. Duponceau, in the Memoirs of the Philosophical Society of America

"A Delaware woman, playing with a cat or a young dog," says this writer, "is heard to pronounce the word *kuligatschis;* which is thus composed; *k* is the sign of the second person, and signifies 'thou' or 'thy;' *uli* is a part of the word *wulit,* which signifies 'beautiful,' 'pretty;' *gat* is another fragment of the word *wichgat,* which means 'paw;' and lastly, *schis* is a diminutive giving the idea of smallness. Thus in one word the Indian woman has expressed, 'Thy pretty little paw.'"

Take another example of the felicity with which the savages of America have composed their words. A young man of Delaware is called *pilape.* This word is formed from *pilsit,* chaste, innocent; and *lenape,* man; viz., man in his purity and innocence.

This facility of combining words is most remarkable in the strange formation of their verbs. The most complex action is often expressed by a single verb, which serves to convey all the shades of an idea by the modification of its construction.

Those who may wish to examine more in detail this subject, which I have only glanced at superficially, should read:—

1. The correspondence of Mr. Duponceau and the Rev. Mr. Hecwelder relative to the Indian languages; which is to be found in the first volume of the Memoirs of the Philosophical Society of America, published at Philadelphia, 1819, by Abraham Small, vol i., pp 356–464.

2. The grammar of the Delaware or Lenape language by Geiberger,

and the preface of Mr. Duponceau. All these are in the same collection, vol. iii.

3. An excellent account of these works, which is at the end of the 5th volume of the American Encyclopædia.

APPENDIX D.—Page 22.

See in Charlevoix, vol i., p. 235, the history of the first war which the French inhabitants of Canada carried on, in 1610, against the Iroquois. The latter, armed with bows and arrows, offered a desperate resistance to the French and their allies. Charlevoix is not a great painter, yet he exhibits clearly enough, in this narrative, the contrast between the European manners and those of savages, as well as the different way in which the two races of men understood the sense of honor.

When the French, says he, seized upon the beaver-skins which covered the Indians who had fallen, the Hurons, their allies, were greatly offended at this proceeding; but without hesitation they set to work in their usual manner, inflicting horrid cruelties upon the prisoners, and devouring one of those who had been killed, which made the Frenchmen shudder. The barbarians prided themselves upon a scrupulousness which they were surprised at not finding in our nation; and could not understand that there was less to reprehend in the stripping of dead bodies, than in the devouring of their flesh like wild beasts.

Charlevoix, in another place (vol. i., p. 230), thus describes the first torture of which Champlain was an eyewitness, and the return of the Hurons into their own village.

"Having proceeded about eight leagues," says he, "our allies halted: and having singled out one of their captives, they reproached him with all the cruelties which he had practised upon the warriors of their nation who had fallen into his hands, and told him that he might expect to be treated in like manner; adding, that if he had any spirit he would prove it by singing. He immediately chanted forth his death-song, and then his war-song, and all the songs he knew, 'but in a very mournful strain,' says Champlain, who was not then aware that all savage music has a melancholy character. The tortures which succeeded, accompanied by all the horrors which we shall mention hereafter, terrified the French, who made every effort to put a stop to them, but in vain. The following night one of the Hurons having dreamed that they were pursued, the retreat was changed to a real flight, and the savages never stopped until they were out of the reach of danger.

The moment they perceived the cabins of their own village, they cut themselves long sticks, to which they fastened the scalps which had fallen to their share, and carried them in triumph. At this sight, the women swam to the canoes, where they received the bloody scalps from the hands of their husbands, and tied them round their necks.

The warriors offered one of these horrible trophies to Champlain; they also presented him with some bows and arrows—the only spoils of the Iroquois which they had ventured to seize—entreating him to show them to the king of France.

Champlain lived a whole winter quite alone among these barbarians, without being under any alarm for his person or property.

APPENDIX E.—Page 36.

ALTHOUGH the puritanical strictness which presided over the establishment of the English colonies in America is now much relaxed, remarkable traces of it are still found in their habits and their laws. In 1792, at the very time when the anti-Christian republic of France began its ephemeral existence, the legislative body of Massachusetts promulgated the following law, to compel the citizens to observe the sabbath. We give the preamble, and the principal articles of this law, which is worthy of the reader's attention.

"Whereas," says the legislator, "the observation of the Sunday is an affair of public interest; inasmuch as it produces a necessary suspension of labor, leads men to reflect upon the duties of life and the errors to which human nature is liable, and provides for the public and private worship of God the creator and governor of the universe, and for the performance of such acts of charity as are the ornament and comfort of Christian societies:—

"Whereas, irreligious or light-minded persons, forgetting the duties which the sabbath imposes, and the benefits which these duties confer on society, are known to profane its sanctity, by following their pleasures or their affairs; this way of acting being contrary to their own interest as Christians, and calculated to annoy those who do not follow their example; being also of great injury to society at large, by spreading a taste for dissipation and dissolute manners;—

"Be it enacted and ordained by the governor, council, and representatives convened in general court of assembly, that all and every person and persons shall, on that day, carefully apply themselves to the duties of religion and piety; that no tradesman or laborer shall exercise his ordinary calling, and that no game or recreation shall be used on the Lord's day, upon pain of forfeiting ten shillings;—

"That no one shall travel on that day, or any part thereof, under pain of forfeiting twenty shillings; that no vessel shall leave a harbor of the colony; that no person shall keep outside the meetinghouse during the time of public worship, or profane the time by playing or talking, on penalty of five shillings.

"Public-houses shall not entertain any other than strangers or lodgers, under a penalty of five shillings for every person found drinking or abiding therein.

"Any person in health who, without sufficient reason, shall omit to worship God in public during three months, shall be condemned to a fine of ten shillings.

"Any person guilty of misbehavior in a place of public worship shall be fined from five to forty shillings.

"These laws are to be enforced by the tithing-men of each township, who have authority to visit public-houses on the Sunday. The innkeeper who shall refuse them admittance shall be fined forty shillings for such offence.

"The tithing-men are to stop travellers, and to require of them their reason for being on the road on Sunday: any one refusing to answer shall be sentenced to pay a fine not exceeding five pounds sterling. If the reason given by the traveller be not deemed by the tithing-men sufficient, he may bring the traveller before the justice of the peace of the district." (*Law of the 8th March*, 1792: *General Laws of Massachusetts*, vol. i., p. 410.)

On the 11th March, 1797, a new law increased the amount of fines, half of which was to be given to the informer. (*Same collection*, vol. ii., p. 525.)

On the 16th February, 1816, a new law confirmed these measures (*Same collection*, vol. ii., p. 405.)

Similar enactments exist in the laws of the state of New York, revised in 1827 and 1828. (See ***Revised Statutes***, part i., chapter 20, p. 675.) In these it is declared that no one is allowed on the sabbath to sport, to fish, play at games, or to frequent houses where liquor is sold. No one can travel except in case of necessity.

And this is not the only trace which the religious strictness and austere manners of the first emigrants have left behind them in the American laws.

In the revised statutes of the state of New York, vol. i., p. 662, is the following clause :—

"Whoever shall win or lose in the space of twenty-four hours, by gaming or betting, the sum of twenty-five dollars, shall be found guilty of a misdemeanor, and, upon conviction, shall be condemned to pay a fine equal to at least five times the value of the sum lost or won ; which will be paid to the inspector of the poor of the township. He that loses twenty-five dollars or more, may bring an action to recover them ; and if he neglects to do so, the inspector of the poor may prosecute the winner, and oblige him to pay into the poor box both the sum he has gained and three times as much beside."

The laws we quote from are of recent date ; but they are unintelligible without going back to the very origin of the colonies. I have no doubt that in our days the penal part of these laws is very rarely applied. Laws preserve their inflexibility long after the manners of a nation have yielded to the influence of time. It is still true, however, that nothing strikes a foreigner on his arrival in America more forcibly than the regard to the sabbath.

There is one, in particular, of the large American cities, in which all social movements begin to be suspended even on Saturday evening. You traverse its streets at the hour at which you expect men in the middle of life to be engaged in business, and young people in pleasure; and you meet with solitude and silence. Not only have all ceased to work, but they appear to have ceased to exist. Neither the movements of industry are heard, nor the accents of joy, nor even the confused murmur which arises from the midst of a great city. Chains are hung across the streets in the neighborhood of the churches; the half closed shutters of the houses scarcely admit a ray of sun into the dwellings of the citizens. Now and then you perceive a solitary individual, who glides silently along the deserted streets and lanes.

Next day, at early dawn, the rolling of carriages, the noise of hammers, the cries of the population, begin to make themselves heard again. The city is awake. An eager crowd hastens toward the resort of commerce and industry ; everything around you bespeaks motion, bustle, hurry. A feverish activity succeeds to the lethargic stupor of yesterday : you might almost suppose that they had but one day to acquire wealth and to enjoy it.

APPENDIX F.—Page 41.

It is unnecessary for me to say, that in the chapter which has just been read, I have not had the intention of giving a history of America. My only object was to enable the reader to appreciate the influence which the opinions and manners of the first emigrants had exercised upon the fate of the different colonies and of the Union in general. I have therefore confined myself to the quotation of a few detached fragments.

I do not know whether I am deceived, but it appears to me that by pursuing the path which I have merely pointed out, it would be easy to present such pictures of the American republics as would not be unworthy the attention of the public, and could not fail to suggest to the statesman matter for reflection.

Not being able to devote myself to this labor, I am anxious to render it easy to others; and for this purpose, I subjoin a short catalogue and analysis of the works which seem to me the most important to consult.

At the head of the general documents, which it would be advantageous to examine, I place the work entitled An Historical Collection of State Papers, and other authentic Documents, intended as Materials for a History of the United States of America, by Ebenezer Hasard. The first volume of this compilation, which was printed at Philadelphia in 1792, contains a literal copy of all the charters granted by the crown of England to the emigrants, as well as the principal acts of the colonial governments, during the commencement of their existence. Among other authentic documents, we here find a great many relating to the affairs of New England and Virginia during this period. The second volume is almost entirely devoted to the acts of the confederation of 1643. This federal compact, which was entered into by the colonies of New England with the view of resisting the Indians, was the first instance of union afforded by the Anglo-Americans. There were besides many other confederations of the same nature, before the famous one of 1776, which brought about the independence of the colonies.

Each colony has, besides, its own historic monuments, some of which are extremely curious; beginning with Virginia, the state which was first peopled. The earliest historian of Virginia was its founder, Capt. John Smith. Capt. Smith has left us an octavo volume, entitled, The generall Historie of Virginia and New England, by Captain John Smith, sometymes Governour in those Countryes, and Admirall of New England; printed at London in 1627. The work is adorned with curious maps and engravings of the time when it appeared; the narrative extends from the year 1584 to 1626. Smith's work is highly and deservedly esteemed. The author was one of the most celebrated adventurers of a period of remarkable adventure; his book breathes that ardor for discovery, that spirit of enterprise which characterized the men of his time, when the manners of chivalry were united to zeal for commerce, and made subservient to the acquisition of wealth.

But Capt. Smith is remarkable for uniting, to the virtues which characterized his contemporaries, several qualities to which they were generally strangers: his style is simple and concise, his narratives bear the stamp of truth, and his descriptions are free from false ornament.

This author throws most valuable light upon the state and condition of the Indians at the time when North America was first discovered.

The second historian to consult is Beverley, who commences his narrative with the year 1585, and ends it with 1700. The first part of his book contains historical documents, properly so called, relative to the infancy of the colony. The second affords a most curious picture of the Indians at this remote period. The third conveys very clear ideas concerning the manners, social condition, laws, and political customs of the Virginians in the author's lifetime.

Beverley was a native of Virginia, which occasions him to say at the beginning of his book that he entreats his readers not to exercise their critical severity upon it, since, having been born in the Indies, he does not aspire to purity of language. Notwithstanding this colonial modesty, the author shows throughout his book the impatience with which he endures the supremacy of the mother-country. In this work of Beverley are also found numerous traces of that spirit of civil liberty which animated the English colonies of America at the time when he wrote. He also shows the dissensions which existed among them and retarded their independence. Beverley detests his catholic neighbors of Maryland, even more than he hates the English government: his style is simple, his narrative interesting and apparently trustworthy.

I saw in America another work which ought to be consulted, entitled, The History of Virginia, by William Stith. This book affords some curious details, but I thought it long and diffuse

The most ancient as well as the best document to be consulted on the history of Carolina is a work in a small quarto, entitled, The History of Carolina, by John Lawson, printed at London in 1718. This work contains, in the first part, a journey of discovery in the west of Carolina; the account of which, given in the form of a journal, is in general confused and superficial; but it contains a very striking description of the mortality caused among the savages of that time, both by the small-pox and the immoderate use of brandy; and with a curious picture of the corruption of manners prevalent among them, which was increased by the presence of Europeans. The second part of Lawson's book is taken up with a description of the physical condition of Carolina, and its productions. In the third part, the author gives an interesting account of the manners, customs, and government of the Indians at that period. There is a good deal of talent and originality in this part of the work.

Lawson concludes his history with a copy of the charter granted to the Carolinas in the reign of Charles II. The general tone of this work is light, and often licentious, forming a perfect contrast to the solemn style of the works published at the same period in New England. Lawson's history is extremely scarce in America, and cannot be procured in Europe. There is, however, a copy of it in the royal library at Paris.

From the southern extremity of the United States I pass at once to the northern limit; as the intermediate space was not peopled till a later period.

I must first point out a very curious compilation, entitled, Collection of the Massachusetts Historical Society, printed for the first time at Boston in 1792, and reprinted in 1806. The collection of which I speak, and which is continued to the present day, contains a great number of very valuable documents relating to the history of the different states of New England. Among them are letters which have never been published, and authentic pieces which have been buried in provincial archives. The whole work of Gookin concerning the Indians is inserted there.

I have mentioned several times, in the chapter to which this note relates, the work of Nathaniel Norton, entitled New England's Memorial; sufficiently perhaps to prove that it deserves the attention of those who would be conversant with the history of New England. This book is in 8vo. and was reprinted at Boston in 1826.

The most valuable and important authority which exists upon the history of New England is the work of the Rev. Cotton Mather, entitled Magnalia Christi Americana, or the Ecclesiastical History of New England, 1620—1698, 2 vols. 8vo, reprinted at Hartford, United States, in 1820.* The author divided his work into seven books. The first presents the history of the events which prepared and brought about the establishment of New England. The second contains the lives of the first governors and chief magistrates who presided over the country. The third is devoted to the lives and labors of the evangelical ministers who during the same period had the care of souls. In the fourth the author relates the institution and progress of the University of Cambridge (Massachusetts). In the fifth he describes the principles and the discipline of the Church of New England. The sixth is taken up in retracing certain facts, which, in the opinion of Mather, prove the merciful interposition of Providence in behalf of the inhabitants of New England. Lastly, in the seventh, the author gives an account of the heresies and the troubles to which the Church of New England was exposed. Cotton Mather was an evangelical minister who was born at Boston, and passed his life there. His narratives are distinguished by the same ardor and religious zeal which led to the foundation of the colonies of New England. Traces of bad taste sometimes occur in his manner of writing; but he interests, because he is full of enthusiasm. He is often intolerant, still oftener credulous, but he never betrays an intention to deceive. Sometimes his book contains fine passages, and true and profound reflections, such as the following:—

"Before the arrival of the Puritans," says he (vol. i., chap. iv.), "there were more than a few attempts of the English to people and improve the parts of New England which were to the northward of New Plymouth; but the design of those attempts being aimed no higher than the advancement of some worldly interests, a constant series of disasters has confounded them, until there was a plantation erected upon the nobler designs of Christianity: and that plantation, though it has had more adversaries than perhaps any one upon earth, yet, having obtained help from God, it continues to this day."

Mather occasionally relieves the austerity of his descriptions with images full of tender feeling: after having spoken of an English lady whose religious ardor had brought her to America with her husband, and who soon after sank under the fatigues and privations of exile, he adds, "As for her virtuous husband, Isaac Johnson,

He tried
To live without her, liked it not, and died."—(Vol. i.)

Mather's work gives an admirable picture of the time and country which he describes. In his account of the motives which led the puritans to seek an asylum beyond seas, he says:—

"The God of heaven served, as it were, a summons upon the spirits of his people in the English nation, stirring up the spirits of thousands which never saw the faces of each other, with a most unanimous inclination to leave the pleasant accommodations of their native country, and go over a terrible ocean, into a more terrible desert, for the pure enjoyment of all his ordinances. It is now reasonable that, before we

* A folio edition of this work was published in London in 1702

pass any farther, the reasons of this undertaking should be more exactly made known unto posterity, especially unto the posterity of those that were the undertakers, lest they come at length to forget and neglect the true interest of New England. Wherefore I shall now transcribe some of them from a manuscript wherein they were then tendered unto consideration.

"*General Considerations for the Plantation of New England.*

"First, it will be a service unto the church of great consequence, to carry the gospel unto those parts of the world, and raise a bulwark against the kingdom of antichrist, which the Jesuits labor to rear up in all parts of the world.

"Secondly, all other churches of Europe have been brought under desolations; and it may be feared that the like judgments are coming upon us; and who knows but God hath provided this place to be a refuge for many whom he means to save out of the general destruction!

"Thirdly, the land grows weary of her inhabitants, inasmuch that man, which is the most precious of all creatures, is here more vile and base than the earth he treads upon; children, neighbors, and friends, especially the poor, are counted the greatest burdens, which, if things were right, would be the chiefest of earthly blessings.

"Fourthly, we are grown to that intemperance in all excess of riot, as no mean estate almost will suffice a man to keep sail with his equals, and he that fails in it must live in scorn and contempt; hence it comes to pass, that all arts and trades are carried in that deceitful manner and unrighteous course, as it is almost impossible for a good upright man to maintain his constant charge and live comfortably in them.

"Fifthly, the schools of learning and religion are so corrupted, as (beside the unsupportable charge of education) most children, even the best, wittiest, and of the fairest hopes, are prevented, corrupted, and utterly overthrown by the multitude of evil examples and licentious behaviors in these seminaries.

"Sixthly, the whole earth is the Lord's garden, and he hath given it to the sons of Adam, to be tilled and improved by them: why then should we stand starving here for places of habitation, and in the mean time suffer whole countries, as profitable for the use of man, to lie waste without any improvement?

"Seventhly, what can be a better or a nobler work, and more worthy of a Christian, than to erect and support a reformed particular church in its infancy, and unite our forces with such a company of faithful people, as by timely assistance may grow stronger and prosper; but for want of it, may be put to great hazards, if not be wholly ruined

"Eighthly, if any such as are known to be godly, and live in wealth and prosperity here, shall forsake all this to join with this reformed church, and with it run the hazard of a hard and mean condition, it will be an example of great use, both for the removing of scandal, and to give more life unto the faith of God's people in their prayers for the plantation, and also to encourage others to join the more willingly in it."

Farther on, when he declares the principles of the church of New England with respect to morals, Mather inveighs with violence against the custom of drinking healths at table, which he denounces as a pagan and abominable practice. He proscribes with the same rigor all ornaments for the hair used by the female sex, as well as their custom of having the arms and neck uncovered.

In another part of his work he relates several instances of witchcraft which had alarmed New England. It is plain that the visible action of the devil in the affairs of this world appeared to him an incontestible and evident fact.

This work of Cotton Mather displays in many places, the spirit of civil liberty and political independence which characterized the times in which he lived. Their principles respecting government are discoverable at every page. Thus, for instance, the inhabitants of Massachusetts, in the year 1630, ten years after the foundation of Plymouth, are found to have devoted 400*l.* sterling to the establishment of the University of Cambridge. In passing from the general documents relative to the history of New England, to those which describe the several states comprised within its limits, I ought first to notice The History of the Colony of Massachusetts, by Hutchinson, Lieutenant-Governor of the Massachusetts Province, 2 vols., 8vo.

The history of Hutchinson, which I have several times quoted in the chapter to which this note relates, commences in the year 1628 and ends in 1750. Throughout the work there is a striking air of truth and the greatest simplicity of style; it is full of minute details.

The best history to consult concerning Connecticut is that of Benjamin Trumbull, entitled, A Complete History of Connecticut, Civil and Ecclesiastical, 1630–1764; 2 vols., 8vo., printed in 1818, at New Haven. This history contains a clear and calm account of all the events which happened in Connecticut during the period given in the title. The author drew from the best sources; and his narrative bears the stamp of truth. All that he says of the early days of Connecticut is extremely curious. See especially the constitution of 1639, vol. i., ch. vi., p. 100; and also the penal laws of Connecticut, vol. i., ch. vii., p. 123.

The History of New Hampshire, by Jeremy Belknap, is a work held in merited estimation. It was printed at Boston in 1792, in 2 vols., 8vo. The third chapter of the first volume is particularly worthy of attention for the valuable details it affords on the political and religious principles of the puritans, on the causes of their emigration, and on their laws. The following curious quotation is given from a sermon delivered in 1663: "It concerneth New England always to remember that they are a plantation religious, not a plantation of trade. The profession of the purity of doctrine, worship, and discipline, is written on her forehead. Let merchants, and such as are increasing cent. per cent. remember this, that worldly gain was not the end and design of the people of New England, but religion. And if any man among us make religion as twelve, and the world as thirteen, such an one hath not the true spirit of a true New Englishman." The reader of Belknap will find in his work more general ideas, and more strength of thought, than are to be met with in the American historians even to the present day.

Among the central states which deserve our attention for their remote origin, New York and Pennsylvania are the foremost. The best history we have of the former is entitled A History of New York, by William Smith, printed in London in 1757. Smith gives us important details of the wars between the French and English in America. His is the best account of the famous confederation of the Iroquois.

With respect to Pennsylvania, I cannot do better than point out the work of Proud, entitled the History of Pennsylvania, from the original Institution and Settlement of that Province, under the first Proprietor and Governor, William Penn, in 1681, till after the year 1742; by

Robert Proud; 2 vols., 8vo., printed at Philadelphia in 1797. This work is deserving of the especial attention of the reader; it contains a mass of curious documents concerning Penn, the doctrine of the Quakers, and the character, manners, and customs of the first inhabitants of Pennsylvania.

APPENDIX G.—Page 48

We read in Jefferson's Memoirs as follows:—

"At the time of the first settlement of the English in Virginia, when land was had for little or nothing, some provident persons having obtained large grants of it, and being desirous of maintaining the splendor of their families, entailed their property upon their descendants. The transmission of these estates from generation to generation, to men who bore the same name, had the effect of raising up a distinct class of families, who, possessing by law the privilege of perpetuating their wealth, formed by these means a sort of patrician order, distinguished by the grandeur and luxury of their establishments From this order it was that the king usually chose his counsellor of state."*

In the United States, the principal clauses of the English law respecting descent have been universally rejected. The first rule that we follow, says Mr. Kent, touching inheritance, is the following: If a man dies intestate, his property goes to his heirs in a direct line. If he has but one heir or heiress, he or she succeeds to the whole. If there are several heirs of the same degree, they divide the inheritance equally among them, without distinction of sex.

This rule was prescribed for the first time in the state of New York by a statute of the 23d of February, 1786. (See Revised Statutes, vol. iii., Appendix, p. 48.) It has since then been adopted in the revised statutes of the same state. At the present day this law holds good throughout the whole of the United States, with the exception of the state of Vermont, where the male heir inherits a double portion: Kent's Commentaries, vol. iv., p. 370. Mr. Kent, in the same work, vol. iv., p. 1–22, gives an historical account of American legislation on the subject of entail; by this we learn that previous to the revolution the colonies followed the English law of entail. Estates tail were abolished in Virginia in 1776, on a motion of Mr. Jefferson. They were suppressed in New York in 1786; and have since been abolished in North Carolina, Kentucky, Tennessee, Georgia, and Missouri. In Vermont, Indiana, Illinois, South Carolina, and Louisiana, entail was never introduced. Those States which thought proper to preserve the English law of entail, modified it in such a way as to deprive it of its most aristocratic tendencies. "Our general principles on the subject of government," says Mr. Kent, "tend to favor the free circulation of property."

It cannot fail to strike the French reader who studies the law of inheritance, that on these questions the French legislation is infinitely more democratic even than the American.

The American law makes an equal division of the father's property, but only in the case of his will not being known; "for every man," says the law, "in the state of New York (Revised Statutes, vol. iii.,

* This passage is extracted and translated from M. Conseil's work upon the Life of Jefferson, entitled, "*Mélanges Politiques et Philosophiques de Jefferson.*"

Appendix, p. 51), has entire liberty, power, and authority, to dispose of his property by will, to leave it entire, or divided in favor of any persons he chooses as his heirs, provided he do not leave it to a political body or any corporation." The French law obliges the testator to divide his property equally, or nearly so, among his heirs.

Most of the American republics still admit of entails, under certain restrictions; but the French law prohibits entail in all cases.

If the social condition of the Americans is more democratic than that of the French, the laws of the latter are the most democratic of the two. This may be explained more easily than at first appears to be the case. In France, democracy is still occupied in the work of destruction; in America it reigns quietly over the ruins it has made.

APPENDIX H.—Page 55

SUMMARY OF THE QUALIFICATIONS OF VOTERS IN THE UNITED STATES.

ALL the states agree in granting the right of voting at the age of twenty-one. In all of them it is necessary to have resided for a certain time in the district where the vote is given. This period varies from three months to two years.

As to the qualification; in the state of Massachusetts it is necessary to have an income of three pounds sterling or a capital of sixty pounds.

In Rhode Island a man must possess landed property to the amount of 133 dollars.

In Connecticut he must have a property which gives an income of seventeen dollars. A year of service in the militia also gives the elective privilege.

In New Jersey, an elector must have a property of fifty pounds a year.

In South Carolina and Maryland, the elector must possess fifty acres of land.

In Tennessee, he must possess some property.

In the states of Mississippi, Ohio, Georgia, Virginia, Pennsylvania, Delaware, New York, the only necessary qualification for voting is that of paying the taxes; and in most of the states, to serve in the militia is equivalent to the payment of taxes.

In Maine and New Hampshire any man can vote who is not on the pauper list.

Lastly, in the states of Missouri, Alabama, Illinois, Louisiana, Indiana, Kentucky, and Vermont, the conditions of voting have no reference to the property of the elector.

I believe there is no other state beside that of North Carolina in which different conditions are applied to the voting for the senate and the electing the house of representatives. The electors of the former, in this case, should possess in property fifty acres of land; to vote for the latter, nothing more is required than to pay taxes.

APPENDIX I.—Page 92.

The small number of custom-house officers employed in the United States compared with the extent of the coast renders smuggling very easy; notwithstanding which it is less practised than elsewhere, because everybody endeavors to suppress it. In America there is no police for the prevention of fires, and such accidents are more frequent than in Europe: but in general they are more speedily extinguished, because the surrounding population is prompt in lending assistance.

APPENDIX K.—Page 94.

It is incorrect to assert that centralization was produced by the French revolution: the revolution brought it to perfection, but did not create it. The mania for centralization and government regulations dates from the time when jurists began to take a share in the government, in the time of Philippe-le-Bel; ever since which period they have been on the increase. In the year 1775, M. de Malesherbes, speaking in the name of the Cour des Aides, said to Louis XIV.*

"* * * * Every corporation and every community of citizens retained the right of administering its own affairs; a right which not only forms part of the primitive constitution of the kingdom, but has a still higher origin; for it is the right of nature and of reason. Nevertheless, your subjects, sire, have been deprived of it; and we cannot refrain from saying that in this respect your government has fallen into puerile extremes. From the time when powerful ministers made it a political principle to prevent the convocation of a national assembly, one consequence has succeeded another, until the deliberations of the inhabitants of a village are declared null when they have not been authorized by the intendant. Of course, if the community have an expensive undertaking to carry through, it must remain under the control of the sub-delegate of the intendant, and consequently follow the plan he proposes, employ his favorite workmen, pay them according to his pleasure; and if an action at law is deemed necessary, the intendant's permission must be obtained. The cause must be pleaded before this first tribunal, previous to its being carried into a public court; and if the opinion of the intendant is opposed to that of the inhabitants, or if their adversary enjoys his favor, the community is deprived of the power of defending its rights. Such are the means, sire, which have been exerted to extinguish the municipal spirit in France; and to stifle, if possible, the opinions of the citizens. The nation may be said to lie under an interdict, and to be in wardship under guardians."

What could be said more to the purpose at the present day, when the revolution has achieved what are called its victories in centralization?

In 1789, Jefferson wrote from Paris to one of his friends: "There is no country where the mania for over-governing has taken deeper root than in France, or been the source of greater mischief." Letter to Madison, 28th August, 1789.

The fact is that for several centuries past the central power of France has done everything it could to extend central administration; it has

* See "Mémoires pour servir à l'Histoire du Droit Public de la France en matière d'Impôts," p. 654, printed at Brussels in 1779.

acknowledged no other limits than its own strength. The central power to which the revolution gave birth made more rapid advances than any of its predecessors, because it was stronger and wiser than they had been; Louis XIV. committed the welfare of such communities to the caprice of an intendant; Napoleon left them to that of the minister. The same principle governed both, though its consequences were more or less remote.

APPENDIX L.—Page 97.

This immutability of the constitution of France is a necessary consequence of the laws of that country.

To begin with the most important of all the laws, that which decides the order of succession to the throne; what can be more immutable in its principle than a political order founded upon the natural succession of father to son? In 1814 Louis XVIII. had established the perpetual law of hereditary succession in favor of his own family. The individuals who regulated the consequences of the revolution of 1830 followed his example; they merely established the perpetuity of the law in favor of another family. In this respect they imitated the Chancellor Maurepas, who, when he erected the new parliament upon the ruins of the old, took care to declare in the same ordinance that the rights of the new magistrates should be as inalienable as those of their predecessors had been.

The laws of 1830, like those of 1814, point out no way of changing the constitution; and it is evident that the ordinary means of legislation are insufficient for this purpose. As the king, peers, and deputies, all derive their authority from the constitution, these three powers united cannot alter a law by virtue of which alone they govern. Out of the pale of the constitution, they are nothing; where, then, could they take their stand to effect a change in its provisions? The alternative is clear; either their efforts are powerless against the charter, which continues to exist in spite of them, in which case they only reign in the name of the charter; or, they succeed in changing the charter, and then the law by which they existed being annulled, they themselves cease to exist. By destroying the charter, they destroy themselves.

This is much more evident in the laws of 1830 than in those of 1814. In 1814, the royal prerogative took its stand above and beyond the constitution; but in 1830, it was avowedly created by, and dependant on, the constitution.

A part therefore of the French constitution is immutable, because it is united to the destiny of a family; and the body of the constitution is equally immutable, because there appear to be no legal means of changing it.

These remarks are not applicable to England. That country having no written constitution, who can assert when its constitution is changed?

APPENDIX M.—Page 97.

The most esteemed authors who have written upon the English constitution agree with each other in establishing the omnipotence of the parliament.

Delolme says: "It is a fundamental principle with the English lawyers, that parliament can do everything except making a woman a man, or a man a woman."

Blackstone expresses himself more in detail if not more energetically than Delolme, in the following terms:—

"The power and jurisdiction of parliament," says Sir Edward Coke (4 Inst. 36), "is so transcendant and absolute, that it cannot be confined, either for causes or persons, within any bounds. And of this high court," he adds, "may be truly said, 'Si antiquitatem spectes, est vetustissima; si dignitatem, est honoratissima; si jurisdictionem, est capacissima.' It hath sovereign and uncontrollable authority in making, confirming, enlarging, restraining, abrogating, repealing, reviving and expounding of laws, concerning matters of all possible denominations; ecclesiastical or temporal; civil, military, maritime, or criminal; this being the place where that absolute despotic power which must, in all governments, reside somewhere, is intrusted by the constitution of these kingdoms. All mischiefs and grievances, operations and remedies, that transcend the ordinary course of the laws, are within the reach of this extraordinary tribunal. It can regulate or new-model the succession to the crown; as was done in the reigns of Henry VIII. and William III. It can alter the established religion of the land; as was done in a variety of instances in the reigns of King Henry VIII. and his three children. It can change and create afresh even the constitution of the kingdom, and of the parliaments themselves; as was done by the act of union and the several statutes for triennial and septennial elections. It can, in short, do everything that is not naturally impossible to be done; and, therefore, some have not scrupled to call its power, by a figure rather too bold, the omnipotence of parliament."

APPENDIX N.—Page 107.

THERE is no question upon which the American constitutions agree more fully than upon that of political jurisdiction. All the constitutions which take cognizance of this matter, give to the house of delegates the exclusive right of impeachment; excepting only the constitution of North Carolina which grants the same privilege to grand-juries. (Article 23.)

Almost all the constitutions give the exclusive right of pronouncing sentence to the senate, or to the assembly which occupies its place.

The only punishments which the political tribunals can inflict are removal and interdiction of public functions for the future. There is no other constitution but that of Virginia (152), which enables them to inflict every kind of punishment.

The crimes which are subject to political jurisdiction, are, in the federal constitution (section 4, art. 1); in that of Indiana (art. 3, paragraphs 23 and 24); of New York (art. 5); of Delaware (art. 5); high treason, bribery, and other high crimes or offences.

In the constitution of Massachusetts (chap. 1, section 2); that of North Carolina (art. 23); of Virginia (p. 252), misconduct and mal-administration.

In the constitution of New Hampshire (p. 105) corruption, intrigue, and mal-administration.

In Vermont (chap. ii., art. 24), mal-administration.

In South Carolina (art 5); Kentucky (art. 5); Tennessee (art. 4); Ohio (art. 1, § 23, 24); Louisiana (art. 5); Mississippi (art. 5); Alabama (art. 6); Pennsylvania (art. 4); crimes committed in the non-performance of official duties.

In the states of Illinois, Georgia, Maine, and Connecticut, no particular offences are specified.

APPENDIX O.—Page 171.

It is true that the powers of Europe may carry on maritime wars with the Union; but there is always greater facility and less danger in supporting a maritime than a continental war. Maritime warfare only requires one species of effort. A commercial people which consents to furnish its government with the necessary funds, is sure to possess a fleet. And it is far easier to induce a nation to part with its money, almost unconsciously, than to reconcile it to sacrifices of men and personal efforts. Moreover, defeat by sea rarely compromises the existence or independence of the people which endures it.

As for continental wars, it is evident that the nations of Europe cannot be formidable in this way to the American Union. It would be very difficult to transport and maintain in America more than 25,000 soldiers; an army which may be considered to represent a nation of 2,000,000 of men. The most populous nation of Europe contending in this way against the Union, is in the position of a nation of 2,000,000 of inhabitants at war with one of 12,000,000. Add to this, that America has all its resources within reach, while the European is at 4,000 miles distance from his; and that the immensity of the American continent would of itself present an insurmountable obstacle to its conquest.

APPENDIX P.—Page 186.

The first American journal appeared in April, 1704, and was published at Boston. See collection of the Historical Society of Massachusetts, vol. vi., p. 66.

It would be a mistake to suppose that the periodical press has always been entirely free in the American colonies: an attempt was made to establish something analogous to a censorship and preliminary security. Consult the Legislative Documents of Massachusetts of the 14th of January, 1722.

The committee appointed by the general assembly (the legislative body of the province), for the purpose of examining into circumstances connected with a paper entitled "The New England Courier," expresses its opinion that "the tendency of the said journal is to turn religion into derision, and bring it into contempt; that it mentions the sacred writings in a profane and irreligious manner; that it puts malicious interpretations upon the conduct of the ministers of the gospel; and that the government of his majesty is insulted, and the peace and tranquillity of the province disturbed by the said journal. The committee is consequently of opinion that the printer and publisher, James Franklin, should be forbidden to print and publish the said journal or any other work in future, without having previously submitted it to the secretary of the province; and that the justices of the peace for the county of Suffolk should be commissioned to require bail of the said James Franklin for his good conduct during the ensuing year."

The suggestion of the committee was adopted and passed into a law, but the effect of it was null, for the journal eluded the prohibition by putting the name of Benjamin Franklin instead of James Franklin at the bottom of its columns, and this manœuvre was supported by public opinion.

APPENDIX Q.—Page 287.

THE federal constitution has introduced the jury into the tribunals of the Union in the same way as the states had introduced it into their own several courts: but as it has not established any fixed rules for the choice of jurors, the federal courts select them from the ordinary jury-list which each state makes for itself. The laws of the states must therefore be examined for the theory of the formation of juries. See Story's Commentaries on the Constitution, B. iii., chap. 38, pp. 654–659; Sergeant's Constitutional Law, p. 165. See also the federal laws, of the years 1789, 1800, and 1802, upon the subject.

For the purpose of thoroughly understanding the American principles with respect to the formation of juries, I examined the laws of states at a distance from one another, and the following observations were the result of my inquiries.

In America all the citizens who exercise the elective franchise have the right of serving upon a jury. The great state of New York, however, has made a slight difference between the two privileges, but in a spirit contrary to that of the laws of France; for in the state of New York there are fewer persons eligible as jurymen than there are electors. It may be said in general that the right of forming part of a jury, like that of electing representatives, is open to all the citizens; the exercise of this right, however, is not put indiscriminately into any hands.

Every year a body of municipal or county magistrates—called *selectmen* in New England, *supervisors* in New York, *trustees* in Ohio, and *sheriffs of the parish* in Louisiana—choose for each county a certain number of citizens who have the right of serving as jurymen, and who are supposed to be capable of exercising their functions. These magistrates, being themselves elective, excite no distrust: their powers, like those of most republican magistrates, are very extensive and very arbitrary, and they frequently make use of them to remove unworthy or incompetent jurymen.

The names of the jurymen thus chosen are transmitted to the county court; and the jury who have to decide any affair are drawn by lot from the whole list of names.

The Americans have contrived in every way to make the common people eligible to the jury, and to render the service as little onerous as possible. The sessions are held in the chief town of every county; and the jury are indemnified for their attendance either by the state or the parties concerned. They receive in general a dollar per day, beside their travelling expenses. In America the being placed upon the jury is looked upon as a burden, but it is a burden which is very supportable. See Brevard's Digest of the Public Statute Law of South

Carolina, vol. i., pp. 446 and 454, vol. ii., pp. 218 and 338; The General Laws of Massachusetts, revised and published by Authority of the Legislature, v. ii., pp. 187 and 331; The Revised Statutes of the State of New York, vol. ii., pp. 411, 643, 717, 720; The Statute Law of the State of Tennessee, vol. i., p. 209; Acts of the State of Ohio, pp. 95 and 210; and Digeste Général des Actes de la Législature de la Louisiane.

APPENDIX R.—Page 290

If we attentively examine the constitution of the jury as introduced into civil proceedings in England, we shall readily perceive that the jurors are under the immediate control of the judge It is true that the verdict of the jury, in civil as well as in criminal cases, comprises the question of fact and the question of right in the same reply; thus, a house is claimed by Peter as having been purchased by him: this is the fact to be decided. The defendant puts in a plea of incompetency on the part of the vendor: this is the legal question to be resolved.

But the jury do not enjoy the same character of infallibility in civil cases, according to the practice of the English courts, as they do in criminal cases. The judge may refuse to receive the verdict; and even after the first trial has taken place, a second or new trial may be awarded by the court. See Blackstone's Commentaries, book iii., ch. 24.

www.ingramcontent.com/pod-product-compliance
Lightning Source LLC
LaVergne TN
LVHW020932110826
845150LV00004B/834

* 9 7 8 1 4 2 5 5 5 2 6 9 5 *